LEADING, MANAGING AND DEVELOPING PEOPLE

Third edition

Edited by Gary Rees and Ray French

The Chartered Institute of Personnel and Development is the leading publisher of books and reports for personnel and training professionals, students, and all those concerned with the effective management and development of people at work. For details of all our titles, please contact the publishing department:
tel: 020 8612 6204
email: publish@cipd.co.uk
The catalogue of all CIPD titles can be viewed on the CIPD website:
www.cipd.co.uk/bookstore

LEADING, MANAGING AND DEVELOPING PEOPLE

Third edition

Edited by Gary Rees and Ray French

Chartered Institute of Personnel and Development

Published by the Chartered Institute of Personnel and Development,
151, The Broadway, London, SW19 1JQ

This edition first published 2010

Typeset and printed by Charlesworth

British Library Cataloguing in Publication Data

A catalogue of this publication is available from the British Library

ISBN 9781843982579

The views expressed in this publication are the authors' own and may not necessarily reflect those of
the CIPD.

The CIPD has made every effort to trace and acknowledge copyright holders. If any source has been
overlooked, CIPD Enterprises would be pleased to redress this in future editions.

Chartered Institute of Personnel and Development, CIPD House,
151, The Broadway, London, SW19 1JQ

Tel: 020 8612 6200

Email: cipd@cipd.co.uk

Website: www.cipd.co.uk

Incorporated by Royal Charter. Registered Charity No. 1079797

Contents

List of Figures and Tables

Chapter 12

Acknowledgements

This textbook has built on the first two editions of *Managing and Leading People* edited by Charlotte Rayner and Derek Adam-Smith, and we would like to thank all colleagues at the University of Portsmouth and CIPD who were involved with these earlier editions which provided excellent building blocks for this new text.

There have been significant developments in business over the past two years, including the financial crisis which has impacted on the work of HR practitioners, and continues to do so with much uncertainty forecast post-2010. Updating existing chapters has therefore involved the inclusion of new and topical material, while we have also devised a number of new chapters for this book. All-in-all authors have worked on individual chapters with great professionalism within a short timeline. We have enjoyed working with all contributors.

We would like to express our thanks to Derek Adam-Smith for his support as Head of the Department of Human Resource and Marketing Management throughout the period encompassing the previous two editions and the development of this new version.

We would like to thank Reed Business Information for the use of their case studies from the XpertHR website (www.XpertHR.co.uk)

Thanks are also due to Ruth Anderson and Kirsty Smy at CIPD Publishing for all their work. We wish to thank, finally, the draft chapter reviewers for their constructive feedback, in particular Stephen Taylor.

We would like to thank Reed Business Information for the use of their case studies from the XpertHR website (www.XpertHR.co.uk)

Gary Rees
Ray French
University of Portsmouth Business School
April 2010

List of contributors

Derek Adam-Smith

Gill Christy

Richard Christy

Ray French

David Hall

Liza Howe-Walsh

Margaret Mackay

Charlotte Rayner

Gary Rees

Sally Rumbles

Simon Turner

Alex Tymon

All the contributors work at the University of Portsmouth Business School, Portsmouth UK.

Walkthrough of textbook features and online resources

LEARNING OUTCOMES

After reading this chapter, you should be able to:

- Appreciate how HR practices may differ across sector types; private, public and third sector.
- Recognise that delivering HR services in smaller organisations differs from those in larger organisations.
- Consider the ways in which the HR function may change as an organisation grows in size.
- Understand the concept of global HRM and its implications for practice in terms of policy and practice for localisation and control from head office.
- Explore the notion of Strategic International HRM; variegations in practice for staffing overseas.

LEARNING OUTCOMES

At the beginning of each chapter a bulleted set of learning outcomes summarises what you can expect to learn from the chapter, helping you to track your progress.

OVERVIEW

This chapter takes theory from Chapter 2 and applies it to the working lives of Human Resource Practitioners (HRPs). In particular we will look at how, while the function of managing human resources is similar in most organisations, the work of the HRPs themselves varies between different organisational contexts; partly dependant on size, and also dependant on the mission of the organisation with respect to profit and not-for-profit. Without doubt the needs of an organisation change as it grows, and although all have to be compliant with the

OVERVIEW

Each chapter opens with an Overview outlining the purpose and content of the chapter.

REFLECTIVE ACTIVITY

Special people, special treatment?

In 2010 the British Prime Minister, Gordon Brown, was caught up in a debate on his 'bullying' behaviour. Several high-profile books on the workings of number 10 Downing Street held consistent reports of the Prime Minister throwing papers and other objects in temper. After several days and a media storm,

it was found that his popularity had actually risen.

In common with all Civil Service departments, an anti-bullying policy applies at Downing Street. To what extent do you think that this situation is unusual? In this case, what are the ethical factors that need to be considered? What should HR do in such circumstances?

REFLECTIVE ACTIVITIES

Questions and activities throughout the text encourage you to reflect on what you have learnt and to apply your knowledge and skills in practice.

 CALL CENTRE IS MY 'DREAM JOB'

CASE STUDY

At 22, Snehal Sampat has landed her dream job.

She works as a customer adviser in Norwich Union's (now Aviva's) call centre in Bangalore, southern India.

In Britain such a job would be considered very ordinary. But in India it is a sought-after position.

Ms Sampat said one of the attractions is the salary.

'The pay is absolutely fantastic,' she said. 'In India, call centres are one of the fastest growing industries. If you perform, you stand to earn a lot of money.'

A lot of money by Indian standards, that is. Ms Sampat earns £40 a week. Her equivalent at a British call centre would be on £250.

But in India, £40 is twice what a teacher earns and about the same as a newly qualified doctor.

Prestige

Ms Sampat and her call centre colleagues, all of whom are graduates, are able to enjoy the fruits of the consumer society: mobile

'About two million people a year come out of Indian universities and technical colleges,' said John Hodgson, the firm's offshoring director. 'Their basic English is at a high level. They seek employment with Western companies because it's seen as a high prestige job, an important stepping stone in their lives.'

Expansion

Indian call centres are 40 per cent cheaper to run than British ones and the number of outsourcing staff is expected to grow tenfold in five years.

It is good news for India, where a third of the population lives in absolute poverty.

Questions

1. How can one account for Snehal Sampat's orientation to work as indicated in this case study?

2. Should Norwich Union be concerned to examine ways of 'enriching' the job of

CASE STUDIES

A number of case studies within each chapter will help you to place the concepts discussed into a real-life context. Accompanying questions encourage you to analyse the case further.

KEY LEARNING POINTS

- The HR function adds value to the organisation in a number of ways through delivering business strategy.
- The HR function adds value, but how it does, and who is perceived as adding value is complex and sometimes a function of internal politics and perceptions of line managers.
- The way in which HR adds value changes as the organisation grows, and also between sectors.
- Outsourcing aspects of HR is common, but needs to be done carefully to ensure the organisation does not lose competitive edge.
- Internationalisation is a current issue for those who recruit, and for those involved in mobilising staff between countries.
- The degree of control from the parent company in the area of international HR presents a challenge which needs to be balanced depending on the context.

KEY LEARNING POINTS

Bulleted lists of key learning points at the end of each chapter are designed to consolidate your learning and pull out key points for you to remember.

REVIEW QUESTIONS

1. Thinking about an organisation with which you are familiar, provide practical examples of ways in which it is operating ethically. Can you relate these examples to the duty, consequences or virtue perspectives on ethics?

2. Discuss the view that an organisation that is providing good value products or services

3. How do HR decisions become conflicted in an ethical sense? Consider situations where you have felt professionally 'torn' between courses of action and analyse your response using ethical frameworks.

4. Given that HR gains much of its power from line managers, how far might this influence the profession's 'honest broker' position?

REVIEW QUESTIONS

Test your understanding of a chapter or topic by tackling these end-of-chapter review questions.

EXPLORE FURTHER

Becker, B and Huselid, MA (2006), Strategic human resource management: where do we go from here? *Journal of Management*, Vol 32, No 6, pp 898–925.

This article is a very effective overview of the strategic issues within HR. Their application of business strategy into the undertaking of HR roles is both thought-provoking and holds a list of key texts should readers wish to pursue the forms of HR delivery within organisations.

Boselie, P, Brewster, C and Paauwe, J

Tharenou, P (2008), *Self-Initiated Careers*. In Baugh, G and Sullivan, SE *Maintaining focus energy and options over the career*, pp 197–224, Information Age Publishing. Howe-Walsh, LJ and Schyns, B (2010), Self-Initiated Expatriates: Implications for HRM, *International Journal of Human Resource Management*, Vol 21, No 2, pp 260–273.

These two contributions give useful insights into the developing area of self-initiated expatriates – a field which is likely to become more important for recruiters in all organisations and one which is not often

EXPLORE FURTHER

Explore further boxes contain suggestions for further reading and useful websites, encouraging you to delve further into areas of particular interest.

ONLINE RESOURCES FOR STUDENTS

- Contemporary accounts of organisational practice – to inspire and inform you
- Questionnaires – assess your motivational skills and leadership attributes
- Annotated weblinks – click through to a wealth of up-to-date information online

Visit **www.cipd.co.uk/sss**

ONLINE RESOURCES FOR TUTORS

- Lecturer's Guide – practical advice on teaching LMDP using this text, teamwork activities and guidance on the in-chapter activities
- PowerPoint slides – build your course around these ready-made lectures

Visit **www.cipd.co.uk/tss**

Leading, Managing and Developing People

The content of this CIPD module is covered as follows:

Leading, Managing and Developing People learning outcomes	*Leading, Managing and Developing People* chapters
1. Review and critically evaluate major contemporary research and debates in the fields of HRM and HRD.	Chapter 1 Introduction Chapter 2 Aims, Objectives and Role of HRM Chapter 3 HRM Contributions in Different Settings Chapter 13 Summary Themes and Future Trends
2. Evaluate major theories relating to motivation, commitment and engagement at work and how these are put into practice by organisations.	Chapter 5 Leadership Chapter 7 Flexibility and the Psychological Contract Chapter 11 Managing the Employment Relationship Chapter 12 Performance Management, Motivation and Reward
3. Debate and critically evaluate the characteristics of effective leadership and the methods used to develop leaders in organisations.	Chapter 5 Leadership Chapter 10 Developing Employees Chapter 13 Summary Themes and Future Trends
4. Contribute to the promotion of flexible working and effective change management in organisations.	Chapter 6 Managing Change Chapter 7 Flexibility and the Psychological Contract Chapter 8 Organisational and Job Design Chapter 9 Recruitment and Selection
5. Critically discuss the aims and objectives of the HR function in organisations and how these are met in practice.	Chapter 2 Aims, Objectives and Role of HRM Chapter 8 Organisational and Job Design Chapter 9 Recruitment and Selection Chapter 10 Developing Employees Chapter 11 Managing the Employment Relationship Chapter 12 Performance Management, Motivation and Reward
6. Assess the contribution made by HRM and HRD specialists in different types of organisation.	Chapter 2 Aims, Objectives and Role of HRM Chapter 3 HRM Contributions in Different Settings Chapter 8 Organisational and Job Design Chapter 9 Recruitment and Selection Chapter 10 Developing Employees Chapter 11 Managing the Employment Relationship Chapter 12 Performance Management, Motivation and Reward
7. Promote professionalism and an ethical approach to HRM and HRD practice in organisations.	Chapter 4 Professionalism and Ethics in Managing People Chapter 11 Managing the Employment Relationship Chapter 13 Summary Themes and Future Trends

CHAPTER 1

Introduction

Gary Rees *and* Ray French

LEARNING OUTCOMES

After reading this chapter, you should be able to:

- identify important themes within the area of leading, managing and developing people through an analysis of two case studies.

- familiarise yourself with the learning features within this book.

- understand the structure of the book in relation to the CIPD Leading, Managing and Developing People Unit (7002).

- locate or 'map' the Leading, Managing and Developing People Unit (7002) learning outcomes to particular chapters in the text.

OVERVIEW

Managing people is rarely dull. In April 2010 news broke that volcanic ash had spread across the skies of northern Europe following an eruption in Iceland. One consequence was an unprecedented closure of UK airspace and resultant ban on commercial flights to and from Britain. Human resource (HR) practitioners are often the first to be directly affected by developments in the world outside work organisations, and so it proved in this case as the ash cloud crisis quickly impacted on their everyday work. The Chartered Institute of Personnel and Development (CIPD) website published guidelines on dealing with the disruption – an estimated 15,000 British workers had been stranded abroad due to the travel chaos caused by the ban on flights.

Volcanic ash had suddenly become a people management issue. Some competing views were put forward on how to deal with staff absence caused by the ash.

While it was claimed that staff stranded abroad would not be entitled to free time off, the Federation of Small Businesses warned members that docking staff pay could lead to employment tribunal cases brought by employees if the organisation did not have a robust absence policy.

Simpson (2010) provided guidelines for employers when dealing with this unusual situation, which include three elements pointing to the need for managers to use discretion, indicating that there were no right answers in responding to the crisis.

- **Leniency.** Although absent workers were not normally entitled to pay if they were unable to perform their duties, HR managers were asked to consider leniency; however, they must be consistent in their approach.

- **Be creative.** Managers were asked to be creative in thinking of alternatives on how missed time could be made up, such as through flexible working arrangements.

- **Be reasonable.** Here, employers were reminded of their duty of care and asked not to place unreasonable burdens on staff who had been away on holiday and were not able to make it back.

By the time you read this book the volcanic ash episode may have blown over – both literally and figuratively. Why have we included it at the very start of our text?

The 2010 ash crisis firstly, points to the inherent unpredictability of managing people and its susceptibility to the impact of outside events. Leading, managing and developing people is fundamentally a topical area. We will provide many examples of the need for those who lead, manage and develop people to keep abreast of trends and developments in the environment – and to respond to them. To take one example, we will examine the growing demand (from employees, governments and other bodies) for flexible working. If we live in a time when flexible working becomes the norm it will need to be managed effectively within the workplace setting.

The guidelines regarding the aftermath of ash disruption secondly show that managing people is not a hard science and contains few right or universally applicable answers. There is often a need for managers to be subtle and creative in the ways they lead, manage and develop employees. We will show that in many topic areas, one size does definitely not fit all. At the same time, there is a need to be fair and equitable and policies can act as a useful way of working towards these aims.

Finally, HR managers wish to nurture their talented or key workers – whether we believe this term applies to everyone who makes a contribution (ie *all* workers) or just to a named sub-group of workers. Employees may seek to work for a 'good employer' and being treated shabbily – at least in their own perception – might adversely affect their psychological contract; a term we go on to explore in our book, and which essentially is the mental picture workers have of how their inputs to an organisation relate to what they receive from it. If employees are disciplined for absence after days stranded abroad due to volcanic ash, or have their pay and other benefits reduced, they may come to see this as a sign that they do not work for a good employer after all, with all the consequences that such a feeling can lead to.

INTRODUCTION

This opening chapter introduces the purpose, content and structure of this book. The third edition has been adapted to meet the requirements of the (new) Leading, Managing and Developing People Unit (7002). We include several new chapters, and have devised relevant and topical reflective activities and case studies. We are also concerned to identify current research evidence and refer to relevant survey reports throughout the book.

A consistent rubric has been developed for each chapter which includes the following key features:

- an overview
- a set of learning outcomes
- an introduction
- reflective activities (activities and case studies)
- a conclusion
- key learning points
- review questions
- explore further (suggested further reading and references).

The text introduces a balance of theory and practice, drawing upon major research work, including theoretical and conceptual models, through to major survey research findings. A combination of reflective activities include case studies (both short and long examples), *vignettes* covering self reflective activities and links to relevant articles. The structure of the text is set out more fully on page 10.

In order to help analyse important concepts such as 'engagement', and 'talent management' within current debates, we shall start by considering a case study from the private sector. We have not assumed that you have an extensive background in HR academic study, just a lively interest in the field, so read the case study and answer the questions before delving into specific chapters in the book.

MANAGING THE WORKFORCE IN A RECESSION

CASE STUDY

David Fairhurst, senior vice president and chief people officer at McDonald's Northern Europe, knows a thing or two about human resources. Recently voted HR's most influential practitioner – one of many accolades over the last few years – he has been responsible for a number of achievements at the fast food chain, including the development of a pan-European talent management programme and its highly successful training programme in which employees can be awarded nationally-recognised qualifications.

Fairhurst is therefore extremely well placed to advise on HR's role in the current recession, especially when it comes to employee engagement.

'You do have to continue to engage with employees because they are going to be with you at the end of a recession and you have to maintain that engagement – so this needs to be thought through,' remarks Fairhurst. 'Think of engagement at its most simple level, which is creating a mutual value between the employer and staff – you do things for me and I do this for you. However, as we ride through the recession we have to re-focus on engaging employees and what we do to engage them will be different and will take some thinking about.'

A different view on engagement

The question is, then, how will it be different? 'Well, for example, is there more financial support that you need to give your employers during this time? Do you need to be more paternal, making sure they don't dip out of pension schemes and that they themselves become too short-term in their outlook? We have to think about all these sorts of things, but the principle is that you have to keep engaging,' he advises.

Equally, HR must also think about the employees that are being 'disengaged' from the organisation, and must ensure it is done in such a way that is perceived to be fair and compassionate by others, he says.

'But there is one challenge I put out there for HR directors – when you look back at the end of this recession, will you be a case study of role model behaviour, values and best practice as an organisation? Will people say, "remember what that business did"?'

This challenge comes back to what Fairhurst dubs as a 'new way' of doing things, in terms of engagement. 'We must not take our eye off this continual experimentation and delivering the results,' he comments.

However, he warns there is a danger that employers can become short-sighted in the current downturn. 'It's too easy to stop doing all these things like engagement, creativity, and experimentation, and go right to the other end and say, now is the time to make sure that people have a desk and you don't bark at them – that's very short sighted. If the profession as a whole can really hold together and focus and help them keep their nerve and remain creative in difficult times, then I think some good can be done in times of recession.'

Managing talent

Another thing that can come under stress during a recession is talent management. Fairhurst points out that there are all types of misconceptions about talent management at the moment, yet talent needs managing, no matter what the market conditions are, he emphasises.

'Organisations that are proactively managed as opposed to "let happen" are the ones that have been more successful, and it's no surprise, if you look at the top priorities from all the research coming out from Harvard and places like that, the key issues are reputation, and the CEO's credibility, and talent has gone right to the top of the CEO's agenda as they have figured out that organisations are about talent and how you manage that talent.'

Fairhurst adds that talent is an organisational resource that needs to be managed in a way that suits the current and future needs of the organisation's strategy, regardless of the economic climate. 'Of course, the fact that we are talking about the lives and livelihoods of individuals here makes this a particularly difficult management challenge – but that is the HR challenge for the 21st century and we have to rise to it.'

HR departments also need to think about their strategic initiatives within the organisation, and must not just view talent management as another term for 'succession planning'. 'Strategic talent management these days is all about projecting the operational income of an organisation – where the business is going to make money, what the talent implications and the gaps are from that, how things need to evolve and where you are going to get it from,' he says.

Therefore, it is not just about 'bums on seats' any more, comments Fairhurst, and who fills what job, it is about keeping up with the fast-moving changing skill set – which leads him on to the subject of the war for talent.

'Some have said the war for talent has eased, but this is misleading as talent supply is dictated by the rate of change in business and the economy – change has never been faster so the war for talent is as alive as it has ever been,' he remarks.

What is McDonalds' secret?

So how does Fairhurst himself ensure staff morale, engagement and productivity levels stay buoyant at McDonald's, during the downturn?

'First and foremost, McDonald's is one of the organisations that has enjoyed positive growth during the current downturn and there are strong business reasons for this. At the same time, we have continued forward momentum with initiatives such as apprenticeships, degrees and LEPs. Maintaining this momentum at a time when it might be argued we could "take our foot off the gas" has undoubtedly enhanced morale, motivation and productivity levels.'

And for HR in general, Fairhurst states that the current recession is the ideal time for HR to step up to the challenge. 'HR has for years wanted the top table position, and if ever there was a time to show what values can be created at the top table, it is now. I like the old joke that leadership is like a teabag – you only know how good it is when it's in hot water. It's the same with HR – you only know how good your HR function is when they show how they adapt and how they maintain focus in the toughest times, and now's the time to step up to the function.'

Fairhurst's top tips:

What should HR focus on during a recession?

- Doing what is right for the business – short and long term.

- Engage those who will ride out the recession with you to ensure they are aligned with what the organisation needs to achieve.

- Treat those who may have to leave the organisation with compassion and fairness.

- If we are judged in hindsight to have done the right things for our organisation, in the right way for our people, we will have done ourselves and our profession an enormous amount of good.

Questions

1. To what extent is McDonald's doing anything different during a recession from what organisations should do during times of prosperity? Give reasons for your answer.

2. What are the fundamental messages that David Fairhurst espouses in terms of HR adding value in practice?

Source: Mitchell (2009)
www.XpertHR.co.uk

Following on from this first case study, which dealt with a large and very well-known (even controversial) private sector organisation, we now turn to look at an example highlighting LMDP issues in the public sector – Wychavon District Council.

CASE STUDY

EMPLOYEE ENGAGEMENT AT WYCHAVON DISTRICT COUNCIL

Introduction

In 2008, Wychavon District Council was awarded top place in the *Times* 'Best Councils to Work For' awards, a ranking that is judged through independent submissions from council staff. This was achieved despite difficult circumstances for employees, who were at the time experiencing the effects of a pay and grading review (part of a nationally negotiated agreement affecting all local authorities).

Internal research also points to consistently high engagement levels. In 2006, when the Council's most recent staff survey was carried out, 70 per cent of employees said they were proud to work there, and 93 per cent said they enjoyed their job.

Having staff who are happy and engaged is not an aim in itself at Wychavon District Council, but it has been a vital ingredient in achieving the organisation's overall goals, according to Jack Hegarty, managing director of the Council, and Fiona Narburgh, head of strategy and communications.

'We have learnt the lesson that you can't deliver well for the residents unless your staff are on board with what you are trying to do, so [our view on staff engagement] is really pragmatic. It hasn't really been to do with a major policy,' explains Narburgh.

Hegarty, who has worked in public sector management for 20 years, adds: 'If you aspire to be a high-performing organisation you won't do it unless your staff are engaged, you just won't do it. You can put processes in, you can put money in, but unless you are working with your people, it won't happen. I've seen this.'

From mediocrity to high performance

Since Hegarty took over the leadership role at Wychavon District Council in April 2004, he has helped take it from what he describes as mediocrity to what has been judged as an outstanding organisation. In 2007, it won the Local Government Chronicle (LGC) 'Council of the Year' position, an award that recognises excellence in councils who take their work beyond the normal level of service provision.

Hegarty describes the challenge he faced when he first took on the leadership role: 'If you are a small, lean council where everyone has got two or three jobs, not just one, how do you get staff to go the extra mile? If staff don't go the extra mile, you remain a mediocre, middle-of-the-pack organisation. There was no chance of us being a failing council, but there was no aspiration at one stage for us to be successful. And that was our starting point.'

Engaging staff

Hegarty says that in order for staff to perform at their best, they have to be heavily engaged with the organisation, feel proud to work for it, and 'feel that they and the organisation are one and the same thing'.

As Narburgh and Hegarty explain, there is no one factor alone that has helped to motivate staff at Wychavon District Council, but a number of elements have helped to shape the way people work, including:

- an open, strong, non-hierarchical leadership style

- a culture where staff are rewarded, supported and listened to

- teamworking as the norm

- clearly communicated, straightforward, shared goals, with a clear focus on customers

- performance management that is clear cut and confrontational when required; and

- clear, engaging communications that help promote a sense of pride, fun and shared values.

Leadership style

Hegarty has a naturally open, accessible style of management, which, coupled with his 'open door' policy helps staff to feel they can bring ideas or issues to him at any time. The style appears to work, as he was ranked 'best leader' in the *Times* 'Best Councils to Work For' special awards.

Hegarty communicates with his staff through regular updates posted on the intranet; briefing sessions for all 420 employees; and – unlike some chief executives (as council leaders are usually known) – he is not afraid to mingle with staff at their desks.

This non-hierarchical style is shared by the Wychavon councillors (or 'members'), who also prefer dealing with employees directly, instead of communicating through management. Staff names are displayed on desks to help facilitate this.

Managers throughout the Council are also expected to work in a similar style with their teams by involving all staff, listening, and sharing information on a regular basis. Team meetings are a regular part of working life. A recent initiative saw several leaders, including the deputy managing director, shadow people such as traffic wardens (known as civil enforcement officers) and waste disposal workers, while some non-management staff shadowed managers.

Teamworking

All managers have access to a shared set of 12 management principles, which include:

'We will maintain good officer and member relationships and the "Team Wychavon" approach.'

Wychavon's 12 management principles are:

- We will continually develop and challenge to remain excellent.

- We will continue to adopt an entrepreneurial not municipal culture.

- We will focus on resident and customer satisfaction as a principal objective and adopt customer insight techniques.

- That the Council will run core services very well and invest in them accordingly – maintain the 'don't fail to succeed' approach.

- Value for money principles will be applied to all policy initiatives and services.

- That application of good performance management will be a cornerstone of the management of the Council.

- That efficiency gains will be driven out by our own actions as an organisation rather than a disproportionate reliance on others.

- We will retain a positive approach, partnership working/joint working with other public and private sector organisations where it improves quality, reduces cost and builds on the Council's reputation.

- We will, where they add value, be engaged in partnerships to help deliver more than we could do above.

- That the approach of 'don't grow the establishment unless you grow the business' be maintained, as will a culture of using skills flexibly within the organisation.

- We will 'invest to save' where there are robust cases to do so.

- We will maintain good officer [staff] and member [councillor] relationships and the 'Team Wychavon' approach.

According to Narburgh, managers consider these principles to be an accurate reflection of how managers work at the Council, as opposed to a remote set of ideals.

The 'Team Wychavon' approach has been a crucial aspect of the Council's success. 'We have learnt that you can't deliver well externally without your staff being part of a team,' says Narburgh. 'And we have to work hard at the "one team, one council" feel,' she adds.

A document that summarises the Council's strategy for the year is central to the ongoing team-building exercise, as it ensures that all staff know what the Council is trying to achieve each year, and keeps the focus clearly on the common aim of helping the residents in the community. This document, known as the 'clear priorities paper', has been created by the leadership team and is used on a day-to-day basis by all departments.

Within the strategy document, the 'priorities' focus on the improvement of the local area. They remain the same each year and act as headlines (Safer, Greener, Healthier, Stronger and Successful). The text beneath each priority, known as the 'promises', changes each year. Copies of the document are displayed on office walls to help focus team planning, and it is used as a basis for each staff member when setting priorities in their performance development reviews.

Employee involvement

A key feature of working life at Wychavon District Council is the involvement of staff in decision-making and new initiatives and, because it is a small council, acting on suggestions can happen quickly. Involvement is encouraged in various ways, including through an employee forum known as the 'sounding board'.

The sounding board was used to shape a new annual staff competition, 'Wychavon Outstanding Service & Colleague Awards' – known now as the 'WOSCAs'. Nominations include best dressed employee, manager and team of the year, and most positive role model.

An initiative known as the 'big ideas' scheme encourages employees to pass on ideas that are 'bigger than the routine issues'. Narburgh is currently working on a feedback initiative so she can let employees know how the organisation has responded to the large number of ideas that have been submitted so far.

'Snap surveys' are also carried out over the intranet, to find out how people feel about particular issues. These are well received, averaging a 60 per cent response rate. As an example, the electronic survey is being used to find out which day employees would prefer to have as an additional day off over Christmas.

Employee motivation

According to the 2006 staff survey, the two most important motivators for staff are a 'sense of personal achievement' and a good work-life balance (both voted as 'very important' by 76 per cent of employees). Coming in third place, 'opportunities for flexible working' was considered a high priority by 68 per cent; while 55 per cent cited pay and benefits.

Flexible working at the Council differs from the public sector norm in that there are no core hours when every employee needs to be present in the office, although each team must make sure that there are enough people available to provide the required service for residents. Using an automated clocking-in system, which is backed up with automated timesheets, each individual can organise their own hours, having liaised with the team, so long as there is cover provided during published office hours.

This means, in practice, that individuals are free to attend school functions and caring appointments, and keep up with other commitments outside work, so long as they make up the time. Conversely, if they work extra hours one week, they can take time off in lieu later. Narburgh believes that flexibility is a two-way process.

Additional Reward Schemes including Health Insurance and Employee Assistance programmes were introduced after 2007.

Performance management

'You can't have good staff engagement if people are working under poor management,' says Narburgh. 'It is impossible, which is why leadership is the most important aspect [of employee engagement], and by that I mean inspiring, open, authentic, leadership. You just can't say you want to be a brilliant council and then tolerate poor management.'

This view is at the root of the tough, focused attitude to performance management at Wychavon District Council. Narburgh continues: 'We are motivating hearts and minds, and so on, and we are training and developing, but actually there is also a hard edge. We are managing performance in a much, much stronger way. We are setting objectives, looking at our targets, being clear about what our strategy is, and a whole host of things.'

Performance development reviews

As part of the ongoing performance management process, all employees are expected to have one formal, annual performance development review meeting with their manager, with two follow-up conversations to chart progress later in the year. This is valued by employees, according to staff surveys, and provides an opportunity to meet the line manager and work through objectives, look at career progression, and assess what help is needed through training. Approximately 1.5 per cent of the staff budget is allocated to each service unit to support performance development.

Culture and communication

A 'values' poster sets out five simple pointers to help employees understand the shared culture, and to get across some of the key points about working at the Council, such as enjoying work, being innovative, and giving a top-rate service to residents while keeping costs down. These are:

- brilliant customer service
- great services every time
- value for money
- fun, motivated and positive
- innovative, always improving.

Conclusion

Narburgh believes that there is no single factor that makes staff feel good about working for an organisation. However, an organisation that fosters an open, honest style of working will encourage employees to do a good job, she adds. This involves management listening and being clear about its expectations; and where there is a simple strategy that fits on to one side of an A4 sheet of paper.

Source: Wolff, C. (2008)
www.XpertHR.co.uk

Questions

1. Consider the extent to which Wychavon's employee engagement approach may make them an employer of choice.

2. In what ways can Wychavon's 12 Management Principles be used by HR to add value to the organisation?

THE STRUCTURE OF THE BOOK

The learning outcomes and content for the Leading, Managing and Developing People Unit can be subdivided into three particular areas, namely contextual factors, core themes and effective practice. Readers need to appreciate the context within which HR operates and how HR can directly or indirectly affect the leadership, management and development of employees. Three core themes of leadership, change and flexibility assist in understanding how the HR function can add value to organisations, whilst the effective practice section addresses how functional aspects of HR can make a direct impact upon organisations and organisational performance.

The text is therefore presented in five parts: (see Figure 1.1)

1. Part One provides the introduction and sets the scene of the text.

2. Part Two addresses the contextual factors which have shaped the nature of HR, and considers the aims, objectives and contribution of HRM across the public, private, third sector and across small, medium, large and multi-national organisations.

3. Part Three addresses the core themes that run through the process of leading, managing and developing people. Leadership, managing change and flexibility form the bulk of these core themes.

4. Part Four considers how HR practitioners and managers can turn relevant and valid theory into practice and use research findings to add value in terms of worker and organisational performance.

Figure 1.1 The structure of the text

5. Part Five comprises the conclusion to the book and makes suggestions about the future of HR by drawing upon various research findings and reports.

Chapters 1 and 13 allow for the text to be introduced and concluded through the use of integrated arguments and contemporary thinking and research.

CONCLUSION

The nature of leading, managing and developing people makes this a highly complex area; challenging and integrative, but also a very rewarding one. Having a good grounding in leading, managing and developing people is core knowledge for those working in HR. We trust that you find the following chapters informative, thought-provoking and a useful framework for understanding leading, managing and developing people.

At this point it is appropriate to introduce brief clarification on terminology. As we will see in Chapter 2, tasks involving leading, managing and developing people often fall to specialist HR managers within work organisations. In an important sense, however, general or line managers need to be involved in managing people too in their day-to-day work. The term 'HR manager' therefore denotes anyone who takes a role in leading, managing and developing people. In some cases HR work is outsourced to specialist providers. In view of this complex picture some writers use the term *human resource practitioner* to encompass anyone whose work touches our subject area. For our purposes, though, the terms 'human resource manager' and 'human resource practitioner' are sufficiently close for both to be used interchangeably, and you will find examples of both terms throughout the book.

CHAPTER 2

The Scope and Nature of Human Resource Management and Human Resource Development

Gary Rees

LEARNING OUTCOMES

After reading this chapter, you should be able to:

- have an appreciation of the role and function of HRM and HRD

- explore approaches to, and models of, HRM and HRD

- be aware of and evaluate models of strategic HRM and HRD

- consider the links between organisational strategy and HR strategy

- understand the interrelationship between line management and HRM/HRD

- identify recent research findings about how HR equates into practice

- assess the value and contribution of HRM and HRD.

OVERVIEW

In Part Two of this book, we examine some of the factors influencing the nature of Human Resource Management (HRM) and Human Resource Development (HRD). The aim is to lay the groundwork for subsequent sections in which we firstly identify *core themes* in leading, managing and developing people (Chapters 5–7), and then go on to examine *effective practice* in selected areas (Chapters 8–12). In Chapter 3, we will highlight the ways in which leading, managing and developing people may vary across different types of organisational settings. In this chapter we will discuss some even more fundamental questions, including how HRM and HRD are defined, who does –

and who should – take responsibility for leading, developing and managing people, and whether HRM and HRD can be regarded as strategic activities. Underlying these questions is the concept of HR practitioners 'adding value', possibly by taking on the role of 'business partner'.

It is useful at this stage to clarify the relationship between the two terms HRM and HRD. They could be considered separate aspects of an overall HR function, while one of these sub-functions may take precedence over the other at any one point. Within academic models, HRD is typically subsumed within HRM when functional aspects are taken into consideration. In this chapter we will explore the HR function in terms of human resource management *and* human resource development, without making judgements as to how these two areas converge or separate themselves. Dependent upon the context, some organisations may combine the HRM and HRD functions into an HR function, whilst other organisations may have a predominance of HRM within the HR function.

HR requires the collaboration of line and senior management. We look at this long-established notion and find support in recent research evidence within the UK. Over the last three years in particular, in the teeth of a global economic recession, measurement of contribution and accountability have been key issues for many business functions, including HR. We attempt to pinpoint the value of HR and, within the overall aims of our book, look at key research findings from recent research, which inform current debates.

INTRODUCTION

Robert Townsend, former CEO of Avis (1981), likened the HR function (Personnel as it was typically known then) to a malignant growth. Townsend claimed that if Personnel people were left unchecked, they would multiply and ultimately take over the company. His controversial and, we can assume, provocative analogy is that of serious and possibly terminal disease. Personnel is therefore by definition, abnormal and pathological, thus requiring 'treatment'. One important task of an organisation according to Townsend is to stem the growth of the Personnel function, and if necessary, cut it out altogether. Denigrating Townsend's notion of Personnel should be an easy task, and we might also question whether such an unpleasant and, for many of us, distressing analogy is appropriate at all. It does shines a light though on the negative reputation that HR or Personnel has sometimes had, and points to the need for HR practitioners to demonstrate clear valued contributions to an organisation.

 REFLECTIVE ACTIVITY

Despite the change of name from 'Personnel' to 'HR', it could be argued that the HR function is still suffering from a lack of status, and like Cinderella, does not get invited to the ball (or top table). Why is it that HR, on the whole, lacks the reputation to make strategic contributions to organisations and establish a strong reputation for itself?

We will argue that the role and function of HR has transformed itself over the last 40 years or so. However, there will no doubt be examples of the full span of traditional 'Personnel' and modern 'HR' in contemporary UK organisations. To what extent can HR be pigeonholed into structural or functional compartments, thereby limiting its scope and impact?

Ulrich, quoted by Brockett (2010, p 11), stated that, 'I think that HR people should see themselves as a professional services group within their own organisation, being a key account manager for the most important clients. Their job is to assess the resources available and use their knowledge to determine how best to transfer those resources to client productivity.'

However, before we look at contemporary HR roles, some historical perspective is useful and it is important to consider the transition from personnel management to HR, and to address definitions in order to make appropriate contrasts.

DEFINITIONS OF PERSONNEL MANAGEMENT, HUMAN RESOURCE MANAGEMENT AND HUMAN RESOURCE DEVELOPMENT

PERSONNEL MANAGEMENT

We begin by considering a widely used definition of personnel management from several decades ago. 'Personnel management aims to achieve both efficiency and justice, neither of which can be pursued successfully without the other. It seeks to bring together and develop into an effective organisation the men and women who make up an enterprise, enabling each to make his/her own best contribution to its success both as an individual and as a member of a working group. It seeks to provide fair terms and conditions of employment, and satisfying work for those employed' (IPM, quoted in Hendry, 1995, p 10).

As we can see here, personnel management is perceived as occupying a neutral position, placed between employers (in the form of management), and other rank and file employees. Its role was reinforced by the development of policies and procedures indicating professional independence and objectivity. An emphasis upon standardisation and equal treatment would often underlie such policies.

HUMAN RESOURCE MANAGEMENT AND HUMAN RESOURCE DEVELOPMENT

Any brief consideration of definitions of human resource management elicits a set of definitions which differentiate HR from personnel – at least in academic terms.

Storey (1995, p 5) defines HRM as 'a distinctive approach to employment management which seeks to achieve competitive advantage through the strategic development of a highly committed and capable workforce, using an integrated array of cultural, structural and personnel techniques'.

However, definitions of HRM are not universal. Boxall and Purcell (2000, p 184) argue that 'HRM includes anything and everything associated with the management of the employment relationship in the firm. We do not associate HRM solely with a high commitment model of labour management or with any particular ideology or style of management.' Whilst a universal and generally accepted definition of HRM is lacking, the same could be said for defining Human resource development.

Human resource development has been defined by Stewart and McGoldrick (1996, p 1) as: 'Human resource development encompasses activities and processes which are intended to have impact on organisational and individual learning. The term assumes that organisations can be constructively conceived of as learning entities, and that the learning processes of both organisations and individuals are capable of influence and direction through deliberate and planned interventions. Thus, HRD is constituted by planned interventions in organisational and individual processes.'

Whilst defining HRM and HRD may prove to be a tricky task, the nature, scope and objectives of HRM and HRD may change considerably in differing contexts. The historical background, senior management philosophy and practice, external forces and internal forces may shape different outcomes as far as what HRM/HRD actually does within the organisation.

In terms of what HR typically 'does', we could include the following as typical: human resource planning, job and organisational design (covered here in Chapter 8), recruitment, selection and induction (see Chapter 9), training and development (see Chapter 10), managing the employment relationship (see Chapter 11), pay, reward and performance management (see Chapter 12), ethical treatment of people including equal opportunities and diversity management (see Chapters 4 and 11), health and safety, knowledge management, mentoring, and disciplinary and grievance-handling to name just some.

Perhaps the most logical argument that determines what HR does in an organisation may be traced back to its historical roots. Who started the HRM process (eg a CEO thought that due to growth of the organisation, a HR function and HR manager needed to be appointed) can be important in tracing its subsequent development. The question of why the HR function was started (perhaps with specific goals in mind, such as identifying training gaps, dealing with increased specialist recruitment etc) is also highly relevant. Following this, identifying key milestones in the development of the HR function may provide further understanding of how HR has evolved (eg the introduction of a performance management system). Whilst each organisation evolves in its own inimitable fashion, generic models of the goals of HRM can, nonetheless, be considered.

HRM GOALS

Whilst the academic debate surrounding the defining of HRM goals continues, Boxall and Purcell (2008, p 20) suggest that there are four underpinning motives in HRM:

- *Cost-effectiveness* – maintaining stakeholder loyalty and trust is essential here, and this may mean running the business within budgetary constraints or maximising profits.

- *Legitimacy* – in essence, the allocation of moral legitimacy and ethical standing in society (see Chapter 4).

- *Flexibility* – in order to cope with change, organisational flexibility is vital for survival. It incorporates both short run responsiveness and long run agility (see Chapter 7).

- *Autonomy* – particularly managerial autonomy and the power to act. The political context may bring about change in managerial behaviour which may need some regulation in terms of corporate social responsibility.

The goals of HRD could be defined simply as developing and improving the performance of individuals and organisations, and we might also include team performance at this point.

Whilst the various goals of HR may differ across private, public and not-for-profit sectors (see Chapter 3), there will also be some similarities. Current UK public sector HR goals may tie in with strategic initiatives linked to the Gershon Efficiency Review (2004) and any other key governmental initiatives – for example, Agenda for Change, Commissioning, Private Finance initiatives and best-value-type initiatives. Ultimately, efficiencies (savings) are sought, with the stated goal of maintaining, or even increasing, service level quality, which means that employees will ultimately have to work harder or, more euphemistically, to work 'smarter'.

Managers in the private sector will already be familiar with the imperative for efficiency gains and, as we will note in the next chapter, the third (or not-for-profit) sector is also facing pressures in this regard.

 REFLECTIVE ACTIVITY

To what extent can an organisation exercise duty of care to all its employees and at the same time drive towards the highest level of cost efficiency? How can HR balance these potentially conflicting goals?

In order to move HR from a mere internal function, we need to analyse the broader strategic context within which it operates to consider whether HR can be strategic in its intent, actions and contribution.

STRATEGY AND HR

Strategy in its most basic sense is a plan of where the organisation would like to go. Although a strategy may take the form of a statement, it is also likely to be supported by strategic plans and imperatives providing the building blocks to meet its planned destination. A strategy should not be envisaged as an end in itself, as there may be a requirement to change course, or to embark on several journeys. One metaphor for business strategy is that of travel. So your strategy might be to travel in a northerly direction. At some points in time people might observe you travelling toward the south. However your long-term strategic intent is still to move northwards and your apparent change of direction might be a short-term retreat or tactical manoeuvre.

De Wit and Meyer (2004, p 50) defined strategy as 'a course of action for achieving an organisation's purpose'.

Taken in its broadest sense, this may not automatically mean profit generation and maximisation, or market domination. Strategy could be determined from more of a bottom-up approach, eg in a workers' collective, than a purely top down approach; or alternatively a range of key stakeholders/shareholders can be involved in making strategic decisions.

There may also be a vision or mission statement to accompany a strategy. The vision is sometimes a means of providing employees with a notion of where the organisation is heading and the values associated with it. The mission statement should reinforce to employees where the company is intending to go, but is often directed at shareholders or customers.

Possessing an organisational strategy and HR strategy is not enough. Strategic fit between HR strategy, HR practices and organisational strategy is paramount (Wang and Shyu, 2008). So how is such strategic fit accomplished? One method is to consider the vertical and horizontal integration of HR policies and procedures. The vertical fit is important in terms of achieving organisational goals through ensuring the alignment of HR activities to strategy. Horizontal fit plays an essential role in making use of these resources. Horizontal integration of HR activities includes aligning different HR activities such as recruitment and selection, performance management and reward so that each activity supports (rather than contradicts/interferes with) other HR activities. Vertical integration includes the way in which these activities fit into and support overall organisational activities, including the organisational vision, mission etc.

In order to assess the extent to which HR as a function can be strategic in its thinking and actions, we need to consider the various approaches/models of HR and the extent to which these align with strategic intent.

MODELS OF HRM AND STRATEGIC HRM

Hall (in Gilmore and Williams, 2009, p 144) defines strategic HRM as 'not any one particular HR strategy, but is a framework for shaping a number of people management strategies'.

Figure 2.1 The hard model of HRM

Source: Fombrun, C. J. *et al.,* 1984:35

While the analysis of the employment relationship and context is important, Beardwell and Claydon (2010) argue that two other issues affect the definition of human resource management. Firstly, the significance of HRM is variable, sometimes with emphasis upon people, strategy, employment relationships etc. Secondly, HRM is derived from a range of antecedents, and depends on the stance and philosophy of the analyst.

These definitions also ally themselves to the *hard* and *soft* models of HRM (Fombrun, Tichy and Devanna, 1984; and Beer, 1984). Hard models emphasise using employees to gain competitive advantage and focus on business and employment strategies by linking HR to business systems. Soft models, contrastingly, emphasise employee commitment and engagement, and attempt to align the interests of employees and management (see also Chapter 11).

Devanna *et al* (1984) suggest that within the organisation there needs to be an alignment of mission/strategy, the organisational structure and human resource management. External to the organisation are forces, such as political, cultural and economic forces, impacting upon the organisation. This approach assumes that HR emerges from the other factors, with strategy as the primary driver, and that HR needs to seek a 'best fit' within this context.

Another approach found within the field of HRM is that of the resource based view of the firm; namely one 'that focuses on the resources and capabilities controlled by a firm as sources of competitive advantage' (Barney and Hesterly, 2008, p 74).

Figure 2.2 The soft model of HRM

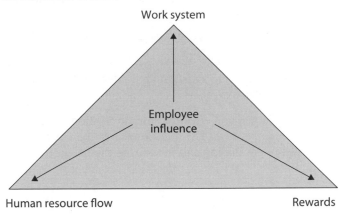

Source: Beer, 1984

Another approach used in HR is that of the 'best practice' model, often referred to as high commitment or high involvement HRM, in which managers consider how bundles of effective HR practice merge together.

CRITIQUE OF BEST FIT AND BEST PRACTICE MODELS

A major criticism of the best fit model is that it may ignore employee interests, and be ignorant of some of the important aspects of the psychological contract (see Chapter 7). The focus of the best fit model may be the pursuit of economic performance to the detriment of everything else. There may also be academic criticisms when addressing the measurement of various HR practices. How *do* we assess the validity of best fit practices? The transient nature of strategy and the need for constant change also makes alignment of current and future needs difficult.

When considering the best practice model, it is difficult to argue that HRM can apply across all organisational settings at all times. To what extent do HR practices transfer from the United States to eastern Europe or the Indian sub-continent for example? Another central concern is the extent to which organisations can adopt a long term approach in reality.

BALANCED SCORECARD

Another model that helps to assess the contribution that HR makes to a business is that of the balanced scorecard. The CIPD Human Capital reporting survey (2004a) argues that the central focus in this model is upon vision and strategy, with four key supporting elements that require targets and measure taken, namely:

- Learning and growth – relating to how we sustain our ability to change and improve (see also Chapters 6 and 12).

- Customer – how we should appear to our customer (see also Chapter 4).

- Financial – how we should appear to our shareholders.

- Internal business processes – to satisfy shareholders and customers, what business processes must we excel at?

This model assumes planned and effective communication (internally and externally) to be a key imperative. The question arises then as to what level HR can become involved in developing and measuring the balanced scorecard.

CASE STUDY

MANAGERIAL PERCEPTIONS OF THE ROLE OF THE HR FUNCTION IN SRI LANKA

Mammam *et al* (2006) investigated the extent to which HRM plays a significant role in organisational strategy processes in Sri Lankan export-oriented clothing manufacturing companies. It was claimed that typically Sri Lankan companies have short term financial objectives which override long term HRM objectives. Complementary to this are line managers' perception of the low importance given to the HR function and its contribution. The HR function derives its direction from corporate plans instead of influencing the plans. Three primary reasons were given for this:

- HR managers failed to provide a quality service.

- HR is unable to operate as effectively in delivering services needed at the standard expected.

- The HR function suffers from structural and managerial limitations, resulting in lack of delivery of quality of service and contribution to individual and organisational performance expected of them.

The key findings of this report are:

- Participation by HR in the decision-making process did not equate to favourable perceptions given to the HR function in the company. Hence, their role was more symbolic than important.

- When comparing local companies and multinational corporations, the transfer of HRM practices is primarily attributed to international buyers demanding high-quality practices and good management practices (the avoidance of a 'sweat-shop' reputation is a driving force).

Question

1. Despite the limitations of the survey (primarily managers' perceptions), what practical steps can the HR function take in order to reduce or possibly eliminate the concerns expressed in the findings?

HRD AND STRATEGIC HRD

However, as we noted at the start of this chapter, 'mainline' HR may not necessarily include HRD and Strategic HRD. HRD may be considered to be a sub-set of HR, and Strategic HRD a sub-set of Strategic HR. But the field of human resource development has grown rapidly in the last 30 years and 'development' as a theme cuts through many traditional HR areas. The current heightened interest in talent management – see Pilbeam and Corbridge (2010) – includes a great deal of debate and research around talent development.

The definition of development carries with it a series of different connotations and meanings. Thomas (2001, p 184) defines development as 'a process of competency attainment and of self-differentiation in the sense of progressively distinguishing oneself from the environment and from other people in order to create a unique self identity'.

Gubbins and Garavan (2009) argue that the primary responsibility of HRD professionals traditionally focused on identifying, selecting and evaluating training programmes. In effect this equates to transactional HR. However, Gubbins and Garavan contend that the role of HRD includes the consideration of environmental forces, and how the development of employees can add to competitive advantage.

Beer and Spector (1989, p 25) define strategic HRD as 'a proactive, system-wide intervention, linked to strategic planning and cultural change. This contrasts with the traditional view of training and development as consisting of reactive, piecemeal interventions in response to specific problems.'

Perhaps the question of where HRD sits as a discipline is a moot point. On a micro level, can HRD be aligned to adult learning and associated psychological theories? On the other hand, at a macro level, where national policy and HRD will be linked, the influence of educational policy and societal impact should be investigated. Wang and Sun (2009) argue that economics, psychology and system theory constitute foundations of HRD.

McCracken and Wallace (2000) devised a model depicting nine key characteristics of strategic HRD. Underpinning these characteristics are a strong learning culture, strategic change focus and a highly mature organisation in HRD terms. These nine characteristics bear similarity with the Strategic HR theory outlined earlier. The first characteristic that McCracken and Wallace identify is that of shaping organisational missions and goals. Secondly, there is top management leadership (including support). Thirdly, the environmental scanning by senior management is in HRD terms. Fourthly, there are HRD strategies, plans and policies in place. Fifthly, strategic partnerships exist with line management. Following that, there are strategic partnerships with HRM. The seventh key characteristic is that trainers act as organisational change consultants. The penultimate characteristic is the ability to influence corporate culture; and lastly, there is emphasis upon cost-effectiveness evaluation.

To what extent are skills, knowledge and core competencies the drivers of innovation and the key sources of competitive advantage (Gratton, 2000)? If core competence leads to organisational capability and competitiveness, then developing employee competence will be a strategic priority.

 REFLECTIVE ACTIVITY

Think of an organisation, and consider the following questions:

● What makes this organisation distinct?

● What precisely is the organisation good at doing (core competences)?

● What has led to the organisation being successful?

● How has any HRD intervention assisted its current competitive position?

The HRD function can play an important part in developing an organisation's culture to learn and aspire to be a 'learning organisation'. However, caution needs to be adopted here, in that we need to continually strive to link learning with performance (Henderson, 1997).

The interplay of HRD and HRM will continue to prove challenging to organisations. In some cases there are obvious structural divides in organisations, for example, a HRM and HRD department who don't particularly work well together, and deliberately separate out the functional aspects. In other cases, there is a strong synergy of activities that seamlessly integrate with organisational practices, and add value, and are seen to be adding value.

THE SHAPE OF HR

Harrison (2009, p 297) provides a useful framework when deciding the shape of the Learning and Development function, which can then be extended to HR more generally.

Firstly, the line managed function, where line-managers are handed the main responsibility for HRD/HRM. Secondly, the HR and HRD function could be outsourced. Thirdly, there is the three legged stool model proposed by Ulrich.

Within the line managed function, there is very much a devolved approach, handing over the majority of responsibility to line managers. The outsourced model may work well for specific aspects of HR and HRD, for example, assessment centres, competence development etc. Some of the key determinants in deciding whether to outsource include cost efficiency, added value, control and partnership.

Previous work by Harrison (2005) cited three other shapes that HRM/HRD could adopt, namely as a cost or profit centre, as a consultancy, or the traditional centralised function.

Operating as a profit centre may prove more attractive to an organisation than viewing HR as a cost centre, which does not necessarily generate its own revenue and therefore is a drain on corporate budgets. The argument of accountability may be less profound if a profit centre is generating sufficient funds. It could be argued that a HR function which can 'sell' its services successfully exhibits a level of professionalism within the market. However, the converse argument could also be true. HR operating as a consultancy service may bring into question the internal/external fit, and to what extent the 'consultancy' aligns with corporate culture and values.

HR BUSINESS PARTNER MODEL

Perhaps one of the more talked about current models is that of the HR Business Partner. Ulrich's original work 1997 emphasised four key roles that HR need to adopt:

- strategic partners
- administrative experts (shared services)
- employee champions
- change agents.

If HR adopts a more business-focused approach, as advocated by Ulrich *et al* 2008, then the emphasis upon customer focus, cost efficiencies, innovation and the ability to respond quickly to changes is highly important.

Business partnership describes the relationship between HR managers (partner) and line/functional managers within an organisation, with an emphasis upon outputs and performance measures, and a view to increasing effectiveness and efficiency of the organisation as a whole.

A research report produced by the CIPD (2007a) found that less than 30 per cent of their respondents had introduced the model in full, with another 30 per cent of respondents having partially introduced the Ulrich model.

Perhaps larger organisations are more likely to adopt the Ulrich model, commonly known as the 'three legged stool', whereby three functional areas of HR include (CIPD Fact sheet, 2010):

- Shared services handling transactional services, such as absence monitoring, payroll etc. The emphasis here is upon low cost and effective HR administration.

- Centres of excellence, consisting of small teams of HR experts with specialised knowledge of leading-edge HR solutions. Competitive advantage is sought through HR innovations, such as reward, learning, engagement and talent management.

- Strategic business partners working with business leaders to influence strategy formulation and strategy implementation. Some activities include organisational and people capability building, resource and talent planning, intelligence gathering etc.

HR BUSINESS PARTNERING IN WHITEHALL

HR business partners in the Civil Service will undergo new training to brush up on their skills ahead of looming budget cuts.

Jacquie Heany, deputy director of the Civil Service's HR professionalism team, reported that Whitehall departments were set to launch a development scheme for all 1,459 Whitehall business partners in order to help create a consistent approach to the change agenda and meet business needs.

In early 2010, the Labour Government revealed plans to slash public sector budgets by £15bn by 2013/2014. At that time, the Conservative Party, as the opposition, pledged to cut Whitehall budgets by 10 per cent if they won the election in 2010.

Hundreds of jobs could be cut across back office roles, including HR, to protect front-line services. Heany added the changes would present 'the leadership challenge of a generation', but Whitehall HR functions had the capability to deal with the task and had been preparing for this over the past 18 months.

'We have some business partners that are fantastic, we have some that are good at some things but not others – it's like any workforce,' she said. 'So what we are trying to do is make sure that, when we know what the [change] agenda is, we have a consistent programme to make sure that

the business function is ready, willing and able to cope with it.'

'As we go forward, and there are so many challenges, I think business partners will really be at the forefront of those challenges.' The new programme launched in January 2010 across the Civil Service.

Business Minister Ian Lucas added private and public sector HR professionals had a 'very demanding agenda' ahead of them. He stated that 'HR people need to look for and identify good leaders. They need to find and identify good practice within their sector and work together, and communicate with other HR directors in different organisations about what works.'

Meanwhile, Heany reiterated that civil service HR teams – totalling 8,823 people – would inevitably shrink as budget cuts took effect. She refused to be drawn on the size of the scale-back expected.

She said: 'The numbers in HR will go down, there's no question of that, just as the numbers in the Civil Service will go down.'

Source: Baker, K. (2009).
www.XpertHR.co.uk

Question

1. Within the context provided (at the time prior to the 2010 election results being known), discuss some of the challenges that HR business partners will face.

WHY DO ORGANISATIONS ADOPT THE BUSINESS PARTNERING MODEL?

The key drivers identified by CIPD 2010(a) include:

- Cost efficiency – smaller teams of HR have to demonstrate their cost efficiency or face being cut back.

- Accelerating competition – with HR central to business competitiveness, delivering skilled, motivated, creative, flexible and creative employees (see Chapters 7, 9, 10 and 12).

- Rising expectations of HR – with an expectation that HR contributes towards strategy, the execution of business plans and delivering tangible commercial benefits.

CASE STUDY

BUSINESS PARTNERING AT THE AA

The Automobile Association has undergone significant change since 2004, with three different owners within this time period. The overriding strategic imperative was to increase profitability. The HR function developed a strategy and HR Business Partner model to support the new business targets and help drive commercial success. In order for Hazel Lee, the HR Manager, to grow profits from £100m in 2005 to £300m in 2008, she had to dovetail HR and business strategy together.

HR business partners were appointed and made responsible for planning the people strategies for the AA's business units. Three senior business partner roles were set up to cover the following:

- corporate, policy and reward
- insurance, driving school, publishing and signs
- road operations.

In addition to this, a communications section was set up to integrate the different functions, which all reported to the HR Director.

A new competency framework identifying key behaviours and experience requirements to operate at business partner level, including commerciality, influencing, operational decision-making and facilitating change, was introduced.

The new look HR function was a leaner department, now operating with 60 employees from the previous 85.

The strategic business themes were:

- Business focus (more profitable business).
- Operational efficiency (lower operating costs with industry-best quality of service).
- Brand differentiation and scale (by leverage of strategic advantage driving sales and market share).

The HR department looked at how HR could deliver value to the business in each of these three areas.

In practice, this meant that Lee and her fellow business partner colleagues were automatically invited to operational management team meetings within their specialist area. In effect, this changed the emphasis towards a much more proactive role for HR, and the expectation from the operational team that HR will make a continuous contribution. The learning curve for all HR business partners was a steep one.

HR's expertise with managing human capital meant that the types of roles and competencies required to meet the business strategies could be created by HR.

According to Lee, some of the critical success factors included:

- HR seizing the business strategy quickly through buy-in.
- Strong leadership within HR.
- Business partners having sound commercial knowledge and focus on the right organisational issues.
- HR strategy developing alongside business strategy.
- Performance measures to demonstrate the tangible benefits of having business partners.
- Some quick wins, and the ability to deliver quickly, then focus on longer-term projects.
- A seat on the board for the HR Director.

Source: Suff, R. (2008)
www.XpertHR.co.uk

Question

Despite the AA being a highly unionised organisation, why did the HR Business Partner model appear to be an appropriate choice in terms of improving the value of HR?

BUSINESS PARTNERING — THE COUNTER ARGUMENTS

Pitcher (2008) argues that the Business Partner model had not resulted in strategic thinking, and was primarily only a change in title. He cites the example of Elizabeth Arden, where the HR Director, Gabriele Arend, disagreed with any model that splits HR professionals into recruiting, training and employee relations experts. Her company is moving towards a traditional structure, where HR employees are trained to develop generalist knowledge.

The CIPD (2010) Factsheet recommends exercising caution when adopting the Business Partner model and suggests that partnering should mean a paradigm shift for most HR functions, resulting in changes to HR's values, operation and skills, and not simply a repackaging of good HR practice.

Perhaps the key question comes down to credibility and contribution, summed up succinctly in a Deloitte Report (2009, p 8):

'The business partners' greatest failing has been their inability to convince senior managers that they have the necessary business acumen to contribute to the strategic debate.'

 HR PARTNERS AT CHRISTIAN AID

CASE STUDY

Bentley (2008) quotes Higgins, a CEO of a human capital company, arguing that 'role fulfilment can only happen if the requisite talent is there.'

This point is picked up by Jane Clark, senior HR business partner at aid agency Christian Aid. She says HR business partners require a whole different skill set compared with traditional HR generalists, and in some organisations HR has been expected to make this transition without adequate support.

'If you re-badge people without giving them training and awareness, you are setting them up for failure,' she said.

For Clark, a strategic HR business partner must be focused on looking forward, 'anticipating change, understanding its impact on the people side of the business and managing this change'. She says they must be comfortable working with senior people from the business on an equal footing and acting as an internal consultant within the business.

Outside experience

But many HR practitioners who have spent all their working life solely within the function will struggle to tick all these boxes, according to Clark. She believes her experience of working outside of HR in an international development role for many years has helped her develop her strategic focus.

She recommends giving HR business partners secondments to other functions in the business as a way of expanding their strategic and commercial nous.

For Jane Clark, strategic HR business partners, who have developed commercial skills, have a choice of career paths.

She said: 'They are well-positioned to move into an HR director's role, but equally could make the step into a senior management position on the top table, and even the chief executive role. Consultancy work is also another option.'

Source: Bentley, R. (2008). www.XpertHR.co.uk

Question

1. With reference to the comments made by Jane Clark, to what extent could it be argued that the Strategic HR business partner is more of a generalist role, incorporating change and strategic decision-making?

For further discussion regarding the future implications of HR, please see Chapter 13.

The shape of the HR/HRD function may evolve through historical developments, or may be deliberately changed to meet the needs of key decision-makers. Perhaps the important factor here is how HR can constantly adapt its HRM and HRD activities, services and interventions to suit critical needs in that particular situation. Flexibility, adaptability and survival of HR remain the key determinants of HR's ability to transform itself to differing contexts. HR does not operate in isolation, and requires management support, sometimes senior management support, but more often, line management support and engagement.

LINE MANAGERS AND HR: EVIDENCE FROM RESEARCH FINDINGS

The question of how much line managers are expected to contribute towards implementing people management activities and practices is a moot one. What is the level of intervention from HR's perspective when they spot errors and mistakes in the way in which line managers operate? If HR is purely acting in an 'advisory' capacity, whereby managers can ignore advice, then by definition, does this not spell the denigration of the HR function?

In a recent survey by the IRS (2009), it was found that in some cases HR took the lead (eg specialist knowledge or expertise surrounding a tribunal claim). In contrast, policies that needed to be applied across every individual employee in the workforce involve greater focus on the role of the line managers (eg performance appraisal reviews etc). The survey found that in 87.3 per cent of tribunal claims, HR took the main responsibility compared to 5.5 per cent who reported a shared responsibility between line managers and HR. The other two areas where HR took on a significant role were equal opportunities and employee relations (see also Chapters 4 and 11). It may be presumptuous to assume that the three key areas avoided by line managers could be considered to be 'dirty work', ie tricky areas that can be drawn out, complex and potentially damaging to the reputation of the individuals concerned. In the IRS 2008 survey on line managers' roles in people management, key findings include:

- Line managers are increasingly expected to implement people management policies, with duties ranging from managing flexible working requests to handling disciplinary and grievance procedures.

- HR practitioners are not always impressed with the way that line managers carry out these responsibilities, and assess their performance as poor in some areas. Line managers are judged ineffective in training and development, absence management and maintaining personnel records.

- HR practitioners believe that training for line managers should be compulsory, and that levels of training and support on offer are inadequate.

- Two thirds of organisations predict the role of line managers to change further in the next three years, and this means taking on more HR functions.

Despite the IRS survey finding that HR use a number of techniques to support line managers in their people management role, such as coaching, meetings advice and support, training and posting information on various channels, the attitude that line managers possess can sometimes inhibit outputs. Some of the problems here may be quite simple – the line manager is taking on too much and may detract from what they perceive as their core function or contribution.

REFLECTIVE ACTIVITY

Consider how a formal arrangement can be made so as to secure a strong working relationship between HR managers and line managers. What key aspects would this arrangement include and how could they be evaluated?

HR IN REALITY: RESEARCH FINDINGS IN THE UK

So what does HRM and HRD actually involve in practice? The following section will consider some of the more recent major research findings in the UK over the last couple of years.

In a recent Knowledge Pool survey (2010, cited in IRS 2010), based on responses from 10,000 managers, they found that where learners receive line manager support, 94 per cent go on to apply what they learned. The role that the line manager plays cannot be under-estimated, and line managers' actions may inhibit or enhance employees' performance. The boss may be the biggest stress factor to an employee, or the strongest motivator to perform.

The Work Foundation Report (2009, p 7) summarised their key findings on people management roles as:

- There are positive associations between good people management practices and organisational performance.

- HR's role in contributing to people management outcomes is ambiguous, uncertain and subject to forces outside practitioners' control.

- HRM is becoming increasingly professionalised.

- Concerns abound surrounding the capability of both the line, and HR professionals to deliver the 'people agenda'.

- It is crucial for effective leadership to include leadership of the values and practices that shape the organisational climate for HRM.

In addition to these findings on people management practices, research related to HRD and employee skills (the National Employer Skills Survey, 2009) has found that:

- Just over two-thirds of employers (68 per cent) had provided any training or development in the previous 12 months – which was level with the proportion recorded in 2007. The pattern of training practice is changing, however, with fewer employers electing to deliver all of their training on-the-job and more combining on-the-job with off-the-job training: the proportion delivering only on-the-job training has fallen from 21 per cent in 2007 to 17 per cent in 2009, while the proportion of employers delivering both off- and on-the-job training has increased from 33 per cent in 2005 and 2007 to 38 per cent in 2009.

- There has also been a decrease in the number and proportion of staff receiving training – from 14.0 million workers (63 per cent of the workforce) in 2007 to 12.8 million workers (56 per cent of the workforce) in 2009 – and a slight decrease in the number of days of training provided per head of the workforce.

- Total employer expenditure on training is estimated to have been £39.2bn over the course of the 12 months prior to NESS09, an increase of just over £500m or 1.3 per cent since 2007. After accounting for inflation, this is equivalent to a decrease in real terms of 5 per cent. The labour costs of those receiving, delivering and managing training form the bulk of this employer training expenditure.

- Although fewer staff are receiving training than in 2007, more is being spent on each person trained. The average annual investment in training per trainee is £3,050, compared with £2,775 in 2007. This means that, per trainee, employers in 2009 spend an average of 3 per cent more on training in real terms (allowing for inflation) than was the case in 2007.

- Although the vast majority of employers regard all staff as fully proficient (81 per cent), in 2009 around one in five employers (19 per cent) reported that they employed staff whom they considered not fully proficient. Around 1.7 million workers or 7 per cent of the total workforce in England were described as having skills gaps.

The NESS 2010 reported on the skills that need improving or updating:

- Employers who identified the need to upskill at least one employee in the next 12 months were then given a range of categories listing types of skills. They were asked which types of skills would need to be improved amongst the single occupation that they felt would be most affected by the need for upskilling. Across all occupation types, the skills that are most likely to need improving or updating in relation to upskilling were technical, practical and job-specific skills, mentioned by 63 per cent of employers who said that they needed to upskill at least one employee over the next 12 months. In some occupational groups such as managers, administration and secretarial roles, and sales and customer service staff, mentions of technical, practical and job-specific skills were less common than average, but skills were mentioned which could be regarded as job-specific for that occupational group (managerial skills for managers, customer-handling skills for sales and customer services staff and general IT user skills for administrative staff).

- Following technical, practical and job-specific skills, a number of skill areas were each mentioned by almost two in five employers needing to upskill staff in the next 12 months: management skills, general IT user skills, customer-handling, problem solving and teamworking skills (each mentioned by between 35 and 38 per cent of employers).

- Communication skills were also quite frequently mentioned (by 32 per cent of those employers identifying the need to upskill). The type of communication mentioned was more often oral than written communication (27 and 21 per cent respectively).

Business planning, training plans and training budgets:

- Almost three-fifths of all employers have a business plan specifying the establishment's objectives for the coming year (58 per cent). Just over two-fifths have a training plan specifying in advance the level and types of training staff will need in the coming year (43 per cent) and just over a third have a budget for this training expenditure (36 per cent). A third of employers (32 per cent) do not have any of these formal plans.

The proportion of the workforce receiving training:

- While the proportion of employers providing training has remained stable since 2007, there has been a decrease in the number and proportion of staff receiving training. Employers reported providing training over the previous 12 months for 12.8 million workers. This is equivalent to 56 per cent of the total current workforce and 63 per cent of the workforce in establishments that provide training. By comparison, in 2007, 14.0 million workers had been trained over the previous 12 months, equivalent to 63 per cent of all workers, and 72 per cent of workers in establishments providing training.

- The proportion of employers that arrange training for the majority of their workforce is high at 70 per cent (of those that provide training) but has decreased from 74 per cent in 2007; and the proportion arranging training for over 90 per cent of their workforce has declined from 44 to 38 per cent (of those that provide training) since 2007.

- The proportion of the workforce trained increases with the size of establishment, from just over two-fifths (43 per cent) in micro-establishments with fewer than five staff to almost three-fifths (57 per cent) of those employed in establishments with 25 or more staff.

- Barriers to providing more training can be grouped into four broad themes: expense; time; training supply; and other barriers. Expense is the most common of these themes (60 per cent), followed by time (54 per cent). Some of these barriers could be generalised across all HR functions and activities.

Whilst the picture presented demonstrates that HRD makes a contribution to business needs, evidence provided in the CIPD Learning and Talent Development survey 2010(b) found that funds available for learning development in the last year have decreased by over half in organisations surveyed. The Human resource development function attracts the same sort of challenges that faces the HRM function, necessitating a need to 'come out of its corner fighting'.

HR SHOWING ADDED VALUE

For HR to maintain its credibility, it not only has to be seen to be doing, but needs to provide evidence through appropriate measurements that it is adding value. The use of HR metrics and other indices like human capital management measures continue to be an aspect of HR. Warech and Tracey (2004) believe that HR is far more than a cost centre, and that being able to communicate assertively affects HR's collective impact on the company's bottom line.

The role of the line manager cannot be overplayed, and both HR and HRD specialists need to engage with line managers in order to establish and maintain a successful business partnership. Cantrell and Benton (2007, p 360) state that their research 'shows that the more involved managers are in employee development, learning and performance appraisals, the better the financial performance of the organisation'. These authors also emphasise the important role that line managers have in active involvement with selection and development of employees.

If we consider the results of the IRS (2010, p 5) survey on HR roles and responsibilities, 'most employers measure the effectiveness of their HR functions, with 72 per cent rating their HR function as very effective or above average based upon their evaluation.' Here HR has contributed towards managing cost cutting exercises, an increased role in developing strategy (with senior managers) and reorganising and restructuring work (in order to save costs).

When it comes to creating a learning culture in organisations, where will this emanate from: who will be the custodian of knowledge management (including knowledge creation and share)?

With regard to HRD showing added value, there is some similarity of arguments presented from HR material earlier. In a study of Indian companies, Rao and Vargese (2008, p 33) found that:

- HRD managers need to recognise stakeholder expectations and understand the overall business and strategic context of their function.

- The HRD function should focus on intellectual capital generation activities and ensure good return on investment on training and other interventions.

- HRD practitioners need to equip themselves with capacity and competencies needed to build the HRD function, and become proactive strategic partners.

- HRD practitioners need to strengthen their partnership and credibility among stakeholders through involvement with policy making.

Ulrich and Smallwood (2004) argue that HRD can create value through building organisational capabilities such as talent, speed of change, shared mindset, accountability, collaboration, learning and leadership.

More recently, the 2010 CIPD Learning and Talent Development report identified that future skills requirements over the next two years include: leadership skills (65 per cent), front-line people management skills (55 per cent), business acumen and awareness (51 per cent) and project/programme management skills (33 per cent). This report argues that the biggest change that is likely to occur over the next five years is a greater integration between coaching, organisational development and performance management to drive organisational change (46 per cent), and greater responsibility devolved to line managers (37 per cent).

CONCLUSION

HR needs to operate effectively at strategic, tactical and operational levels. Rees and McBain (2004, p 25) argue that in order for HR to maintain its importance, it needs to:

- participate in strategic decision-making, demonstrate added value, and act as a business partner

- move from assuming full responsibility for all HR managers and engage with line managers (and develop the capability of line managers)

- shift the focus from internal to external, including benchmarking against other organisations, and collecting data on competitors. This includes keeping in touch with business trends and how these impact upon people management practices within the organisation

- become more anchored in, and central to, the contribution to business, thereby building commitment from employees

- move away from reactive supporter to proactive strategic adviser, anticipating required changes.

This model echoes the principles of Business Partnership, but is less concerned with structural issues and focuses upon the role and contribution of HR more. This 'internality' argument on meeting customer needs is explored by Jenner and Taylor (2007, p 8), where HR views employees (and potential employees) as internal customers, and 'anticipating, identifying and satisfying customer requirements'.

The IRS 2010 survey results contradict some of these aspirations, and bring HR back to its transactional role. The two most prominent measures assessing HR effectiveness are absence management and staff turnover data. Employee surveys follows this, then spending against budget, and disciplinary and grievance data after that, followed by exit interview feedback.

It appears that we have gone full circle, with the continuum ranging from notions on how HR can act as a strategic business partner, to a transactional cost cutter. However, given the current economic climate and what 'has to be done', HR has an opportunity to further demonstrate its worth and contribution, and more importantly measure and communicate this effectively to major stakeholders. If it does not, it is unlikely that Cinderella will be attending the ball!

KEY LEARNING POINTS

- The HR department or function has changed considerably in the last 40 years, and tends to adopt a managerialist (corporate) position nowadays.

- HR needs to take time to evaluate and justify itself as a function or face attack or possibly outsourcing or replacement.

- Where HR sits within corporate planning is pivotal to its involvement with strategic and mainstream business activities.

- HRD and Strategic HRD play an important function in the development of employees to adding to business success.

- The HR Business Partner model carries with it a series of potential benefits and limitations, and should therefore be adapted according to the organisation and context, and possibly face up to the fact that it simply won't work as a model.

- Despite the theory, there is a great deal of evidence to suggest that HR does receive the attention and support that it requires as a key function within organisations. The interplay between line management and HR is crucial in obtaining the right business outcomes.

REVIEW QUESTIONS

1. To what extent can there be a 'perfect shape' to an HR function in an organisation? Consider the arguments both for and against this proposition.

2. Does the HR Business Partner role sit most comfortably within private, public or third sector organisations? Support your answer with practical benefits.

3. How can the HR /HRD function build relationships with line managers so as to put improved working practices into effect?

4. What is meant by 'Strategic HRD'? Evaluate the major components of Strategic HRD.

EXPLORE FURTHER

Aston Centre for Human Resources (2008) *Strategic Human Resource Management, Building research based practice*. London: CIPD.

Boxall, P. and Purcell, J. (2008) *Strategic and Human Resource Management*. 2nd ed. Basingstoke: Palgrave Macmillan. This textbook is strong on theory surrounding strategic HR.

Gilmore, S. and Williams, S. (2009) *Human Resource Management*. Oxford: Oxford University Press. This book provides grounding on many aspects of HR.

Caldwell, R. (2008) HR business partner competency models: re-contextualising effectiveness, *Human Resource Management Journal,* Vol 18 (3), pages 275–94. This article provides useful arguments around the Business Partner model.

CHAPTER 3

HRM Contributions in Different Settings

Charlotte Rayner *and* Liza Howe-Walsh

LEARNING OUTCOMES

After reading this chapter, you should be able to:

- appreciate how HR practices may differ across sector types; private, public and third sector

- recognise that delivering HR services in smaller organisations differs from those in larger organisations

- consider the ways in which the HR function may change as an organisation grows in size

- understand the concept of global HRM and its implications for practice in terms of policy and practice for localisation and control from head office

- explore the notion of Strategic International HRM: variations in practice for staffing overseas.

OVERVIEW

This chapter takes theory from Chapter 2 and applies it to the working lives of human resource practitioners (HRPs). In particular we will look at how, while the function of managing human resources is similar in most organisations, the work of the HRPs themselves varies between different organisational contexts; partly dependent on size, and also dependent on the mission of the organisation with respect to profit and not-for-profit. Without doubt the needs of an organisation change as it grows, and although all have to be compliant with the law, small businesses often only seek involvement by HR to ensure such compliance, commonly using external consultants. After growth, generalist internal HR managers are typically appointed and with further success and growth, specialists, policy designers and strategists broaden the input from HR. Their continued tenure means they are perceived as adding value to the organisation – although naturally the nature of value added varies between roles.

Public sector and third sector (not-for-profit) HR practitioners can sometimes feel undervalued in academic research, which typically focuses on those organisations seeking profit. In this chapter we argue that all HR managers 'add value', and we will explore this notion in depth with examples.

Taking the concept of context further, we explore international and 'global' HRM, presenting the practical issues of locus of control (how far the organisation controls from 'head office' or allows localisation), and the movement of staff overseas by the use of expatriates and other forms of staffing (Judge, Naoumova and Douglas, 2009). Some expensive techniques are used by organisations for staffing overseas, often with little understanding of the benefits accruing to the organisation. In all sections of this chapter, the relationship of HR practice and the interface between line managers and specialist HRPs is discussed, as we regard this link as a highly salient issue for the management and leadership of people in all types of organisation.

INTRODUCTION

Chapters 1 and 2 have outlined the main influences on HRM and HRD with regard to managing and leading people. In this chapter we will seek to change the focus in several ways. First we will concentrate on how HR adds value, initially examining what it is to add value. Quite often it is perceived that value is only added by the introduction of high quality products and services. Although value can be added in this way, it can be added in many other ways too. In this chapter we examine the original concept of 'value added' which demonstrates that cost-cutting, efficiencies and simply resolving value-losing conflicts can add to the offering of the organisation. HR practitioners may not have headline visibility in these achievements very often, but are usually important players in the success of initiatives as part of their daily work (Paauwe and Boselie, 2005). Hence we will explore the notion of adding value through a narrowing of focus to specific types of organisation and also using examples, and illustrate how the nature of the challenge within HR can vary enormously dependent upon the context one is working in. In the second section of the chapter we will broaden our scope to an international focus in order to examine the management and leadership of people in multi-country organisations. It is not only when operating from sites in other countries that international understanding is needed. When one is sending employees abroad to work on assignments, or using staff employed by organisations based in countries offshore, there is a need to understand the HR implications of increasing geographical scope. With the success of Internet-based selling and recruitment, the need for international HRM is now not just the province of large multinationals, but a real possibility for many smaller organisations and the third sector. Hence practitioners' competence in international and global HR becomes more prevalent than unusual.

HR IN DIFFERENT CONTEXTS

It is essential that all staff contribute to the organisational effort. The work output of some staff such as those in sales is highly tangible and their contribution to the organisation's goals obvious. But what of HR practitioners? As a service function, one needs to be explicit in order to identify the organisational benefit from their work (Wright and McMahan, 1992). Human resource management as a profession is connected to employees and their outputs regarding the organisation (Huselid, 1995). Our understanding of how employees contribute is largely driven by the 'resource based view' (see Boxall and Purcell, 2008 for a full description), where the value of the organisation is created from resources, of which one is employees, and HR practitioners are intricately involved in delivering such value (Paauwe and Boselie, 2005).

The notion of 'value' in contemporary strategic thinking was developed by the strategist Michael Porter who saw those in the organisation adding value in a cumulative 'value chain' (1985). As an economist he saw 'value' being related to profits. This view is reflected in a recent CIPD Employee Outlook survey (CIPD, 2009a), where around half of those asked saw their purpose at work as enhancing profits. But how does an internal service function enhance profits? Porter would suggest that value is added in two ways: either by reducing costs (hence leading to higher profit margin) or by adding features and benefits which clients and customers value and are willing to pay for and, although they cost more to deliver, can be charged for at a premium, hence adding to the profit margin. Applying Porter's guidance to the HR context of managing and leading people reveals a multitude of ways in which added value can be achieved.

Although public sector and third sector organisations do not usually seek to make profits, they are immensely budget conscious and hence we need to pay some attention to how they can use Porter's fundamentals of adding value. Being publicly funded, such organisations have to take care with all expenditure. Given that many public sector institutions carry a staff cost of at least 50 per cent of their overall budget as they are usually in a service capacity, the role of HR should be fundamental (Gould-Williams, 2003). Value can be added by a reduction in overall expenditure or doing more with the same staff after savings are made in an area, or by developing staff so that the service they provide outweighs the cost of the development.

Let us consider the public sector. Given that wages are such a major cost, HR can impact added value by contributing to projects which reduce staff costs. This might be through helping line managers reorganise work so that the same can be done with less. For example, local councils conduct much business using IT contact with their residents, meaning initial investment in website design, equipment and training existing staff, but eventual savings as automation takes effect. Paying parking tickets online rather than sending in a cheque (to be processed by staff and incurring bank charges) or visiting Council offices (with the accompanying costs of being met and dealt with in person) are two examples. The Ordinance Survey office has recently moved to a much smaller building after recruiting and training staff (over a long period) competent in technologically based mapping so that they simply didn't need their paper-based library of maps and bulky equipment. The long-term savings from the smaller new building should be significant. The new generation of staff can do more with less space. Value has been added through a very tangible change of operations stemming from the blend of HR enabling new technology.

Truss and Gill (2009) investigated the process that HR delivered in the UK public sector, exploring the issues of social capital, perceived added value and HR process through in-depth interviews at two NHS hospitals and two local councils. Their study found both value-adding and value-reducing examples. Perceptions of value reduction included poor union-employer relationships which led to stagnation and blocks to change. Poor time boundaries with recruitment were an example where line managers saw HR as reducing value through the loss of good candidates (Truss and Gill, 2009, p 679) and inconsistency in HR personnel in providing their internal services was always seen negatively (Truss and Gill, p 680). One can see how this would add to costs as line managers and senior staff sought to use HR department members who they trusted and had a reputation for delivering processes, whilst avoiding those less reliable. Timely responses by the HR department in the delivery of processes were perceived as value adding by non-HR managers in all areas. It appeared that a visible and proactive HR leader was highly influential on how HR was perceived. In most cases the HR strategic contributions were acknowledged as solid. It was in the detail of more day-to-day process where value was not positive, and also through inconsistency of personnel. Their study included HR practitioners where they correlated stronger performances with a strong sense of identity and purpose such that even if HRPs were working at a level of isolation, they knew the HR strategy and understood their contribution. HR departments which were led less well and had a poor sense of identity and cohesion amongst members were perceived less well. These lessons are likely to be useful in non-public sector contexts too.

The CIPD has recently carried out a study on high-performing HR departments in large organisations that includes the public sector (Sears, 2010). It sought to discover how HR might function in the future. The report suggested that to provide sustainable value a mind-shift away from tactical short-termism was needed. This provides a genuine challenge for the public sector, where government departments may change leadership with elections, meaning longer term visions are avoided. Service providers such as health, education and welfare frequently have funding changes, meaning a context where risk-taking on larger projects might be shunned.

What comes across in the CIPD research is the embeddedness of these high achieving HR departments in the 'business' of their organisations. As such 'HR initiatives' were rarely undertaken; instead, the organisation (or a segment) has a new thrust which involves HR as OD consultants or being involved in delivering changes connected to the new direction. Hence the notion of HR being strategic had become so much enacted that they were natural and obvious players in any change. The study demonstrated how Surrey police undertook a strategy that allowed local managers more discretion, and the ability to reach into all parts of the operation. HR policies were reviewed, reduced and rewritten 'with broad principles rather than detailed dictat' (Sears, 2010, p 9).

REFLECTIVE ACTIVITY

Consider the example of Surrey police provided above. In what ways do you think the relationship between line managers and HR may have changed as a result of the new approach? How would staff in your HR department react to enabling more managerial discretion? Discuss the strengths and weaknesses of devolving power to the line manager in the public sector.

Turning now to the private sector, costs are clearly important, and they are more likely to track profits stringently, albeit the rhetoric does not always match reality (Woodall *et al*, 2009). There are several large studies which have examined the link between HR strategy and business strategy (eg Wang and Shyu, 2008) and these are based on private sector organisations, often taking 'top performing' organisations in a financial sense and then asking about HR practices. It is becoming clear that although researchers do find positive relationships between HR alignment with business strategy and performance, the causal direction is less clear. That is, are the better financial performers just better organised and integrated, or is there something special about the alignment of HR?

An aspect which emerged for the private sector in particular in the recent CIPD research (Sears, 2010) was the need for HR to challenge all types of managers. Naturally one has to already have a culture where challenging the status quo (and also those with status) does not carry penalty to be able to challenge. However, if one does, HR is uniquely positioned to add value as it reaches into all corners of the organisation.

The ongoing debate regarding bankers' bonuses is a good example. Investment decisions are made in banks by individuals using skills (bringing together market knowledge from a range of sources), experience and professional judgement, contributing a key set of competencies that are central to the organisation's strategic success. A highly complex set of (often incomplete) data means the skill of bankers is at a premium. For a bank struggling with debt, there is an argument to pay more for skilled people who will create wealth (value) far beyond the cost of bonuses. This balance has to be weighed carefully and is one in which HR plays a role, bringing their own skills and knowledge and understanding of the implications on all parts of the business of 'perceived excess' in one area. Human resource development (HRD) can be the lynchpin for the achievement of strategies where redeployment of tasks is an aspect of implemented business strategies.

Garden centres now have cafés. Supermarkets now sell clothes as well as their traditional food lines. Couriers now drop off and pick up parcels, entering parcel movements into the computer directly through mobile terminals, multi-tasking and upgrading their responsibility in a fundamental way to add value through cost efficiency and using high performance working practices (Katou and Budhwar, 2009). All these strategic changes are designed to contribute to profit and will involve complex processes of change that result in redeployed staff re-training and quite possibly new terms and conditions of service. HR is involved in achieving strategic change, and although it may never serve a customer directly, adds value (Ulrich, Younger and Brockbank, 2008) through implementing business strategy.

The differences between the public and private sectors may not be great in many instances. Getting nurses to upgrade their skills to take over responsibilities previously the domain of qualified doctors is an increasing trend throughout the NHS. How far this is different in principle from the job redesign of the courier in the private sector is questionable. Both are about empowerment, learning and training so that responsibilities can be flattened in the hierarchy with cost savings. The value added might be spent in different ways; the hospital may do more with the same number of staff, the courier firm might expand using the savings from their strategy or pay higher dividends to shareholders. But the strategy is the same, and HR has played a key role, even though the spending of the value added might be very different.

The final sector we consider is the third sector (charitable and voluntary organisations) which often operates in fragile environments, vulnerable to changes in funder behaviour. The National Society for the Prevention of Cruelty to Children (NSPCC) has seen great changes in its activities over the years and although they have always provided care and protection for young people, they have extended their operations into training and advising local authorities, and now supervise the activities of Childline, one of the largest telephone helplines in the UK which employs highly skilled staff to deal with children who may be in extremely difficult circumstances. The need to turn their activities towards different streams of funding has meant they have had to be as nimble as any commercial organisation, but are constrained in ways not experienced by for-profit companies. The sector has expanded as government has retracted from providing direct services, such as in elderly care where there are now far fewer council-run sites with provision being delivered by private and third sector organisations (Wainwright *et al*, 2006). There is a blurring between public, private and third sector (eg Rodwell, Noblet, Stean, Osborne and Allisey, 2008). We now turn to the challenges for HR to add value in the third sector context.

Without doubt, issues to do with recruitment can be especially tough in this sector. The handling of volunteers is a specialism many charities have to manage, and input from HR into the parameters one needs to provide for such unpaid workers to engage in a way traditionally associated with that where an employment contract exists, can be tricky. It is usually the case that third sector pay at all levels, being open to scrutiny by funders and the public alike, is low (Cunningham, 2008). How does one attract and retain talent in such contexts? How does one fund training and other learning opportunities in order to develop staff when budgets are commonly connected in discrete ways to deliverable projects? How far can 'rewarding work' be used or abused? The sector is poorly researched from an HR perspective, and one must question how far such organisations are able to voice concerns for fear of upsetting funders and users alike.

Central to issues around funding and reward of employees is the relationship between the third sector group and other agencies with which it partners. In elderly care the partner might be a local council; in education, a government department; in research it may be the NHS or specific benefactors. It is common that funders impose terms and conditions on those agencies which deliver services (Marchington, Vincent and Cooke, 2005) thus leaving the third sector provider little room for movement. In addition, competitive tendering for third sector contracts may mean those involved with negotiating contracts have to be very lean with their highest cost factor – employees (Cunningham, 2008). As funding is based on contracts typically lasting one to two years, substantial long term investment or investment in potential new areas of work through HRD can be difficult to resource. Cunningham's study in the Scottish voluntary sector identified three types of agencies: those who aligned with local authority terms and conditions and developed reputation and quality consistency, serving many clients (hence dependent on few); those who compromised on some terms and conditions and were quite hand-to-mouth on contracts; and finally those who were 'struggling to care' (Cunningham, p 1041) for employees, being dependent on few large contracts and in poor bargaining positions.

To add to the pressure, third sector organisations have to protect their reputation with great care. The notion of employer branding has been used very well by those in the sector to bolster the non-financial rewards of employment and also provide an enhanced image for funders. It is essential to deliver on any promises made in branding in this sector, as so much funding is local and bad news can travel fast.

REFLECTIVE ACTIVITY

Funding HRD activities in the third sector can be problematic, especially providing learning events for the many staff who are on low wages. The Children's Society takes advantage of a strong link with the trade union UNITE. In several instances, the Society has enabled a few employees (who are often workplace representatives) to attend UNITE training, who then cascade the knowledge and skills through the Society at a far lower cost than external providers but to exacting standards.

The Children's Society is quite a large charity. How might a small charity enable learning and development to be funded or delivered at low cost?

Some areas of HR add value directly in any organisation, for example in the provision or overseeing of administrative tasks connected to people: wage systems, pensions, employment records, benefits and rewards systems. These are fundamental to the functioning of all organisations. However, they are often seen as 'hygiene factors' and so are not necessarily valued when everything goes well, but heavily criticised when they fail to perform. Few employees are grateful for being paid on time, but most would be unhappy if wages arrived late! Their effectiveness provides value and ineffectiveness causes cost, thus reducing value.

Without doubt HR adds value through some of the roles described by Ulrich and Brockbank (2005). It is always valued for its contribution in keeping the organisation in compliance with legal requirements (the HR expert), and in having specialists who provide policy advice and implementation at a strategic level (HR strategists).

The data for the performance value (financial and otherwise) created by HR professionals is difficult to study with certainty (Paauwe, 2009) because if one uses broad brush measures (such as return on capital employed) many non-employee components are involved, thus making a 'straight line' between HR involvement and organisation-level performance measures impossible to measure with certainty or at least to be treated with extreme caution (Wright and Haggerty, 2005). Many HR initiatives concern longer term development where an outcome (such as learning) might take many years to impact directly (Anderson, 2007) and hence shorter term value might be perceived in more fluid terms as a function of 'return on expectations' by senior and line managers.

REFLECTIVE ACTIVITY

Please consider a recent major change in your organisation. Could this have been undertaken without HR input? What was the nature of that input (with regard to your specific type of organisation) and did it add value through reducing costs further or achieving the change more efficiently or effectively?

HR ROLES AS THE ORGANISATION GROWS: SMES

The function of HR is needed in all organisations beyond the simple formation of a partnership between two or more individuals. Many small organisations do not see the need to employ an HR specialist and, forever cost conscious, tend not to directly employ HR assistance until it is really needed – perhaps as a result of hygiene factors not being met. Instead HR might be outsourced to an HR consultant retained for policy and administrative tasks with their legal expertise enabling the small organisation to adhere to regulations. The small business is very reliant on the skills and knowledge of the consultant, and as such somewhat vulnerable unless the provider is effective. Many HR consultants do excellent work with small businesses, often beginning with a limited and legalistically-geared brief and patiently expanding their role into Organisational Development, HRD and other facets of delivery as the organisation is successful. Indeed, contact with HR consultants is sometimes the only space when owner-managers of small businesses take time away from their operational focus to consider their staff in a systematic and future-oriented manner.

The next evolutionary step is to hire an HR generalist to service the small firm, and logically occurs when it is cost effective to do so. A small business generalist needs by default to be a jack-of-all-trades (perhaps with the exception of legal support) and undertake (or at least coordinate) all HR roles. HR generalists may not be providing very sophisticated services, but it is likely they will be closely aligned with the 'business' as their day-to-day activities are immersed with those connected to clients, suppliers and the product/service to be delivered. Short lines of communication and close contact with seniors should mean fast delivery of change. Naturally the agenda will be limited in scope and also limited through limited funding, but the capacity to add value focused on the business is very high. Greiner (1972) suggests that as organisations grow they pass through a series of crises. Almost like a squeeze-box movement, the locus of control is central. Most small business owners like to have control, but this can become more difficult as the organisation grows, failing to deliver optimal effectiveness as the owner-manager becomes a bottle-neck of decisions and checking employees' work. In some senses many small businesses reflect the 'hard HR' model (for the Michigan Approach, see Boselie, Brewster and Paauwe, 2009 for a review). A resolution of this early Greiner crisis for small businesses sees a middle line of managers having more autonomy to enable growth. It is possible at this time one moves into more development as typified by the 'soft HR' Harvard school (*ibid*), although hard HR may predominate. But greater autonomy risks fragmentation as the organisation may grow in different ways under the direction of a team of sub-unit leaders, leading to a crisis of control. Greiner's next crisis is therefore a need to pull things back into a more coherent whole again. Even at this stage, as often SMEs do not devolve much decision-making, the HR generalist has only a few key managers to deal with. Unitarism is assumed, and the atmosphere is often still patriarchal (Legge, 2005), especially if the owner-manager is still in charge. If a full time HR professional has not been hired before now, it is likely this crisis sets the scene for the change.

In what way can the generalist HR practitioner provide value for the SME? Becker and Huselid (2006) are clear that beyond the standard HR administration, the focus of any HR activity, if it is to be aligned into the organisation strategy, needs to focus in areas rich in human capital. Hence HR can provide insight on focusing effort on those who create the value which is essential for strategic success. Thus an importer geared to growth through extending market share can focus on rewards connected to performance targets with appraisal and feedback to those sourcing and selling products as the nexus of Strategic Human Resource Management (SHRM). A professional firm of knowledge workers may have a different focus such as that of HRD opportunities and an emphasis on life-balance as a means to recruit, retain and foster performance in the professionals who are key to delivering the organisational offering. In the medium-sized organisation HR professionals thinking through these 'bundles' (Gould-Williams, 2003) for the organisation can add great value. It should be noted that Becker and Huselid concur with others that not all employees add strategic value to the organisation and they argue the SHRM architecture needs to be built around the human capital which adds the crucial value for the organisation's strategy. Their evidence concerns operational delivery of HR, holding interest to generalists especially, and they suggest 'workforce strategy' is a good term to use as everyone can grasp its significance, including line managers who can partner in its formation.

As the firm grows, it is likely that so too will the number of HR professionals, with evolution into the better defined roles (as described by Ulrich) as a progression. However, as the medium-sized organisation works its way through the growth cycles, the final stage Greiner suggests is a 'crisis of red tape' as bureaucracy has been used to coordinate the organisation – a complaint which will not surprise any seasoned HR practitioner!

 REFLECTIVE ACTIVITY

Quicksilver has 200 employees and is a leader in yacht insurance worldwide, and is based in Cowes on the Isle of Wight. Careful stewardship through early years, and the retraction of mainstream insurers from the niche has allowed steady growth. Internet and magazine advertising links customers to the call centre (100 staff) which also deals with initial claims. Each staff area has a Board Director. There is an underwriting and claims group (40 staff), the marketing department works with IT (15 staff), and the finance department (18 staff) is under the direct control of the CEO who is a qualified accountant. Quicksilver has a differentiated strategy, not the cheapest in the market, but reliable for reasonable claims. The firm employs three HR practitioners who also oversee the building and non-IT facilities. One looks after recruitment, with call centre staff being a main headache; one deals with HR administration and facility issues; and Sylvia Norris is the HR Director dealing with policy and strategic issues, and also helps out her line-reports. Call centre staff are trained by an external provider. The credit crisis did not affect their own financial standing, but customers are looking for cheaper deals and 'dodgy claims' are increasing. This has led to a stagnation in growth and internal tensions are rising in the firm as non-payment of claims has affected their reputation. Sylvia has been challenged that the once positively regarded 'professional' practices in HR (clear job descriptions, target-setting and performance appraisal systems for example) are tying everyone down far too much as 'belts need to be tightened'.

www.XpertHR.co.uk

Question

1. How can Sylvia respond to these pressures?
2. In what other ways can she and her team add value at this time in the growth of the firm?

The larger organisation holds different challenges for HR. Diversification may mean different strategies in different sub-units and human capital investment may vary across the organisation (Boxall and Purcell, 2008). The drive for efficiencies through standardisation of processes and policies may mean over-bureaucratisation in some cases and insufficient support in others (*ibid*). In larger organisations there are many decision makers and coordination within the HR department may become paramount to gather issues and focus effort (Sears, 2010; De Vos and Meganck, 2009). As the distance between key areas for attention and HR increases, so gaps may appear. It is perhaps not surprising that the seam of 'critical HR' research (which includes examination of dysfunction between HR effort and what is valued) is undertaken almost always in large organisations (eg Truss and Gill, 2009; De Vos and Meganck, 2009). One might see that coordination activities within HR cost salaries, but the effect a synergistic team can provide can make a real difference (Becker and Huselid, 2006, p 907).

There has been a trend over the last decade away from vertical integration (where one owns all aspects of the organisation) towards outsourcing and supply-chain management. A common technique in large organisations, how far can HR be outsourced? The strategy literature suggests that when outsourcing, it is only those aspects of the organisation that do not contribute to strategic success which should be considered – otherwise one has competitive competency owned by others. Many surveys from the CIPD show that wages are commonly outsourced by organisations of all sizes – a specialist firm can often provide payroll cheaper than in-house. Other aspects of HR are far more contentious. How far should training and other learning events be outsourced? If knowledge is central to the product or service being offered, surely HRD must be provided in-house? Opinions differ, and there are bold examples of outsourcing such as at Hampshire County Council when the whole HR department was outsourced.

 REFLECTIVE ACTIVITY

Visit the CIPD website at www.cipd.co.uk. Look through its collection of surveys and related articles on outsourcing. Pick one function of HR that is contentious in terms of being outsourced.

Questions

1. Are the factors to be considered the same for large private and large public sector organisations?

2. Should HR ever be entirely outsourced?

3. What are your views as to the aspects of HR which should always remain in-house?

Outsourcing in HR is a debate that will no doubt continue. An interesting set of data is shown by Wahrenburg, Hackethal, Friedrich and Gellrich (2006, p 1747), displaying variation across the portfolio of HR activities. As one would expect, clerical functions are far more likely to be outsourced than top management advice. They found variation between industries with some commonality within industry (they examined finance in particular). We would argue that if the whole of HR is outsourced it is seen as a commodity adding no strategic value and then in some senses the profession has failed (Priem and Butler, 2001). One must recognise that some strategic advice will come from consultants who have broadened activities from being auditors and advising on finance to helping with cost and value-added. If HR is entirely outsourced, clearly the message from the architects of the organisation is that HR as a function is not seen as central to the management and leading of people in providing competitive advantage (Woodall *et al*, 2009). Clearly this argument has many decades to run.

The shift into and out of outsourcing has provided a highly diverse situation for HR practitioners and those seeking a career in HR. Opportunities for roles exist within all sectors, either fully employed by an organisation or acting as a consultant independently or as part of an outsourced agency. In the end the HR function is delivered. But how the value is created and by whom varies as to the context one is examining and the choices the organisation has made (Boselie, Brewster and Paauwe, 2009).

REFLECTIVE ACTIVITY

A small law firm is having difficulty attracting and retaining lawyers in a provincial office overseas, they currently have no in-house HR function. The partner in charge has decided to introduce flexible benefits in line with the larger competitors.

Brief the management team on how the benefits could be introduced and managed.

How could they utilise HR input to assist with their goal?

EXPANDING OUR BORDERS: THE GROWTH OF INTERNALISATION

This millennium is seeing the world connected internationally through the use of the Internet, changing the scope for recruitment, working and operations at a fundamental level. Such advances mean that national borders are being crossed by even small organisations who now find foreign markets hold the staff they need, or hold customers who might want their organisation's products and services. Thus the portfolio of skills needed in managing and leading people is becoming an international arena, and one for which the HR professional needs to be prepared. It is to the international context that our attention now turns.

Why do we need to explore global strategy in HRM? HR as part of the strategic component delivering organisational strategy is increasingly breaking national borders (Sparrow *et al*, 2005). With wider globalisation, HR is under pressure to deliver policies and practices that will support the business objectives of the organisation and demonstrate results in an increasingly competitive economic environment. Working alongside the other business functions such as finance, operations and corporate departments, HR have to understand how they can help to deliver the vision to the business in an international context.

Changes to demographics, such as an ageing workforce and the emergence of developing countries, mean that looking towards future staffing may require an international approach. We see more organisations requiring staff to be internationally mobile. Organisations compete for talent across the globe as individuals broaden their search for the best employment opportunities, globalising recruitment markets. Those organisations with sites overseas require an understanding of the complexities involved with managing staff internationally and the impact this has upon the global HR strategy.

Global staffing can play a key role in shaping the competitive position of multinational enterprises (MNEs) via individuals' transfer of knowledge across the organisation, which is often cited as one of the main reasons to undertake an international assignment. Additionally the widely accepted reasons for transferring staff from one country to another include developing the individuals' management or leadership skills, knowledge of markets or products or strengthening the organisation's international competencies (Strack *et al*, 2007).

Much of the research in international human resource management (IHRM) focuses upon the management of staff within MNEs and involves the study of expatriates, but can also apply to small and medium-sized enterprises (SMEs) and a broader definition of international staff.

STRATEGIC INTERNATIONAL HRM

The trend over the last few years has been to attempt to link international human resource management (IHRM) to the strategy of the organisation in line with fulfilling the company's global strategy (SIHRM).

 REFLECTIVE ACTIVITY

HSBC defines itself as 'the world's local bank' in its marketing. Visit its websites and examine its corporate messages.

Questions

1. What effect does this international branding have on HR in the UK?

2. Given HSBC's messages, how would you approach someone in a London office of the firm to undertake an overseas assignment in a subsidiary in Detroit for two years?

DEFINING STRATEGIC INTERNATIONAL HRM

In order to highlight the context of SIHRM, a definition is needed. Schuler *et al* (1993, p 422) define SIHRM as:

> human resource management issues, functions, and policies and practices that result from the strategic activities of multinational enterprises and that impact the international concerns and goals of those enterprises.

The definition brings together a number of factors that include literature from international business and management, as well as international human resource management. 'In essence, MNEs are firms that need to be global and local (multi-domestic) at the same time' (Schuler *et al*, 1993, p 421).

Schuler *et al* (1993) explore this notion through the development of an integrative framework to further our understanding of strategic international human resource management (SIHRM). The development of a framework leads to including three major components: issues, functions, and policies and practices, which in turn are influenced by MNEs' Strategic activities. These will now be discussed.

SIHRM issues

The organisation needs to decide how much control it allows the local business whilst considering that this may vary dependent upon the local environment. Cultural differences play a part in the decision as to which approach the organisation will pursue. Human resource management plays an important role within the organisation in terms of integrated or differentiating practices.

SHIRM functions

The function relates to human resource orientation: the time, energy and financial resources operating the human resource organisation and the locations of the resources. There are several ways that the company may choose to manage its human resources. For example, all HR policy and practice activities are handed down from headquarters of the MNE. In contrast, local divisions are able to tailor HR practices that are more locally accepted such as the promotion criteria.

SHIRM policies and practices

Policies and practices involve developing general guidelines on how individuals will be managed and developed within the organisation. For example, the HR policy may outline the reward structure and instruct all sites to pay the local median for certain grades of employees. However, it may be part of the company's overall strategy to take into consideration the nuances within a particular environment. For example, it will provide specific practices that are appropriate to the local market, such as incentivised pay schemes for specific talent sectors. Indeed, there may be particular local requirements that will impact upon HR policy and practices in terms of legislation, such as the minimum wage etc. Therefore, a single policy acts as a guide whilst consideration is provided as to local terms and culture.

It can be seen that a thread throughout the issues, functions and policies described above is that of the degree of localisation allowed by the parent office. Organisations vary enormously as to how far this is granted, and it may not be standard across the whole organisation.

But how does international or global HRM differ from domestic HRM? Evolution to IHRM complicates HRM practices (Kiessling and Harvey, 2005). There are different types of employees to consider such as host-country nationals (HCNs), parent-country nationals (PCNS) and third-country nationals (TCNs).

CASE STUDY

IBM

Let us use the illustration of IBM, where the parent organisation is based in the USA. It has offices in the UK, where British employees would be seen as HCNs. It might also have staff from the USA (PCNs), and employ specialist staff from anywhere in the world who are neither British nor American nationals (TCNs). The international context introduces different ways in which these employees are employed, such as: expatriates (for IBM, the USA manager takes a two-year job in the UK but is still employed by the parent office); inpatriates (coming from a subsidiary into headquarters – in our example a UK manager taking a two-year contract to work in IBM in the USA but still employed through the British office); hybrid arrangements or on local conditions where a foreign national decides to be employed directly by the local organisation.

REFLECTIVE ACTIVITY

Your organisation, a UK-based telecoms company employing 100 people, wants to expand their market share in South Africa and they decide to open a dedicated office in Johannesburg as part of their long term strategy. The office will provide the hub for future training of local employees. Advise the organisation on which strategy would achieve their aims to introduce the headquarter's culture and ethos in terms of work practices to the new office. The current HR function is served by one consultant with part-time administration support. Which of the following approaches would you advise and why?

- Use a two-year long term assignment, a traditional expatriate package.
- Use a short term assignment.
- Hire someone locally and provide them with some headquarters training.
- Employ someone from headquarters on local terms and conditions.

It is useful at this point to highlight the various staffing strategies that global organisations utilise. Influences towards staffing strategies were first addressed by Perlmutter (1969) and later extended to provide the following approaches to global staffing (Heenan and Perlmutter, 1979):

- Ethnocentric – strategic decisions are made by the headquarters by parent country (PCNs) expatriates. It is thus accepted that all policies and practices emanate from headquarters. Arguably, the advantage is that qualified managers are available from the home country (precluding any local labour shortage). However, this approach does limit the opportunity to promote host-country nationals to senior managerial positions, hence risking the loss of staff with this potentially short term view.

- Polycentric – generally the operations would be managed by host-country nationals (HCNs) with the intention that they remain in the host country precluding the use of expensive expatriates from the parent company. There are disadvantages to this approach in the limiting of assignments by home or host, reducing knowledge transfer and management.

- Geocentric – this approach seeks to resource the best person for the position regardless of their nationality.

- Regiocentric – some autonomy is reflected in this approach towards decision-making. This approach is likely to facilitate more local responsiveness towards operation and form regional boundaries according to geographical locations such as Eastern Europe, the Mediterranean, Northern USA etc.

Both polycentric and regiocentric approaches allow for more local responsiveness, with less corporate integration. However, the danger is that there is knowledge being built in subsidiaries by HCNs which the parent does not benefit from, at a risk of losing competitive edge.

Many of these strategies ask people to work overseas. The term 'expatriate' refers to someone who is temporarily assigned to an overseas location from their home organisation. Some organisations refer to such individuals as international assignees. Traditionally, expatriate assignments are considered to fall into either long term assignments over 12 months to a maximum of four years; short term assignments of three to twelve months; or business trips typically lasting no longer than three months.

Long term assignments are considered to be over 12 months in duration and offer a full compensation package whereby the expatriate is provided host housing, living allowances, removal etc. Often long term assignments incorporate arrangements for a partner and children. In terms of cost it is generally accepted that an assignment will cost the organisation three to four times the expatriate's salary (GMAC, 2008).

 REFLECTIVE ACTIVITY

If the costs for the use of expatriates are so high, what arguments are there for such assignments to be used by organisations?

The rationale for an overseas assignment should always be considered. MNEs often favour a long term assignment when the objective is to commence business operation in an overseas location. However, a smaller organisation may not have the resources to utilise a long term assignment as that individual is intrinsic to the home company. Therefore, the strategy of staffing may well differ depending on the size of the organisation.

AGILENT TECHNOLOGIES

The move to reduce costs has seen a decline in the number of long term assignments with organisations utilising short term assignments instead. Agilent Technologies has seen an overall reduction in headcount in line with many MNEs over the last few years in order to reduce costs. This led to reducing its multimillion-dollar expatriate programme (Workforce Management, 2004). In order to understand the cost involved with their expatriate programme, Agilent outsourced the administration of their expatriates. In 2000 Agilent had approximately 1,000 expats costing $72 million. Over the next three years, the company reduced the number of expatriates to around 300 expats. In order to achieve this large reduction in headcount Agilent looked at alternative ways of resourcing positions, favouring the local market. In addition a review of their policy and expatriate package has seen a large scale reduction in benefits offered, to reduce costs by 70 per cent to $23 million.

Agilent's example raises some interesting points. Until the company decided to outsource their expatriate programme they had not considered the actual costs; they knew expatriates were expensive but did not realise the extent. The challenge of tracking expatriates is echoed by many MNEs (Workforce Management 2004).

Questions

1. How would you recommend Agilent assess the success of its programme, other than the reduction of cost for its expatriate programme?

2. What do you think the effect of reducing the number of expat opportunities could have been at Agilent head office?

3. How would you be able to track such effects?

4. What effect might you want to look for in the various subsidiaries?

5. How might you measure the impact?

SHORT TERM ASSIGNMENTS

The move towards cost reduction has contributed towards the increase in short term assignments. Recent data found 70 per cent of international assignments were scheduled for one year or less, compared to only 13 per cent planned for that duration in previous years (GMAC, 2008). Instead of providing an expatriate package that allows the employee to take their immediate family on assignment, the organisation supports only the assignee. Costs are saved by precluding education costs as well as reduced housing costs (as the expat is not accompanied by their family) and further allowances associated with a long term assignment such as family health care insurance. Thus the employee is sent overseas with minimal support and cost.

REFLECTIVE ACTIVITY

Consider this description:

> Avaya Inc, a provider of communication systems, started sending more employees on short term assignments. Typically assignments last for six months and are managed as a business trip. The employee stays in a hotel or company apartment and is reimbursed for meals and trips home every other month, eliminating the need to pay costly housing allowances and costs related to moving the employee's family (Workforce Management, 2004).

Questions

Assume the previous system was one of two-year assignments accompanied by a family.

1. What effect would this change have had on the type of applicants for the job?

2. What effect would the change have had on recipients of the services of these assignees in the host country?

3. Would any of these changes worry you from an HR perspective?

4. How would you advise Avaya to proceed?

THIRD-COUNTRY NATIONALS

A third-country national (TCN) is an individual who works for an international organisation whose nationality is different from that of the company, and of the country in which the organisation operates – for example, a UK manager working for a Spanish subsidiary of an American company. The advantages of TCNs from the company's point of view are that they need to provide very limited additional assistance for a limited period such as housing, education tax etc. There is an increased trend towards this type of employee and companies such as Avaya have increased TCNs by over 50 per cent during the last decade (Workforce Management, 2004).

LOCALISATION

Another alternative to an expatriate assignment is the use of localisation. This is where expatriates move permanently to local terms and conditions, and this has seen an increase over the last decade (GMAC, 2008). This could be at the end of a long or short term assignment at the choice of the individual. Or an individual may be sent on assignment with the expectation that they would localise with minimal support from the company. The move towards recruiting expatriates on the basis that they will localise from the beginning is not new, especially within the 20-year-old plus market. However, what has changed is the push to hire employees locally and not use expatriates at all – here the local employer might take on someone who lives only miles from the parent company but who is never employed by the parent. The benefit to the organisation is the significant saving in expatriate terms and conditions, especially education costs for children as well as cost of housing. An emerging trend of hybrid packages allows expatriates access to some of the expatriate package initially to set them up in the new country and then gradually removes the benefits during the year, such as help with rented accommodation.

SELF-INITIATED EXPATRIATES

An area relatively under-explored is the increase in self-initiated expatriates (SIEs) (Howe-Walsh and Schyns, 2010). A self-initiated expatriate independently moves to another country for employment. As such, a self-initiated expatriate does not receive any additional support from their home country employer. However, there are opportunities to manage this growing pool of resources more effectively. Research has shown that self-initiated expatriates themselves note several combined reasons for pursuing an overseas appointment: career development; location of vacancy; no family ties; dissatisfaction with current lifestyle; timing (Fitzgerald and Howe-Walsh, 2008).

Who manages these types of staffing arrangements can often become blurred. Whilst the self-initiated expatriate will be treated as an ordinary new joiner, other support mechanisms can be put in place to support their initial move. There are additional considerations to explore regarding the level of support the HR function can offer during the recruitment phase. In a traditional expatriate assignment services such as cultural training would be offered prior to the assignment.

Howe-Walsh and Schyns (2010) show how different types of adjustment require the use of differing HR practices. In order to make the most of self-initiated expatriates, consideration of how the organisation can aid their initial adjustment can provide a strategic advantage over companies that do not provide support by attracting good candidates. The following points are highlighted as areas to explore in order to improve the process of recruitment and retaining self-initiated expatriates:

- Recruitment strategy: developing the reputation of the organisation as an employer of choice attracts candidates, assisting with recruitment of talent (Glen, 2006). Selecting the right candidates poses challenges for any organisation. Self-initiated expatriates offer additional benefits to the organisation during the early stages of their employment as they are already receptive to working in an overseas location, so the likelihood of them having problems adjusting to the local culture diminish (Tharenou, 2008). In addition, they have chosen the organisation and the position offered, rather than being sent on an assignment.

- Training and mentoring: whilst new joiners are often provided with some sort of induction training it is unlikely that a self-initiated expatriate will be offered any cultural training for reasons outlined before. However, the benefits of mentoring should be considered. One area a mentor can provide assistance with is in helping the self-initiated expatriate to gain a greater working knowledge of the organisation, again akin to the services offered to any new joiner.

- Non-work support: the types of activities that HR would traditionally support for an expatriate should also be considered in terms of self-initiated expatriates. Finding accommodation can be one of the most stressful parts of relocation. HR can provide support in terms of facilitating the search for properties as well as assistance with tenancy agreements. Other forms of support include opening bank accounts, social security and residence registration, communication connections and expatriate social groups. Facilitating these types of support enables the SIE to start work faster and add value to the organisation.

GLOBAL/INTERNATIONAL HR AND THE SME

The discussion so far has revolved around MNEs. However, arguably, much of the business conducted today is undertaken by small to medium-sized firms (SMEs), many of whom have a global dimension, often levered through the Internet, but with implications for the HR function (Engle *et al*, 2008). IHRM is mainly focused upon MNEs and as such there is an argument to say that transferring the HRM practices from MNEs to SMEs is limited (Festing, 2007).

Drawing upon the research of MNE organisations, SMEs pose different challenges (Anderson and Skinner, 1999). SMEs are more dependent upon environmental situations in different countries. Anderson and Boocock (2002) suggest this relates to:

- The importance of the founder/owner. Within any organisation there are links to how the organisation is perceived and its leader (Festing, 2007). Within an SME the owners' entrepreneurial style, the way they conduct business, can be part of the attraction of working for the organisation.

- Recruitment, selection and retention within an SME is likely to be managed without the assistance of an HR function and more informal processes are therefore utilised.

The most striking difference between MNEs and SMEs is that the SMEs do not have the same human resources department infrastructure capability, as previously mentioned. Sending managers overseas to open or start new business ventures is thus not supported by an HR function locally or any specialists at the parent organisation. Being able to construct value-adding arguments for managing a limited number of staff overseas becomes more difficult in such circumstances (Bowen and Ostroff, 2004).

WHO IS RESPONSIBLE FOR INTERNATIONAL HR POLICY?

Traditionally within an MNE, IHR policy and practice is undertaken by specialists, either as part of the HR team, or partially or fully outsourced, as outlined with Agilent Technologies. The decision as to what policies the company choose to adopt towards their international workforce ultimately rests with the organisation's overall strategy. Nearly two thirds of companies (64 per cent) have no specific procedures in place to measure the success of their expatriate benefit programmes (Mercer, 2008/9). Thus there are issues with retention and monitoring from the outset of the expatriate's career path.

DEVOLUTION TO LINE MANAGERS

With increased devolution to line managers it is important to consider the perceptions of more than one stakeholder. We have already noted that HR delivery of international services may be internal to the HR function, a separate specialised function or outsourced. It is increasingly becoming the norm with MNEs that HR policy and practice delivery is undertaken by the line manager (Perry and Kulik, 2008). Within an international context the likelihood within an MNE is that there will be a duplication of organisational stakeholders within the home country and host country. The multiple stakeholders involved in managing individuals across more than one country add another dimension to managing people. A greater understanding of the stakeholders highlights the necessity for clear and transparent strategy supported by HR policy and practice.

 IHG

CASE STUDY

Asia is a rapidly developing continent and the ubiquitous 'war for talent' is accentuated for the Intercontinental Hotels Group (IHG) with rival hotels from China constantly approaching staff with job offers. HR's biggest challenge, according to Ricky Wong, HR director, IHG Hong Kong, is finding and keeping the right people in such an aggressive labour market.

'I'm really concerned that our staff will be poached by competitors,' Wong says. 'Managers from hotels In Macau come to our hotel and sit in the lobby to check out the staff they want to poach. The particular hotel I'm talking about has 3,000 rooms and they need experienced managers.'

So where will they find them? 'They'll find them at the five-star hotels in Hong Kong – hotels like ours,' says Wong. As a result of such measures, he takes career development very seriously. Many of IHG Hong Kong's employees have been at the company for several years, and while he cannot promise promotions, on-the-job learning with greater participation in

management decisions is a must to keep staff engaged.

'Many employees are looking for personal development. They can suggest how to do the job better, and we encourage that. They can disagree with managers – and that's not easy in the traditionally hierarchical culture of Asia. We "allow" them to disagree and to have a sense of involvement,' says Wong. This mature approach to managing employees seems to be working. IHG's staff turnover is at 12 per cent, a hefty 8 per cent lower than that of its main Hong Kong competitor (another five-star hotel), according to Wong. (Xperthr, 2008)

www.XpertHR.co.uk

Questions

1. Identify and appraise the attitudes and approaches adopted in this excerpt.

2. What other tactics might be employed to further enhance the achievement at IHG?

3. In what ways is the HR strategy adding value to the organisation?

CONCLUSION

In concluding this chapter, one can see that approaches for delivering support for managing and leading people become more complex as the organisation expands in terms of the number of employees, the scope of the organisation and its geographical reach. We have examined how the emphasis on what an HR practitioner actually does varies with the size, stage in development and sector of the organisation being served. Adding value from HR is possible in all circumstances. Although much is made of HR aligning with the strategy of the organisation (eg Wang and Shyu, 2008), this becomes more difficult as the organisation grows and the physical and psychological distance between HR and decision makers becomes greater. No doubt an area for development in research is the political skills HR practitioners need to develop in order to influence and ensure that their value-adding ideas are tried by the organisation (Dany, Guedri and Hatt, 2008), and that their work receives sufficient profile to make sure it is perceived as value-adding (Sears, 2010).

We have seen that cutting costs through outsourcing is a common trend, and likely to continue as vertical integration is lessened. HR is not immune from these trends, but if it is to remain a strategic component of success, aspects of HR need to be kept in-house (Woodall *et al*, 2009). The level of outsourcing affords many varied career opportunities for HR practitioners working in providers of services. There is a danger though that career paths in these directions may be limited to 'being efficient' only in cost-effective terms rather than adding value in more subtle ways.

Less and less are international issues the prerogative of large multinationals. Globalising job markets as well as the opportunities that the Internet provides for selling products and services abroad means that complexity can arrive sooner rather than later for many in the HR function.

KEY LEARNING POINTS

- The HR function adds value to the organisation in a number of ways through delivering business strategy.

- The HR function adds value, but how it does, and who is perceived as adding value is complex and sometimes a function of internal politics and perceptions of line managers.

- The way in which HR adds value changes as the organisation grows, and also between sectors.

- Outsourcing aspects of HR is common, but needs to be done carefully to ensure the organisation does not lose competitive edge.

- Internationalisation is a current issue for those who recruit, and for those involved in mobilising staff between countries.

- The degree of control from the parent company in the area of international HR presents a challenge which needs to be balanced depending on the context.

REVIEW QUESTIONS

1. Do you think HR professionals at all levels can demonstrate value-added - or is this an issue only for people at the top?

2. What would you see as the challenges of someone changing job from being a business partner in HR in the private sector to one in the public sector? How would you suggest such an individual prepares for their new role?

3. The chapter has considered outsourcing. Assuming there are financial gains for providing an outsourced HR service, what other parameters would you consider when evaluating this issue?

4. Why is adding an international dimension to one's operation so challenging for HR? Use the example of a UK organisation setting up a sales office in Canada as an example to illustrate your ideas. In this operation some local Canadian staff would be employed, but need Head Office help during the set-up period.

EXPLORE FURTHER

Becker, B. and Huselid, M. A. (2006) Strategic human resource management: where do we go from here? *Journal of Management*, Vol 32, No 6, pp 898–925.

This article is a very effective overview of the strategic issues within HR. The application of business strategy into the undertaking of HR roles is both thought-provoking and holds a list of key texts should readers wish to pursue the forms of HR delivery within organisations.

Boselie, P., Brewster, C. and Paauwe, J. (2009) In search of balance: managing the dualities of HRM, *Personnel Review*, Vol 38, No 5, pp 461–71.

This paper provides an excellent overview of the Strategic HR issues and constructs in contemporary thinking with an excellent reading base for further exploration. This can be compared to the CIPD-sponsored research (Sears, 2010) which is drawn from large organisations where the notion that practice outstrips thinking and academic work is put forward.

Tharenou, P. (2008) Self-Initiated careers. In Baugh, G. and Sullivan, S. E. *Maintaining focus, energy and options over the career,* pp 197–224, Information Age Publishing. Howe-Walsh, L. J. and Schyns, B. (2010) Self-initiated expatriates: implications for HRM, *International Journal of Human Resource Management*, Vol 21, No 2, pp 260–73.

These two contributions give useful insights into the developing area of self-initiated expatriates – a field which is likely to become more important for recruiters in all organisations and one which is not often studied.

Woodall, J., Scott-Jackson, W., Newham, T. and Gurney, M (2009) Managing the decision to outsource human resources, *Personnel Review,* Vol 38, No 3, pp 236–52. This article provides a very good literature review of outsourcing HR and a fascinating study of practice in contemporary UK-based organisations. Tracking through their references, readers will find key evidence regarding the need for HR not only to undertake an effective role, but also to be seen to do so.

CHAPTER 4

Professionalism and Ethics in Managing People

Charlotte Rayner *and* Richard Christy

LEARNING OUTCOMES

After reading this chapter, you should be able to:

- understand the concept of business ethics

- explain the difference between the duties, consequences and virtues approaches to ethics

- comprehend what may be meant by an 'ethical dimension' to the management and leadership of human resources

- identify the link between ethics, equal opportunities and diversity management

- appreciate the role of ethical codes of conduct

- understand the role of professional associations

- consider the implications for professional leadership in HRM.

OVERVIEW

Professionalism is not just what you do; it includes the principles behind what you do. People in organisations detect signs of what is acceptable and the tenets by which the organisation works from their line manager, as well as their basic upbringing (Wiley, 2000). Human resource (HR) practitioners play a key role in standard-setting. Naturally they get involved when situations go wrong, but their key work is in preventing misbehaviour through their own role modelling, the advice they give to line managers, and the type of attention they pay to policies.

In this chapter we will examine ethics in general terms and the professional leadership that HR practitioners can bring. We will suggest that being ethical is part of a professional identity. We begin this chapter by considering ethics in a general sense and applying ethical decision-making to the workplace. We use a variety of examples including an illustration of equal opportunities and the potential for positive discrimination – no doubt a debate set to run for some time. Finally we focus on the role of the HR practitioner as a professional, examining the key elements of professionalism (including the role of the CIPD) and discussing some contemporary ideas on the HR profession.

INTRODUCTION

One way to think about business strategy is to see it as the way in which an organisation deploys its resources in order to achieve its goals. To be successful in a changing environment, an organisation needs to keep all of its resources aligned to the chosen strategy, which may involve acquiring new resources, developing existing resources and disposing of resources that are no longer of value to the organisation and its strategy (Caligiuri, Lepak, and Bonache, 2010). These days, the phrase 'human resources' is in general use, so we might pose the question: is it acceptable for an organisation to treat its human resources in the same way as other non-human resources? If not, why not, and what rules should apply?

Thinking about these issues is important because the ethics of managing human resources will depend to some extent on the nature of the relationship between an employer and its employees. A firm's delivery van, for example, could be defined as part of its 'transportation resources'. This van is exclusively available to the firm, can be used (within the law) as the firm sees fit, can be rented out or sold when no longer needed or scrapped when no longer useful to the firm. Is the same true of the firm's human resources? One might reasonably assume not, but why not?

The first point to make is that employers do not actually own their human resources, otherwise the word would be 'slavery' rather than 'employment'. The actual arrangement is a contractual one between two parties, who choose to take on certain rights and duties towards each other – see also Chapter 11. It is quite true, of course, that human resources (employees) can be motivated and otherwise persuaded to act in the interest of the employer, sometimes to an astonishing degree, but they remain individuals who choose to act in that way. This aspect of the relationship, however obvious, is central to effective human resource management (HRM).

It is also usually true that the employment relationship is a continuing one. A continuing relationship brings benefits for employers, in terms of reduced transaction costs, such as recruitment and training. It also brings benefits for employees, for example by providing a more stable income stream. Furthermore, the employment relationship needs – from an ethical point of view – to be seen as different from other buyer/seller relationships because of the great asymmetry of power between most employing organisations and individuals. Employers are usually economically more powerful than individual employees and have ready access to far more specialised resources: it is perhaps not surprising that laws and other controls have emerged to provide special protection for the 'sellers' in employment transactions (Gilmore and Williams, 2009).

Above and beyond these practical points about people as employees, there is a strong sense that humans are special: that they have rights that other inanimate resources do not have, purely by virtue of being human (we will side-step the question of animal rights in this chapter). Humans are individuals and citizens as well as employees, meaning that they can reasonably demand to be treated in certain ways by employers, whether or not those rights are reinforced by law.

Thinking about the nature and purpose of the employer/employee relationship helps to illuminate how that relationship should be conducted ethically (by both parties). Before examining how ethics can be applied to the main aspects of HRM, we review briefly the fundamental perspectives on ethics.

APPROACHES TO ETHICS

The study of ethics seeks a systematic and defensible understanding of good and bad. In Western philosophy, this is usually considered to have resulted in three main perspectives on ethics:

- Ethics seen as duties: things that should be done or refrained from, because they are good or bad in their own right.

- Ethics seen as consequences: good acts are those that lead to good results, and bad acts are those that lead to bad results.

- Ethics as virtues: the desirable qualities or character traits that are possessed by good people.

For a long time, strong arguments have been made to support each of these main outlooks and most readers will recognise the role that each plays in day-to-day ethical reasoning. However, the question of what is good and bad in human behaviour remains complex and difficult, with the possibility of contradictory answers from the different perspectives (Crane and Matten, 2010).

Duty-based views of ethics (known as 'deontological' ethics) see goodness or badness as inherent in the act itself, rather than in the consequences. If lying is bad, for example, it is because the act of deliberately saying something that the speaker knows to be false is bad in itself, plain and simple. Deontological ethical frameworks offer a set of duties or principles which must be respected, irrespective of the consequences. The German philosopher Kant (1724–1804) has been one of the leading voices in duty-based ethics: in his view, ethics are based on the duties that we owe each other as fellow members of a rational species. We should, for example, only act in ways that could reasonably be adopted by anyone in similar circumstances (which is close in meaning to the golden rule: 'do as you would be done by'). Keeping promises, for example, is required, because not to do so would render the idea of a promise absurd. Also, people should always be treated as being of value in themselves, rather than simply used as a means (to achieving someone else's desires): people should be treated with respect for their equal status as moral beings and not subjected to degrading or humiliating treatment, coercion or abuse.

The general problems with an exclusively duties-based view of ethics involve:

- excessive rigidity, which can result from taking no account of possible consequences of following a principle or duty

- complexity: if principles are made more detailed in an attempt to deal with the wide range of real-life situations, then the resultant algorithms can become very unwieldy; and

- priority: which principles should take precedence over which others and what is the principle that governs this precedence?

Those who see ethics only in terms of consequences look for good or bad in the results of the act, rather than in the act itself. A deliberate untruth, for example, is neither good nor bad in itself – it depends on the consequences. From this point of view, the ethics of stealing, or even killing, can only be judged by asking what happens as a result of the particular act. One familiar form of consequentialism is utilitarianism, which looks for the greatest good for the greatest number. In its original form, utilitarianism tries to assess the change in happiness for everyone affected by a proposed act (later forms sought to consider the consequences for those affected if the proposed action were to become commonplace). There are two main types of difficulty in an exclusively utilitarian view of ethics:

- methodology: while measuring changes to happiness may sound like a good idea, it is extraordinarily difficult to do so with any precision or consistency, as a moment's thought will confirm; and

- justice: as Mackie (1977) points out, the problem with this approach is that it can allow undeserved bad consequences for one group to be offset by good consequences for another group, as long as the net change in happiness is positive. This can be potentially very bad news for minorities, in particular.

The contrasting views of duty-based and consequences-based ethics are reflected in the quote ascribed to Machiavelli: 'The end justifies the means.' 'Ends' are results and 'means' are principles or methods, and the argument between the two views has been running for centuries.

 REFLECTIVE ACTIVITY

You are running late for a meeting in which job redundancies are being discussed, and you wish to protect your own department from this threat. The only parking space available near the meeting location is restricted for disabled access (you do not have a disabled sticker).

Confronted with this dilemma, explain your thought processes and actions with reference to both the duty-based and consequential approaches to ethics.

Virtue ethics is a separate way of thinking about good and bad. Virtues are desirable character traits, exhibited by good people. For Aristotle (384–322 BC), human virtues are those qualities that allow us to fulfil our highest purpose as humans: these qualities lie between undesirable extremes (as 'courage' lies between 'cowardice' and 'foolhardiness') and wisdom is required to recognise the virtuous approach.

REFLECTIVE ACTIVITY

In recent years, a number of 'ethical' investment products have been marketed, which explicitly avoid any contact with businesses in a potentially wide range of categories (for example, tobacco, armaments, alcoholic drinks, gambling and so on). To what extent should the purpose of an organisation be taken into account in judging the ethics of those who work in that organisation? For example, is it still virtuous to display loyalty towards an organisation whose outputs are seen by some as bad? Give examples to illustrate the points you make.

The virtues approach is about how people should live their lives, in order to realise their highest potential. This takes time and experience: rather than propose a series of rules or principles, the main way of becoming virtuous is to study the lives of good people and learn to imitate them.

 REFLECTIVE ACTIVITY

Special people, special treatment?

In 2010 the British Prime Minister, Gordon Brown, was caught up in a debate on his 'bullying' behaviour. Several high-profile books on the workings of number 10 Downing Street held consistent reports of the Prime Minister throwing papers and other objects in temper. After several days and a media storm, it was found that his popularity had actually risen.

In common with all Civil Service departments, an anti-bullying policy applies at Downing Street. To what extent do you think that this situation is unusual? In this case, what are the ethical factors that need to be considered? What should HR do in such circumstances?

ETHICS IN THE WORKPLACE

How useful are these ethical perspectives in thinking about the ethics of managing people at work? Plainly, all three approaches have some relevance:

- Most would agree that there are some ways of treating employees that are just plain wrong, whether or not they are also illegal. Bullying and intimidation, for example, are plainly unacceptable. Duties-based thinking also underlies the establishment of employees' rights (and corresponding duties on employers).

- Similarly, an organisation can hardly avoid considering the consequences of proposed actions, for the organisation, for its employees and for third parties.

- Discussions of leadership often consider what are, in effect, virtues. Yukl (2009) describes the 'qualities' or 'traits' approach to understanding leadership and lists characteristics such as self-confidence, initiative and self-belief. These qualities are very like the idea of virtues – each could be seen as a desirable point between undesirable extremes, for example.

However, if we define business ethics as the study of good and bad in business conduct (an approach that can be extended to non-business organisations as well), then the ethical approaches that have been developed for personal ethics may not be adequate to apply at the 'business' level, because organisations are not people. Organisations are, however, different from completely inanimate objects for two reasons:

- they do behave with intent, in pursuing their objectives through strategies

- they are, from one point of view, groups of individual people, who singly or jointly make the organisation's decisions and who do so as human beings, with the ability to reason ethically. Employees generally do not leave their own values at the door when they go to work and they retain a capacity to imagine the effects on other people of the choices they make at work.

 REFLECTIVE ACTIVITY

Utilitarian thinking

In recent years, there have been many reports of financial services and other companies 'outsourcing' call centre or back-office work from the UK to lower-cost Anglophone locations such as India or Sri Lanka. This has led to controversy, since the outsourcing initiatives are often accompanied by redundancies in the UK.

This phenomenon provides an opportunity to explore the utilitarian approach to ethics. Imagine a hypothetical case of a large UK-based insurance company that is proposing to outsource its customer service call centre from a medium-sized town in the north of England to Bangalore. The UK centre is to be closed and there will be several hundred redundancies.

Make a list of the groups of people who will be affected by this initiative and then:

- describe the likely nature of the effects for each group; and

- take a guess at the likely size of each group.

How useful is this approach in illuminating the ethical implications of the proposal? Is it possible to judge the 'greatest good for the greatest number'? What difficulties would arise in trying to make this analysis more detailed and precise? Putting these methodological difficulties to one side, how satisfactory does the utilitarian approach seem to be as a way of assessing good and bad in this case? If it seems to be unsatisfactory or incomplete, what is missing?

THE PURPOSE OF AN EMPLOYING ORGANISATION

An important additional factor to consider, when thinking about the ethics of HRM, is that of the aims and purpose of the employing organisation (Ellesworth, 2002). Organisational purpose relates directly to ethics in HRM because organisations can be taken to employ people primarily in order to pursue that purpose. The idea of organisational purpose is an important one in trying to understand the ethics of actions taken by an organisation: an investment bank, for example, has a very different purpose (or set of purposes) from a university. Some types of organisation have multiple purposes: local governments, for example, have many different demands to satisfy, while others, such as small businesses, are in principle simpler.

Business organisations generally might be thought to have a simpler purpose, but this is a subject of some controversy. One school of thought defines the business purpose as that of maximising owner (shareholder) wealth, on the basis that this is the aim of shareholders in investing their money. There is therefore a duty on the directors of the company to pursue this aim in their running of the company, and co-incidentally a recent CIPD Employee Outlook report found that 49 per cent of participants saw their purpose as 'making the most profits for investors and owners' (CIPD, 2009a).

Friedman (1970) provides a succinct and often-cited summary of the view that the social responsibility of business is to make as much money as possible for the owners, within the law and the rules of competition. If this definition of purpose is accepted, then for a company to spend shareholder funds in ways that cannot be shown to be consistent with maximising owner wealth is unethical. This amounts to an ethical objection to some of what companies do under the heading of corporate social responsibility (CSR), unless, of course, the CSR programme has the aim or effect of increasing or safeguarding the company's profit (see below).

Sternberg (2000) proposes a three-way test of business ethics, in which an action proposed by a business has to be:

- consistent with the business purpose (which is defined in a similar way to Friedman)

- consistent with the requirement of ordinary decency (eg not cheating, stealing, coercing and so on); and

- consistent with the requirement for distributive justice (that rewards should be proportional to contribution to reflect fairness).

However, many define the business purpose much more broadly, suggesting that a business has a wider responsibility to the society in which it operates and that the task of a manager must recognise additional duties associated with the needs and claims of various stakeholder groups (eg Springett, 2004). In the original sense, stakeholders were disinterested individuals who safeguarded the stake in a bet, but the word has now become used to denote any groups with an interest in an organisation – those that may affect or be affected by the actions of the business. In business organisations, shareholders are one such group, but so are employees, customers, the local community, suppliers and so on. Public sector organisations usually have a keen sense of their stakeholders. The task of a manager, from this point of view, is to 'balance' stakeholder needs, which provides a very different ethical yardstick for a business from Friedman's view (and some practical difficulty in knowing when that balance has been achieved) and enables similarities to be drawn between profit-making and non-profit-making concerns.

Donaldson and Preston (1995) discuss the various ways in which businesses can respond to stakeholder groups, pointing out that a company may decide to engage with stakeholder groups because it is a more effective way of making money for shareholders. Alternatively, a 'normative' approach to stakeholder theory recognises duties towards stakeholders that must be discharged even if those actions are not clearly consistent with maximising owner wealth. One example of the latter might be a company's involvement in local community projects, in which the expenditure cannot be shown to be maximising owner wealth. This is not say that there will be no commercial benefits from this type of expenditure – customers may approve of the venture, for example, and so switch more of their purchases to the sponsoring company – but it may be very difficult to convert those benefits into forecast cash flows. In a normative view of stakeholder theory, an organisation will acknowledge duties to get involved in this way, even if the commercial benefits are partly unclear.

 REFLECTIVE ACTIVITY

A mobile phone provider plans to install a new mast in order to improve network coverage. Identify the stakeholder groups who would have an interest in this decision.

Since employees are one stakeholder group, the potential importance of the distinction between a shareholder and stakeholder approach should be clear. In the shareholder view, employees are one of the resources deployed by the organisation in its efforts to maximise owner wealth, usually in competition with other organisations trying to appeal to the same market. In the stakeholder view, the employee stakeholder group is one of many whose interests and needs are part of the organisation's agenda, to be balanced in some way with the needs of other groups. At first glance, the 'shareholder' approach to HRM may seem to require the lowest possible salaries, barely-legal working conditions and a generally oppressive and exploitative approach to the management of employees. However, the first impression may be misleading: the shareholder-focused company can only make money for its owners by successfully developing and marketing products and services in competition with other suppliers. It will, therefore, have to find ways of attracting, retaining and motivating good staff, in order to stay competitive. A 'stakeholder' approach to HRM might make different claims about its motives, but on any given day might also look remarkably similar to the HRM practised by a shareholder-focused company.

As a special survey in *The Economist* pointed out (22 January 2005), CSR has become an accepted part of the corporate dialogue with the rest of the world although the debate on the scope of activities continues (eg Porter and Kramer, 2006). As Crook (2005, p 3) comments:

'It would be a challenge to find a recent annual report of any big international company that justifies the firm's existence merely in terms of profit, rather than "service to the community". Such reports often talk proudly of efforts to improve society and safeguard the environment – by restricting emissions of greenhouse gases from the staff kitchen, say, or recycling office stationery – before turning hesitantly to less important matters, such as profits. Big firms nowadays are called upon to be good corporate citizens, and they all want to show that they are.'

Readers would be correct to infer from the sardonic tone of this quote that *The Economist* special survey raised some concerns about the way in which the notion of CSR is developing. Companies are now called upon to report according to a 'triple bottom line', in which economic results (profits) are joined by effects on the natural environment and on social well-being. This raises methodological difficulties – while there are clear conventions for measuring profitability, it is much more difficult to find generally-accepted yardsticks for environmental protection or social justice (Vilanova, Lozano and Arenas, 2009).

However, assuming that these methodological difficulties can be overcome in due course, concerns are also expressed about the principle of this type of CSR. Friedman (1970) expressed doubts that companies have the expertise to undertake non-business projects and opined that social projects should be the domain of elected governments, rather than unelected boards of directors. This perspective echoes Adam Smith's concept of the 'invisible hand', through which individuals pursuing their own interest are guided to benefit society, even though they had no such intention. However, CSR in its broader sense is now the accepted orthodoxy: for as long as customers expect the firms they buy from to give an account of their effects on society and the environment, then prudent companies will be likely to comply (Porter and Kramer, 2006). Many companies are genuinely seeking to do much more than toe the line in their CSR programmes, of course, with clear positive effects for many communities.

EQUAL OPPORTUNITIES AND ETHICS

To discriminate originally meant to distinguish between one thing and another. Strictly speaking, therefore, the word 'discrimination' is ethically neutral – indeed, HRM activities such as recruitment or promotion must entail discrimination (between the one that is to be appointed and the others, for example); see also Chapter 9. However, discrimination has recently acquired a pejorative sense, alluding to the exercise of prejudice, which is clearly unethical, and often illegal. In this sense of the word, it is 'unfair' or 'irrelevant' discrimination that is objectionable: the introduction into the process of factors that have no connection with the work to be done. Discriminating against lazy or dishonest people is thus acceptable (and perhaps even advisable), but discriminating on the basis of gender, ethnic origin or age is unethical.

The principle of equal opportunity (EO) requires that people should be recruited on the basis of their ability to do the job, with no other factors intruding into the decision (Noon in Beardwell and Claydon, 2010). In what ways can this be said to be ethically desirable (ie whether or not it is also legally obligatory)? In this case, both duty-based and consequentialist ethical arguments can be made to support the equal opportunities principle. The duty-based ethics point is clear: to treat employees on some basis other than EO (for example, to allow ageist or homophobic sentiments to enter into decisions about them) is to fail to show respect for their equal status as fellow members of the moral community. As discussed by Boatright (2000), prejudice also treats people only as members of groups, rather than affording them the individual treatment that they should reasonably expect. Making recruitment, promotion or redundancy decisions on the basis of prejudice is therefore manifestly unjust to those who are disadvantaged.

From the employer's point of view, a strong consequences-based case in favour of EO can also be made. Organisations that rule out candidates from a whole group on the basis of prejudice are depriving themselves of a significant pool of talent in the labour market, and this failure to engage with diverse groups is likely to lead to non-optimal performance (Von Bergen, Soper and Parnell, 2005; Hunt, 2007). Organisations may therefore be damaged by the exercise of prejudice, irrespective of any legal penalties to which they may be exposed. However, anti-discrimination legislation is commonplace in modern economies, which suggests that the market-driven response to prejudice has been found to be inadequate. This may be because in real life, some employers might perceive enough scope to exercise their prejudices without significant disadvantage, unless legal penalties were also in prospect. Also, not all employing organisations are subject to competition and thus, in the absence of prohibitive legislation, would suffer little or no penalty for unfair discrimination. Alternatively, a government may find that the theoretically purgative effect of competition is taking too long to eliminate unfair discrimination and decide that legislation is desirable for utilitarian reasons.

It would be wrong, however, to infer from these arguments that equal opportunities is the sole – or even the pre-eminent – ethical principle at play in contemporary HRM. In large numbers of businesses around the world, the owners or managers may regard it as perfectly normal and desirable to prefer to recruit or promote an acceptably competent member of the same family over a better-qualified stranger. This is not the place to debate the relative merits of the two principles, but rather to suggest that EO is often not the sole governing principle in HRM, however strong the deontological and consequence-based arguments in its favour.

Even in Western employing organisations, the EO principle is made more complex by the growing interest in two other ideas – diversity management and so-called 'positive' discrimination, in which measures are taken to improve the chances of a particular group that is seen as being disadvantaged. A moment's thought will show that these two ideas could each have the practical effect of diluting or directly contradicting the EO principle in some cases. This should not be surprising – EO is a proposition about justice in the process of things like deciding on job offers or promotions. However, both diversity management and positive discrimination make separate arguments about justice that start from the observed end-result of the process.

Arguments about positive discrimination have been going on for several decades. We review them briefly here because they provide an example of the complexity of ethical arguments in practice, and also because they seem to be becoming more prominent in some European countries, having been much more familiar in the United States up to now. For example, the Norwegian government introduced legislation to make it a requirement from 1 January 2008 that 40 per cent of main board seats in public companies should be held by women. This rule, first announced in 2003, was virtually completely achieved by the deadline: by contrast, the average proportion of women board directors for Europe as a whole was reported by the BBC as just 8 per cent. In the UK, the Government announced an Equality Bill in June 2008, whose aims include that of allowing positive discrimination in certain circumstances in the interests of increased equality. In each case, these measures seem to envisage cases in which some groups will be given preferential treatment of some sort, in order to address end distributions that are seen as lastingly unfair: in effect, EO in the process of appointment has to be modified or even suspended in some cases, in order to have an end result that is more satisfactorily equal.

Respectable ethical arguments can be made to justify this type of discrimination. Boatright (2000) reviews three main types of argument in favour:

- Compensation: some groups have been unjustly discriminated against for a long time and this injustice calls for the compensation that positive discrimination can offer.

- Equality: where distributive injustice has been entrenched for a long time, the gap between the majority and the disadvantaged minority may require to be closed through legislative action, in order to allow EO policies to operate fairly.

- Utilitarian: positive discrimination in some circumstances can be justified as a means of addressing urgent social problems.

However, the arguments against positive discrimination are also considerable: at the individual level, it can amount to unfair discrimination and each of the arguments about EO discussed above must apply. Those who are (rightly or wrongly) perceived to be 'filling quotas' in recruitment or appointment may also face the problem of unkind (if unspoken) assumptions about their individual abilities and there may also be a risk of being seen to patronise the disadvantaged group as a whole. Perhaps the vexed question of which type of ethical argument should be given primacy over the others is one that is best left to the interplay of democratic forces in society.

REFLECTIVE ACTIVITY

In the UK it is illegal to discriminate against a job applicant on the grounds of demographic characteristics such as gender, race or religious affiliation. However in exceptional cases, there may be grounds for exemption under section 9 of the Employment Act (2000). Rayner and Rumbles, in Gilmore and Williams (2009), noted that it was thus acceptable to select Connie Fisher, a white female actor, to play the part of Maria in the musical *The Sound of Music*. More seriously, it is legal and acceptable to appoint a female to work in a women's refuge for victims of domestic violence. Likewise one could legitimately select a male to counsel male victims of abuse.

Think of an example where there would be very strong arguments for and against using section 9 of this act for recruiting and selecting job applicants.

By contrast, Diversity Management (DM) as an idea is not centrally concerned with the arguments for and against positive discrimination. The idea of DM is mainly about organisational performance. As one definition (Hays-Thomas, 2004, p 12) explains:

'...we will use the term "diversity" to refer to differences among people that are likely to affect their acceptance, work performance, satisfaction, or progress in an organisation. When we speak of "managing diversity", we mean the purposeful use of processes and strategies that make these differences among people into an asset, rather than a liability, for the organisation.'

As the same author later observes, a policy context of affirmative action (such as has applied in the USA since 1965) is relevant to DM, since it will have the effect of increasing the diversity to be managed. However, the idea of DM is that diversity is to be desired by an organisation in its own right, irrespective of any legislative context. The DM proposition is essentially instrumental – learn to promote and manage diversity effectively and your organisation will perform better. The reason for this is that a diverse set of human resources will far better equip an organisation to sense, understand and respond to changes in its business environment, with benefits in terms of successful innovation, better risk management and in greater resilience to environmental turbulence. As such, the proposition seems to be irresistible to a business – who would not want the bottom-line benefits that are seen as the reward for effective DM? Some caution needs to be exercised with this simple equation, however: for example, effective DM is likely to require far more than just lip service and to take time to achieve. This may be one reason why the evidence of bottom line benefits is sometimes mixed, as suggested by Von Bergen *et al* (2005). We should perhaps not be surprised to find that the DM task is complex and that success is unlikely to be instantaneous. In terms of ethical human resource management, DM is a proposition that is mainly justified in terms of its beneficial consequences, although the more respectful treatment of individual employees that can result from effective DM is also desirable from a deontological point of view.

CASE STUDY

An organisation that does pay attention to diversity issues may be seen, and indeed brand-marketed, as ethically aware. Recent in-store advertising by the Tesco organisation showed employees who are from diversely categorised groups advertising relevant services, but always promoting the Tesco brand. The lay customer may, albeit perhaps subconsciously, perceive the organisation as non-discriminatory and therefore ethically 'good'. The Tesco diversity statement reads:

Staff Diversity benefits a business in many ways, including greater customer and staff loyalty ... We are committed to ensuring that at all times and in every aspect of employment, including recruitment, training and development, everybody receives the same treatment. Both internal and external applicants are considered on individual ability, regardless of factors such as gender, age, colour, creed, race, ethnic origin, disability, marital status, religion or belief, trade union membership or sexual preference and orientation.'

Source: http://www.tesco.com

Question

Consider the following questions:

1. What are the potential advantages of an organisation actively considering such an approach to diversity management?

2. What could be the potential barriers to the effective adoption of such an approach?

3. How could these be constructively addressed?

ETHICS IN BUSINESS — THE ROLE OF HR

The view that 'good ethics means good business' is one that would probably be shared by both shareholder and stakeholder-focused enthusiasts, although they might well differ on the precise meaning of 'good ethics', as discussed above. If this is so, then all organisations have strong prudential reasons for promoting ethical conduct by their employees. Given the importance of ethical conduct in business, what contribution can or should a human resource professional make to an organisation's ethical policy?

There is no doubt that much of the work of HR professionals involves ethical issues, from crafting employment and benefit policies to advising managers in undertaking performance management processes in acceptable ways. The 'expert' role outlined by Ulrich (1997) has implications for the discussions of legal compliance in this chapter: HR can be valued as keeping those who are directly managing people on track regarding employment law. We have suggested that the law is a minimum requirement and that those organisations which desire to be competitive (in any sense) for people, customers, league tables or funding may be well-advised to do more than the law requires and take ethical issues seriously. Given that HR reaches into all corners of the organisation, there is an opportunity for HR to provide leadership in crafting policies and advising on practice which creates a positive environment for competitive recruitment and solid retention of staff. In many ways one might see ethics as good professional practice as much as 'good business'.

In pursuance of good ethical standards, the Chartered Institute of Personnel and Development, as the professional association for the UK HR profession, has a Code of Professional Conduct and Disciplinary Procedures (2008a), to which all members must conform. In this way the CIPD is fulfilling its role as a professional institution. Before we return to the code, it is important to have an idea of the importance of ethical and practice codes in professions.

Perkin's review of professional associations (1989) shows the development of some occupations included a system of quality control whereby users of that occupation could know the practitioner met certain standards. For example, one cannot practise as a medical consultant in most countries without certain qualifications and experience, and neither can one claim to be a 'lawyer' without certain credentials. Professional associations continue to perform the role of providing credibility to their members through the control of membership (Farndale and Brewster, 2005) although our understanding of 'professions' is broadening (Hanlon, 1998).

The CIPD, like many professional associations, allows different grades of membership contingent on the completion of learning (or equivalent proof) to signify a level of competence, through the CIPD qualification framework (Gilmore and Williams, 2007). In this way the CIPD seeks to raise standards of practice, as more employers use the CIPD's quality-controlled qualifications to recruit HR practitioners (as reflected in current recruitment advertisements). Embedded in the qualification process are ethical issues and standards of practice which promote 'professionalism' and include the development of ethical understanding. If the HR practitioner can advise and model ethical behaviour, then they can contribute to raising the standards of practice in all managers. This approach does not come without caveats. Given the recent push towards enabling line managers to undertake some functions, one might argue that the HR profession has diluted itself, and in addition many of those practising at board and other senior levels do not have CIPD qualifications or indeed membership (Caldwell, 2008; Wright, 2008).

Being a member of the CIPD and 'acting as a professional' entails far more than passing exams, as indicated in the CIPD Code (*ibid*). It includes continuing to update professional knowledge, uphold legal thresholds and 'exercise integrity, honesty, diligence and appropriate behaviour in all ... business, professional and related personal activities' (p 3). It is clear the CIPD intends no exceptions to positive professional behaviour in all aspects of working life. Those embracing such standards may use it as a frame for 'professional identity' where the standards become part of their working self (Alvesson and Willmott, 2000).

In a world in which ethical choices about the treatment of employees are increasingly being transformed – through the growth of legislation – into legal obligations, one part of the HR role must clearly be that of ensuring that the organisation remains within the law in its dealings, briefing and offering support to line management accordingly (Ulrich and Brockbank, 2005). But of course they do this with other employees, many of whom will themselves be members of professional associations. As noted above, employees are human beings and must be expected to introduce their own values into the way they perform. Mahoney (1994) discusses the 'moral resources' that are available to organisations and employees, including external resources such as codes of conduct, the law and religion, together with internal resources such as conscience and personal moral development. In the United States a survey found that although most managers suggested they learned ethical decision-making at home (from their family or church), professional organisations showed a high influence (55 per cent) as did business colleagues (60 per cent) (Wiley, 2000).

A code of conduct can allow an organisation to signal to its employees or members the standards of behaviour it requires. Naturally one might, as an employed professional, have more than one standard to uphold – for example those in part time CIPD study may have a student code, an employer's code, that of the CIPD together with any other professional memberships. Besides providing guidance to employees/members about the expected standards, these published codes also send a clear signal to the outside world: 'these are the standards by which we are happy to be judged.'

From the point of view of ethical theories, codes of conduct are certainly partly deontological in nature, since they will usually include principles or duties to be respected by those covered by the code. However, it is usually true that the principles in the code have been developed by senior members of the industry, profession or organisation, based on their extensive experience of the outcomes of different courses of action, which is an example of consequentialist thinking. One reason why a well-written code of conduct can be so valuable to employees is that, at any given time, it may be very difficult to forecast exactly which course of action is going to be in the best interests of the organisation, even for individuals who are strongly committed to acting in an ethical way (Foote, 2001).

REFLECTIVE ACTIVITY

A professional code

Locate the CIPD's Code of Professional Conduct and Disciplinary Procedures (for example from the CIPD website at http://www.cipd.co.uk).

Consider the standards of professional conduct. In what ways do these standards seem to reflect the influences of deontological (duty-based), consequentialist and virtues approaches to ethics?

As with any professional code of conduct, the CIPD code has to cover a potentially very diverse range of real-life situations. Read through the code and discuss the role these standards and requirements would be likely to play in helping CIPD members to identify ethical courses of action in their work.

Even the best codes of conduct, however, cannot possibly cover every possible situation that will arise, particularly when organisational environments are changing so quickly. Role modelling and a clear commitment to ethical behaviour from the top of the organisation is essential (Wiley, 2000). This clear commitment is not simply a matter of communicating in words and actions to employees – feedback channels are also important. As Sternberg (2000) points out, good corporate governance should include the provision of effective communication channels, through which possible whistleblowers can make potential problems known to those at the top of the organisation (ie those who are in a position to do something about the issue). The problems that worry potential whistleblowers are of general public concern – damage to the natural environment, for example – but should also be of direct concern to the management of the organisation, not least because of the potential damage to the organisation's reputation.

Many corporations have established specialist ethics officers, who are responsible for fostering ethical conduct throughout the organisation and for providing guidance in difficult cases. This source of advice will often be a valuable part of an organisation's ethical mix, but it is most likely to work effectively in a culture that involves every employee in the organisation's ethical policy. The same could perhaps be said of an organisation that relies heavily on its HR department to develop and implement an ethics policy.

REFLECTIVE ACTIVITY

Choose one example from the last three years of cases of unethical conduct by businesses: these may be connected with health and safety, customers, suppliers or financial mismanagement or misbehaviour. Collect information about what happened from published sources such as news organisation websites (the BBC site, for example, at http://www.bbc.co.uk is particularly useful in this respect). How far was this 'led from the top'? Identify the key turning points of what was done. What should (not) have been done, and which professionals should have acted differently? Discuss how, with hindsight, the problem might have been avoided using HR-designed policies and practices.

As suggested above, there is much that HR professionals can do to brief, train and communicate in the area of ethical conduct, but there are a number of reasons why an organisation's ethical policy will work best if it is accepted as the responsibility and part of the identity of every employee. For example, the HR department will have as its principal focus the treatment of employees: however, an organisation deals with people in many other categories – customers, for example, or suppliers – and ethical considerations must apply to them too. Experience also suggests that major ethical problems for an organisation can have their origins in the way that work is carried out at a relatively junior level, way beyond the visibility of a central HR department, however diligently it carries out its role. If corporate ethics is allowed to become the concern of a few specialists, rather than the responsibility of all, then the risk of major problems will remain high.

Newspapers often contain current stories of unethical behaviour by individuals at all levels of employment. Very often the focus is on the individual whistleblower or the alleged perpetrator of the unethical action. Often there are many more players involved; those who suspected, those who knew and did nothing, and those who could have taken action. Subsequent publicity affects all employees, and potentially in a serious way through reductions in loyalty, pride and commitment, and ensuing drops in performance. Abusing ethical standards may have repercussions from one's professional association (Fournier, 1999), and impact one's career and private life. Integrity is a key attribute of the true professional, and integrity requires a serious and lasting commitment to high ethical standards.

CONCLUSION

Professionalism and ethics are topical in this period of financial recovery. As the recovery continues, we will no doubt see further reflection and analysis of the 'credit crunch', hopefully to learn lessons from poor judgement prior to the crisis. The last few years have served to highlight the importance of solid ethical practice in the leadership and management of people. There are some guidelines one can follow from ethical theory which inform the choices we make. However, ethical principles need to be kept in mind as there can be conflicts of interest and a need to balance outcomes for a variety of stakeholders. Demonstrating good ethical practice means thinking decisions through in a careful manner.

One common problem is that managers fail to perceive the ethical implications of a decision or action at the start. In this area Human Resource Management professionals can contribute uniquely across the organisation. By setting ethically-screened policies they can attempt to provide a framework within which managers can operate that precludes some unethical choices. By working with partner line managers, they can bring an independent 'third party' view to bear on decisions where the manager might not have considered the ethical implications fully. Embedding ethical principles in training and learning events, the HRD specialist can prompt all employees to be more aware of the nature of their professionalism and the role of ethics within it.

There are codes of conduct provided by professional and industry bodies to which professionals affiliated to them need to comply. These codes are a welcome addition to guide practice. However codes, by their very nature, operate with a broad brush. There is a need for all professionals, and especially those in HR able to influence at the heart of the organisation, to pay close attention to both micro and macro decisions such that high standards of practice are set in professional ethical practice for others to follow.

KEY LEARNING POINTS

- In this chapter we have outlined areas that are becoming of increasing urgency in the HR field and which relate to ethical practice generally and professionalism specifically. These are not easy topics, and possibly require all staff to reflect at a deeper level than previously.

- There are a variety of approaches to analysing situations from an ethical point of view. Sometimes these can lead to very different logic and actions.

- Often employees do not analyse the ethical principles they employ.

- There is a strong case that good ethics makes sustainable business sense.

- Some issues (such as equal opportunities) are enshrined in law and regardless of one's personal feelings, one must facilitate the adherence to these rights, promoting them and leading the organisation through changing policies and practice.

- HR and line managers have an important role to play in influencing the level and type of integrity observed beyond the law and thence adopted by others.

- The CIPD plays an important role in the HR profession. Regardless of one's specialism, membership of the CIPD involves needing to abide by its Standards.

REVIEW QUESTIONS

1. Thinking about an organisation with which you are familiar, provide practical examples of ways in which it is operating ethically. Can you relate these examples to the duty, consequences or virtue perspectives on ethics?

2. Discuss the view that an organisation that is providing good value products or services to its customers, paying its bills and treating its staff decently over a long period of time is acting as ethically as anyone can reasonably expect.

3. How do HR decisions become conflicted in an ethical sense? Consider situations where you have felt professionally 'torn' between courses of action and analyse your response using ethical frameworks.

4. Given that HR gains much of its power from line managers, how far might this influence the profession's 'honest broker' position? Does this matter?

5. Can one be an 'HR professional' without being a member of the CIPD?

EXPLORE FURTHER

Crane, A. and Matten, D. (2010) *Business Ethics*, 3rd ed. Oxford: Oxford University Press. One of a number of well-written texts on business ethics. Crane and Matten provide a balanced and accessible discussion of the various viewpoints.

Sternberg, E. (2000) *Just business*, 2nd ed. Oxford: Oxford University Press. This book is recommended as a strongly-argued account of the importance of a purpose-based view of business ethics.

The conflicts that confront HR professionals are explored in the articles by Wright and Caldwell in the reading list. Read any one of these along with the CIPD Code and consider how you might be impacted as a professional.

Part 3: Leading, Managing and Developing People: Major Contemporary Themes

CHAPTER 5

Leadership

Gill Christy

LEARNING OUTCOMES

After reading this chapter, you should be able to:

- explain the difference between the terms 'management' and 'leadership'
- identify the significance of leadership for a variety of types of organisation
- understand the key theoretical approaches to the study of leadership
- apply knowledge of these approaches to the work of the personnel/HR professional
- suggest development activities to support the changing nature of organisational leadership.

OVERVIEW

In Part Three of this book, we turn to examine key themes within the area of leading managing and developing people. Central in this regard is the concept of leadership. The purpose of this chapter is to introduce the reader to the main theoretical approaches to the study of organisational leadership, and to provide an awareness of the strengths and shortcomings of these approaches. Current areas of academic research are briefly outlined to indicate the dynamic nature of the research agenda and possible future developments.

The chapter begins with a discussion of the terms 'management' and 'leadership' and relates both to the strategic purpose and direction of an organisation. Seven key approaches to the study of leadership are presented and discussed, with the aim of providing a critical awareness of their implications. Important links are made between organisational leadership in general and the role of the human resource (HR) professional in particular. Finally, some of the newer approaches to the study of leadership are briefly outlined, again with reference to the role which might emerge for both the specialist human resource professional and everyone who is involved in working with people in the more general sense.

INTRODUCTION

This chapter focuses on leaders in a business or organisational context, and views leaders as key players in both devising and implementing organisational strategy. It considers how existing theories and frameworks help to address the question of what exactly makes a leader effective in a business or a working environment. Some concepts and models clearly derive from, and apply to, other areas of human activity such as politics, sport and warfare. The notion of leadership provides an enduring fascination; not only to academics such as psychologists and political or social scientists, but also to journalists, biographers, authors, dramatists and film-makers for whom it provides a rich source of material both factual and fictional. As we shall also see, many terms and metaphors associated with the study of leadership derive from sporting and military contexts. However, when we enter the more usual organisational arenas – businesses, public sector and governmental organisations, non-profit-making organisations such as charities – we tend to encounter the term 'manager' more frequently than the term 'leader' as the one to describe such key players. It is, therefore, important to start by considering how far these two related concepts, leadership and management, overlap.

 REFLECTIVE ACTIVITY

Before we delve into the academic literature on leadership, it may be helpful to review your own views on the topic through consideration of some prominent business leaders, for instance, James Caan (of TV's *Dragons' Den*), the late Dame Anita Roddick, Michael O'Leary,

Ingvar Kamprad or Jacqueline Gold. Conduct brief research into your chosen leaders' business careers. Can you identify common traits among these leaders? What style of leadership do you associate with these people? Have they always been successful?

MANAGEMENT OR LEADERSHIP?

There seems to be a certain revival of interest in the concept and application of leadership in recent years. Two decades ago, ambitious candidates for top-flight jobs in the world of business and public affairs might have enrolled on programmes to become 'Masters of Business Administration' or to take diplomas in management studies. Today there is a burgeoning market in postgraduate degrees such as leadership studies, or business development and leadership. The Management Standards Centre (MSC) included the term in its revised National Occupational Standards for Management and Leadership; and in 2003 Investors in People UK launched its supplementary 'Leadership and Management' model, discussed further below. Similar thinking has also led to the development of the CIPD's own Leadership and Management Standards, now integral to the professional development and qualification programme. So an initial question to consider is why there is such renewed interest in the concept of leadership, and how this fits with traditional ideas about organisational management. Perhaps part of the answer is to do with changing patterns of organisational life and similar changes in social expectations within the working environment.

Traditional organisations with strongly hierarchical structures are becoming rarer, and newer forms of both commercial and public sector organisation tend to be more flexible and task- or client-focused. What Handy (1976) described as 'matrix' organisations are generally considered to be more effective in a highly fluid commercial or operating environment; and the 'shamrock' style of organisation (Handy, 1989) charts the move towards further operational flexibility. This type of organisational flexibility was also described by Atkinson (1984) in his model of the flexible firm, which disaggregates different organisational requirements and builds in a further form of organisational flexibility by outsourcing or subcontracting a number of its activities. This kind of articulated organisational structure works against the maintenance of strong hierarchies based around position (or legitimate) power (Mullins, 2010), and often requires individual managers to exercise a different form of authority from that conferred simply by virtue of status or rank. Similarly, wider social attitudes towards authority have changed and, as in other walks of life, people generally expect to be consulted and involved in their work rather than simply instructed. In some circumstances these expectations are now supported by the law, for instance through the Information and Consultation of Employees (ICE) Regulations of 2005 which now apply to all businesses with more than 50 employees. Together, these trends may have renewed the interest in leadership as an important skill for those attempting to 'get things done through other people'.

Mullins (2010) suggests that there is a close relationship between the two concepts (management and leadership) and recognises that at least some authors and commentators dislike attempts to separate the two (*ibid*). Other writers, such as Hollingsworth – someone with both military and commercial experience – and Kotter (Bloisi *et al*, 2003; Huczynski and Buchanan, 2007), make a very clear distinction. Kotter describes leaders as those who set a direction, align people to the vision and motivate them; whereas managers plan, organise, control and resolve problems. In Hollingsworth's model, leadership involves innovation, development, a focus on people, inspiring trust, having an eye on the horizon and 'doing the right things'. By contrast, management is associated with administration, maintenance, systems/structure, control, paying attention to the bottom line and 'doing things right'. This distinction is also reflected in the National Occupational Standards for Management and Leadership which appear to show a transition between operational and/or supervisory levels of management at levels 2 and 3, and a more strategic approach at levels 4 and 5 (Management Standards Centre, 2008). It is, therefore, a useful means of organising further discussion of the subject in terms of organisational people management practice.

For the purposes of this chapter, strategic leadership is taken to mean the activities involved in the initial creation of an overall business or organisational strategy, then directing and energising organisational resources towards the achievement of that strategy. Insofar as it then relies on others to carry out the strategy it may involve some management, but it is primarily about business vision and mission. This means 'doing the right thing', creating the differentiators which, in people terms, involve becoming an employer of choice, an organisation which is able to encourage outstanding performance from its workforce and thus achieve superior results. On the other hand, managerial leadership is taken to mean activities surrounding the creation, maintenance and development of an appropriate infrastructure for business operations, including that which involves organising the work of other people. It means creating a working environment that can help a business or other organisation to achieve its objectives. In this sense management includes leadership to some degree: it is about 'doing things right'.

STRATEGY AND LEADERSHIP

As we saw in Chapter 2, the term 'strategy' is conceived as a means of identifying the ways in which an organisation seeks to pursue its purpose, or achieve its objectives. A prominent view of business strategy is 'resource-based', that is to say, mainly to do with identifying the key resources that give the organisation a distinctive capability and finding ways of applying those capabilities to parts of the market that offer the best prospects (Johnson *et al*, 2007; Legge, 2005; Boxall and Purcell, 2003). Following from this, the key tasks in the strategic planning process could be said to be:

- analysing the organisation's environment and the changes that are expected over the plan period
- identifying and evaluating the organisation's key resources: those that are distinctive (by comparison to competitors) and those that are also important to delivering value to customers, taxpayers or client groups
- considering strategic options: ways of matching organisational resources to particular parts (segments) of the market, looking for the approach that is forecast to create maximum added value for shareholders, or to achieve the most effective use of public or donor money
- choosing the preferred strategic option
- re-aligning the organisation's resources (human and others) behind the chosen strategy: acquiring new resources, modifying existing resources and getting rid of those that cannot be economically reconfigured (which, of course, opens up questions about the ethical treatment of human resources)
- directing and energising those resources towards implementing the strategy, and
- responding to unexpected events during implementation.

Most of these activities are focused at the higher levels of a business or organisation, and are often the province of a single individual (for instance in a small business or owner-managed enterprise) or a small group such as a company chief executive and board of directors. In the public sector, strategic management will be in the hands of those who exercise political power and the professional experts who advise them and find appropriate means of executing political decisions. They are activities which are primarily about making informed strategic choices, in other words responding to the question 'What is the right thing to do?' They are also about convincing and energising others to put their effort behind the chosen strategy, and in this sense involve many leadership skills. In terms of people management, this level of leadership is about defining approaches to ensure that appropriate talent is recruited and motivated to achieve superior results.

REFLECTIVE ACTIVITY

Look up the following article by Sean Coughlan on the BBC business news website: http://news.bbc.co.uk

'MBAs must drop the machismo' 28 February 2005

This summarises some research carried out by Brunel University Business School. What light does this research shed on the changing nature of organisational leadership and management? What are the implications of this research for universities and business schools who deliver MBAs?

MANAGEMENT AND LEADERSHIP

As mentioned earlier, in 2003 Investors in People UK launched its supplementary 'Leadership and Management' model, which seeks to help organisations create and maintain effective leadership skills amongst managers (Investors in People website: www.investorsinpeople.co.uk). This emphasises the important links between the two functions as well as indicating the increased significance of developing leadership within UK organisations. Leadership ability is defined as one of the attributes of the successful manager, along with the intellectual skills required for the assimilation of information, analysis and planning, technical and professional knowledge of the business area or sector, and a clear understanding of the specific organisation and its capacities.

Similarly, the Management Charter Initiative (MCI), which developed as a result of the recommendations in the Handy and Constable and McCormick reports of the late 1980s, undertook a major analysis of the nature of management for the purposes of establishing a clear framework for managerial qualifications. Its work resulted in the adoption of a competency-based approach which quickly became highly influential in the field of management development in Britain (Frank, 1991). The 1997 edition of the occupational standard was based around four major components: managing operations, managing finance, managing information and managing people, only the last of which could be clearly seen as requiring leadership skills. More recently, the MSC has researched and developed a new set of standards, which also provide a functional map and set of units of competence which encompass the important knowledge and skill components of effective management. The significance of leadership is more clearly emphasised in the title of the new standards themselves: the National Occupational Standards for Management and Leadership. The six basic elements of the new standards, which can be viewed at the MSC website (http://www.management-standards. org), are:

1. Managing self (depicted as a central aspect of the remaining five standards)

2. Providing direction

3. Facilitating change

4. Working with people

5. Using resources

6. Achieving results.

Leadership ability can be firmly associated with the second, third and fourth of these elements; and indeed the term 'working with people' has replaced 'managing people' in a way which might indicate the reducing of emphasis on formal control and the increased need for collaboration in present-day work environments noted above.

The CIPD Professional Standards recognise that soft skills are just as important as technical ones, and so these are better represented and thus reflect more fully aspects of leadership which are essential to good management practice. Nevertheless, these functions are qualitatively different from those required of strategic leadership which, as we have noted, appear at the higher levels of organisations. The majority of the Standards are much more concerned with 'doing things right' in the sense of providing an effective structure within which people can achieve high levels of performance for their organisation.

It is now possible to turn to some of the concepts and theories about leadership, and to identify how well they might support the development of effective people management, either at a strategic or at a more operational level.

LEADERSHIP: THEORETICAL FRAMEWORKS

It is useful at this point to remind ourselves of some of the key frameworks which have developed for the analysis and study of leadership. A summary of differing academic approaches to the subject is offered by several writers including Mullins (2010), Bloisi *et al* (2003), Hersey *et al* (2001), Huczynski and Buchanan (2007), Kreitner and Kinicki (2001) and Yukl (2006). Most offer a framework for leadership studies which identifies the following main schools of thought:

- The qualities or traits approach
- The functional or group approach
- The approach which sees leadership as a behavioural category
- The leadership styles approach
- The situational approach and contingency models
- Transformational leadership
- Inspirational leadership.

(See Mullins, 2010, p 376.)

Taking each of these approaches in turn we can examine the general principles and models involved, and comment on their suitability in relation to either strategic leadership or managerial (operational) leadership. Some comments about the implications of each model for the development of effective organisational leaders are also included.

QUALITIES OR TRAITS APPROACHES

This approach is essentially the 'great person' theory of leadership, and takes an approach which tries to identify the significant features of acknowledged leaders. Early approaches to the study of leadership (mostly undertaken before and shortly after the Second World War) dwelt on the personal qualities and characteristics of successful leaders in an attempt to isolate the 'magic ingredients'. They have not generally agreed on a common set of characteristics, although one or two, such as self-confidence and intelligence, did figure in a number of models (eg Kreitner and Kinicki, 2001). Indeed, it is possible that the very act of selecting successful leaders for study introduces a form of bias which prejudices the results of any subsequent analysis. For instance, the absence of women from many research samples may well reflect the social constraints of the time rather than indicating that women lack innate leadership qualities. Indeed, it has been argued (Alimo-Metcalfe, 1995) that studies of women leaders actually identify a different range of effective leadership qualities compared with studies of men; and that it is important to: 'challenge the dangerous implicit assumption that identifying the criteria for leadership positions from groups of senior managers, all or most of whom (chances are) are male, may well lead to gender-biased criteria for the subsequent assessment process' (Alimo-Metcalfe, 1995, pp 7–8).

Her research also has relevance when considering the contrast between so-called 'transactional' and 'transformational' styles of leadership and is discussed further below.

Similarly, it is also important to note that the characteristics that have been proposed as significant may not be universally applicable. Cultural factors, for instance, may result in very different values being placed on a specific personal quality, (such as willingness to take risks, to 'break the rules' in pursuit of an objective, or to act openly in pursuit of personal ambition) in different societies. Hofstede's model (2001) has identified dimensions of cultural difference which he termed 'uncertainty avoidance', 'power distance', 'masculinity/femininity' and 'individualism/collectivism', and he described how combinations of these formed the characteristics of particular cultural environments. Clearly some cultures might accept and applaud qualities such as personal ambition and risk-taking where others would be more likely to value behaviours which support collective achievement or stability and a sense of social inclusion. The importance of cultural difference in relation to appropriate leadership styles and behaviours is developed more fully under the heading of situational or contingency theories of leadership.

As a result, we might consider that trait theories offer few pointers which can help aspiring managers assess their potential other than by trying to decide if they possess the appropriate qualities, or can develop (or even simulate) them. Trait theories offer little help in terms of suggesting how managerial leaders can prepare and adapt themselves to the reality of work to be performed.

Furthermore, little connection is made with the variety of organisational circumstances where leadership needs to be exercised, including those circumstances where leadership shifts from the operational to the strategic levels of activity. The high public profile of both political and business leaders who operate at strategic level may well tempt us to analyse their qualities, but our information is imperfect (even about high-profile individuals) and of course the same individual can be both successful and unsuccessful during her or his career.

Adoption of the 'traits' approach also has implications for the role of people management in an organisation. If the development of successful organisational leaders is largely a matter of identifying those individuals who possess the desired characteristics and then offering the selected potential managers opportunities to develop and exercise these abilities, then the focus of people management will probably be on devising appropriate tests (such as psychometric or aptitude tests) which will help identify the 'right stuff', and devising systems of training and promotion which will support their development.

THE FUNCTIONAL APPROACH

The functional approach to leadership studies generally considers what leaders do to be effective, rather than examining what they are. One of the main exponents of a functional approach in the UK is John Adair, an author with a military background, and the influence of his theory of action centred leadership (Adair, 1983) derives from its adoption by the Industrial Society (re-named the Work Foundation in 2002) as a central plank of their management and leadership training programmes in the 1980s. He suggested that there are three main areas of managerial leadership activity: those concerned with building the team; those concerned with developing the individual within the team; and those which are directed at the achievement of the task. This type of approach has an important appeal in that it suggests that leadership skills can be acquired, and that pre-existing characteristics are less significant that the ability to learn how to act in such a way as to balance the three key areas of activity. From the people management perspective, it places less emphasis on selection and more emphasis on training than trait theory would imply. It gives individuals a better framework for self-selection into managerial roles, and a clear set of development tasks to help them to create a successful infrastructure as managers. Adair's approach has proved highly successful as the basis for a robust and accessible system of training for supervisors and middle managers. However, it has little to say about the type of leadership that is involved in actually creating and driving organisational strategy. This is not to suggest that Adair himself has nothing to say about strategic leadership in other contexts (see, for instance, Adair, 2003).

The approach taken firstly by the MCI and now the MSC in their review of management standards is that of functional analysis, and the resulting functional map forms the basis for the 56 units which comprise the current standards. It is similar to action centred leadership in the sense that it provides a general prescription and one which has been thoroughly researched in a variety of sectors, for managerial competence. In terms of people management, yardsticks such as these have significant value in terms of setting required performance standards for supervisors and managers, identifying both individual and job-related managerial training needs, developing career structures, and of course can be used for selection purposes. What all functional approaches might fail to recognise sufficiently well, however, is the significance of such elements as tacit knowledge regarding effective performance: the sort of knowledge of and 'feel' for organisational context which generally only results from experience (Pilbeam and Corbridge, 2006). It is possible that leadership and management are a more integrated set of activities than competency-based or unitised approaches might lead us to believe. Leadership, and strategic leadership in particular, may be more than the sum of its parts.

REFLECTIVE ACTIVITY

Gladiator

Watch the opening scene of Ridley Scott's 2000 film, *Gladiator*.

It shows the preparation for a battle (stop it when the first arrows are fired – about eight to ten minutes in). Analyse Maximus' behaviours during the pre-battle preparations using Adair's 'Task, Team, Individual' model of leadership.

If you aren't squeamish, watch the rest of the film; then consider and analyse the different leaders (listed below) who emerge, using ideas discussed in this chapter. You might consider

situational factors, behaviours and characteristics.

- Maximus the general (played by Russell Crowe)
- Marcus Aurelius, the old emperor (played by Richard Harris)
- Commodus, the young emperor (played by Joaquin Phoenix)
- Gracchus, the 'republican' senator (played by Derek Jacobi); and
- Lucilla, the daughter of Marcus Aurelius (played by Connie Nielsen).

THE BEHAVIOUR OF LEADERS

Behavioural theories extend the basis of study beyond the leader himself or herself, and have as their basis a consideration of the effects which leaders have on the actual performance of groups by examining leader behaviours and relating them to outcomes. The Ohio State studies and those of the Michigan Institute for Social Research in the 1960s and 1970s pioneered this approach and produced remarkably similar results. Mullins (2010, p 380) summarises these as being leader behaviours concerned with task functions (the 'structure' dimension in the Ohio State studies and 'production-centred' supervisory behaviour in the Michigan one) and leader behaviour concerned with maintenance functions ('consideration' in the Ohio State term and 'employee-centred' behaviour in the Michigan one). He further relates them to McGregor's 'Theory X and Theory Y' managerial assumptions and the dimensions of concern for production and concern for people first proposed in Blake and Mouton's (1964) managerial grid and now revised and renamed the leadership grid (Blake and McCanse, 1991).

Behavioural studies have the advantage of offering would-be managers some options regarding behaviours which can be effective, rather than a single prescription for success. Whilst the studies concluded that there was no universally superior style, and that the circumstances of leadership might have an important influence on the effectiveness of one style over another, they did conclude that a balance between these two dimensions of behaviour seemed to be important in achieving success. In this respect they have much in common with situational or contingency theories, which have more to say about the way in which behaviours can be matched to circumstances. Once more, this type of approach offers a wider range of options for the use of training and development techniques as a means of encouraging managerial leadership capacity. In relation to strategic leadership, 'consideration' and 'structure' are both relevant to strategic tasks, but in general behavioural theories have little explicit to say about leadership at this level of organisational life.

LEADERSHIP STYLES

Approaches to the study of leadership which analyse the differences between leadership styles are generally focused upon the leader's attitude towards people and the resulting behaviours which they exhibit in their day-to-day dealings with members of the team. This generates a range of possibilities, and the resulting classifications usually identify a range of styles, perhaps most succinctly described by Tannenbaum and Schmidt (1973). They focused on the relative strength and power of managers and non-managers (ie subordinates) in terms of decision-making. At one end of the resulting continuum is 'boss-centred' (autocratic) decision-making where a manager largely decides what is to be done in a specific circumstance, and others accept and follow the decision. At the other end is joint (or democratic) decision-making, where a manager will define a problem or situation and then participate in the decision-making simply as a member of the team. This model recognises the need for an understanding of the relationship between specific managers and their teams from a basis of both leader and follower characteristics (such as personality, relevant knowledge and experience, sense of security, etc) and permits the inclusion of circumstantial considerations (organisational and societal factors, etc) in the equation. In this respect it bears considerable similarity to the contingency models discussed in the next section. Insofar as it examines the skills and requirements for leading a team, the approach is not prescriptive, and is an appropriate tool for analysing and identifying the range of successful managerial leadership styles. It also offers some important messages about the importance of flexibility in terms of managerial style. Like the behavioural theories discussed earlier, these approaches have significant value in terms of management development; but also have similar shortcomings when it comes to the consideration of strategic leadership.

SITUATIONAL AND CONTINGENCY MODELS OF LEADERSHIP

While traits-based and functional models of leadership concentrate on the leaders, and behavioural models examine the effect on the led, situational perspectives add a third dimension: that of the circumstances, both organisational and environmental, in which the leadership activity occurs. This allows the development of what is generally termed the contingency approach to leadership; in other words an approach which might answer the question 'What type of leadership actions and behaviours are appropriate?' with the phrase 'It depends on the circumstances.' Contingency approaches thus suggest a wide range of different but equally valid ways of leading and managing people. Some, such as Hersey and Blanchard's model of situational leadership, (see Hersey *et al*, 2001) focus on the appropriate leadership styles for groups or individual followers who are at different stages of 'readiness' or 'maturity' to achieve a task; readiness being defined as a combination of both ability, willingness or confidence to carry out the task in question. As these vary over time, so the leader needs to choose and use the most appropriate style to fit the circumstances. The four styles suggested in the situational leadership model are summarised from Hersey *et al* (2001, pp 182–87) as follows:

- S1 – telling – provides high amounts of guidance and direction but little supportive behaviour. This style is most appropriate for low follower readiness; including situations where followers are unable and/or unwilling. The leader structures the task and concentrates on step-by-step help and instruction.

- S2 – selling – requires high amounts of both directive (task) and relationship behaviours. This style is most appropriate for low to moderate follower readiness; particularly when followers are willing but still not fully capable of performing. The leader encourages more dialogue to achieve 'buy-in' amongst the followers.

- S3 – participating – shows high levels of two-way communication and supportive (relationship) behaviour but low amounts of guidance (task behaviour). This style is most appropriate for moderate to high follower readiness: in other words situations where followers are competent but inexperienced, or competent but de-motivated. The leader should focus on discussion, encouragement and facilitation rather than instruction.

- S4 – delegating – involves little direction or support, in other words low levels of both task and relationship behaviours. This style is most appropriate for high follower readiness, in other words situations where managerial intervention is largely unnecessary (unless there are significant problems), and can focus on monitoring.

For instance, a human resource assistant who is who is highly capable and confident about carrying out selection interviews would respond well to a delegating style of management in relation to this work. However, if they then find themselves in changed business circumstances and need to carry out redundancy interviews without having had much relevant experience, then a 'selling' style of managerial leadership might be more suitable, or possibly a 'telling' style if the individual was particularly resistant to carrying out the new task. There is also evidence that contingency approaches to leadership have particular relevance when considering inter-cultural situations. Kreitner, for instance, suggests that national culture is an important contingency and that cultural analyses such as those of Hofstede can be helpful in identifying appropriate styles for the needs of different cultural groups (Hofstede, 2001; Kreitner, 2001; Kakabadse *et al*, 1997).

There seems, from Kreitner's research, to be some indication that the most widely applicable style is the participative one. It is well suited to many national cultures but particularly those such as that of the US and Sweden where there is limited 'natural' respect for hierarchy and seniority: what Hofstede would term a 'low power distance' culture. Nevertheless, it can be successful in a wider range of cultures than the directive style. The latter is more specifically suited to 'high' power distance cultures where status automatically commands respect (Kreitner suggests French and Indian cultures), and where subordinates will generally expect their managers to have the answers by virtue of the expertise which has enabled them to achieve their status. The directive style translates poorly into 'low power distance' cultures or those where joint regulation or co-determination is the norm (for instance the German one). He explains, however, that:

> 'Participative leadership is not necessarily the best style; it simply is culturally acceptable in many different countries . . . directive leadership turned out to be the least appropriate leadership style.' (Kreitner, 2001, p 613)

Moving more directly into the area of strategic leadership in a business context, Clarke and Pratt (1985) and Rodrigues (1988) both consider the importance of the stage of growth which a business has reached and suggest that this too can be an important contingent factor with relation to the choice of strategic leadership style. Taking a basic model of the business growth cycle such as the 'Boston box', which identifies four developmental stages of an enterprise – start-up, growth, maturity and decline – these authors suggest that there are matching styles of strategic leadership: champion, tank commander, housekeeper and lemon-squeezer. The start-up organisation or venture needs a 'champion' style, a leadership style which is prepared to fight for the enterprise on a variety of fronts, thus suggesting the need for an energetic individual with a wide variety of technical management skills. An example of a 'champion' might be the founder of easyJet, Stelios Haji-Ioannou. At the end of 2002, having developed this very successful low cost airline, he stepped down as chairman in order to use his talents in what he considered to be the most effective manner, involving himself in new ventures, entrepreneurial innovation and similar 'no frills' developments in other markets. His easyGroup (see www.easy.com) has initiated a wide variety of new ventures including mobile phones, low-cost cinemas, car rental and, more recently, pizza delivery and Internet cafés.

The skills of the champion relate closely to those of the tank commander, whose strategic role is to develop strong teams that can drive the business forward once it has entered a growth phase. The housekeeper needs fewer entrepreneurial skills but must be able to achieve more in the way of planning, cost control and the formalisation of processes and organisational structures such as reward and training systems. The lemon-squeezer, who is trying to extract the best from a declining business and if possible turn it around, needs a range of skills which are more to do with taking tough and difficult measures as effectively as possible than fostering and encouraging growth. Possible examples of this type of leadership might include Sir Stuart Rose at Marks & Spencer between 2004 and 2006, and Justin King at Sainsbury's in late 2004–5. Such circumstances are common in business life; examples which came to prominence at the start of 2008 include the challenges faced by the new management of Northern Rock, and for Tata following its purchase of the Jaguar and Land Rover brands from Ford. Clarke and Pratt consider that most managers have one primary style and are not necessarily suited to all stages of business development.

The contingency approach to leadership emphasises contextual factors as an important influence on leader success. Professor Joseph Nye, in a BBC interview ahead of the UK publication of his book *The Powers to Lead: Soft, hard, and smart* in May 2008, stressed the relationship between contextual knowledge and leadership power, explaining that contextual knowledge helps leaders to determine what balance they should strike between the use of what he terms 'hard' power (issuing commands) and 'soft' power (the ability to attract and retain followers). Contingency approaches remain highly relevant for the exercise of leadership in modern organisations, having perhaps two main implications for organisational leadership and its development. First of all, training for management and leadership skills needs to include the use of tools and techniques which can enable those in managerial and leadership positions both to identify salient circumstantial features, and then choose the right method to match those circumstances. It might also suggest that leadership can, and perhaps should, change hands in response to changed circumstances if one person's skills are more appropriate than another's, which clearly has implications for management structures and individual careers. It also has particular relevance for strategic leadership. Radical change in organisational circumstances might necessitate such a significant change in strategic direction that a leader who is firmly associated with the former strategy may be far less able to lead in the new direction (Rajan, 2002). High profile examples of this phenomenon would be the changes in leadership of all three of the main political parties in the UK since 1980.

STUART ROSE AT MARKS & SPENCER, 2004–2010

Stuart Rose took charge of the fortunes of one of Britain's favourite high street retailers in May 2004. He became CEO during a turbulent time, as company profits had taken a serious knock, and the business was the subject of a hostile takeover bid by Sir Philip Green of the Arcadia group (one of Rose's former bosses). Rose won the highly public boardroom battle for M&S's independence, but the real challenge was to turn round a company which had seen its profits drop from £1 billion in 1998 to less than 20 per cent of that figure in five years.

Writing in the *Harvard Business Review* in 2007, Rose describes the key problems of his early tenure. The business was looking tired, the staff feeling uncertain and the management team suffering from a plethora of strategic initiatives, mostly introduced by external consultants. He had worked at M&S earlier in his career, and so his understanding of the company (and his affection for it) was an important cornerstone of his leadership ability. Realising that M&S needed to get back to the core values which had made it great and to reconnect with its customers, he identified three key objectives which would form the basis for his turnaround plan: improving the product, refreshing the stores and revitalising the service.

The first two of these objectives involved an overhaul of the supply chain to streamline and speed up the delivery of the company's essential fashion products. The second involved a major de-cluttering exercise (skips at each store were filled with unnecessary cardboard signs) followed by a longer term refurbishment programme. The third objective was, in many ways, much tougher since it involved re-motivating a management team which had lost its way and had to be slimmed down to save costs, whilst at the same time trying to encourage the frontline staff and enhance their customer service skills. There was a major overhaul of the company's pay structure, which meant moving away from rewarding length of service to rewarding performance;

this was not likely to be popular. Rose also wanted to introduce standardisation into the staff contracts, to reduce the 300 different types of contract down to a core of three. This facilitated a review of the company career structure and the development of much clearer promotion paths which, it was hoped, would improve staff retention rates. On top of this, a big and expensive sales training programme covered all 8,000 staff and a system of company coaches was created to ensure the learning wasn't lost.

The change programme attracted criticism from both staff and the trade union which operates in the retail sector (USDAW). However, the success began to show through in 2006, and the staff shared a significant bonus that year.

The years following the turnaround have not always been easy. In 2007 recession hit the high street early and hard, at a time when M&S had committed itself to an expensive environmental campaign (Plan A). Rose angered some shareholders when he combined the roles of CEO and Chairman in 2008, a move which was seen as both arrogant and bad corporate governance. Then, in 2009 he announced that he planned to retire in the spring of 2010, and the search was on for his successor. The baton passed to Marc Bolland, who left his post as CEO of Morrisons in December 2009 in preparation for the challenge of leading this British icon into the next decade.

Questions

1. Using one of the models included in the chapter so far, analyse and describe Stuart Rose's leadership style.

2. What would the situational leadership model tell us about the differing leadership characteristics which were necessary in 2004 when the company was in crisis, and in 2007 when it was successful?

3. What advice might you offer to Marc Bolland about leading M&S in 2010?

TRANSFORMATIONAL LEADERSHIP

Recent literature on leadership has noted the difference between so-called 'transactional' forms of leadership and 'transformational' ones. This contrast relates back to ideas about the nature of leadership in a society which no longer accepts 'authority' as the basis for command. If authority and 'position power' (French and Raven, 1968) no longer works, what are the alternatives? One approach is to bargain: in other words to appeal to the self-interest of the followers. So-called transactional forms of leadership rely on the leader's capacity to negotiate appropriate follower behaviours based on legitimate rewards or punishments – although there is, of course, an inherent assumption that the leader has the appropriate authority to offer such rewards or administer punishments. Alimo-Metcalfe (1995) notes the findings of Rosener (1990) that the men she studied were more likely than the women to adopt transactional styles, and suggests why women have tended to be more participatory:

> 'The fact that most women have lacked formal authority over others . . . means that by default they have had to find other ways to accomplish their work.' (Rosener, 1990, p 124)

This is contrasted with transformational leadership, which is a process by which leaders create high levels of motivation and commitment by generating and communicating a clear vision and, often, appealing to higher ideas and values amongst followers. Rosener (1990, p 120) defines it as motivating others by 'transforming their individual self-interest into the goals of the group' and by trying to make people feel part of the organisation. Whilst recognising this apparent gender difference, Alimo-Metcalfe (1995) warns against too close an association between female management styles and transformational leadership, suggesting that even here there are gender differences in the use of transformational techniques (such as empowerment). In her view, the 'female' version of transformational leadership is mainly focused on the creation of a sense of belonging, inclusiveness and connectedness with others in the organisation as well as its goals, whereas the same technique used by men is more focused on separateness and autonomy in pursuing organisational aims. Thus she suggests that a more general move within organisations to adopt such transformational approaches is not necessarily a means by which women can expect to achieve status and leadership positions more readily, despite an initial expectation that it might.

Legge (2005) explains how this focus on a shared vision and personal commitment was, in the 1980s, part of a transformational leadership style which was characteristic of successful Japanese companies. It was re-integrated into American management culture (which was more focused on transactional leadership) via the work of the 'excellence' gurus like Peters and Waterman, or Ouchi. She charts the appeal of this style of leadership, and in particular its association with the 'American dream' and thus some of the 'soft' human resource management practices which facilitate the growth of an enterprise culture. She also offers a critique of this essentially paternalist and unitary approach to the management of people, which (when push comes to shove) will always prioritise business needs over individual or workforce needs, thus perhaps laying managers open to charges of hypocrisy when individual and corporate interests clearly do come into conflict.

These concepts are clearly relevant to many strategic situations: for example, can an organisation that develops its own leaders respond effectively to discontinuous external change? Also, this set of ideas helps to illuminate the process of realigning the organisation's resources described above, as well as bringing new insight to the strategic analysis of the organisation's external and internal environments.

 REFLECTIVE ACTIVITY

Return to the previous case study about Marks & Spencer. Explain whether you think transactional or transformational leadership was most appropriate during 2004–5. Stuart Rose, like other CEOs, is accountable to shareholders as well as having responsibility for staff. What might be the implications of this dual role for his approach to leadership?

INSPIRATIONAL LEADERSHIP AND 'AUTHENTIC' LEADERSHIP

Finally, it is impossible to discuss questions of leadership without considering the concept of inspirational leadership, which has regained some currency in recent years. In some ways this brings us back to concepts associated with trait theories, and in particular the characteristic usually described as 'charisma'. Inspirational leadership, we are told by Adair (2003) and others, is about creating and communicating vision, having a passion and a dynamism that drives the leader and engages the enthusiasm and efforts of the led; even exhibiting unconventional behaviour and performing heroic deeds (Conger, 1999). It includes the ability to take a long-term view, to inspire trust and confidence, which unlocks talent and enables the organisation to achieve exceptional performance. A recent trend in the world of management training and development that reflects this renewed attention to the highly personal nature of leadership, and in particular strategic leadership, is found in the growing interest in emotional intelligence as a relevant and learnable management skill.

Mullins (2010) and Legge (2005) both sound notes of caution in their consideration of inspirational leadership and draw attention to some of its drawbacks. Certainly it is difficult to see how charismatic leadership can be developed effectively. This is not to deny that many business founders have been charismatic and inspiring individuals, but their skills have often been better described as those of the 'champion' which, as we have seen, relies on a wide range of business skills as well as the ability to protect and nurture a project. It is also less than wholly evident that inspirational leadership in itself results in significant benefits for organisational performance; in some cases it may be that the loss of the visionary results in the dissolution of the organisation. A specific attack on the cult of the inspirational leader was made by Beverly Alimo-Metcalfe at the HRD 2008 event, where she was reported (Evans, 2008) as saying that:

'Organisations shouldn't be choosing leaders who were "charismatic and inspirational" because these qualities in the hands of some people can be lethal. People at the top who are charismatic get there through the demise of others – they emasculate everybody else along the way. This kind of leadership can be toxic.'

Adrian Furnham has also written about arrogance and egotistical leadership behaviour using the legend of Daedalus and Icarus (Furnham, 2005). Inspirational leadership relies on a certain degree of emotional manipulation, and so its ethical status as a general management strategy might be open to challenge. It may also inspire less desirable characteristics in the followers, such as a high level of individual dependence on the approval and support of the leader; a fear of 'going against the grain' or groupthink; and a degree of enthusiasm for the 'vision' which could encourage people to act in ways which stray beyond the boundaries of what might be considered ethical, or even legal (Conger, 2002). Inspirational leaders can be bullies as well as visionaries; and the more powerfully they communicate their values, the less space there is for reasoned doubt or even opposition.

It is sometimes difficult to separate the concept of charismatic or egotistical leadership (with all its potential failings) from another idea which seems to have a more positive image – that of 'authentic' leadership. Authentic leadership is sometimes described as 'an expression of the leader's true self' – although of course the *perception* of authenticity might simply result from good acting (Ladkin and Taylor, 2009). Techniques from the world of performance art are often discussed in this context; for instance the Stanislavski method (*ibid*) and classically rooted concepts such as mastery and congruence (Ladkin, 2008). All this might suggest that followers can never really know if the leader's display of their 'true self' is anything more than an illusion. However, illusions can be powerful things, and some researchers have noted that the outcomes of 'authentic' leadership on followers' attitudes and behaviours can have significant predictive validity in terms of enhanced trust, job satisfaction and job performance (Walumbwa *et al*, 2008).

LEADERSHIP; THE RESEARCH AGENDA

Writing in the February 2008 issue of *Impact*, Linda Holbeche, the CIPD Director of Research and Policy, noted the evolving nature of management and leadership, and suggested that some important new themes are emerging from current research. Amongst these are the challenges created by the need to lead in situations of increasing complexity, ambiguity and uncertainty; the idea of building 'communities of leaders'; and the influence of leader values in shaping the behaviour of those around them. These ideas have clear implications for HR practitioners, who are often charged with the responsibility for developing organisational leaders.

It is also evident that the question of leadership remains an important area for academic research. The growth of 'virtual' organisations and teams has led to an interest into the practice of 'e-leadership', and this is likely to be of growing significance as technology offers more and better opportunities for work to be organised using geographically dispersed expertise (Avolio *et al*, 2000). Ilze Zigurs has developed some ideas about the transfer of traditional team roles into a virtual environment, including that of leadership. If physical presence is an important means of signalling and reinforcing leadership in traditional teams, what happens when there is no such presence? The concept of 'telepresence' becomes relevant here; but as she explains:

> 'being telepresent is more than just keeping up a steady stream of email messages to team members. Leaders need to learn how to use the vividness and interactivity of media to make their presence felt in a positive way.' (Zigurs, 2003, p 344)

She goes on to suggest ways in which aspects of leadership, such as communicating vision, motivating, mentoring and building trust, can be transferred from face-to-face to virtual environments, and makes specific recommendations for leadership in virtual teams.

There is also significant focus on cross-cultural leadership, most notably in the continuing work of Project GLOBE (Global Leadership and Organizational Behavioral Effectiveness), which involves over 160 researchers working in 62 societies (see French, 2010). An in-depth study of some of the project's findings has examined culture and leadership styles in 25 of the countries under review, and uses Hofstede's (2001) model as the basis for comparative analysis (Chhokar *et al*, 2007). From other perspectives, the relationship between leaders and followers continues to generate new ideas and approaches, including developments based on the theory of 'leader-member exchange' (LMX). This examines the two-way or dyadic relationships between a leader and a follower (rather than a leader and the group as a whole):

> 'LMX theory of leadership focuses on the degree of emotional support and exchange of valued resources between the leader and members. Thus, LMX leadership theory's main focus is to diagnose this relationship so a higher quality can be developed in this relationship, enabling improved performance.' (Kang and Stewart, 2007, p 532)

Kang and Stewart detail the significance of trust and empowerment in high quality leader-member exchange, and suggest that LMX might have important implications for the practice of human resource development.

It is scarcely surprising that some of the more recent contributions to the field have been concerned with failures of leadership, particularly in the financial services organisations which, in 2007, sparked major disruption to the global economy. Concern with the psychological flaws of chief executives has led to a line of research based on ideas of hubris, overconfidence and narcissism. This is well summarised by Bollaert and Petit (2010), whose exploration of the work seeks to move beyond an examination of this 'dark side' of executive psychology and appeals for a better understanding of (amongst other things) its causes:

> 'We believe that it is important to understand the contextual factors which may cause or aggravate hubristic tendencies, including the possible 'hubrisizing' effect of the executive function, as preventive measures could

then be discussed in the context of corporate governance reform.' (Bollaert and Petit, 2010, p 12)

Human resource professionals might be well placed to contribute to processes that attempt to identify the antecedents of hubristic behaviour and contribute to the necessary elements in corporate governance systems that would help to control their growth and impact.

Whether we are concerned with traditional, virtual, inter-cultural, good or bad leadership, the academic field can offer the practitioner insights into useful approaches, as well as extending the range of knowledge and understanding about effective leadership in new contexts and situations.

REFLECTIVE ACTIVITY

Locate and read the following article by Beverly Alimo-Metcalfe and Margaret Bradley about a recent research study into the link between leadership and employee engagement: Cast in a new light, *People Management*, 24 January 2008, 38–41.

What appears to be the most significant dimension of leadership in this study, and why? What are the implications of this research for organisational leadership development initiatives, for instance the use of competency-based programmes such as the MCI?

CONCLUSION

It is clear that there is a renewed sense of the importance of good leadership amongst those most concerned with setting standards for today's managers, be they in business, the public services, or elsewhere. This comes from both social and political changes, which have encouraged more individualism and less obedience to traditional forms of authority. It also stems from the need, as Handy predicted in 1989, for organisations to become more federal than monolithic, and for new styles of management and leadership to emerge to suit the changed environment, including the virtual one. It reflects a growing public interest in the standards of behaviour of those who run businesses and direct our lives through political decisions, and their competence to carry out the tasks entrusted to them. In this respect it links firmly with discussion about ethical standards and organisational practices considered elsewhere in this book.

Personnel and HR professionals will be concerned to ensure good people management and leadership in their organisations, to improve both the performance of the organisation itself and to enable it to attract and keep good staff. This means choosing appropriate frameworks for the selection of potential leaders, their initial training, managing the performance expected of them once in the job, appraising, developing, and rewarding them, facilitating their careers and, sometimes, removing them. A coherent, fair and equitable approach to these tasks is thus essential.

In terms of their applicability to managerial leadership, functional approaches, such as those developed by the MSC, have a lot to offer in terms of managerial leadership and professionalism. They are accessible to all, and can be used for a variety of organisational people management purposes. They offer a valuable way of ensuring that we 'do things right'. In terms of strategic leadership, and particularly when considering international and cross-cultural ventures, contingency theories seem to have more currency, offering a means by which those in charge of organisational strategy can ensure that they make the sort of choices which connect successfully to their business environments: 'doing the right thing in the circumstances'.

KEY LEARNING POINTS

In the light of the main theories and their implications for the personnel professional, the key learning points which emerge are:

● That the relationship between leadership and management is a close one and the two concepts should be considered different in nature but mutually reinforcing in effect.

● That leadership is essential to the successful strategic management of any organisation.

● That the way in which we analyse and understand leadership has important implications for personnel professionals, particularly with respect to the selection and training of organisational leaders.

● That an over-emphasis on charismatic leadership can result in undesirable organisational outcomes.

● That the increasing complexity and virtuality of organisations may be changing the very nature of what we understand by leadership qualities.

CASE STUDY

AYO GURKHALI

Patsy Stone, the dissolute, beehive-haired 'fash-mag slag' star of *Absolutely Fabulous*, might appear an unlikely candidate for the leadership of a major national political campaign, but in 2009 the actress Joanna Lumley (whose portrayal of Patsy catapulted her back to fame in the 1990s), found herself doing exactly that.

Lumley grew up in Northern India, the daughter of a Major in the 6th Gurkha Rifles. Her family background and experience gave her an unshakeable respect for the Gurkhas, and so she was a natural ally for the campaigning organisation which had, for many years, been attempting to win Gurkha veterans the right to live in the UK. During 2008, she became the public face of this campaign,

which ultimately achieved its main objective in 2009 amid a frenzy of political and media activity. On the face of it, the Gurkha Justice Campaign was not taking place in a favourable environment; the UK government was under pressure to tighten immigration controls and there had been recent disputes in the construction sector which centred on the use of foreign labour in Britain during a period of recession and rising unemployment. Yet the plight of the elderly Gurkhas, for many of whom time was clearly running out, appealed to the British sense of support for the underdog. What Lumley brought to the table was a significant element in its success, although she was quick to acknowledge the efforts of others who had been more closely involved in the day-to-day management of the campaign.

What contributed to her successful leadership of the campaign? Firstly, her face was recognised with affection by members of several generations, including those who held political power; indeed, opposition politicians seemed keen to associate themselves with the campaign and appear alongside her in the press. Secondly, her media appearances showed her to be articulate, attentive and single-minded, and someone who would seize opportunities when more reticent players might hesitate. Her terrier-like pursuit of Phil Woolas, the Home Office Minister, through the BBC studios on 7 May 2009 exemplified this tenacity. The result was an extraordinary impromptu press conference during which the minister agreed to a number of key requests, and the whole incident became a popular YouTube item. Finally, while she clearly felt very strongly about this issue, she focused on the facts and she clearly resisted any public emotion; anger, cynicism but above all, tears were to be firmly resisted. This mix of popularity, intelligence and single-mindedness, together with a restrained and respectful manner (no Geldof-like swearing for her!) gave her access to the Prime Minister himself, whom she skilfully praised as 'a man of integrity' at a time when his support was essential but far from guaranteed.

After the ruling which gave the rights the veterans had been seeking, she visited Nepal, where she was hailed as a goddess. After her return, and as the MPs' expenses scandal broke, she was sometimes asked during interviews if she would like to seek political office, but rejected the idea saying she would be 'hopeless' in that type of job.

She did, however, accept a role as ambassador for the Child Welfare Scheme charity which works with children and their mothers in Nepal.

A number of the press conferences and public statements made by Lumley and others during the Gurkha Justice Campaign can be found on YouTube.

Questions

1. What leadership traits do you think Joanna Lumley exhibited during the campaign?

2. How many of the functions of a leader do you think she displayed, and which appear to be missing?

3. To what extent do you think her leadership style could be characterised as 'feminine', and why?

4. Joanna Lumley is a well known and experienced actress who took on a very public leadership role. Do what extent do you think her leadership was 'authentic' and did this affect her success?

REVIEW QUESTIONS

1. What do you see as the significant differences between leadership and management? Must all good managers be good leaders? Do all business leaders have to be good managers?

2. Imagine you are in charge of devising a management development programme for a large commercial organisation. What would you include on the subject of leadership and how you would teach this topic? How would you do things differently if you were designing a management development programme for a local authority? (You might like to consider one recently developed leadership and management training programme described by Rebecca Johnson in the 23 August 2007 edition of *People Management*.)

3. Think about someone you know who you would describe as a good leader, preferably in an organisational context. What makes them good in your view? Would the skills and attributes you identified earlier be suitable in all contexts?

4. Are you a member or leader of a virtual team? If so, try to analyse what sorts of leadership behaviour appear to be effective in this environment. If not, what challenges might exist for leaders of such teams, and how could a personnel specialist help to identify them? You might like to consider if any lessons can be learned from the way in which virtual communities such as Facebook or Second Life operate.

EXPLORE FURTHER

Mullins, L. (2010) *Management and Organisational Behaviour*, 9th ed. Harlow: FT/Prentice Hall. This text offers comprehensive descriptions and discussion of all major conceptualisations of both management and leadership, including those relating to gender, as well as relevant case studies.

Yukl, G. (2006) *Leadership in Organisations*, 6th ed. London: Prentice Hall. Another comprehensive review of the nature of leadership in an organisational setting.

A recent addition to the literature, *The Powers to Lead* (2008) Oxford: OUP, by Harvard professor of international relations Joseph Nye considers leadership styles and skills, and also discusses the transferability of leadership between different arenas such as the military, politics and business.

Avolio, B., Walumbwa, F. and Weber, T. (2009) Leadership: current theories, research and future directions in the *Annual Review of Psychology* Vol 60, pp 421–49 offers a summary of recent directions in academic leadership research.

French, R. (2010) *Cross-Cultural Management in Work Organisations*, 2nd ed, includes a chapter on the implications of national culture for organisational leadership as well as some information about key authors on cultural difference, and the relevant findings of Project GLOBE.

Information about Project GLOBE (Global Leadership and Organizational Behavior Effectiveness) can be found at the project's website, hosted by the Thunderbird School of Global Management, and located at http://www.thunderbird.edu/sites/globe/

CHAPTER 6

Managing Change

David Hall *and* Gary Rees

LEARNING OUTCOMES

After reading this chapter, you should be able to:

- explore the nature and types of change
- examine the context, process and content of change
- explore and examine change interventions
- examine change leadership and change capability
- examine the role of HR and change.

OVERVIEW

Change continues to take a front stage role in both academic research and industrial practice. Whilst it is difficult to gain a universally accepted definition of change, we are reminded that change management is not a distinct discipline with rigorous and defined boundaries, but more that the theory and practice of change management draws upon a number of social science disciplines and traditions (Burnes, 2004, p 261). This chapter encapsulates the major theories in the field of change, adopting a strategic perspective, and considers how HR can impact upon change in organisations.

The appropriateness of change planning and intervention is dependent to some extent on how we fit theory into practice and vice versa. Grint (1997, p 1) sums the argument up particularly well:

'Theory is where you know everything and nothing works;
Practice is where everything works, but nobody knows why;
Here we combine theory and practice:
Nothing works and nobody knows why'.

Whilst it is unlikely that any one change model fits perfectly, there is scope to consider a more hybrid approach to change. There needs to be a move away from 'static' models of change, which stress the content and substance of change,

(Nelson, 2003) to the dynamics of change, with the expectation that change occurs within a less certain environment, where flexibility is required to maintain or enable competitive advantage. These issues will be explored throughout this chapter.

INTRODUCTION

DEFINING CHANGE AND CHANGE MANAGEMENT

Small-scale and relatively simple changes that can typically be categorised as 'hard' problems, are usually managed within the day-to-day operational management activity. This type of change is not usually referred to as 'change' by managers, and the process of managing it is not described as 'managing change' or 'change management' within organisations.

Managers have to consider the many factors involved in a complex and dynamic situation, before making decisions that provide the basis for implementing actions that will influence the effectiveness, efficiency and ultimately the sustainability of their organisations.

Brech (1975, p 19) defines management as:

> 'A social process entailing responsibility for the effective and economic planning and regulation of the operations of an enterprise, in fulfilment of given purposes or tasks, such responsibility involving:
>
> (a) judgement and decision in determining plans and in using data to control performance and progress against plans;
>
> (b) the guidance, integration, motivation and supervision of the personnel composing the enterprise and carrying out its operations.'

Brech describes the four main elements of management as being planning, control, co-ordination and motivation. Fayol (1949) describes the function of management in similar terms proposing five elements of management: planning, organising, commanding, coordinating and controlling.

Management can be described as, essentially, an intervention for controlling operational performance outcomes in line with an organisation's purpose and objectives.

In carrying out their responsibilities, managers are dealing with change on a day-to-day basis, which raises an interesting question: when does management become 'change management'? Is this purely an academic question (it will be for many managers) or is it helpful from a management and organisational perspective to understand what, if anything, differentiates the two?

Change may be defined simplistically as making things different, but the definition needs to make explicit mention of actual and perceived change(s).

Fincham and Rhodes (2005, p 525) define change management as 'the leadership and direction of the process of organisational transformation – especially with regard to human aspects and overcoming resistance to change'.

The Society for Human Resource Management defines change management as:

'The systematic approach and application of knowledge, tools and resources to deal with change. Change management means defining and adopting corporate strategies, structures, procedures and technologies to deal with changes in external conditions and the business environment.'

Therefore, managing change or 'change management' is a form of management control through the application of systematic management interventions that involve people to achieve a desired future state with defined performance outcomes in line with the organisational strategy.

From this definition, it is clear that there is a strong and inextricable link between organisational change, performance and strategy.

TYPES OF CHANGE

Dependent upon the perspective that has been adopted, a variety of models and concepts can be utilised in order to consider the types of organisational change. This chapter will consider the level of change, the size and scope of change, the nature of change and the momentum of change.

THE LEVEL OF ORGANISATIONAL CHANGE

Carnall (2003, p 174) suggests that there are three levels of strategic change. Firstly, organisation-specific changes, such as a new information system. Secondly, generic organisation-wide change programmes, such as business process re-engineering (BPR). And thirdly, generic multi-organisational change programmes: for example, mergers and acquisitions.

THE SIZE AND SCOPE OF CHANGE

Child (2005) provides a useful model on how to differentiate between the scope of change and type of change – see Figure 6.1.

It must be borne in mind that whilst radical and incremental change may be defined and measured, often it is the perceived scale of change that may be more important than the actual scale of change.

THE NATURE OF CHANGE – PLANNED OR UNPLANNED?

Whilst it may be assumed that all organisational change is both rational and planned, with control of nearly all processes and resources, there may be

Figure 6.1 Child's approaches to organisational change

Approaches to organisational change

	Planned	Emergent	
	BPR	Organic development (eg start up company)	whole org.
Radical	Merger of departments	Changes to selection of new members made by teams	part org.
	Annual targeted improvements	Organisational learning	whole org.
Incremental	Changes agreed in staff performance plans	Continuous improvement through project teams	part org.

Source: Child, J. (2005) *Organisation*, Blackwell

occasions when a less planned and logical method may be adopted. A parallel argument is one of adopting an organic approach to change (Burns and Stalker, 1994) versus an expected mechanistic approach. If it is assumed that change can emerge, then one approach by management may be to throw a metaphorical hand-grenade into the organisation, and then see what emerges.

For example, an organisation may deliberately set about rumour-mongering around restructuring and job cuts, then formally notify employees that all jobs have been red-circled and that employees have to make applications for new posts. During this time, communication and consultation is deliberately kept to a minimum. Management then see what emerges after a period of time. A less contentious scenario could also be envisaged, where the management of an organisation simply let things run, without obvious intervention.

Expectedly, change models tend to centre around planned change, which in itself will determine the various factors or characteristics that are then compared to, for example, strategic/tactical and operational change, radical, transformational and incremental change, the rate of change (change momentum), and hard versus soft change.

However, complex large-scale changes, usually driven by external factors and having a significant 'soft' change element, are planned and coordinated. The terms 'managing change' or 'change management' can be used to describe the application of systematic interventions to implement a planned change within organisations to achieve a desired future state. In the following section, several key change management models are considered.

THE NATURE OF CHANGE – HARD AND SOFT CHANGE

Managing task elements of change is often referred to as the 'hard' elements, which are defined and measured. 'Soft factors', such as culture and motivation, may be more difficult to assess. Emphasis may be placed upon managing task factors at the expense of soft factors during change interventions. However, Sirkin *et al* (2005) argue that four hard factors are correlated to the outcome of change interventions, namely: duration (length of time), integrity (reliance on managers), commitment (of all involved in change) and effort (within the opportunity of time allowed).

When characterising change, we have considered the speed and magnitude of change, and related this to the problem of complexity. The problems that change presents to an organisation can be perceived by managers as 'difficulties', which are 'bounded' in that they can be well-defined (specified) and can be dealt with without involving or impacting on the wider organisation.

Another category of problems is those which cannot be well-defined and are 'unbounded' in the sense that the wider organisation is implicated and needs to be involved in dealing with these types of problems.

THE NATURE OF CHANGE – TOP DOWN VERSUS BOTTOM UP

Top-down change could stem from a managerial prerogative for maintaining control throughout the change. Change could be driven through by management, and resistance controlled and eliminated. Here change can become more of a political issue (Gioia and Thomas, 1996). Lupton (1991) argues that a bottom-up approach has its benefits in that employees at all levels have skills and expertise that are often lost in change processes. A third option is a combination of top-down and bottom-up approaches.

CHANGE MOMENTUM: MAGNITUDE AND SPEED

The momentum of change, ie the combination of speed and magnitude of change, is a useful concept to analyse and characterise different types of change. As we have seen, change momentum is not always easy to predict but if it can be anticipated (in many cases it can be), interventions to manage change may be considered from the options available. In other words, if managers are able to characterise the type of change an organisation will experience, this can be helpful in considering appropriate interventions to manage change in an effective way. We will consider change management interventions later but let us return to characterising change. Figure 6.2 below represents a model of change momentum based on the two key variables of speed and magnitude.

'Smooth' and 'bumpy' change are both characterised by relatively small (and less complex) change but differing in speed of implementation, with 'smooth' change happening over a longer period of time than the latter. Smooth change happens in small steps and is often described as being 'incremental', being barely noticeable in the day-to-day business of an organisation. Relatively minor

Figure 6.2 Model of Change Momentum

Magnitude of change

'Planned' Large change Slow change	*'Big Bang'* Large change Fast change
'Smooth' Small change Slow change	*'Bumpy'* Small change Fast change

Speed of change

changes to policies and procedures would be examples of this type of change. This type of change is typically driven by internal factors.

'Bumpy' change is more noticeable, as the speed of change is fast and, therefore, requires a quicker response time by managers and employees in dealing with this type of change. This type of change is typically driven by external factors which require an organisation to move quickly to respond. Examples of this would include organisations responding to crises, which require significant investment or changes in practice, eg health, safety and the environment, regulatory reform or legal proceedings. Companies involved in fast moving markets often have to manage this type of change as consumer opinion and tastes quickly change.

Grundy (1993) describes three types of change related to speed of change. The first is 'smooth incremental change' as change that evolves slowly in a systematic and predictable way. He also describes 'bumpy incremental change' as periods of relative calm, ie little or no change, that is punctuated by accelerated change. The third type of change described by Grundy is 'discontinuous' change, which he defines as '*change which is marked by rapid shifts in strategy, structure or culture, or in all three*' (Grundy, 1993, p 26). This would equate closely to 'Big Bang' change in terms of change momentum.

Grundy's 'discontinuous change' and 'Big Bang' change describes many of the characteristics of what has become known as 'transformational' change – a type of change that involves the values, attitudes and behaviours of people that contribute towards shaping the culture of an organisation. This form of complex change focuses on the motivation and commitment of employees and their contribution towards performance outcomes. Leadership which emphasises these employee attributes in managing change is described as 'transformational leadership' (Bass, 1985) which we shall return to later.

In conclusion, a range of differing variables have been used to examine the different types of change. However, there may be other more relevant comparators than the ones presented. It is necessary to examine the context of change as well in order to assess whether the most appropriate comparators have been used.

ANALYSING THE CHANGE CONTEXT

The question as to why organisations change is often determined by a combination of both push and pull factors. Organisations sometimes have choices as to whether they want to change, or are sometimes forced to change because of legal or other reasons. The importance of why organisations change is linked to the timing of change.

Whilst there may be a range of comparators with which to analyse change dimensions, a potential metaphor is one which considers a combination of change interventions running concurrently – see Figure 6.3. The metaphor shows a range of change interventions, some of which start anew, some end, and all of which may impact upon each other.

Whilst classic change models may posit a start, middle and end part of the change process, it is important to have to start at some point in terms of determining where the organisation is now and where it wants to arrive at in terms of change. Change models can either adopt a reactive approach (this is why we need to change), or adopt a proactive approach (where do we want to get to as an organisation?).

Figure 6.3 Combination of concurrent change interventions

New change processes introduced

Flow of tide (change)

External changes impacting

Each strand represents a different change process

External changes impacting

Change processes terminating

Combination of change interventions running concurrently

Figure 6.4 The iterative nature of change, and planning for change

Adapted from De Wit and Meyer (2010)

With strategic change, we may start with a strategic plan, or possibly a vision or mission statement, which leads to a strategic plan. When analysing why organisations change, there is often a 'trigger for change'. The CIPD (2009) quotes the following triggers for change:

- challenges of growth, especially global markets
- challenges of economic downturns and tougher trading conditions
- changes in strategy
- technological changes
- competitive pressures, including mergers and acquisitions
- customer pressure, particularly shifting markets
- challenges to learn new organisation behaviour and skills
- government legislation/initiatives.

When it comes to analysing the strategic context, a range and models can be utilised. Both the internal and external context need to be analysed.

EXTERNAL DRIVERS OF CHANGE

A useful tool to examine the external drivers of change involves the PESTLE taxonomy. The earliest known reference to a framework for describing the external business environment is by Aguilar (1967) who presents 'ETPS' as a mnemonic to represent the four sectors: **E**conomic, **T**echnical, **P**olitical, and **S**ocial. Variations of this include 'PEST' and 'PESTLE' which adds the Legal and Environmental dimensions – see Figure 6.5.

Figure 6.5 PESTLE framework

Factor or driver	Typical considerations
Political	<ul><li>Taxation and other policies</li><li>Current and future political support</li><li>Funding, grants and initiatives</li><li>Trade organisations</li><li>Internal and international relationships</li></ul>
Economic	<ul><li>Economic situation</li><li>Consumer spending</li><li>Levels of government spending</li><li>Interest rates, inflation and unemployment</li><li>Exchange rates</li></ul>
Social	<ul><li>Demographics and social mobility</li><li>Lifestyle patterns and changes</li><li>People's attitudes and actions</li><li>Media perception and influence</li><li>Ethnic and religious differences</li></ul>
Technological	<ul><li>Research, technology and innovation funding</li><li>Consumer behaviour and processes</li><li>Intellectual property</li><li>Global communication technological advances</li><li>Social networks</li></ul>
Legal	<ul><li>Legislation in employment, competition and health and safety, etc</li><li>Changes in legislation</li><li>Trading policies</li><li>Regulatory bodies</li><li>International protocols</li></ul>
Environmental	<ul><li>Clean technologies and processes</li><li>Waste management and recycling</li><li>Attitudes of government, media and consumers</li><li>Environmental legislation</li><li>Global warming and emission protocols</li></ul>

The PESTLE taxonomy provides a useful external environment scanning framework and a methodology for identifying and analysing factors that shape the external business environment. When combined with a SWOT (Strengths, Weaknesses, Opportunities and Threats) analysis, this evidence-based approach provides valuable information for strategic decision-making.

The external environmental factors identified from a PESTLE are typically considered opportunities or threats in a SWOT analysis. Strengths and weaknesses are usually regarded as internal organisational factors which can be considered against the external opportunities and threats. This 'looking out' and 'looking in' approach provides a basis for internal-external organisation analysis and is an important part of the strategic management process, if carried out in a purposeful and rigorous manner.

INTERNAL DRIVERS OF CHANGE

Not all organisational change can be attributed to managers responding to a business environment comprised of external factors. Internal drivers of change can also play a major role in initiating change and these include:

- new leadership
- new strategy
- new structures
- new business model
- organisation growth
- redesign of jobs
- redesign of business processes
- outsourcing
- change of location
- installation of new technology and systems
- changes to employees' terms and conditions
- being acquired or merged with another organisation
- redundancies.

These changes can be and often are influenced by external factors, but they can also be triggered by decisions which are not made as a response to changes in the business environment.

Pettigrew and Whipp (1993) argue that environmental assessment is only one of five factors that determine the success of managing change. The other four factors are: leading change, linking strategic and operational change, considering human resources as both assets and liabilities, and a central factor in all of this – coherence – pulling the other four factors together.

REFLECTIVE ACTIVITY

Duty of care

Change has been equated to bereavement (Marris, 1988). Constant change may not allow employees time to grieve. It could be argued that organisations have a duty of care to ensure that the welfare of their employees is paramount and thereby limit constant and dramatic change. If an organisation does not constantly seek employee feedback and make an assessment through an organisational stress thermometer, how will it know how much employees can take? What are the implications for organisations when deciding upon the nature and type of change, and upon how change should take place?

It is important to differentiate between external and internal factors when considering change, with the key difference being that organisations and managers may have little, if any, control over the external factors. However, internal factors are typically management decisions which are designed to exert some form of control aimed at achieving certain performance outcomes.

Organisations lobby governments on many issues in an attempt to influence politicians' decisions and the outcomes that define the external factors which ultimately shape the business environment in which they operate. Climate change and the environment are examples of contemporary issues that continue to attract the lobbyists in the early part of this century.

Control is the primary motivation for doing this because if organisations can be a factor in shaping their business environment, this enables them to predict more accurately what this environment will look like. This, in turn, puts these organisations in a stronger position to be able to make informed strategic decisions to control their future direction and performance.

The UK government's 'modernisation programme' of public services described in the White Paper of 1999 (www.cabinetoffice.gov.uk/moderngov/whtpaper/index. htm) set out a ten-year change programme aimed at delivering more responsive and high-quality public services which can be measured by better results. The National Health Service (NHS) is probably the most widely publicised example of the 'modernisation agenda' having been subjected to a plethora of change initiatives and performance targets. A combination of external and internal factors typically drive this type of change in organisations.

CHOICE OF CHANGE INTERVENTION

After the context has been analysed, the choice of change intervention needs to be considered. Five different change management tools and techniques will be introduced in order to provide an understanding of how the organisation can manage change.

TROPICS test

The Open University (1985) describes two types of problems as 'difficulties' and 'messes'. Paton and McCalman (2000) use the terms 'hard' and 'soft' respectively to describe these same sets of problems.

Paton and McCalman (2000) devised the 'TROPICS' test as a guide to help determine the nature of change in terms of a continuum from hard to soft (see Figure 6.6).

This test provides a useful reference framework to help characterise and understand the parameters involved when facing change. It is important to recognise that this is a continuum, and many change programmes will combine elements of hard and soft change.

Figure 6.6 The TROPICS test

Hard	Soft
Time-scales clearly defined/short to medium term	Time-scales ill-defined/medium to long term
Resources needed identified	Resources uncertain
Objectives specified and quantified	Objectives subjective and ambiguous
Perceptions of the problem shared by all	No consensus of problem
Interest in problem limited and defined	Interest in problem widespread and ill-defined
Control within managing group	Control is shared with people outside of managing group
Source of the problem is within organisation	Source of the problem is outside the organisation

With knowledge and understanding of the issues involved when faced with a change scenario, managers are in a better position to be able to assess the situation and decide on an appropriate course of action to help control and manage the change process.

Lewin's three-phase change model

One of the earliest known models applied to managing change was a three-phase model which focused on the psychological aspects of behaviour modification by Kurt Lewin (1951):

1. Unfreezing: lowering resistance to change by recognising and accepting the need for change.

2. Movement: developing new attitudes to encourage behaviours necessary for change to occur.

3. Refreezing: stabilising, supporting and reinforcing the new change conditions.

This model presents a systematic approach to change management, describing a sequence of well-defined and interrelated processes. The premise for this model was that by identifying and understanding the key stages involved in the change process, the likelihood of effective change management was increased – by managers making better informed decisions about which interventions to use in managing change.

Lewin was also responsible for developing force-field analysis (Lewin, 1947), a diagnostic technique which considered the forces or 'drivers' for and against change. At any time, there will be a number of forces in play that resist change and support the 'status quo', and forces that encourage change. These can be internal or external forces, or as is usually the case, a combination of both types of forces.

Figure 6.7 Lewin's force-field analysis

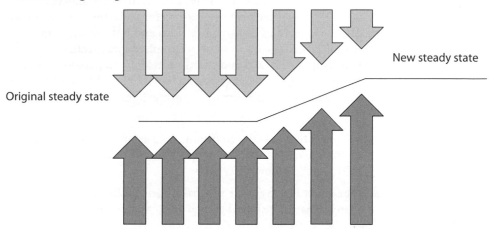

Forces resisting change

Original steady state

New steady state

Forces driving change

When the sum of the forces 'for' and 'against' change are equal, they cancel each other out resulting in equilibrium, ie a steady state. However, when the forces driving change are greater than the forces of resistance (either by the driving forces increasing or the restraining forces decreasing), change will occur, and the organisation will inevitably change and move to a new state, as shown in Figure 6.7.

Although Lewin's model is criticised for oversimplifying change by describing a sequential linear process, its three stages of change are reflected in other more contemporary change management models. French, Kast and Rosenzweig (1985) list eight components of a planned-change effort which can be related to Lewin's model:

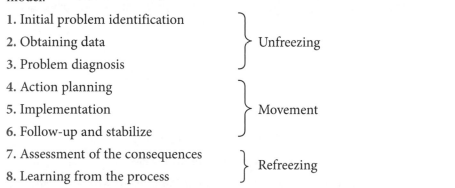

1. Initial problem identification
2. Obtaining data   } Unfreezing
3. Problem diagnosis

4. Action planning
5. Implementation   } Movement
6. Follow-up and stabilize

7. Assessment of the consequences   } Refreezing
8. Learning from the process

The other main criticism of Lewin's model and other linear change models is that they describe the process of change transforming from an initial state to a final stage. Today, change is widely recognised as being a constant and continuing phenomenon for all organisations, albeit at a faster rate for some compared to others.

RESISTANCE TO CHANGE

A multitude of factors could contribute to resistance to change. Prahalad, quoted in Allio (2008:12), cites three primary reasons for resistance to change in organisations. Firstly, the logic of management actions and behaviours is not always obvious. Secondly, if change occurs, the accumulated intellectual experience of the players gets devalued and change is taken as a personal threat (so a safety net is needed). Thirdly, managers need to have their hand held while they are learning. Prahalad emphasises the need for managers constantly learning new skills.

French *et al* (2008) suggest that in order to minimise resistance in such cases, the change agent should make sure that the people affected by the change know specifically how it satisfies the following criteria:

- *Benefit.* The change should have a clear relative advantage for the individuals being asked to change; that is, it should be perceived as 'a better way'.

- *Compatibility.* The change should be as compatible as possible with the existing values and experiences of the people being asked to change.

- *Complexity.* The change should be no more complex than necessary. It must be as easy as possible to understand and use.

- *Triability.* The change should be something that people can try on a step-by-step basis and make adjustments as things progress.

 REFLECTIVE ACTIVITY

Your organisation (or an organisation of your choice) has decided to introduce job evaluation and performance management organisation-wide, and at the same time operate a recruitment ban and pay freeze. As the HR Business Partner, use Lewin's model to identify some of the potential forces acting for and against this change initiative.

Kotter's eight-stage change model

John Kotter (1996) described an eight-stage change process for managing change in large organisations following his research into US organisations who had failed to manage change effectively:

1. Establish a sense of urgency – *the need to change*

2. Create a guiding coalition – *with authority and credibility*

3. Develop a vision and strategy – *a clear aim and way forward*

4. Communicate the change vision – *promote understanding and commitment*

5. Empower broad-based action – *enable people to act and overcome barriers*

6. Generate short-term wins – *to motivate and ensure further support*

7. Consolidate gains and produce more change – *maintain change momentum*

8. Anchor new approaches in the culture – *new values, attitudes and behaviours.*

This model appears to be a linear and sequential set of processes, and has been criticised for these reasons. However, in the final two steps, Kotter attempts to address the problem of the 'refreezing' stage in Lewin's model by encouraging organisations and their employees to develop attitudes and values which help to promote the behaviours required to encourage and support further change. In developing an organisational culture that is proactive to change, this helps to create a feedback mechanism which transforms a linear change model into a continuous process.

Many change management programmes applied in organisations are based on systematic change management models comprised of sequential processes similar to the examples outlined above. However, a common modification to these models in practice is to introduce an additional process at the end which provides a feedback step from the final to the initiating stage. With this modification, these models describe a cyclical and continuous change management system.

A significant feature of Kotter's model is the role of leadership, particularly in developing and communicating the vision for change, which is critical to effective transformational leadership, and management of change in large-scale organisations (Bass, 1985).

This type of approach to change tends to be effective for change that is predominantly 'hard' by nature, ie as characterised in terms of the TROPICS test. Objectives, milestones and performance can be quantified and applied within the boundaries of a specific change programme, thereby offering a means to assess progress of the managed change programme.

Organisational development

There is another approach for intervening to improve organisational performance through managing change called organisational development (OD) that offers appropriate solutions to the 'softer' aspects of change. We must remember that hard and soft change form part of a continuum, and that the majority of change scenarios involve both aspects. When managing change, organisations will apply a range of interventions often using both approaches described in this chapter. These different approaches are not mutually exclusive.

There are many definitions of OD, but the following definition is particularly useful in helping to develop understanding of the context, content and processes involved in OD as a change and organisational performance intervention.

French and Bell (1999, pp 25–26) define OD as:

> 'a long term effort, led and supported by top management to improve an organisation's visioning, empowerment, learning and problem-solving processes, through an on-going, collaborative management of organization culture – with a special emphasis on the culture of intact work-teams and other team configurations, using consultant-facilitator role and the theory and technology of applied behavioural science, including action research'.

The CIPD (2009b) offers the following succinct definition of OD as a 'planned and systematic approach to enabling sustained organisational performance through the involvement of its people'.

OD emphasises the management of culture and employee behaviour as the central interventions for sustaining organisational capability to deal with long-term change and improve performance. An examination of several definitions of OD reveals a number of common features which highlight the distinguishing characteristics of the OD approach to change:

- It is has top management support and involvement – it is participative.

- It deals with change over the medium to long term – it is strategic.

- It applies to an entire organisation and its component parts – it is systematic within institutionalising change.

- It draws on the theory and practice of behavioural science – such as leadership, group dynamics and work design.

- It emphasises the transfer of knowledge and skills through training and developing people – using action research and organisational learning methods.

- It is concerned with planned change but is adaptable to new situations – rather than prescribing a rigid process which must be followed.

- It is uses data to inform decision-making and progress – it is 'evidence-based'.

- It often makes use of 'change agents' or OD practitioners to facilitate the OD process.

- It is aimed at facilitating planned change and improving organisational performance over the longer term.

The roots of OD can be found in the motivation theories of the 1940s and 1950s which gave rise to the Human Relations School of management and organisation. It became popular towards the end of the last century as an alternative approach to the 'hard' systems approach shaped by the models which flourished in the 1980s and 1990s. These models struggled to deal with the complexities and often unknown factors that were common components of the 'unbounded' soft and messy problems organisations faced as their environments rapidly changed.

OD focuses on managing organisational culture by promoting values and attitudes associated with personal and professional development, problem-solving, openness, engagement and commitment. The premise of this approach is that if an organisation's employees share such common values, this will manifest in desirable and normative behaviour at all levels – individual, team and organisation.

An example where the application of the OD approach would be particularly relevant would be in developing a 'high performance culture' within an organisation. Establishing a shared set of values which employees, particularly managers, agree to adhere to in the work environment provides a guide for what is regarded as acceptable employee behaviour, which, over a period of time becomes regarded as normal behaviour by most employees.

The set of values would typically include values related to learning and improvement, working with others, being honest and respectful, etc, which ultimately influence an individual and group behaviour to enable performance improvement. These values would typically be applied in performance management interventions, recruitment and selection, career development and progression, reward schemes and leadership development, to facilitate and embed an evasive organisational culture that encourages and supports high levels of commitment to performance.

This is a sophisticated and complex form of organisational control based on influencing normative behaviour which is acceptable to managers and employees. The principles of OD also facilitate management of the psychological contract which is defined by Guest and Conway (2002) as '...the perceptions of the two parties, employee and employer, of what their mutual obligations are towards each other'.

Guest and Conway propose in their model of the psychological contract that the implicit nature of the contract is moderated by the employees' and employers' sense of fairness and trust, and the belief that the employer will honour the unwritten 'arrangement' between them. It is suggested that a healthy psychological contract will promote employee commitment and satisfaction and have a positive influence on performance.

How employees experience and perceive the workplace, and their relationship with managers and colleagues, will play a role in shaping their attitudes and consequent behaviour. Organisational development, with its emphasis on values and attitudes as a means of managing culture and change, also presents an opportunity for employers and employees to develop positive psychological contracts to the benefit of both parties.

Although OD is an intervention for managing change and improving performance, because it focuses on the culture of an organisation influencing the attitudes and values (and ultimately behaviour), it pervades all areas and activities of an organisation. With an emphasis on learning and improvement, at individual, group and organisational levels, through techniques such as action learning, it develops and sustains the performance capability of an organisation through its people asset (human capital) and prepares an organisation for dealing with continuous change: ie it develops a state of enduring 'readiness' for change.

In doing this, OD shapes the culture of an organisation to encourage managers and employees not to resist change but to be accepting and even embrace change, and approach it in that way. In other words, OD influences the ethos of an organisation and its people in dealing with change. It is an approach which addresses the 'soft' and often intangible aspects of managing change which, because of the complexity involved, the rationality-based linear change models do not adequately accommodate.

Organisations who take the OD approach towards managing change tend to rely less on specific and explicit change programmes, but approach change as a normal part of everyday business. In the UK, the NHS has attempted to take this approach having undergone radical change since the inception of the 'modernisation programme'. The OD approach implies that normal business is about change, and dealing with change is implicit in what organisations and their people do – it is 'business as usual'.

This makes a lot of sense because if we accept that organisational change is a permanent phenomenon, employees will soon become exhausted and de-motivated if they are presented with one change programme after another, and sometimes multiple change programmes at the same time.

That is not to say that organisations who adopt the OD approach cannot and do not roll out specific projects for introducing change. This would be a particularly appropriate approach for managing 'hard' changes which are specific and contained, and lend themselves to being managed as a project with clearly defined and measurable objectives

IMPRESS – MEETING COMPANY GOALS THROUGH STRATEGIC ACQUISITIONS

CASE STUDY

Impress is a privately owned worldwide manufacturer of metal food cans, operating in 21 countries, with 8,000 employees, and a turnover of 1.6 billion Euros in 2006. Impress as a legal identity is based in the Netherlands, but has its head office in Paris, and operates primarily throughout Europe. Their strategy is to be the best metal can manufacturer as opposed to the most profitable or biggest, and place great emphasis upon values surrounding operational excellence. The corporate culture centres around trust, transparency and teamwork.

Impress adopts an acquisition strategy in order to meet company objectives, and not as a purpose in itself. After Impress has considered acquiring another organisation and has evaluated if there will be a resultant strategic advantage, questions around the target company's readiness to change are considered. All relevant parties are brought to the table, and human resources, finance, legal, production, management and technical teams are consulted in an unaggressive and unobtrusive way.

Impress managers seek to understand the culture and management model of the organisation and its capacity for change, as well as explore the leadership of the change process. The reputation of the company in the local area is considered, employee behaviours and skills are analysed and

consideration given to company values and how they are communicated through the company.

During the post-acquisition process, welcome meetings are arranged, existing signs and logos are replaced by the Impress brand, plans for integration of the two company structures set out, synergies and benchmarking sought, and restructuring plans made. Information is communicated as clearly and widely as possible in order to keep all relevant parties informed. Management changes are made as quickly as possible and a vision developed for the acquired company.

Impress uses a 'learning by doing' framework for acquisitions, which facilitates the integration process and creates enough flexibility to allow processes and values to be influenced by the cultures of the company that it acquires and the countries in which it operates.

Source: case taken from Ursula Huws and Brie O' Keefe, Managing Change in EU cross-border mergers and acquisitions. Case example Impress. The European Foundation for the improvement of living and working conditions, 2008.

Question

Consider the extent to which Impress adopts Kotter's approach when managing acquisitions and change.

Figure 6.8 A systems model of change

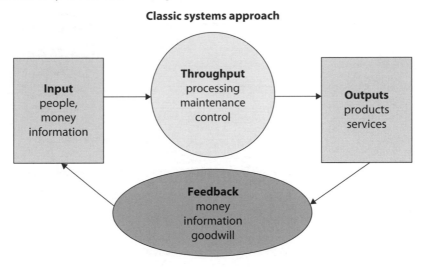

Classic systems approach

A systems approach to change

Whilst the concept of a systems approach may on the face of it appear simplistic, systems models allow for a great deal of complexity and data to be analysed. Figure 6.8 demonstrates the key components of a process model of change.

Whilst there is a range of systems models available to the change agent, Mayon-White (1993), cites the example of Systems Intervention Strategy as a useful tool for undertaking change. The diagnosis phase asks 'Where are we now?' – and then 'Where do we want to be?' which evolves the identification of objectives and constraints. The question 'How will you know when you get there?' is addressed by the formulation of metrics for our objectives. In the design phase, we ask 'How can we get there?', where we generate a range of options, then ask 'What will it be like?' where we can model options selectively. During the implementation phase, we consider whether we will like it, and then evaluate options against metrics. Finally, we ask 'How can we carry it through?' then consider the design of implementation strategies and then carry through the planned changes. Figure 6.9 demonstrates how the 'problem owners' fit within this model. Whilst McCalman and Paton (1992) argue that the problem owner may clearly define the nature of change, those affected by the change, the boundary and scope of the change and the relationships affected by the change, it could be contested that establishing who is affected by the change is not always apparent. 'Affected' could be considered in terms of job, role, task, function etc, but may not account for emotional or cultural ties etc.

Mayon-White (1993, p 136) provides a chart showing the types of action and tools and techniques that are used in Systems Intervention Strategy (Table 6.1).

Figure 6.9 Systems Intervention Strategy

A range of models have been presented, some of which show signs of overlap – for example, Systems Intervention Strategy includes Lewin's force-field analysis. The choice of model(s) is up to the change agent and key stakeholders. It is possible to combine aspects of different models – for example, having a combination of OD and SIS – but caution needs to be expressed so that there is no confusion as to what the process actually involves.

LEADING CHANGE

The choice of change agent is critical to the success of any change intervention. Whilst a universal definition of a change agent proves impossible to locate, characteristics, competences and skills can differentiate across change agents.

In simple terms, Rosenfeld and Wilson (1999, p 294) define change as 'the individuals or groups of individuals whose task it is to effect change'.

What does a change agent look like?

Whilst the determination of choice of change agent will be determined by a range of factors, Lessem (1989) provides a range of change agent characteristics:

Table 6.1 The key features and methods of SIS

The three phases of the strategy	The steps of the strategy phases	What kinds of actions are appropriate to each step?	What tools and techniques are available to help?
Diagnosis	0. Entry	Start by recognising that change is a complex process.	Make use of the concepts of 'mess' and 'difficulty'.
	1. Description	Structure and understanding the change in systems terms. Get other points of view on the change problem or opportunity.	Use diagrams. Set up meetings (NGT, Delphi, etc). Create a model of things as they are.
	2. Identify objectives and constraints	Set up objectives for the systems that you are examining. Think of the objectives of the change itself.	Set up an 'objective tree'. Prioritise your objectives for change.
	3. Formulate measures for your objectives	Decide on ways of measuring if an objective is achieved.	Use '£s' or quantities where possible. Scaling or ranking methods elsewhere.
Design	4. Generate a range of options	Develop any ideas for change as full options. Look at a wide range of possibilities. Your objectives may suggest new options.	Brainstorming. Idea writing. Interviews and surveys. Comparisons with best practice in other organisations.
	5. Model options selectively	Describe the most promising options in some detail. Ask of each option: what is involved? Who is involved? How will it work?	Diagrams are simple models. Cost-benefit analysis. Cash flow models. Computer simulations.
Implementation	6. Evaluate options against measures	Test the performance of your options against an agreed set of criteria.	Set up a simple matrix to compare the performance of your options. Score each option against the metrics.
	7. Design implementation strategies	Select your preferred options and plan a way of putting the changes into place.	Look for reliable options. Check back to 'problem owners'. Plan time and allocate tasks.
	8. Carry through the planned changes	Bring together people and resources. Manage the process. Monitor progress	Sort out who is involved. Allocate responsibility. Review and modify plans if necessary (CPA etc).

(Mayon-White, B. and Mabey, C. (1998) *Managing Change* 2nd ed. Open University Press)

- *You are professional*, with an in-depth knowledge and experience in a particular field, and often with greater loyalty to your profession than to your organisation.

- *You learn from change*, by observing, conceptualising, experimenting and validating. Also, by accommodating through flexible communications.

- *You troubleshoot*, rapidly identifying opportunities for change, and coming up with alternative courses of action to exploit them.

- *You adapt to change*, by mapping out the internal and external environment, and by creating systems and procedures for dealing with change.

- *You experiment with change*, continually forming temporary project groupings. Also, by solving ongoing problems in interdisciplinary teams.

- *You plan for change*, by constructing long-term plans with contingencies built in. Also, by monitoring changes and adapting plans accordingly.

- *You embody the spirit of change*, and are respected as a free thinker. You also embody the organisation's cause.

 REFLECTIVE ACTIVITY

Question

To what extent can the HR function adopt Lessem's seven characteristics and demonstrate these during a change process?

Doz and Prahalad (1988) cite a range of tools that change agents can select from and use. Firstly, data management tools concern the manipulation of information, systems, resource allocation procedures, strategic planning and budgeting arrangements. These tools are used to guide decision-making. Secondly, manager's management tools are a combination of 'hard' and 'soft' approaches. 'Hard' tools involve manipulation of key appointments, career planning and reward systems. 'Soft' tools include changes to management development and socialisation patterns. These tools decide the rules of the game. Thirdly, conflict management tools involve relocation of decision responsibility, formation of business teams, task forces and co-ordination committees, the appointment of 'integrators', and establishment of procedures to resolve issues. These tools may be used more predominantly at different stages of a change intervention: data management tools may prove most useful at the early stages of change, whereas conflict management tools may be used throughout some change interventions or perhaps during the 'movement' and 'refreezing' stages of a change process.

Buchanan and Boddy (1992) identified 15 competences that change agents adopt, clustered into 5 areas, namely: goals, roles, communication, negotiation and managing up. These competences sit within a framework which emphasises the political dimension. The importance of both front stage and back stage activity

Figure 6.10 The expertise of the change agent

Source: Buchanan and Boddy (1992)

emphasises how the change agent has to manage their position continuously so as to ensure their tenure and sustainability through the change intervention. Figure 6.10 displays the three critical agendas that may impact upon the determination of the change agent, where the content agenda relies upon technical competence (similar to Doz and Prahalad's data management tools), and the process agenda matches implementation skills, where communication, consultation, team-building, influencing and negotiation skills are key (similar to Doz and Pralahad's conflict management tools).

It could be argued that the more strategic the change, the more politically charged it will be and thereby draw upon more power bases. Balogun *et al*'s research (2005) supports Hardy's argument (1994 and 1996) that change agents address and engage the 'power of the system', mobilising existing powers to negotiate power interdependencies to enrol staff to their cause. This parallels with Kotter's (1999) notion of forming powerful coalitions so as to affect a change agenda. Kotter (1999) argues that managers typically form powerful coalitions through network-building and setting both business and personal agendas.

When making an assessment as to whether change agents could be recruited internally within an organisation, perhaps an evaluation of whether there is a critical mass of the various skills within this context can be carried out. If not, perhaps the necessary skills can be bought in.

The choice of who leads the change is a critical one, and should not rely purely on technical expertise. Endemic to this change process may be the setting of a vision or visioning statement by key player(s). If HR is to remove its reputation of being the bridesmaid, rather than the bride, then it needs to adopt strategic positioning, understand the business completely (business partnership), and adopt a leadership role (business leader).

 HM REVENUE AND CUSTOMS (HMRC)

CASE STUDY

'Only 11 per cent of employees thought that the changes had been managed well' (Churchyard, 2010). The resulting low morale and employee engagement scores added to Lesley Strathie's concerns (HMRC Chief Executive) when she was confronted with this survey finding in front of a sub-committee of MPs.

In an article from *The Times* (2010), Chris Mills argues that the radical change encountered by HMRC resulted in ineffective change management, attributed to the leadership rather than general competence.

Mills goes on to say that since the merger of the Inland Revenue, and Customs and Excise since 2003, the organisation focused more upon tax-raising at a strategic level, but lost the sense of purpose lower down. Involvement of operational staff, where they drive the process quickly and effectively, was lacking. What is required includes strategic goals and a 'comprehensively thought-through model of the entire organisation, which encompasses vision, strategic performance measures, organisational structures, projects and business-as-usual activities, together with the right combination of skills, competencies and behaviours needed by all staff'. Mills continues this line of argument by stating that the need to demonstrate

clear alignment between all of these factors is crucial. The extent to which senior managers are more likely to be focused on building the profile of their own area (and themselves) may contaminate the effectiveness of the change process, despite having an overarching strategy and vision.

Another potential compounding factor is the Government's efficiency agenda, which attempts to maximise resources and ultimately save costs. Mills posits that senior civil servants are often criticised for their apparent inability to translate good strategies into effective action, and sometime overuse consultants and other external staff in order to make things work, rather than providing the bursts of expertise for which they are better suited.

Sources: Mills, C. (2010) HMRC running out of time to regain its sense of purpose, *The Times*, 14 January 2010, and Churchyard, C. (2010) MPs 'alarmed' by low morale at HMRC, *People Management*, 10 March 2010.

Question

Consider how the use of a change intervention, such as Organisational Development or Systems Intervention Strategy, can assist in ensuring the strategic to operational alignment required to bring about effective change at HMRC.

HR VALUE ADDED AND CHANGE

Can HR establish and maintain a strategic level involvement in organisations? The danger of pigeon-holing functions is that some form of reductivism may result. If strategy was determined at a resource and capability level, then HR could perhaps fit more readily within strategic decision-making in the organisation. However, Warren (2009) argues that Organisational Development needs to start with the business and HR's role is to facilitate it. HR and Organisational Development should be one and the same. It depends upon the level of importance that Organisational Development has within organisations as to whether OD impacts upon (and possibly guides) strategic planning. For HR partners to take a leadership and proactive role, they will need to contribute towards key strategic decisions, and to do this, understanding of strategic change and change interventions is critical.

When bridging the strategic and tactical level, CIPD research (2009) has identified various aspects that HR professionals can undertake in order to make a successful contribution to change projects, namely:

- involvement at the initial stage in the project team
- advising project leaders in skills available within the organisation – identifying any skills gaps, training needs, new posts, new working practices etc
- balancing out the narrow/short-term goals and broader strategic needs
- assessing the impact of change in one area/department/site on another part of the organisation
- being used to negotiating and engaging across various stakeholders
- understanding stakeholder concerns to anticipate problems
- understanding the appropriate medium of communication to reach various groups
- helping people cope with change, performance management and motivation.

There are perhaps many other areas where HR should impact upon change in organisations, such as learning from change, capturing appropriate knowledge and knowledge share. Similarly, HR can facilitate team-building. Arrata *et al* (2007) argue that three critical elements are crucial to any change programme – thoughtful design, careful recruitment and development of personnel, and close integration between the change agent team and the organisational areas targeted for change. Successful communication underpins the effectiveness of the change team.

CHANGE: THE FINANCIAL INDUSTRY IN 2007

CASE STUDY

Paralysis within the financial sector following the 'credit crunch' of 2007 saw the first run on a major British bank in more than a century, which eventually led to Northern Rock being nationalised the following year. Nearly a year later, the US banking sector experienced a tumultuous weekend in September 2008 when Merrill Lynch was acquired and 'saved' by the Bank of America, while Lehman Brothers was left to its own demise by the US Treasury and went into liquidation.

The consequences of these events would be felt all over the world, as governments provided unprecedented financial 'rescue' packages to stabilise the global banking sector and support their economies. However, this rescue attempt could not prevent many developed countries slipping into recession in 2008 while politicians and media commentators debated how long the recession would last.

In the UK and in many other countries, the cost of the financial meltdown is being shared by businesses, public sector services and taxpayers. Since the financial crisis, many companies have struggled to survive and have responded by cutting costs, wages and jobs. Public sector budgets have been cut as governments attempt to manage the enormous budget deficit acquired as a result of the bank bail-outs.

The financial crisis of 2007 was a dramatic and major change but it is important to recognise that it is still only part of a continuum of change, which, at any moment in time has historical lineage, current context and future implications.

This recent episode in change also serves to illustrate how the business environment is shaped by external factors outside the control of most organisations, and even outside the control of institutions who thought they were in control!

There are not many organisations that will remain unscathed by the fall-out from the events described above. Organisations, in order to survive and sustain, will have to respond to the dynamic business environment they operate in by 'managing change'.

Managing change is nothing new to organisations but the scale and speed of change in the business environment may present situations and challenges that are difficult to respond to, as was the case for Lehman Brothers in 2008. Lehman Brothers found that in the rapidly changing environment it was engulfed in, it could not exert control or manage change to sustain the organisation.

The causes of the financial crisis outlined above were a complex combination of political, economic, social and technological factors which shaped the external business environment.

These drivers of change had their roots in the USA going back to 2002 when the relaxation of financial regulations; available cheap debt and the desire of individuals to own or improve their homes, all came together to shape a business environment that provided opportunities for financial institutions to create and sell new loan products known as sub-prime mortgages. These mortgages were sold to many individuals with poor credit standing who had little chance of repaying their loans.

Complex computer software programs and global communication networks enabled this sub-prime debt to be repackaged and sold on as investments on the global mortgage bond market.

The difficulties incurred by banks which either sold these mortgages or invested in the repackaged sub-prime mortgage debt led to what became known as the 'credit crunch'. The crux of the problem was the financial institutions did not identify the risk that they were exposing themselves to because they did not fully understand the nature of the business environment they were operating in. In other words, they did not recognise the external factors that would eventually impact on their business.

Had the financial institutions understood the risk they were engaging in, they might have made smarter decisions and avoided the difficulties they got into, or they could have taken steps to manage the risk better than they did. With better knowledge and understanding of the business environment, organisations can – if they choose to – make better informed strategic decisions in order to minimise risk and optimise performance. In other words, good information and how to use it makes for better decision-making and management control.

There were a number of key internal factors involved in the financial crisis of 2007, which, when combined with the external drivers described, provided an inevitable path to disaster for many of the organisations involved, as outlined below.

First, there was the decision of the banks to repackage sub-prime mortgages as collateral debt obligations or 'CDOs', a type of asset-backed security, and sell these as investments on the mortgage bond market, which represented a new business model for dealing with mortgages. This had the affect of spreading high-risk investments amongst the financial institutions who decided to engage in this business model – but not in a good way. The CDOs were so complex that the banks who had bought them were unable to gauge the amount of risk they were exposed to through these products.

Internal management decisions were taken by (a) the banks providing the mortgages to take advantage of a business opportunity they saw as a new marketing strategy, and in turn (b) other banks and financial institutions to invest in CDOs as an investment strategy.

Another major internal driver of change in the financial crisis was the practice of incentive schemes based on large cash bonuses to reward employees for selling and investing these products. This powerful driver encouraged the proliferation of these activities.

Questions

1. What were the triggers for change within the context described?

2. To what extent was the change depicted as a 'Big Bang' approach to change?

CONCLUSION

Lloyd and Maguire (2002, p 149) argue that 'In future, the critical focus for sustainable organisational success will build on what the organisation knows about itself and its environment, and not on the transient structure and detailed processes. The successful organisations of the future will not be managing change but rather facilitating conversations for organisational learning and individual responsibility'. Hence the emphasis here is upon individual and team development, which sits comfortably within the scope and domain of Human Resources.

'Change is ultimately about people – if they do not change, nothing significant happens' (Miller, 2004, p 10). Perhaps the argument for organisations having stronger and more sophisticated Organisational Development processes can never be understated. A positive employee attitude towards change is vital to a successful outcome. Tan and Tiong (2005) found that the highest correlated success factor was optimism, which they define as attitude towards change. HR, in partnership with line management, need to ensure that organisational change is planned, communicated and executed successfully on an ongoing basis in order to sustain business survival.

- There are numerous ways in which change can be analysed as far as the scope and nature of change is concerned.
- HR professionals need to have an appreciation of the complex nature of several (sometimes contradictory) change interventions operating concurrently.
- The context of change needs to be analysed in order to decide upon whether and which type of change intervention is needed or appropriate.
- Organisational Development is a change intervention particularly suited to changing employees' values and organisational culture.
- HR has a significant contribution to make to strategic change interventions, particularly when collating knowledge and learning emanating from change interventions, which can be used on subsequent change interventions.
- Change agents typically have to exhibit a range of skills and competences in order to demonstrate their credibility as change agents, and simultaneously be aware of the political context within which they operate.

REVIEW QUESTIONS

1. Discuss the extent to which a vision and mission statement is important when an organisation is going through cultural changes.

2. Consider a change intervention with which you are familiar and consider what some of the barriers to change were, and where resistance to change was encountered. Try to classify these barriers and resistance factors into key categories.

3. What are some of the key skills that a change agent needs to exhibit? To what extent are these skills context-specific?

4. Think about how you could apply Lewin's change model to a change scenario of your choice. To what extent were there critical moments that defined the unfreezing, movement and refreezing?

EXPLORE FURTHER

Hughes, M. (2010) *Change Management: A critical perspective*, 2nd ed. CIPD. A sound textbook presenting a range of approaches to change.

Senior, B. and Swailes, S. (2010) *Organisational Change*, 4th ed. Pearson. The chapters on Systems Change and OD

are particularly useful reading.

Price, D. (ed) (2009) *The Principles and Practice of Change*. Palgrave Macmillan. Provides a range of different perspectives on change by presenting some key articles and works on change.

CHAPTER 7

Flexibility and the Psychological Contract

Simon Turner

LEARNING OUTCOMES

After reading this chapter, you should be able to:

- define flexibility and understand the different meanings attached to this concept
- evaluate the importance of the psychological contract on employees' behaviour
- understand how flexibility and the psychological contract, are inter-related; and
- explain how psychological contracts and flexibility can link with improved organisational performance.

OVERVIEW

This chapter aims to explore the connections between organisational performance and two topics in the current Human Resource Management spotlight: the policies of flexibility by which organisations respond to the need for continuous improvement, and the slippery concept of multi-faceted psychological contracts which might help us to make sense of workers' commitment and associated attitudes towards the employer.

There are connections between these topics. The level of commitment displayed by workers can be related to their psychological contract, and the state of the contract in turn influences workers' attitudes towards providing flexibility. Employers' desires for these concepts to be 'got', or controlled, are linked with the creation of HR policies designed to improve organisational performance. There is much debate in the HR field surrounding the approaches and activities designed to secure improvements in outcomes and performance, including recommendations by the Chartered Institute of Personnel and Development (CIPD), the UK professional body. It has been observed (Marchington *et al*, 2005) that there is a tendency for these concepts to become conflated with their anticipated results, so that the descriptions become prescriptions, accepted as conventional wisdom.

We also find tensions within this field. The desire for organisations to integrate HR policies with business objectives may sit uneasily with the move towards

Atkinson's (1984) flexible firm, with decentralised responsibilities and externalised workers. The client organisation in an outsourcing arrangement may find it difficult to manage, or influence, the policies of the supplier of labour. Gilmore (2009) records that flexible approaches to workforce deployment have often been coupled with an increase in part-time working, fixed-term contracts and outsourcing, making it potentially more difficult to secure organisational commitment. It has been noted that in much of the HR management literature, the typical focus is on the remaining core activities and not on how non-core activities are provided (Marchington *et al*, 2005).

The concepts set out and discussed in detail in this chapter are central to the core themes of our book, based around effective leadership and management of people. As such, material presented in this chapter is linked with themes and topics introduced elsewhere in the text. To take one example, the broad term *flexibility* encompasses organisational and individual elements. In Chapter 8 we will see how people's experiences of work are affected by the organisational structure in which they operate, and of course, by the nature of work they do. In an important sense, therefore, organisational and job design lay out the context within which flexibility can be achieved. At the same time, the individual aspect of flexibility must be understood with reference to the subject of motivation – which we address fully in Chapter 12.

Meanwhile the promotion of all aspects of high-performance working, including flexibility, was addressed in Chapters 2 and 3. What can be said is that flexibility operates on both an organisational and individual level and that organisations and individuals (including managers and leaders) will have a keen interest in the topic.

We have, finally, an interesting issue regarding terminology and language throughout this chapter. How we choose to refer to the people – as employees, workers, or individuals is context-bound, and arguably influences (or is influenced by) our thinking. Much of the current literature focuses on employees inside the organisation, yet as we will see, so-called networked organisations rely also upon people outside: agency and outsourced workers, and the pseudo-employed.

INTRODUCTION

It is commonly stated that the management of people in organisations has recently been carried out against a backdrop of a rapidly changing and turbulent environment. In many advanced economies there has been a move away from mass production of standardised products or even routine white-collar administrative work, with many such jobs moving to countries such as China and India. Concurrently it has been suggested that people in organisations increasingly aspire to work more flexibly and wish to work in more autonomous and creative roles. A search for work-life balance by many employees results in a need for support from employing organisations in order to prevent burnout and maximise their work performance (French *et al*, 2008). Accelerating globalisation and technological advance has meant that the environment of organisations – both in the private and public sectors – has changed rapidly, resulting in a need for greater flexibility from organisations, their leaders and other workers (Thomas, 2009; Thompson and McHugh, 2009).

In this chapter we will examine a range of terms which have emerged as both diagnoses of current work practices and solutions to problems of managing people in the current competitive environment. Words and phrases such as *flexibility, work-life balance* and *work intensification* will be defined, analysed and their benefits and disadvantages highlighted. The debate on flexible responses to trends such as globalisation, technological advance and the 'marketisation' of public sector provision now has an established body of knowledge from Atkinson's (1984) notion of the flexible firm through to the CIPD 2010 report on sustainable organisation performance. The area under consideration in this chapter continues to be academically relevant, topical and of personal interest to many of us.

REFLECTIVE ACTIVITY

KPMG avoids redundancies through flexible working

Writer and researcher Charlotte Wolff notes how international professional services firm KPMG was particularly concerned to avoid employee redundancies following the economic downturn of 2008. David Conder, Head of People at KPMG, noted that: 'When we made redundancies alongside other, similar, firms in 2002/3, it constrained growth when the upturn came and it was also a very painful process for the organisation to go through.' KPMG's strategy now is to do the right thing for its clients, its people and the business. This means retaining talent, intellectual capital and the motivational level of its teams, thus ensuring continuity and top quality service.

KPMG's strategy now includes a 'flexible futures' programme using reduced hours and sabbaticals to manage the workforce flexibly during times when business is quiet.

Source: Wolff (2008)

Question

Provide three reasons why we might reasonably anticipate that redundancies would hinder an organisation's performance following an economic upturn.

FLEXIBILITY

Flexibility has been frequently identified as a key human resource policy goal, along with strategic intention, quality, and employee commitment, in order to ensure an adaptable organisation structure (Guest, 2004). These HR goals are in turn held to generate

> '. . . a range of positive organizational outcomes, such as high job performance, high quality problem solving, successful change, lower turnover, absenteeism and grievance levels and high cost-effectiveness.'
> (Iles *et al*, 1996, p 18)

On the one hand employers, encouraged by governments and non-governmental bodies, such as the International Monetary Fund and the World Bank, press the case for workforce flexibility in the hunt for efficiency, and on the other hand it is claimed that individual employees look for flexibility in working hours as they attempt to juggle the demands of home and work lives. It seems that the two agendas might meet in a unitary, though stressful, work-life balance (CIPD 2008b; Taylor, 2002; Pollitt, 2003) where employers' flexibility requirements can coincide well with the wants and needs of a great many employees. An outcome, it is claimed, is that 'flexible working has a positive impact on employee performance and helps to reduce stress . . . [and] that flexible workers [are] found to have higher levels of commitment and job satisfaction than other employees' (CIPD, 2008b).

Four main types of flexibility can be identified (after Blyton and Morris, 1992):

1. task or functional flexibility, where employees may be multi-skilled

2. numerical flexibility, using different types of employment contracts and sub-contracting, as in Atkinson's (1984) core-periphery concept

3. temporal flexibility, where the number and pattern of hours worked varies, for example zero hours, and annual hours

4. wage flexibility, where wages are individualised, and may be performance related.

A notable early contribution to an understanding of contemporary attempts to change work and workers allocation was Atkinson's (1984) flexible firm model. This painted a heroic picture with committed core employees being highly regarded, well paid, who have improved career prospects, and who offer in return functional flexibility, often through multi-skilling. On the periphery are the distanced externals: the 'atypical', 'non-standard' or 'non-core' workers (described in negative terms) with low security to ease the organisation's needs for adjustments to market forces. There are important ethical undertones to such a distinction with Clegg *et al* (2008) suggesting that the periphery itself comprised two sub-groups. These were firstly workers who were semi-skilled operating in the lower rungs of the supply chain and who could be easily dismissed and re-employed according to cost and demand fluctuations. The other sub-group was an underclass working (possibly illegally) in poor conditions outside the formally recognised labour market. Such workers do not show up in official statistics or most research studies so remain outside the scope of most discussions of worker flexibility – but they are real nonetheless. Later in the chapter we look again at the dark side of flexible working.

Current observations are that organisational forms are changing, with bureaucracies being dismantled and replaced by looser, networked organisational forms and processes, featuring partnerships and contracting-out of activities. 'In the name of right-sizing, de-layering and concentrating upon core competencies, the outsourcing of services continues to expand' (Marchington *et al*, 2005, p 2) as organisations move from vertical towards horizontal integration. With this, come changes in the employment relationship. Marchington *et al* (2005, p 18) present an additional dimension to the understanding of employment flexibility, namely the extent to which the employment contract is under the influence of a single employing organisation or subject to control or influence by multiple employers, as might be the case with agency workers (Figure 7.1). This axis is added to the previously accepted continuum depicting variations in the internalisation or standardisation of the employment contract (as in the core-periphery concept).

As the authors describe, the internalised, standard employment relationship is seen in the bottom left-hand corner. In the top right-hand corner is self-employment, 'where there is no contract of employment and where the self-employed individual sells his or her skills to a range of organisations and is, therefore, not dependent on a particular organisation for income' (*ibid*:18).

The horizontal axis, from employees to non-employees, depicts the shift away from internalised full-time employees to a diversification of contracts including part-time, casual, temporary, and self-employed workers. 'Part-time work might be considered to be close to the standard contract as there is nothing in principle stopping part-time work being organised on the same basis as internalised, full-time work with the same social rights and same regularity of employment' (*ibid*:18). At the extreme of where the guarantees of employment and income are, at best, short term, are the so-called pseudo self-employed workers, who often work at a distance from the employer – such as homeworkers and freelancers – 'but who may be highly dependent upon one employer, even if there is no formal contractual guarantee of continuous employment or minimum income' (*ibid*:19).

In the centre of the field we find temporary agency workers, in ambiguous circumstances: self-employed yet employed, where the agency is commonly regarded as the legal employer, even though it is the client who exercises control.

Figure 7.1 The twin dimensions of employment flexibility

Source: Marchington, M. *et al* (2005). By permission of Oxford University Press

'The employing organisation, which acts as host to the temporary agency workers, directs their work activities side-by-side with those of direct employees on similar tasks ... This employment relationship ... [involves] both deviations from the status of direct employees, and control from more than one employing organisation' (*ibid*:19).

The top left-hand side '... covers an area where employment is internalised but where there is more than one employing organisation that can be considered party to the relationship.' Here 'there is a direct employment relationship but other employers – acting as agents or suppliers – may be involved in the employment experience, and even in controlling the employment relationship' (*ibid*:18–19).

WORK INTENSIFICATION AND WORK-LIFE BALANCE

Recent years have seen an increasing number of organisations in the UK offering a range of flexible working options to their employees. For many employers this has been a response to increasing interest in work-life balance, the need to be competitive in the labour market, and the introduction of legislation giving parents of young or disabled children and, more recently, carers, the right to request flexible working arrangements (Kelliher and Anderson, 2010, pp 83–84).

In a more critical vein, attention is drawn to other aspects of the work-life balance concept by Eikhof *et al* (2007) where 'beyond working time and the provision of flexible working practices to enable child care, there is little in the debate about the need to change work *per se.*' These authors also comment that the work-life debate 'narrowly perceives "life", equating it with women's care work, hence the emphasis again of family-friendly policies'. (*ibid*:326).

We can detect that flexibility, lying at the heart of the wage-work bargain, means different things to the different parties to the deal. Whilst conventional definitions are expressed from the point of view of the employer or organisation, descriptions of the consequences for the worker are required in the interests of balance.

It is possible to glimpse an unanticipated consequence of adopting flexible working practices – that of work intensification. Whilst reporting evidence that flexible workers record higher levels of job satisfaction and organisational commitment than their non-flexible counterparts, Kelliher and Anderson (2010) also report evidence of work intensification being experienced by both those who work reduced hours and those who work remotely. It is suggested that the apparent paradox of high job satisfaction and organisational commitment alongside work intensification can be explained by employees trading flexibility for effort. Employees respond to the ability to work flexibly by exerting additional effort, in order to return benefit to their employer.

Three means by which intensification may take place have been identified (*ibid*, p 86). Increased effort may be imposed (as when workloads may increase following downsizing) or enabled (because flexible working patterns facilitate the exercise of increased effort), or it may be a reciprocal act on the part of employees in exchange for discretion over working arrangements. See the current research section for further examples.

Intriguingly, Kelliher and Anderson (2010, p 99) suggest that in contemporary workplaces, with a 'prevailing rhetoric of greater personal autonomy', employees often see themselves as responsible for their own work intensification. To some extent the professional workers saw themselves as partly responsible and therefore did not voice opposition. However, other studies have also found that employees do not always respond negatively to intensification, especially where they believe they will gain some benefit as a consequence (*ibid*, p 99).

 ## REFLECTIVE ACTIVITY

Current research: experiences of intensification

Kelliher and Anderson's (2010) interviewees, in a number of UK private sector organisations, vividly illustrate the three means of intensification.

Imposed intensification

Workers describe why imposed flexible working, on reduced hours contracts, has resulted in work intensification. Their workloads had not decreased in line with their hours when they moved to a reduced hours contract and consequently they were doing something akin to a full-time job, but in fewer paid hours. This could result in both increased extensive and intensive effort.

One interviewee commented: 'There is enough workload to keep me busy for five days, but I only have three days to do it in, so I either work late, which I do sometimes, or I try and delegate some of it.'

Others described that they felt the need to be available at times when they were not scheduled to be working, but when the business was operating. This took the form of being prepared to take phone calls and checking emails at times they were not working.

For example one interviewee reported: 'On a Monday, when I'm not at work, I'll typically put in forty minutes to an hour just checking my emails to make sure that I'm on top of any issues that come up, or that came up over the weekend . . . so I check the email at least once if not twice during the Monday.'

Enabled intensification

By contrast others, typically remote workers, describe that working flexibly enabled them to work more intently, exercising both greater intensive and extensive effort. For example: 'It's much easier to maintain your energy levels and enthusiasm if you're working for three days or four days, than if you're working for five days . . . and keep your efficiency up if you're just maintaining it over three or three and a half days, rather than five.'

Intensification as reciprocation and exchange

Commitment levels of remote and reduced hours workers are reportedly higher than those who did not work flexibly. The impact of commitment on effort is illustrated by this worker who reported greater extensive effort when she worked from home:

'So you have this kind of loyalty I guess, which is very deep seated to be honest, if people are prepared to treat you as a human being more . . . . I'm not some kind of machine that has to be at the office at nine and five thirty, I actually do see myself in a more human way, which is around the commitment . . . When companies support you, you are naturally more loyal and more committed.'

Source: Kelliher, C. and Anderson, D. (2010)

THE BUSINESS BENEFITS OF FLEXIBLE WORKING

We commonly hear managerial descriptions, in unitary terms, of flexible working arrangements featuring options which allow employees to strike a work-life balance which fits with their needs, and yet gives the employer a say in the decision-making process (Wight, 2007). Elsewhere we find descriptions of flexible working delivering improved business performance on service delivery and customer satisfaction, efficiency savings, and reduced recruitment and retention costs (Thomson, 2008). Examples of this flexible working include part-time work, job-sharing, flexi-time, working school hours, nine-day fortnights, mobile working, and team rotas, which are claimed to give the employees choice in how, when and where they work (see the following case study).

CASE STUDY

BENDING THE RULES: SURREY COUNTY COUNCIL EMBRACES FLEXIBLE WORKING

Surrey County Council has taken steps to ensure that its workers can complete their daily tasks from spaces other than their desk at the office. There have been investments in technology which allow workers to log in at any PC or any telephone on a certain network, and all social workers have a tablet PC to carry when out of the office. Anything the social worker records on the tablet is instantly added to a database back at the office and is therefore accessible to other staff. Staff are able to check their work emails from home, allowing the option of working from home, and also reducing the dependence on physical office space. . . Working from different offices or at home, working while travelling, and hot-desking in an office environment can all add flexibility to the working day.

The importance of giving the employees choice in how, when and where they work has led to an improvement in Surrey Council in terms of productivity, reduced sickness levels and financial gains. There has been a 4 per cent reduction in staff turnover, and there are now 700 fewer full-time posts, leading to a decrease in staff costs. The Council has been able to rationalise the property portfolio and standardise IT systems. It has also seen an increase in morale amongst employees as they are given more freedom to choose their working hours, and it shows trust in the employees that they will manage to strike a successful work-life balance.

Taking a broader view, the issue of flexible working has become an increasingly important topic as the Government re-evaluates the employment laws in the UK. All employees, regardless of circumstance, have a right to request a flexible working pattern from an employer. The employer has to weigh up the effect the application would have on the business as a whole. The employer has the right to reject an employee's flexible working request if it would be of detriment to the business.

Source: Wight, G. (2007)

Questions

1. Give examples from your own experience of flexible working.

2. Were your feelings towards flexible working positive or negative – or a mix of the two – and why?

3. How can organisations balance greater employee freedom within flexible working with customer requirements?

CASE STUDY

FLEXIBILITY — THE IMPORTANCE OF MANAGEMENT INTERVENTIONS

Shift-pattern switch improves staff turnover and recruitment at Seeboard: high-risk initiative brings rich rewards

Seeboard Energy Ltd is a utility company with around 1.8 million customers, mainly in south-east England (Seeboard has since been taken over by EDF energy). Its customer-contact centre operates from 8 am to 10 pm (Saturday 8 am to 6 pm). Staff answer around 3,000,000 calls a year and respond to around 800,000 letters or emails from customers.

Three-week rolling shifts

In 1999, the company introduced three-week rolling shifts to cover the contact centre's main hours of operation. The shifts were:

● early: 7.30am–3.30pm or 8am–4pm;

● core: 8.30am–4.30pm, 9am–5pm or 9.30am–5.30pm; and

● late: 10am–6pm, noon–8pm or 2pm–10pm.

The change led to a significant rise in employee turnover, particularly among women. The company also experienced increasing difficulty attracting potential employees – again, particularly women. Commercially, at an average cost of £3,000 to recruit and train an employee, it was proving an ineffective use of the company's resources.

Staff focus groups were set up in July 2000, and team leaders and managers asked employees to give their views. In addition,

questionnaires were sent out to staff. Findings indicated one major issue: the three-week rolling shift pattern did not provide staff with enough stability with which to balance their home and work commitments. In particular, this was an issue for women with childcare responsibilities, as it made arrangements for childcare much more complex.

Fixed-shift pattern

The company's solution was to introduce fixed shift patterns. It piloted the approach in an area of the organisation that had the highest number of vacancies (150).

Measuring the impact

Under the three-week rotational shift system, staff turnover was 20 per cent, with more than 65 per cent of this figure being women. By April 2001, under the fixed-shift system, this had halved to 10 per cent, with 50 per cent of this figure made up of women. In addition, over a one-year period, the response rate to recruitment advertisements improved significantly, and many of the applicants were women.

Source: Pollitt, D. (2003)

Question

Why do you think response rates to job advertisements improved over the period in question? Do you think the same positive response would still be found ten years after the rotational shift patterns were introduced? Give reasons for your answers.

The Seeboard example shows clearly the importance of effective *management* of flexible working and, in particular, consultation with the employees who will actually experience the changed arrangements. The importance of monitoring reactions, post-implementation, is clearly demonstrated in this case.

NEGATIVE ASPECTS OF FLEXIBILITY

We have already drawn attention to the dark side of flexible working and this was highlighted in the UK context by Toynbee (2008) – see below.

Appalling conditions

Labour MPs representing the poorest places see how appalling conditions under bad employers can be. They see where agency workers are brought in to undercut existing wages – remember Gate Gourmet (the airline catering firm Gate Gourmet was involved in a high-profile dispute with employees at London Heathrow airport in 2005). Or where workers who want to be taken on permanently are fired and rehired to prevent them acquiring rights. They see outsourced NHS cleaners, and workers throughout the public sector, are denied a chance they once had to work their way up. Agencies don't train people to fill higher-level jobs for which they are not contracted (Toynbee, 2008).

An alternative to the conventional wisdom regarding the economic necessity of flexibility, at both global and individual levels, is provided by Giles *et al* (2010) in the following case study.

 THE FAILINGS OF FLEXIBILITY

CASE STUDY

For years, it has been the settled view in economics that, in most cases, flexible labour markets are best. More jobs might be lost in a downturn, but this cost was far outweighed by the benefits of flexible pay and the ease of reallocating jobs from dying industries to dynamic ones. Nobody was more closely aligned with such recommendations than the Organisation for Economic Co-operation and Development, the Paris-based club of developed nations.

But now the OECD is modifying its view. 'We have been promoting flexibility, not for the sake of it, but for economic performance and for workers to get into new jobs,' says Stefano Scarpetta, the OECD's head of employment analysis.

This motivation is allowing a change of view. 'Judging from the outcomes so far, short-time working schemes [such as in Germany, in which people work fewer hours while the government tops up their pay, although there are questions about whether this merely delays job losses] seem to have been rather successful in containing the job haemorrhage,' he says, adding that even his organisation is 'a little bit more positive on public works programmes: we argue that as part of a labour market approach, they might be worthwhile'.

While this is not a wholesale repudiation of the OECD's former views, it reflects the fact that, according to the organisation's own analysis, the gains in employment flexibility of recent years have failed to protect employees from the economic crisis. 'There do not appear to be any clear grounds for concluding that workers, generally, are any better or worse prepared to weather a period of weak labour markets than was the case for the past several recessions,' the OECD concluded in its latest Employment Outlook.

Some top economists argue that the theory of superiority of flexible labour markets applies only at full employment. It will not work well when there has been a large shock to demand, output is well below potential and jobs are effectively rationed. In these circumstances, German-style institutions that cushion and spread the pain are probably superior.

Question

Identify the stated view taken on flexible labour markets by the main UK political parties. Can you identify significant differences between them?

Source: Giles, C., Guha, K. and Atkins, R. (2010)

THE BENEFITS OF BEHAVIOURAL FLEXIBILITY

Most attention has been given to organisational and labour market flexibility rather than personal flexibility. For firms to be flexible they depend on the flexibility of the workforce: an orientation, attitude, or style among employees, including team-oriented, lateral and autonomous perspectives (Iles *et al*, 1996, p 21). Anell and Wilson (2000, p 168) suggest the following qualities might be required in employees:

> '... a desire to seek feedback on performance, a desire to improve, an ability to see multiple perspectives, a broad vision, an ability to visualize relationships, a readiness to accept responsibility for decisions, self-confidence, proactivity, a liking for change and a desire for co-operative independence.'

Among senior managers, personal and strategic flexibility and internal characteristics such as problem solving or creative thinking are desirable. These authors describe elements of 'behavioural flexibility' in managers in terms of the ability to manage complexity and uncertainty, adaptability, tolerance of ambiguity, openness, empathy, non-judgementalism, interest in others, and willingness to acquire new behaviours and attitudes. Sennett refers to 'a particular strength of character – that of someone who has the confidence to dwell in disorder ... who flourishes in the midst of dislocation' (1998, p 62).

In his book, *The Corrosion of Character* (1998), Richard Sennett examines the consequences for workers of the need for organisations to operate in highly competitive markets. He suggests that the flexibility they need to display, the willingness to accept change, and the loss of security that results, can have damaging effects on personal character.

Character, he argues, is an emotional experience that involves loyalty, mutual commitment and the pursuit of long-term goals. As society pursues immediate needs and businesses seek to respond to the consequent short-term goals, organisations find themselves regularly needing to restructure and redesign. In such a new economy he suggests that character traits are damaged with negative effects on workers' morale and motivation. People thus co-operate but without any underlying commitment: 'superficial co-cooperativeness'.

CASE STUDY

PWC INCREASES EMPLOYEE FLEXIBILITY

Professional-services firm PricewaterhouseCoopers (PWC) is described as a knowledge-driven organisation. When its employees leave, the firm not only loses the training and knowledge they have built up, but also the client relationships they have developed.

PWC now has a strategy based around choice for its employees, whose average age is only 27. There is a generous scheme of maternity and paternity leave, childcare vouchers for returning mothers and other benefits. Moreover, most employees are equipped to be able to work from home, and almost all of them choose to do this at least once a month.

The company has launched an in-house concierge service. Employees are offered a wide range of domestic services at discount price. They include activities (such) as waiting in for plumbers, builders and electricians. Take-up appears to be greatest among company consultants, who often work offsite for months.

PWC has also introduced the notion of 'paid time off', rather than the more restrictive 'annual leave'. Employees can use their paid time off allocation for short-term illness, child care and jury service, as well as holiday.

According to the author, the strategy appears to be successful. Despite skill shortages in the consultancy sector, staff retention at PWC has improved by between 4 and 5 per cent over the last year.

Source: Perry, M. (2001)

Questions

1. What does this case show us about the benefits of flexibility to organisations and staff?

2. Is this type of flexibility restricted to the type of professional worker employed by PWC or could and should it have wider application?

The parties' responses to each other's requests for flexibility within the wage-work bargain, worker and 'employer', are likely to be inextricably inter-linked. The concept of the psychological contract provides us with a suitable lens through which to view this aspect of leading and managing people.

THE PSYCHOLOGICAL CONTRACT

Although questions have been raised about its meaning and value (Guest, 1998) the concept of the psychological contract has become a central theme of people management. It describes the employment relationship in terms of mutual expectations or obligations, in order to make sense of the range and degrees of commitment that flow in both directions. It is here that organisational policy and procedures mix with individual managerial and employee attitudes and behaviours, with complex outcomes.

There are two main definitions of the psychological contract (Marks, 2001). The first is derived from the work of Argyris (1960) and Schein (1978) and refers to the perceptions of mutual obligations held by the two parties in the employment relationship, the organisation and the employee (or worker). The second definition, which is based on the work of Rousseau (1995, p 9), asserts that the psychological contract is formulated only in the mind of the employee and is therefore about 'individual beliefs, shaped by the organisation, regarding terms of an exchange between individuals and their organisation'.

According to Rousseau (1995, p 1) the ideal contract details expectations of both the employee and the employer, but these contracts are incomplete and so become 'self-organising'. A contractual continuum is commonly offered, from transactional (covering incentive pay and well-specified performance levels) to relational (including loyalty and concern for employee well-being). Transactional terms are exemplified by 'a fair day's work for a fair day's pay' and focus on short-term (and usually monetary) exchanges. The relational contract 'focuses on open-ended relationships involving considerable investments by both employees (company-specific skills, long-term development) and employers (extensive training)' (*ibid*, p 91).

A useful typology is offered by Rousseau (Figure 7.2), using the dimensions of time-frame and performance requirements, who (1995, p 98) says that four types of contract emerge 'with distinct behavioural implications for workers':

- transactional contracts – of limited duration with well-specified performance terms

- transitional or 'no-guarantees' contracts – essentially a breakdown in contracts, reflecting the absence of commitments regarding future employment as well as little or no explicit performance demands or contingent incentives

- relational contracts – open-ended membership but with incomplete or ambiguous performance requirements attached to continued membership

- balanced contracts – open-ended and relationship-oriented employment with well-specified performance terms subject to change over time.

Figure 7.2 Types of psychological contracts

Performance terms

Duration	Specified	Not Specified
Short term	Transactional (eg retail checkout operators employed during Christmas season) ● Low ambiguity ● Easy exit/high turnover ● Low member commitment ● Freedom to enter new contracts ● Little learning ● Weak integration/identification	Transitional (eg employee experiences during organisational retrenchment or following merger or acquisition) ● Ambiguity/uncertainty ● High turnover/termination ● Instability
Long term	Balanced (eg high-involvement team) ● High member commitment ● High integration/identification ● Ongoing development ● Mutual support ● Dynamic	Relational (eg family business members) ● High member commitment ● High affective commitment ● High integration/identification ● Stability

Source: Rousseau, D. (1995)

In other words, the 'psychological contract' is a term for describing what is implicit in terms of reciprocity and exchange within the employment relationship.

It is suggested (CIPD, 2005a, p 3) that employers have been encouraged to take the psychological contract seriously due to changes ranging from the need for externalised workers to display functional flexibility, to the survivors of downsizing carrying 'more weight', and 'human capital' becoming more critical to business performance.

IMPLICATIONS FOR THE MANAGEMENT OF PEOPLE

The CIPD (2005a, p 6) describes 'getting' commitment from employees by drawing on the motivators contained within Herzberg's two-factor theory, outlines what organisations 'need' to do, and draws attention to the importance of the line manager role, in these terms:

> 'Research suggests that in order to feel committed employees must feel satisfied with their work. Job satisfaction is more likely to be achieved where the employer offers employees what they want. Surveys consistently show that employees generally want interesting work, opportunities to develop, fair treatment and competent management. The line manager has a key role to play in maintaining commitment. Employers need to focus on tapping in to what employees are looking for and how they feel about their work. They need to involve and engage them. And they need to train line managers in how to manage people.'

We might consider to what extent employers can indeed offer what employees want in many sectors of the economy. A flavour of the confidence to be found in some HR literature is provided by Hiltrop's (1996) reassurances, lack of doubt and claims for what employers must, and should, do.

Recent work has emphasised the notion of *engagement*. This is defined by the CIPD (2010) as 'employees internalising and emotionally connecting to the organisation's core purpose'. This CIPD survey emphasised the role of line managers in motivating via an engaging team-management style, following on from the 2005 work cited above.

There is no doubt that increasing competition and changing expectations among employees have prompted a growing disillusionment with the traditional psychological contract based on lifetime employment and steady promotion from within. Consequently, companies must develop new ways to increase the loyalty and commitment of employees.

For instance, given the pressure to do things better, faster and cheaper, reward systems should recognise contribution rather than position or status. Reward strategies may also be used to rebuild commitment for survivors in downsizing organisations.

In addition, considering the shift towards decentralisation and empowerment, it is essential that individuals and groups are given more responsibility over salary decisions. Furthermore, rewards should be based on continuous performance and continuous improvement, rather than single events or past achievements.

CONTRACTS

Theories of the psychological contract have been built around full-time permanent employment and there is discussion about the extension of the concept to incorporate the experience of contingent workers. As Marchington *et al* (2005, p 78) point out:

> 'temporary agency workers attempt … to satisfy their obligations simultaneously to two employers – the agency and the client. This simultaneity raises questions about organisational commitment and loyalty.'

'Forced' changes to contracts

Earlier in this chapter, 'imposed intensification' of work was noted when employees were subjected to reduced hours contracts. Saunders and Thornhill (2006) explore the implications for employees' psychological contracts in conditions of a forced change from permanent to temporary employment status for some employees within an organisation. They suggest that permanent employees generally continue to exhibit relational forms of attachment to the organisation. These, 'the employees believe', are reciprocated by the organisation. Reactions from forced temporary workers are more varied. After a period of denial, some develop a more calculative approach to their interactions. Others maintain aspects of their previously developed relational attachments. Only some temporary workers appear to recognise that their future direction is no longer a concern of the organisation. Although only based upon one organisation, Saunders and Thornhill (2006) suggest that the process of psychological contract adjustment is likely to emerge through gradual re-interpretation, rather than through re-negotiation.

Since commitment within the psychological contract is assumed to be based on 'volition', then a lack of volition, and conflicts of loyalty, will have an effect on psychological contracting among contingent workers. We might expect non-permanent staff to show a more transactional approach, and show less commitment, than permanent staff. Research evidence provides ambiguous results. In a call centre environment, Biggs and Swailes (2006) found that agency workers had a significantly lower level of organisational commitment compared with permanent workers. However, this is not necessarily the case according to MacDonald and Makin (2000, p 89) who suggest 'the observance and commitment to the norms, symbols, and rituals of desirable groups is often higher among those just outside, but wishing to join, the group than it is among established members.' From the same authors we hear of higher levels of organisational commitment and job satisfaction among some temporary staff.

One possible explanation, it is suggested, may lie in the short tenure of non-permanent staff within the organisation.

Contract breach

To what extent can we come to understand the concept of the psychological contract through examining its being breached or violated? Coyle-Shapiro and Kessler (2000) describe a situation in which the majority of employees have experienced contract breach, in a large local authority directly responsible and accountable for a range of public services including education, environmental health and social care to the local population. This view was also supported by managers, as representatives of the employer, who further indicated that the organisation, given its external pressures, was not fulfilling its obligations to employees to the extent that it could. Overall, the results indicate that employees redress the balance in the relationship through reducing their commitment and their willingness to engage in organisational citizenship behaviour when they perceive their employer has not fulfilled its part in the exchange process.

A range of individual responses

There is a 'complexity of feelings' towards, and reactions resulting from, becoming a temporary worker, according to Saunders and Thornhill (2006, p 452) where the attractions associated with obtaining greater freedom have also been associated with greater insecurity, potentially lower control over hours of work and working patterns, and a continuing need to find new work. These ideas of preference for temporary work have been linked to workers' skill and knowledge levels to produce a typology of temporary contracts (Marler *et al*, 2002; cited in Saunders and Thornhill, 2006, p 452):

- boundaryless worker: high preference for temporary work and a high skills/ knowledge level
- permanent temporary worker: high preference for temporary work and a low skills/knowledge level
- transitional worker: low preference for temporary work and a high skills/ knowledge level
- traditional worker: low preference for temporary work and a low skills/ knowledge level.

This typology 'implies that personal preferences for temporary work are likely to influence feelings towards different types of psychological contracts. In particular high preferences for temporary work would seem likely to accentuate positive feelings towards transactional-oriented psychological contracts, whereas low preferences for temporary work would accentuate negative feelings towards transactional-oriented psychological contracts' (*ibid*, p 452).

Table 7.1 The distinction between 'old' and 'new' characteristics of psychological contracts

Old contract	New contract
Organisation is 'parent' to employee 'child'	Organisation and employee enter into 'adult' contracts focused on mutually beneficial work
Employees' identity and worth are defined by the organisation	Employees' identity and worth are defined by the employee
Those who stay are good and loyal; others are bad and disloyal	The regular flow of people in and out is healthy and should be celebrated
Employees who do what they are told will work until retirement	Long-term employment is unlikely; expect – and prepare for – multiple relationships
The primary route for growth is through promotion	The primary route for growth is a sense of personal accomplishment

OLD AND NEW PSYCHOLOGICAL CONTRACTS

The terms of the new contract are still unclear, though the material so far in this chapter has provided us with insights, but Maguire (2002) presents a number of distinctions between the old and new psychological contract which are shown in Table 7.1.

As Maguire (2002, p 8) puts it:

> 'The key differences between the "traditional" and the "new" psychological contract relate to the decreased expectation of paternalistic human resource practices, the replacement of the concept of organisational worth with "self-worth", the substitution of personal accomplishment for promotion as the route to growth, and the decreased importance of tenure.'

REFLECTIVE ACTIVITY

Thinking about the organisation you work for or one with which you are familiar, to what extent is employment characterised by 'old' or 'new' contracts?

To what extent do you envisage your career developing with multiple employers? If you find this picture realistic, will your loyalty to any *one* employer be diminished?

The CIPD suggest (2005a, p 4) that the 'old' psychological contract is 'in fact' still alive, and that surveys show the majority of employees feeling satisfied with, and not worried about losing, their jobs. However, these surveys also show there are concerns about long hours and work intensity, and levels of trust in the organisation have fallen, particularly in the public sector.

It is commonly heard that the 'old' psychological contract, with its emphasis on employment security, has been held to have been violated because of extensive downsizing among white-collar employees from the late 1980s and early 1990s (Mumford, 1995). This proposition has been examined by Beaumont and Harris (2002), using data from UK manufacturing industries for the years 1978–95. The authors call into question the view that historically high and sustained downsizing among white-collar employees was a leading cause.

Examining the psychological contract in terms of the parties' fulfilment of their obligations to each other highlights gaps in what employees expect and receive from their employer as well as what employees feel they owe the employers and actually give. This is illustrated in Simon Caulkin's findings set out below.

Loyalty of young workers: the new psychological contract?

Simon Caulkin reports on research by the Work Foundation on the motivation of the newest generation of workers, the 18- to 24-year-olds

'Employers need to understand better how Generation Y, as the Work Foundation researchers term them, differs from previous cohorts of workers, and what that means for employment policies. For young workers, the new implicit contract of employability, rather than a job for life, is the only one they have known. And they have learned its lessons fast. Accordingly, they have developed a much more instrumental approach to employment than their predecessors. They have high expectations of careers development and gaining early responsibility and attach substantial importance to the employer's "brand" – not just out of desire to work for a company that matches their own values, but also with an eye to improving their CV.

The Work Foundation terms this "gold-dusting" – buffing their record to attract other employers. Loyalty to the organisation lasts only as long as they are achieving personal goals.'

Source: Caulkin, S. (2003) How to catch a rising star, *The Observer*, Business pages, 9 November, p 15. Guardian Newspapers Ltd.

We can conclude that contextual factors are key to understanding the psychological contract. If the employer is felt to have breached the contract, should we automatically assume that employee behaviour will necessarily be affected negatively? It seems that, in times of high job insecurity, employees may be less inclined to display negative behavioural outcomes due to the power disparity between the employer and employee, or to fear of redundancy, though attitudes towards the employer will be changed, if not translated into action.

CASE STUDY

THE PSYCHOLOGICAL CONTRACT AND RETENTION

Roger Eglin, writing in the Sunday Times, suggests that emotional ties – rather than just money – are vital in getting good managers to stay with their employers.

A group of 476 Henley alumni were questioned about their relationship with their employers. Of the replies, 11 per cent were couched in what are described as transactional terms, while a compelling 52 per cent came down in favour of a relationship contract. 'They want a more effective relationship with issues such as aspiration, equity and community remaining important . . . For those who have the talent and can make a choice this is what counts.'

With some jobs set to move to India, Barclays Bank has struck a deal with the Unity trade union to help those affected. But rather than losing people through redundancy, Barclays is offering them training-and-development opportunities to make them more 'marketable' within the bank.

Source: Eglin, R. (2004) Cash is not king in holding on to staff. *Sunday Times* (London) Appointments, 15 February, p 7. Times Newspapers Ltd.

FLEXIBILITY, PSYCHOLOGICAL CONTRACTS AND PERFORMANCE

The concepts of flexibility and the psychological contract are essentially transactional involving reciprocal views concerning the quality of relationship between employee and organisation. It is now appropriate to revisit the links between people management and organisational performance.

Organisations seek to identify the link between people and performance (Purcell *et al*, 2003), and the concept of high-performance working (HPW) (CIPD, 2003a; CIPD, 2004b; DTI, 2005) is characterised by references to flatter, non-hierarchical structures, moving away from reliance on management control, towards teamworking and autonomous working based on high levels of trust, communication, and involvement. Whether the focus is on profit and shareholder value in the private sector, or on outputs and service levels in the public sector, performance is the topical currency.

Purcell *et al*'s (2003) study on the impact of people management on organisational performance was intended to show the way in which HR practices – or what the CIPD terms 'people management', meaning all aspects of how people are managed – impact on performance. The study was conducted within a framework which claims that performance is a function of people's ability (knowledge and skills), their motivation, and the opportunity they are given to deploy their skills (referred to as AMO). The authors concluded that a range of 11 HR policies and practices are required to turn this into action and a model was devised, covering recruitment and selection, training and development, career opportunity, communications, involvement in decision-making, teamworking, appraisal, pay, job security, job challenge/job autonomy, and work-life balance.

'These performance-related HR policies encourage people to exercise a degree of choice on how and how well they do their job. In other words, they help induce discretionary behaviour which makes people work better and improve performance. This happens because the HR policies and practices develop positive employee attitudes or feelings of satisfaction, commitment and motivation.' (Purcell *et al*, 2003, p ix)

This material is taken from *Bringing Policies to Life: The vital role of front line managers in people management* by Sue Hutchinson and John Purcell (2003), with the permission of the publisher, the Chartered Institute of Personnel and Development, London.

Figure 7.3 The people and performance model

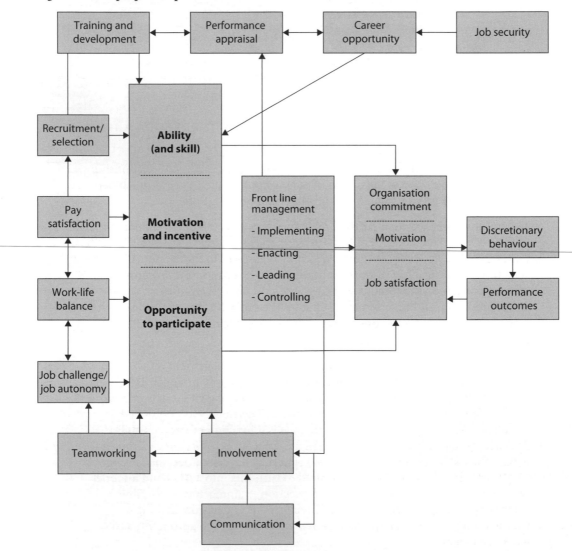

Some HR policies and practices were shown to be particularly important in terms of influencing employee outcomes like commitment, job satisfaction and motivation. These were those concerned with career opportunities, job influence, job challenge, training, performance appraisal, teamworking, involvement in decision-making, work-life balance, and having managers who are good at leadership and who show respect.

Among the implications for HR policy and practice is 'operational measurement' rather than 'remote' measures of profit:

> 'Proving that HR contributes to performance is not a major issue, and measures which use profit or shareholder values are too remote from the practice of people management to be useful. What is important is operational measurement where a close link can be observed, and the regular collection of these measures covering people, operational, financial and customer areas is commonly done in the best firms.' (Purcell *et al*, 2003, p 72)

We can conclude that the responsibility for enacting the policies rests with front-line managers, since these are the people with whom workers theoretically interact. In Hutchinson and Purcell's (2003) framework, 'organisation process advantage' – the way these policies are implemented – is what makes a difference. Put another way: it's not what you do, it's the way that you do it.

The CIPD (2007b) Standards for Leadership and Management are placed in the language of performance infrastructure ('critical failure factors') and differentiators ('critical success factors'). The former describes what is needed to do things right (efficiency) and deliver acceptable levels of behaviour and legal compliance, although it is observed that mere adherence to process seldom generates high-performance outcomes. The latter describes what is needed to do the right things (effectiveness) and, the proponents claim, deliver 'genuine' people involvement, commitment, engagement and added-value contribution. There are connotations of Herzberg's two-factor theory of motivation, which we discuss in Chapter 12, here: 'infrastructure' linking with hygiene factors and 'differentiators' involving motivators. The 11 policy areas (Purcell *et al*, 2003) are seen as the performance infrastructure requirements, while the ways in which front-line managers deliver the policies – implementing, enacting, leading and controlling – are seen as the differentiators. It is claimed that these are 'directly related to the levels of commitment, motivation and satisfaction that employees report, and this, in turn, is linked to the vital area of discretionary behaviour' (Hutchinson and Purcell, 2003, p 3).

In 2010, the CIPD's report on sustainable organisational performance concluded that sustainable organisations would need to have a balanced short- and long-term focus and, crucially, agility to adapt to challenges and opportunities. It is clear that the notion of flexibility coupled with the need to ensure engagement via positive psychological contracts is crucial in this regard. The same report emphasised the need for leaders who regard employees as a core asset. We have seen that the management of flexible working should have at its centre a preoccupation with the people involved and should both be implemented and reviewed through consultation with those most closely involved.

There are very clear and important links between understanding the concepts, putting them into operation via effective management and subsequent organisational performance.

CONCLUSION

Organisations concentrate upon meeting the needs of their stakeholders: shareholders and customers in the private sector; government and service users – now increasingly 'consumerised' – in the public sector. Responsiveness to the 'whip' of the market, previously a private sector concern, is also now increasingly required in the public sector as it becomes 'marketised.' The organisation and its workers, internal or external, core or contingent, are required to focus on performing.

Agile response is the order of the day as time-frames are shortened, and so flexibility is sought, from collective and structural flexibility, to individual and behavioural. As organisations are re-engineered, and downsized, and spans of control are increased, management attention is devoted to the increasingly autonomous worker, without losing control. To better understand the discretionary element of employment relationships, the psychological contract, and its management, has become a focus of attention.

It seems that the air is filled with managerial information and messages, suggesting what might or should be done. There are confident, sometimes strident, assertions and claims, based on research findings and examples of what appears to be best practice, and some of these might remind us of Pollert's (1991) 'desperate search for panaceas.' Amongst this traffic it is possible to detect strengthening signals, describing increasing intensification of work and workers feeling pressurised. Where there is not a readily available pathway for workers to transmit signals of this sort, the alternative is to send messages through changed behaviour or attitudes. The reader, and the HR practitioner, then has the difficult task of listening and making sense of the sometimes conflicting information at his or her disposal.

KEY LEARNING POINTS

- Developments in the global economy have resulted in a need for greater flexibility from organisations.
- There are different types of flexibility including task, numerical, temporal and wage flexibility.
- There are documented examples of unintended consequences of flexible working, and negative aspects of this notion more generally.
- Managers can usefully be aware of the concept of the psychological contract, in order to enhance worker commitment and engagement.
- A number of HR policies and practices, frequently carried out by line managers, influence worker commitment, loyalty and engagement.

REVIEW QUESTIONS

1. Critically assess the respective advantages and disadvantages to organisations and to employees of the different forms of workplace flexibility.

2. Identify and evaluate the specific actions that managers can take that will improve employees' psychological contracts with the organisation.

3. Evaluate the role of front-line managers in influencing the discretionary performance of individuals within the organisation.

4. How might the performance of outsourced workers be managed or controlled in order to sustain satisfactory outcomes for customers and service users in 'networked' private and public sector organisations?

EXPLORE FURTHER

Guest, D. (2004) Flexible employment contracts, the psychological contract and employee outcomes: an analysis and review of the evidence, *International Journal of Management Reviews* 5/6 (1) pp 1–19. This article provides a thorough review of evidence about the characteristics and consequences of flexible employment contracts and the role of the psychological contract.

Sennett, R. (1998) *The Corrosion of Character: The personal consequences of work in the new capitalism*. London: Norton. Sennett's account of the social consequences of flexibility is recommended to all readers.

Rousseau, D. (1995) *Psychological Contracts in Organizations: Understanding written and unwritten agreements*. London: Sage. Readers are referred to this publication for a comprehensive account of the psychological contract.

Pilbeam, S. and Corbridge, M. (2010) *People Resourcing and Talent Planning: HRM in practice*. 4th ed. Harlow: FT Prentice Hall. This book includes a comprehensive description of the various forms of flexibility.

CHAPTER 8

Organisational and Job Design

Ray French

LEARNING OUTCOMES

After reading this chapter, you should be able to:

- assess the potential importance of organisational design and job design as part of the process of leading, managing and developing people

- recognise the contribution both concepts can make to the development of flexible and committed employees

- identify the possible negative impacts and/or unintended consequences of organisational design and job design

- point to the prevalence of post-bureaucratic structures and 'enriched' jobs in reality within the 21st-century global workforce.

OVERVIEW

In this chapter we examine organisational arrangements, in particular the ways in which organisations can be structured and jobs designed. It is argued that managers can exercise a degree of choice in both areas and that structural arrangements and the design of jobs will have a strong influence on organisational performance. From the perspective of leading, managing and developing people, organisational and job design are key concepts since peoples' experience of work will be profoundly affected by the structure within which they operate and, of course, the nature of the work that they carry out. In Chapter 12 we examine the literature on motivation which frequently emphasises the psychological processes involved in influencing the degree of effort and commitment exhibited by employees. In this chapter we will see how people's attitudes and behaviour are also shaped by their working context – including structure and job design.

The topics examined in this chapter can appear abstract and even 'dry' and less engaging than areas such as leadership and ethical considerations. However, organisational and job design are important concepts on several levels. If two friends, one working in a classic bureaucracy, the other in an 'adhocracy' (we will define these terms in more detail), compare their everyday experiences of work they will find that their working lives are indeed very different. As we will also see, organisation and job design are core principles underlying strategies of people management, so they are of interest to existing and future HR managers as well.

It is important to recognise that attempts to enhance performance through the application of design principles can founder through the law of unintended consequences. Linstead *et al* (2009) and Watson (2006) for example, both highlight what are termed 'dysfunctions' of bureaucracy. Bureaucratic structures are intended to foster efficient working through stability, predictability and fair treatment (both of employees and clients or customers). Bureaucracy is essentially conceived as a rational system of organisation. However, the very features which are supposed to aid efficiency can result in reality in negative behaviour – for example defensive or even 'jobsworth' style behaviour among employees, resulting from over-adherence to rules, and moderate or 'get-by' performance as a consequence of slow and rigid promotion procedures. In this chapter we will advise against any assumption that implementing changes in organisation or job design will automatically result in positive outcomes. Notwithstanding this point, organisation and job design can be powerful tools for change.

We will, finally, show how recent work in organisation and job design has often sought to use these ideas to promote flexible working – an important theme within leading, managing and developing people in the 21st century. Gilmore (2009:354) notes that 'the theme of flexibility permeates issues of employment and labour utilisation, as well as the concept of post-bureaucratic organisation. . .' The same author goes on to state that flexibility is associated with interesting tensions arising in the employment relationship. Preece (2009, in Gilmore and Williams, p 75) records that one reason for organisation re-design – in the form of post-bureaucratic structures – is to allow the job of managing human resources to focus on: 'ensuring that the benefits of working with this more flexible, temporary workforce are maximised, and with ensuring that workers' knowledge and skills are deployed in ways that add value to the firm'. The links between organisational design, job design and flexibility will be further drawn out in this chapter.

INTRODUCTION

We begin this section with a definition of some of the key terms which form the basis for an understanding of organisational arrangements.

ORGANISATIONAL DESIGN

Organisational design is defined as a planned activity in which designers – usually managers, maybe in conjunction with specialised consultants – attempt to adjust the formal shape of their organisation. There are many types of organisation and consequently many choices in organisational design (Wood *et al*, 2010). Organisational design is defined by French *et al* (2008, p 329) as: 'the process of choosing and implementing a structural configuration for an organisation'. We see therefore that organisational design and structure are not synonymous but in a fundamental sense are linked concepts. Organisational design creates organisational structure, defined as the intended pattern of tasks, responsibilities, lines of authority and networks of communication in an organisation.

It can be seen from this categorisation of structure that we are in essence dealing with formalised features of organisations. The classic way to depict an organisation's structure is via scrutiny of a chart or other diagram, in effect taking an impersonal view of what *should* happen in that organisation. The term *informal organisation* denotes what actually happens in a workplace, which can deviate from what should occur within formal arrangements – for example if people habitually ignore a bureaucratic rule or procedure.

'Organisation structure' as a term has several different sub-components within this overarching definition. These are set out below:

Formalisation

Formalisation refers to the extent to which an organisation stipulates the way work or particular roles comprising a job should be carried out. One guide to ascertain the degree of formalisation is the existence of procedural manuals or job descriptions preordaining working styles and practices.

Specialisation

This aspect of structure refers both to the extent to which work roles involve a range of specialist activities and to the ways in which workers with similar or related roles and tasks are grouped together. Many organisations have historically operated in a highly specialised manner, typically by setting up discrete functionally-based departments.

Vertical differentiation

This sub-set of structure links to power and authority. An organisation could specify many levels within a hierarchy each with distinct reporting responsibilities, or it might be designed as a relatively 'flat' organisation, with few hierarchical levels. The concept of span of control in which the ratio of workers reporting to managers is prescribed is also relevant here.

Centralisation

This deals with decision-making, in particular whether responsibility in this regard rests with senior managers, as against where it is cascaded throughout the organisation. Closely associated with this central idea is the degree to which tight control is exercised by a head office or whether, contrastingly, greater autonomy is granted to operating units or divisions.

Line and/or staff functions

In this element of structure there is a distinction between 'line' functions which are intimately connected with the primary purpose of the organisation, and contrasting (although complementary) 'staff' functions which supplement and further the aims of the organisation through the provision of ancillary services. In a large college, for example, the organisation's prime objective will be the education of students – so that lecturers form part of the 'line', while an HRM department may be categorised as a 'staff' function. We have looked at the implications of this distinction for HR in Chapter 2. The relationship between line and staff (and their relative importance) raises issues of horizontal (as opposed to vertical) co-ordination and control.

Later in this chapter we will examine the ways in which organisational design – and hence structure – can be utilised in a positive way within the overall project of leading, managing and developing people.

REFLECTIVE ACTIVITY

Look again at the elements of organisational structure listed above. What type of structure do you think would be most appropriate for a hospital? Give reasons for your answer.

JOB DESIGN

Job design as defined by French *et al* (2008, p 207) is 'the planning and specification of job tasks and the work setting in which they are to be accomplished'. The authors elaborate on their definition by proposing that much contemporary writing on the subject views the objective of job design as facilitating meaningful, interesting and challenging jobs and that, within this perspective, a manager's responsibility is to design jobs that will motivate an individual employee. This finding underpins much academic research in this area which often posits a link between aspects of jobs and employees' psychological well-being. We will examine several examples of work within this tradition in this chapter. However job design, as we will see, does not presuppose the design of enriched jobs – it can also lead to the splitting of tasks into routine, repetitive and unskilled work.

Watson (2006) draws a distinction between the terms 'job design' and 'work design'. He notes that job design refers to task patterns that could occur in any part of a work organisation, while work design is underpinned by more broadly defined principles which could reflect that organisation's culture and structure. This refining of terminology is useful in that it highlights the role of managerial choice in devising principles for organising work. Thus job design, and beyond this, work design can form part of a more strategic approach to managing people. Watson (*op cit*) makes the distinction in this context between *direct* and *indirect* control principles. In the former case, there is a stress on prescribed task procedures with only a minimal level of commitment required from employees. In contrast, indirect control principles emphasise far greater discretion for employees in the way they perform tasks; this in turn is dependent on their higher levels of commitment, leading to mutual trust between members of the organisation in question.

It would be true to say that for much of its history job design, and the broader concept of work design, has been associated with principles of direct control. In reading earlier work on this subject, one finds particular resonance of these ideas in the work of Frederick Taylor and his model of *scientific management* often subsequently referred to as Taylorism. As we will see, Taylor's work, together with principles associated with Henry Ford, contain assumptions that jobs can be designed on a rational basis in order to maximise workers' efforts with a view to quicken production, radically reduce costs and increase output to a very significant extent. It can be argued that mass production and consumption patterns have been predicated on these principles. At the time of the millennium several commentators promoted the case for Ford as one of the key influential figures of the 20th century, in part because of his impact on social trends due to the production of affordable cars, but also because many millions of people worked in jobs that bore the stamp of his (and Taylor's) vision. This tradition within job design has either minimised the issue of workers' motivation or put forward a model of needs at work which centre on maximising income, for example the concept of rational economic man.

Leach and Wall (2004) link different views of job design with specific epochs, making the distinction between traditional job design – which emphasises the design of jobs in order to minimise skill requirements and training times – and more contemporary *job redesign* which, contrastingly, recommends increasing the number of tasks carried out by an individual worker such as through job rotation and 'enlarging' and/or 'enriching' individual jobs. We will explore these concepts in greater detail later in the chapter.

FLEXIBILITY

We have referred to this concept on several occasions already in this book and examined it in greater detail and depth in Chapter 7. This broad term refers to several discrete areas of business operations. It can be applied firstly to flexible forms of organisational structure –inferring a move away from a rigid bureaucratic form to one that can respond more speedily to demands emanating from its environment (Rollinson, 2009). At the same time it refers to attempts to enrich workers' jobs through multi-skilling, greater autonomy and responsibility with the general aim of fostering both better performance and greater commitment to the employing organisation. We will primarily examine the notion of flexibility with reference to these twin themes.

The term 'flexibility' is also, however, used in the area of employment itself, resulting in greater prevalence of such arrangements as part-time and fixed-term working, casual employment, outsourcing and teleworking. For some commentators (Bratton and Gold, 2007) increasing flexibility of employment has led to heightened distinctions between a core and peripheral workforce.

REFLECTIVE ACTIVITY

A CIPD survey (2009c) included data on why employers chose to outsource parts of their employee resourcing activities such as recruitment advertising and candidate sourcing and screening. Some of the more oft-cited reasons given for outsourcing included: increasing efficiency, reducing costs, freeing up HR managers to concentrate on more strategic activities and increasing resourcing flexibility to meet peaks and troughs of demand.

One can see that there are powerful reasons for outsourcing work beyond individual organisations. However, some of the same reasons given for outsourcing – particularly increasing efficiency and reducing costs – were given as a justification for keeping activities in-house. There are no right answers, and individual circumstances intervene – for example, a particular relationship with an external provider might make it advantageous to outsource.

MODELS OF STRUCTURE

Having defined key terms used in this chapter, we now turn to look more closely at the topic of organisational structure, which is an essential component of organisational design.

BUREAUCRACY

Bureaucracy has been a highly influential and long-lasting form of organisation structure – some writers see examples of it as far back as ancient Greek and Roman civilisations. In modern times, its key features were articulated by the sociologist Max Weber, who constructed an ideal type of bureaucracy – ie what it would look like in an extreme or idealised form.

WEBER'S MODEL OF PURE BUREAUCRACY

- Tasks are allocated according to certified expertise, with resultant specialised (for example, departmental) structure.
- Jobs are defined through clear and often simplified routine tasks.
- Control is exercised through a hierarchical structure, typically with many layers denoting levels of authority.
- Rules and procedures are clearly set out in the form of written documentation.
- There are pre-set formal systems of communication via specified channels with hierarchical authority paramount.
- Employees are appointed and, where appropriate, promoted on the basis of clear criteria often relating to their qualifications.
- Managers are salaried officials and do not have a financial stake in the organisation.

- Rules are set and all decisions made rationally in an attempt to eliminate non-rational elements such as emotional involvement or personal preference.

In the late 19th century Weber claimed that organisations (in Europe) came to lay particular stress on rational decision-making. It was claimed that this distinguished them from the ways in which previous communities' workplaces operated more on the basis of traditional authority. Watson (2006, p 38) states that 'Out of this major cultural shift came bureaucracy. And bureaucracies are what modern organisations are.'

ALTERNATIVES TO BUREAUCRACY: ADAPTING TO 'CONTINGENCIES'

From the 1950s onwards, a wave of critical comment emerged centring on a perceived inability of bureaucratic structures to cope well in the face of changing circumstances. The underlying idea that organisation structures are influenced by 'external' factors, to which they must be adapted to ensure high performance, is commonly referred to as *the contingency approach*. Before examining the factors that have been identified as relevant situational events or contingencies, it is timely to look at some alternative structures which are either extensions of bureaucracy or radical alternatives.

Project team structures

Project teams are normally seen as temporary structures set up for a specific purpose where cross-functional expertise is required (see Needle, 2004, for further detail). In some sectors – for example, consultancy – such structures could be seen as the norm, groups of employees from different functional areas routinely being assembled to provide an integrated service for a particular client. Another possible scenario in which such a structure would be relevant is where a project group comprising potential users of a new IT system, including representatives from different functional departments, work together to consider the implications of the new system for their own sub-unit. One advantage of such a structure is that it encourages workers to consider their contribution to organisational goals from a variety of perspectives and can therefore facilitate cross-fertilisation of ideas.

The matrix

Matrix structures are by no means recent phenomena, having been identified in significant numbers from the 1970s onwards. The key defining point of a matrix structure is multi-reporting, in that employees are required to consider at least two aspects of their job – typically their functional specialism and the products or services provided as part of their work. We have already referred to the distinction between 'line' and 'staff' functions, which is addressed directly in the matrix form, the notion of facing in different directions being reinforced in the structure of the organisation itself. Many students and academics reading this book will be familiar with the idea of the matrix since it is by no means uncommon in the higher-educational sector (the author can identify examples from a number of different countries). A lecturer may form part of an academic department based on his or her academic subject area but may also have to report to senior managers whose remit could be courses (the product), or quality assurance, or international developments, or knowledge transfer. In such a case the individual lecturer could report to five separate managers.

Advantages of matrices are similar to those put forward for project teams in that they allow for easier collaborative working – and even synergy. On the other hand, the major criticism of matrix structures has centred on their potential for ambiguity and even outright confusion in reporting. The matrix idea could readily lend itself to transnational or global working – and this aspect is pursued more fully later in this chapter. The concept of a matrix is indeed similar to the ideal type of the 'global firm' based on divisional structure.

Divisional structure

The divisional form of structure, also known as the multi-functional model, was originally conceived as an alternative to the functional bureaucracy. In this form, entire divisions are set up to deal with all aspects of a product or service. It can be argued that the focus of such a structure is on *outputs* – that is, the end product – rather than on the inputs (all resources including human skills, knowledge and effort) needed to turn the end product into a tangible entity. General Motors (GM) for many years provided an example of this type of strategic approach to structure. GM's divisions were based on brand names and associated products. Individual divisions were largely self-contained and operated as profit centres. However, headquarters – sometimes known as 'the centre' – co-ordinated overall strategy and centralised other activities. The divisional nature of this multinational company became evident in 2009, when GM, following financial problems caused by global economic turbulence, sold off whole divisions of the company hosted outside the USA.

Organic structure

This model was originally put forward by the researchers Burns and Stalker (1961) as an idealised counterpoint to the classic bureaucratic structure. As we shall see in the following section examining the impact of contingent factors on organisational form, Burns and Stalker found that this type of structure, or rather its component features, would be effective when organisations operated in a 'turbulent' environment of rapidly changing technology, fierce competition and uncertain customer demand. The features of this abstract model were:

- network (as opposed to hierarchical) structures of control and communication
- knowledge spread throughout the organisation (rather than located at the top)
- employee commitment to their tasks (compared with loyalty to the organisation)
- knowledge, skills and experience applied to diverse tasks (compared with long-term specialisation)
- communication flowing up, down and across the organisation rather than essentially top-down.

Burns and Stalker's organic structure is characterised overall by informality and flexibility. Originally applied to the fast-changing micro-electronics sector of the 1960s, it has increasingly been advocated in other areas of the private and public sectors because their environments are perceived as more turbulent as a result of economic, political and technological change.

Adhocracy

The adhocracy shares important features of the organic form. However, it may go further in that it can be defined as an organisational type that is not planned in the first instance; rather it develops spontaneously or in an *ad hoc* manner, hence the name (Clegg *et al*, 2008).

CONTINGENT FACTORS

There are many potentially distinctive forms of organisational structure: we have only outlined some general principles here. As suggested earlier, the essence of the contingency approach is that particular types of structure should be *designed* in the light of the contingent factors acting on the organisation in question. Although contingencies are by definition framed by unique circumstances, overarching factors usually put forward are listed below.

Technology

The work of Joan Woodward, published in 1965 (but based on research carried out in the mid-1950s), identified a link between technology – here referring to production methods – and the ways in which the companies she studied were organised. Woodward's conclusion was that the production systems used by the companies she researched resulted in differences in those companies' structures. Woodward, in addition to demarcating forms of structure and linking them to technology, also, and very importantly, concluded that there was an optimal situation in which organisations that aligned their structures according to the technologies they used would be the most efficient. In other words, the structure would have to fit with this particular contingent factor.

Size of organisation

A research team from Aston University in England proposed that an organisation's size would be the most important determining factor in terms of its optimal structure (see Pugh and Hickson, 1976, for an account of the research by members of the original group). The Aston researchers examined the extent of specialisation, the degree to which formal policies influenced work in reality, and standardisation in terms of procedures. The Aston academics then identified a number of points for comparison, all deriving from Weber's ideal type of bureaucracy, finally correlating these with statistical data from their own research sample. Their conclusion was that the independent variable which most strongly impacted on the dependent variable of organisational structure was size. The *post hoc* logic which purports to explain these findings was fundamentally that as organisations grow in size there is considerable pressure for them to become more bureaucratic – see also Chapter 3. Once again, the influence of a contingent factor pointed to an ideal structure depending on the nature of the specific organisation.

Organisational environments

As we have already noted, Burns and Stalker (1961) proposed their dichotomy of *mechanistic and organic structures*. The mechanistic category is very similar to Weber's model of bureaucracy, while the diametrically opposite organic form is flexible, is network-based and requires commitment – in addition to compliance and loyalty – from employees within this structure. The key contingent variable for Burns and Stalker was the particular environment facing the organisation. The more turbulent the environment, in terms of technological advance, competition and customer or client demand, the more organic the organisation should be, if it were to prosper and even survive in such a challenging milieu. Burns and Stalker identified organisations that had failed to adapt via changed structures, thus adding weight to their central proposition.

In conclusion, organisational design offers a degree of choice to decision-makers who should consider the contingent factors faced by their organisations before deciding on structural arrangements. Nonetheless, such choices are themselves constrained as it has been shown that different structures tend to be more effective in particular circumstances – ie depending on factors like size, technology and environment.

APPROACHES TO JOB DESIGN

Traditionally job design principles have emphasised job simplification (Taylor, 1911), interpreted critically by some writers as de-skilling, while more recent contributions to the subject area have typically recommended expanding jobs in order both to increase employee job satisfaction, or at least to reduce boredom, and to engender greater *flexibility* in a workforce, (Hackman and Oldham, 1980). It is often proposed that such flexibility is desirable in view of changes in the wider business environment. In the UK context, Hutton (2004, p 1) presents this argument as follows: 'Britain's fundamental economic structures are changing; industries and services built around knowledge are growing, while those built around mass industrial production and raw muscle power are declining. Work is becoming more intelligent and an intelligent workforce is going to be one that wants to be intelligent about how it organises itself. The more autonomy and control it can have, the more content it will be.'

One should be wary of assuming that there is, or will shortly be, a proliferation of 'intelligent' work. On the contrary the emergence of increasing numbers of workplaces such as fast food outlets and call centres have mainly been associated with standardised repetitive 'Taylorist'-style jobs. Beyond such work with its associated routine tasks, one also finds what Clegg *et al* (2008) refer to as 'grunge jobs' comprising both work carried out in the lower reaches of the supply chain supporting global business, and that performed by an underclass of sometimes illegal workers operating in very poor conditions outside the formally recognised and regulated job market.

Nonetheless, there is also evidence that increasingly many workers will be required to act as thinking performers and this segment of the workforce will form the main focus in this chapter. In such an environment it is posited that organisations seeking distinctive high performance should be involved in job design, which contributes towards a positive psychological contract between employer and worker. This, it is suggested, can also aid and reinforce successful organisational performance. We discussed both the issue of flexibility and the psychological contract in more detail in Chapter 7.

It is also necessary for all organisations to engage in job design as an 'infrastructure' task, to ensure that work is allocated into suitably-sized role descriptions capable of being carried out effectively. At the same time, it is essential to ensure suitable demarcation of roles both vertically (in terms of skill, knowledge and hierarchical level) as well as horizontally (in functional terms). This aspect of basic job design is a prerequisite for minimal threshold standards of performance by organisations and is needed to avoid fundamental problems relating to the nature of work and roles.

It is possible to locate key developments in the approach to job design, although while these have been developed in particular epochs, each can still be applied to current work situations. It is now time to look at these approaches in more detail.

SCIENTIFIC MANAGEMENT

As indicated earlier, for its most famous proponent Frederick Taylor, scientific management involved organising tasks into highly specialised jobs. Managers should take on responsibility for planning, co-ordinating and monitoring work, with the task worker restricted to the level of operative. Recruitment and training are simplified and workers are grouped together in large units such as factories or call centres, enabling a high volume of chiefly standardised goods or services. One example is the Fordist production line system, which, in addition to demarcating jobs, also controlled the speed of work. It is difficult to over-emphasise the significance of this model of job design. Henry Ford, in laying the conditions for mass production of cars, was able to reduce costs very substantially, which in turn led to greatly increased levels of car ownership in the USA. This led to him being considered one of the pivotal figures of the 20th century in the industrialised world.

Scientific management as a driver for job design has attracted much controversy and a good deal of criticism in the areas set out below:

● It can lead to product inflexibility.

● It has been criticised as dehumanising and for failing to recognise 'higher order' human needs such as self-actualisation.

- It may foster compliance and an instrumental view of work as a means to an end, as opposed to engendering commitment and loyalty.

- Monotony and boredom can result in reduced performance outcomes.

More generally, scientific management is perceived by some commentators as a particularly direct form of control of work and workers by management. Braverman (1974) is prominent among writers who go on to assert that this concept of job design is fundamentally associated with an attempt to 'de-skill' workers. One need not accept Braverman's class-based analysis to recognise that managers as a group are, in the nature of their role, concerned to control and regularise jobs and work. Nonetheless, not all jobs have been subject to this version of job and work design and the ability of particular groups of workers to retain or even enhance skill levels remains an important factor in job design.

Adler (1999) has put forward an interesting restatement of the impact of simplified 'Taylorist' jobs on employees' attitudes to their work situation. His research indicated that under conditions of scientific management, employees could still be motivated by a sense of a 'job well done'. For example, they were found to respond positively to managers' encouraging them to compete with co-workers, both in terms of quality and output. When they were respected and trusted by managers, the workers under study reciprocated with commitment and loyalty.

JOB REDESIGN

Job redesign emerged in part as a reaction to the perceived negative effects of scientific management. Its academic roots lie in the so-called 'human relations' school which emphasised people's social needs which, it was claimed, could and should be met in the workplace. Herzberg's two-factor theory of motivation proposed that pure motivation derived from the content of work as opposed to 'hygiene' factors such as pay, physical working conditions and quality of supervision. Hygiene factors, for Herzberg, were sources of dissatisfaction which could be lessened if, for example, pay was improved. However, workers would only be truly motivated if their job or work met their needs for recognition, autonomy and achievement. Herzberg's view was that virtually all human beings would respond to work which was rich in motivating factors, if they had the ability to do the job and the opportunity to carry out meaningful work. We will, however, question this near-universal perspective later in this chapter.

In a highly significant contribution to this topic area, Hackman and Oldham (1980) proposed, on the basis of research, that five key characteristics could be used to identify the extent to which a job would, in reality, be motivating.

- skill variety – if different and diverse activities demanded the exercise of a range of skills and abilities

- task identity – the extent to which a job involves a whole and identifiable piece of work with a tangible end result

- task significance – the perceived value and effect of a job on other people

- autonomy – where a worker is free to schedule the pace of his or her work, have some choice in how the work is carried out and is relatively independent of supervision

- feedback – the degree to which a worker gets information about the effectiveness of his or her performance. This feedback could be gained through observation of the work outcomes.

It is argued that each key characteristic is linked to a positive psychological state which, in turn, leads to desirable work outcomes. For example, task significance could result in a feeling of satisfaction in the meaningfulness of work undertaken, with positive outcomes of work motivation and effectiveness following on from this psychological state. In summary, Hackman and Oldham stated that intrinsic motivation is dependent on individuals' experiencing *three* critical psychological states: experienced meaningfulness (as noted above), experienced responsibility for work and knowledge of the results of work activities.

Hackman and Oldham recognise that individuals can respond to the characteristics differently; they are after all a function of the individual's perception, so the motivating potential of a job may vary between people. Several factors will influence the manner in which any one individual will respond to changes in their job design.

- Growth-need strength. It is suggested that people vary in the extent to which they desire accomplishment and autonomy at work. People high in this category will therefore respond positively to enriched jobs; contrastingly, other workers might find newly enriched jobs a source of anxiety.

- Knowledge and skill. People who perceive they can perform adequately (known as a sense of self-efficacy) respond more positively to enriched jobs. This highlights the importance of individuals' perceptions and also the development of knowledge and skills at work.

- Context satisfaction. Hackman and Oldham found that employees who were more satisfied with contextual factors such as pay and working conditions would be more likely to respond positively to job enrichment than fellow workers dissatisfied on these measures.

However, despite recognising potential differences in the ways particular workers might respond to job enrichment, in overall terms Hackman and Oldham's model sets out a clear agenda for managers and others to devise meaningful and varied jobs.

 REFLECTIVE ACTIVITY

Question

1. How can Hackman and Oldham's model be applied to the following jobs?

    - Dentist

    - Railway ticket collector

    - University lecturer

    - Tiler

    - Your current or previous job (assuming this is not one of the above).

The job redesign approach attempted to put forward a model which, through increasing the scope of jobs, could result both in greater efficiency and output (however defined) while also increasing the motivation of a workforce. Hackman and Oldham, while stressing the importance of 'moderating factors' which depress levels of motivation – for example, lack of knowledge or skill, 'low growth-need strength' and other negative factors in the work context – clearly advocate the design of jobs which can lead to psychological well-being among the people who perform them.

We have noted that Hackman and Oldham question whether, and to what extent, jobholders are likely to respond positively to jobs that are 'redesigned' in this way. Their approach in addressing this issue is essentially a psychological one focusing on presumed needs and other psychological characteristics of human beings which could vary. It may be, however, that individual workers can also *choose* work that, although comparatively meaningless, may offer the prospect of other desired rewards including pay, for wider reasons based on their calculation of costs and benefits. Support for this notion is provided by the work of Goldthorpe and Lockwood (1968) who identified a category of workers who took an instrumental attitude or *orientation to work*. Formed outside the workplace and influenced by, among others, family and peers, the instrumental orientation regards work as a means to an end, and workers within this category often make a conscious decision to enter psychologically unfulfilling but highly-paid work. Thus many workers meet their higher-order needs off the job. With 168 hours in every week, work rarely consumes more than a third of this time for most people. There is ample opportunity for individuals with strong growth needs to find satisfaction beyond their place of work

This is not to say that decision-makers should make no attempt to design satisfying work for jobholders; there may be considerable practical benefits in so doing. It is useful, however, to adopt a contingency perspective in this area: that is, to understand that the nature of job design may depend on a variety of factors including the work itself and the chosen orientations to work as well as the psychological needs of the workforce.

It should finally be noted that enriched work, with its hoped-for concomitant high commitment, can itself be regarded as a form of subjugation due to the demands it imposes on employees working within its precepts. Grey (2009, p 82) notes that: 'What now appears quite normal and natural is that managers will work long hours, do whatever needs to be done to get the job done and are motivated to do so by the intrinsic interest of their work, the payment they receive and, in general, a sense of responsibility and professionalism.' Grey goes on to paint a picture of managers stressed out by endless demands and locked into a particular set of corporate imperatives which, while in many respects preferable to that endured by workers in less enriched and self-managed jobs, themselves involve considerable sacrifices in many respects.

CASE STUDY

CALL CENTRE IS MY 'DREAM JOB'

At 22, Snehal Sampat has landed her dream job.

She works as a customer adviser in Norwich Union's (now Aviva's) call centre in Bangalore, southern India.

In Britain such a job would be considered very ordinary. But in India it is a sought-after position.

Ms Sampat said one of the attractions is the salary.

'The pay is absolutely fantastic,' she said. 'In India, call centres are one of the fastest growing industries. If you perform, you stand to earn a lot of money.'

A lot of money by Indian standards, that is. Ms Sampat earns £40 a week. Her equivalent at a British call centre would be on £250.

But in India, £40 is twice what a teacher earns and about the same as a newly qualified doctor.

Prestige

Ms Sampat and her call centre colleagues, all of whom are graduates, are able to enjoy the fruits of the consumer society: mobile phones, DVDs, Western clothes and smart rented flats.

By the end of the year Norwich Union will employ 3,500 people in Bangalore, Delhi and Pune.

'About two million people a year come out of Indian universities and technical colleges,' said John Hodgson, the firm's offshoring director. 'Their basic English is at a high level. They seek employment with Western companies because it's seen as a high prestige job, an important stepping stone in their lives.'

Expansion

Indian call centres are 40 per cent cheaper to run than British ones and the number of outsourcing staff is expected to grow tenfold in five years.

It is good news for India, where a third of the population lives in absolute poverty.

Questions

1. How can one account for Snehal Sampat's orientation to work as indicated in this case study?

2. Should Norwich Union be concerned to examine ways of 'enriching' the job of customer adviser in its Indian call centre operation? Give reasons for your answers.

Source: Bond (2004)

LESSONS FROM JAPAN

Any overview examining how job design has developed as a concept would not be complete without acknowledging the influence of ideas originating in, and imported from, Japan. The purpose here is not to provide an account of how Japanese techniques came to be commended to UK organisations from the 1980s onwards. Neither will we undertake a detailed analysis of what is a highly complex concept of management underpinned by deep assumptions within Japanese society. Rather we will concentrate on how Japanese management principles have impacted on the specific area of job design, where it is claimed the following factors are particularly relevant:

- Teamwork. Japanese management techniques have often advocated the grouping of workers into teams, even in areas of work which would otherwise be organised on an individual basis. This concept can be extended to encompass task decision-making – for example, through quality circles.

- Multiskilling. The physical grouping of workers can also be extended to enable more similar job descriptions – that is, setting a context of work in which employees are required to have generalised job skills. It follows that these jobs are minimally demarcated. We see here an early embodiment of the principle of flexibility.

- Total Quality Management (TQM). For our purposes the key element of TQM is the principle that quality control should be the concern of all workers and therefore form part of every employee's job role. This could be seen as one manifestation of job enlargement, building both additional duties and responsibilities into their jobs.

REFLECTIVE ACTIVITY

TQM

Derived from Japanese management methods, and in contrast to other methods of monitoring the quality of a business's output, such as inspection and quality control, TQM is said to be a means of ensuring customer satisfaction through a process involving the continuous improvement of all work operations. Importantly for the study and leadership of people, to be successful its advocates point to the need for all employees to be involved in TQM. It requires creative thinking, and the use of teamwork to solve problems and meet customers' needs. From this standpoint, competitive advantage and differentiation can be achieved through recognising the, often untapped, resource that organisations have in their workforces.

Question

To what extent could your own job, or one with which you are familiar, benefit from TQM applications? Give reasons for your conclusions.

Japanese work design principles have been incorporated within a wider philosophy, including 'single status' employment conditions and lifetime, or at least long-term, tenure of employment. Some elements are not unique to the Japanese context: for example, Swedish car-makers had also (quite independently) introduced small-group working into their production processes along with aspects of job enlargement. Nonetheless the Japanese system, as described, can be said to be a distinctive and coherent view on job design; the latter might be seen as a differentiating factor. There have been well-publicised instances of Japanese practices being introduced to the UK, for example in the Nissan and Toyota car production facilities. Some of the principles outlined here have been widely adopted. While the economic difficulties experienced by Japan since the 1990s have cast some doubt on the extent to which they can be regarded as a panacea, many employers now assume that quality issues should be the concern of all workers and that this should be operationalised through job design.

One should take a realistic view of the extent of improvements emanating from such approaches to job design. These it is claimed centre on the twin benefits of greater productivity and more positive attitudes among jobholders. Important and commendable as they are, these benefits will not outweigh other factors affecting the organisation. One example is provided by figures indicating the comparatively strong productivity of Japanese-owned car plants in the UK. Rhys (Murray-West, 2002), in acknowledging their excellent productivity, noted nonetheless that measuring performance by productivity was 'using only a Soviet Union measure of performance. Productivity is a necessary condition of performance, but it is in no way sufficient to guarantee profitability. It hasn't stopped Nissan slipping into loss-making, which indicates the pressure they are under from the strength of sterling.' He also referred to the crucial importance of the desirability of the product itself!

BUSINESS PROCESS RE-ENGINEERING (BPR)

This concept, we will argue, should also be examined when considering approaches to, and influences on, job design. BPR emerged in the 1990s and is associated with Hammer and Champny (1993) and Davenport (1993). These writers advocate a radical approach to organisational development. In effect they recommend ignoring past and current practice when considering how to both structure an organisation and design work. They place a strong emphasis on processes, and attention to these at the same hierarchical level. Such chains of process are thus horizontal and often cross traditionally functional boundaries.

The focus on an absolute need to serve the customer can result in very dramatic changes to work processes and jobs. Buchanan and Wilson (1996) conducted a 'patient trail' in a British hospital. They found that a hospital patient might routinely have dealings with between 50 and 150 different members of the hospital's staff, becoming at different times the responsibility of most of the hospital's functional departments in the course of diagnosis, on-site treatment and after-care. Problems that arose from this complex process were attributed to hospital staff being, quite naturally, concerned primarily with what happens at their own stage of the patient's journey. Staff working within such a fragmented environment were not always aware either of what had gone on before or what would subsequently happen to the patient.

Examples such as that given above suggest that organisations should re-structure away from vertical or functionally-based departmental structures if there is to be a true focus on the customer (this ignoring the debate over whether patients can be truly thought of as customers). But in addition to organisational re-structuring, BPR also implies that jobs themselves should also be re-organised around principles of customer care and that employees should increasingly be empowered to make the decisions affecting a customer's relationship with the organisation.

GOAL-SETTING AND JOB DESIGN

Mullins (2010) notes that seemingly diverse methods of job design can in reality be inter-connected with some extent of overlap between them. He also brings the concept of goal-setting into view as another approach to job design. This conclusion is also drawn by French *et al* (2008), who suggest that as goal-setting involves developing, negotiating and formalising employees' targets and objectives, it can readily be expanded to encompass goal-setting results in specific task goals. Locke's work on goal-setting suggested that specific and difficult goals supported by task feedback are more likely to lead to higher performance, although they should not be seen as too difficult or impossible, and they would in any case only be effective if the worker had feelings of self-efficacy.

CASE STUDY

CALL CENTRES NEED NOT BE SUCH A NIGHTMARE

Companies that treat staff like battery hens and keep customers on the line for ages do themselves no favours, writes Roger Eglin.

When Bernard Marr, a research fellow at Cranfield School of Management, was approached by DHL, the parcels giant, to measure performance at its call centres, he was shocked by the conditions he found.

Marr began by interviewing people to identify what made for best practice, and he has just produced a study on call-centre management.

'You wouldn't believe what it was like in some of the call centres I visited,' he said. 'The conditions were little different from what a chicken must experience at a factory farm. There was almost an army-like atmosphere. There were huge queues of customer calls and managers were running about shouting at staff to reduce the queues. It was very scary.'

He had personal experience of the abysmal service that has given call centres such a bad name with consumers. 'I wanted to change my broadband supplier,' he said. 'There was no direct line to the cancellation department, so I had to find the best way in. I waited in the queue for 45 minutes to get through. Then when they put me through, I had to wait another 30 minutes. It was clear they had no idea of what customers were experiencing.'

Marr said that the problem with call centres was that they were run as separate business units, with managers spending all their time trying to control the time and cost per call. They were not seen as part of the company, although they had become the primary point of contact for customers.

'One centre wanted to produce better customer satisfaction. Staff were given a target of settling a call within two minutes, but customer satisfaction still went down because after two minutes staff would just pull the plug or pass calls to other departments. This was producing the wrong sort of behaviour and they didn't achieve any of their strategic objectives.'

Marr said companies ended up monitoring the number and length of calls because it was easy to do, but they failed to realise it was a pointless exercise because it focused on measuring efficiency without understanding what the business was about.

'A successful centre is one that really talks to the customer', said Marr. 'Yet only a few companies understand this. They just want to reduce the numbers. The staff do not like it. If you interview front-line staff who are given time to talk to the callers, they will tell you they work harder. If someone has a bad experience with the call centre, it shapes his or her perception of the company. If things are really bad, they will never go back to that company.'

'Doing something about it is commonsense but it doesn't filter through to top executives. They don't understand the importance of call centres or that they are a company's public face.'

But Marr had a surprise at Fujitsu, the Japanese IT company. There he found happy staff at call centres in Crewe and Stevenage that contributed greatly to the company's success. 'The atmosphere was so different,' he said. 'People were enthusiastic, trying to understand what customers wanted.'

Fujitsu started developing its call centres in 1999 when Stephen Parry joined the company. It now employs 4,000 staff in call centres worldwide.

Much of Fujitsu's success stems from the close relationships it develops with clients. Instead of focusing on the time it takes to deal with a call, Fujitsu explores whether the call was necessary in the first place. It aims to cut down the number of calls and create more time to answer the ones that matter.

'Sometimes it can be difficult to establish the customers' problems because they are reluctant to discuss the details of their business with an outsider. It took time to overcome the reluctance of a fast-food company to let Fujitsu explore why it was making so many calls. Eventually a team from Fujitsu spent an afternoon there and

discovered that the restaurants were having trouble accessing the company's system because of inadequate server capacity.' 'They should have learned sooner,' said Marr. 'It was costing them a lot of money.'

Questions

1. How did a preoccupation with customer relationships impact on the jobs of Fujitsu call centre workers?

2. To what extent do you think the call centre staff at Fujitsu are truly 'empowered'?

3. Identify the difficulties managers could face in attempting to change the ethos of a call centre towards the Fujitsu model as set out in the case study.

Source: Eglin (2004)

CONCLUSION

ORGANISATIONAL DESIGN, JOB DESIGN AND HIGH-PERFORMANCE ORGANISATIONS, A CONTINGENCY VIEW

The argument for linking principles of organisational design and job design to high performance and commitment workplaces can be summarised as follows:

- Organisational design can achieve an organisational structure best suited to deal with that organisation's circumstances or *contingent factors*.

- A constantly changing and ever more competitive business environment means that work organisations in all sectors require multi-skilled, proactive and customer-focused staff in order to be successful. These staff can be characterised as thinking performers.

- An increasingly educated workforce, used to exercising discretion and choice in other areas of their lives will, in any case, demand jobs which are psychologically fulfilling.

- High performance work organisations will therefore increasingly need to design (or enable their workers to design) jobs that provide variety, scope for initiative and autonomy and empower jobholders.

Noon and Blyton (2002) group these arguments under the heading of the 'upskilling thesis'. These writers go on, however, to question the extent to which this thesis is borne out in practice, proposing that there remain very wide differences both in terms of the range of tasks undertaken by workers and the degree of autonomy experienced across the labour market.

A contingency approach to the area, while recognising the value of 'humanising' jobs, would suggest that different models of job design are appropriate in different situations. For example we should critically address the proposition that work has largely become more 'intelligent'. A large-scale research project, carried out by Professor Peter Nolan into work patterns in the UK, identified a more complex and subtle picture. Nolan (quoted in Wignall, 2004) records that 'we still have 10.5 million manual workers in this country. That's 40 per cent of the workforce. They're in warehouses, filling envelopes, filling shelves. Stacking shelves is something like the eighth quickest growing occupation. . . . People think we now have a service economy where everyone sits at a computer, and that's just not true. Jobs are being created by new technologies, but those jobs are the same kind of jobs that people were doing before.'

It is not the intention here to dismiss the possibility that all jobs can be enriched or made more customer-focused. This is certainly true to an extent and managers should continue to seek ways in which this may be achieved. However, one should recognise the role of rhetoric – or even hyperbole – in some literature in this subject area, and the relatively unchanging nature of many people's work.

One can also put forward a view that organisational effectiveness can be achieved through different models and indeed conceptions of organisational design. The fast food sector provides a notable example of continuing simplification of tasks, albeit within a teamworking framework. Here we have classical contingency principles operating – that is, the optimal structure of the organisation will all depend on the level of predictability required (both product and service) hierarchical relationships and the expectations of a workforce, many of whom in this case may have only short-term plans regarding their work and employment. In contrast, the nature of organisations and work in other sectors may lend itself far more easily to flat structures or even adhocracies, encouraging greater initiative and autonomy on the part of jobholders. Organisational design remains an important area. As Clegg (2009:528) notes: 'Organisation design matters just as much as any other kind of design. . . Ugly organisation design produces bad managing.'

As we saw in Chapter 7, it has been argued that organisations should seek to implement and maintain functional flexibility, this concept encompassing job rotation, multi-skilling and, where appropriate, teamworking as part of an overall strategy of flexibility or adaptability. Other aspects of flexibility included numerical flexibility, the precursor of many instances of downsizing, and financial flexibility which, in an attempt to control salary costs, has seen numerous examples of subcontracting work, zero hours contracts and even the wholesale movement of jobs to other parts of the world. However, even this seemingly inexorable logic may be contingent on particular circumstances. Clark (1993) suggests that there might be instances where workers' specialist knowledge is perceived as sufficiently important to justify retaining and bolstering it. The same author also notes that a worker's commitment to high quality work can emanate from a feeling of 'ownership' of that work or job. There is, in conclusion, a range of strategic choices available to organisational decision-makers when approaching the area of both organisational and job design.

KEY LEARNING POINTS

- People's experience of work is affected by the organisational arrangements in which they operate and the nature of the work they do.

- A variety of organisational structure models have been put forward in order to enhance performance.

- Job redesign emphasises increasing the scope of jobs in order to increase efficiency and foster high levels of worker motivation.

- Large numbers of people continue to work in jobs designed under principles of 'Taylorism' or scientific management.

- A contingency approach to both organisational and job design, stressing the importance of recognising situational factors, is recommended.

REVIEW QUESTIONS

1. Provide a list of five advantages of the bureaucratic model of structure, and five disadvantages.

2. With reference to real-world examples, assess the usefulness of the contingency approach to organisational design.

3. Assess the importance of job design within the overall process of managing people. Give reasons for your answer.

4. How strong is the evidence that meaningful work will motivate a workforce?

EXPLORE FURTHER

Hackman, J. R. and Oldham, G. R. (1980) *Work Redesign*. New York: Addison-Wesley. Read this source text for an in-depth discussion of how job characteristics can affect workers' attitudes.

Watson, T. J. (2006) *Organising and Managing Work*. Harlow: FT Prentice Hall. Chapter 8 provides an interesting wide-ranging summary of issues relevant to job – and work – design, illuminated by cases and conversations deriving from the author's own research.

Grey, C. (2009) *A Very Short, Fairly Interesting and Reasonably Cheap Book About Studying Organizations*, 2nd ed. London: Sage. This book provides a thought-provoking and entertaining account of the development and application of many of the principles dealt with in this chapter.

CHAPTER 9

Recruitment and Selection

Ray French *and* Sally Rumbles

LEARNING OUTCOMES

After reading this chapter, you should be able to:

- comprehend the potential importance of recruitment and selection in successful people management and leadership

- identify aspects of recruitment and selection which are needed to avoid critical failure factors

- understand recruitment and selection policies and procedures which are said to be asociated with high performance, commitment and successful organisational outcomes

- evaluate selection methods according to criteria of professionalism including reliability, validity and fairness

- appreciate the links between recruitment and selection and other activites which integrate workers within an organisation and ensure their longer-term successful working.

OVERVIEW

In this chapter we examine the important role of recruitment and selection within the process of leading, managing and developing people. Recruitment and selection is pivotal in this regard in certain important respects. At the most basic level our focus in this book is on people management within the employment relationship. Those charged with recruiting people to posts in work organisations take a crucial 'gatekeeper' role; only those people selected for employment can be led, managed and developed. So in the most fundamental sense the decision to employ (or not) underpins the whole area of managing people. Issues associated with exclusion from the workplace also highlight the need for professionalism, fairness and ethical behaviour on the part of those engaged in this activity.

Recruitment and selection also has an important role to play in ensuring worker performance and positive organisational outcomes. It is often claimed that selection of workers occurs not just to replace departing employees or add to a workforce but rather aims to put in place workers who can perform at a high level and demonstrate commitment (Ballantyne, 2009). We will elaborate on the sometimes complex linkages between recruitment and selection and performance later in this chapter.

Recruitment and selection is characterised finally by potential difficulties and it is necessary to keep abreast of developments in research in the field. Research from the CIPD (2009a), for example, concluded that organisations should increasingly be inclusive in their employment offering as younger generations have grown up with the notion of flexible working, while older people have an interest in flexible working as an alternative to retirement. This is just one example of how current research can inform practice and also shows the critical importance of the social context in which recruitment and selection takes place.

INTRODUCTION

Recruitment and selection forms a core part of the central activities underlying human resource management: namely, the aquisition, development and reward of workers. It frequently forms an important part of the work of human resource managers – or designated specialists within work organisations. However, and importantly, recruitment and selection decisions are often for good reason taken by non-specialists, by the line managers. There is, therefore, an important sense in which it is the responsibility of all managers, and where human resource departments exist, it may be that HR managers play more of a supporting advisory role to those people who will supervise or in other ways work with the new employee.

As Mullins (2010, p 485) notes: 'If the HRM function is to remain effective, there must be consistently good levels of teamwork, plus ongoing co-operation and consultation between line managers and the HR manager.' This is most definitely the case in recruitment and selection as specialist HR managers (or even external consultants) can be an important repository of up-to-date knowledge and skills, for example on the important legal dimensions of this area.

Recruitment and selection is often presented as a planned rational activity, comprising certain sequentially-linked phases within a process of *employee resourcing,* which itself may be located within a wider HR management strategy. Bratton and Gold (2007, p 239) differentiate the two terms while establishing a clear link between them in the following way:

> 'Recruitment is the process of generating a pool of capable people to apply for employment to an organisation. Selection is the process by which managers and others use specific instruments to choose from a pool of applicants a person or persons more likely to succeed in the job(s), given management goals and legal requirements.'

In setting out a similar distinction in which recruitment activities provide a pool of people eligible for selection, Foot and Hook (2005, p 63) suggest that:

> 'although the two functions are closely connected, each requires a separate range of skills and expertise, and may in practice be fulfilled by different staff members. The recruitment activity, but not normally the selection decision, may be outsourced to an agency. It makes sense, therefore, to treat each activity separately.'

Recruitment and selection, as defined here, can play a pivotally important role in shaping an organisation's effectiveness and performance, if work organisations are able to acquire workers who already possess relevant knowledge, skills and aptitudes and are also able to make an accurate prediction regarding their future abilities. If we accept this premise (which will be questioned to some extent in this chapter), recruiting and selecting staff in an effective manner can both avoid undesirable costs – for example those associated with high staff turnover, poor performance and dissatisfied customers – and engender a mutually beneficial employment relationship characterised, wherever possible, by high commitment on both sides.

A TOPICAL AND RELEVANT AREA

Recruitment and selection is a topical area. While it has always had the capacity to form a key part of the process of managing and leading people as a routine part of organisational life, it is suggested here that recruitment and selection has become ever more important as organisations increasingly regard their workforce as a source of competitive advantage. Of course, not all employers engage with this proposition even at the rhetorical level. However, there is evidence of increased interest in the utilisation of employee selection methods which are valid, reliable and fair. For example, it has been noted that 'over several decades, work psychology has had a significant influence on the way people are recruited into jobs, through rigorous development and evaluation of personnel selection procedures' (Arnold *et al*, 2005, p 135). In this chapter we will examine several contemporary themes in recruitment and selection including what is human as the competency approach and online recruitment.

Recruitment and selection does not operate in a vacuum, insulated from wider social trends, so it is very important to keep abreast of current research. A CIPD annual survey report, *Recruitment, Retention and Turnover* (2009d), showed how the financial crisis was biting in the field of HRM. The survey concluded that half of the companies surveyed claimed that the recession was having a negative impact on their employee resourcing budgets and activities. 56 per cent of organisations were focusing more on retaining than recruiting talent, while four out of ten said that they would recruit fewer people in the forthcoming year. Interestingly, 72 per cent of respondents thought that employers would 'use the downturn' as an opportunity to get rid of poor performers and bring about culture change. These specific findings epitomise the very close link between recruitment and selection and the wider social and economic context.

This aspect of employee resourcing is characterised, however, by potential difficulties. Many widely-used selection methods – for example, interviewing – are generally perceived to be unreliable as a predictor of jobholders' performance in reality. Thus it is critically important to obtain a realistic evaluation of the process from all concerned, including both successful and unsuccessful candidates. There are ethical issues around selecting 'appropriate', and by implication rejecting 'inappropriate', candidates for employment. Many organisations seek to employ people who will 'fit in' with their organisation's culture (French *et al*, 2008) – see also the IKEA case study below. This may be perfectly understandable. However, it carries important ethical overtones – for example, whether an employing organisation should be involved in shaping an individual's identity. We put forward the view in this chapter that, notwithstanding the moral issues and practical difficulties outlined here, recruitment and selection is one area where it is possible to distinguish policies and practices associated with critical success factors and performance differentiators which, in turn, impact on organisational effectiveness in significant ways.

 WHY WORK AT IKEA?

CASE STUDY

The following extracts are taken from the IKEA Group corporate website 'Why work at IKEA?' section.

Because of our values, our culture and the endless opportunities, we believe that it's important to attract, develop and inspire our people. We are continuously investing in our co-workers and give them sufficient opportunities and responsibility to develop.

What would it be like to work at ikea?

You'd be working for a growing global company that shares a well-defined and well-communicated vision and business idea.

You'd be able to develop your skills in many different ways, becoming an expert at your daily work, by taking new directions in other parts of the company, or by taking on greater responsibility, perhaps even in another country.

Human values and team spirit are part of the work environment. You'd not only have fun at work, you'd be able to contribute to the development of others.

At IKEA you'd be rewarded for making positive contributions.

You'd have the chance to grow and develop together with the company.

Values at the heart of our culture

The people and the values of IKEA create a culture of informality, respect, diversity and real opportunities for growth. These values include:

Togetherness and enthusiasm

This means we respect our colleagues and help each other in difficult times. We look for people who are supportive, work well in teams and are open with each other in the way they talk, interact and connect. IKEA supports this attitude with open-plan offices and by laying out clear goals that co-workers can stand behind.

Humbleness

More than anything this means respect. We are humble towards our competitors, respecting their proficiency, and realising that we constantly have to be better than they are to keep our market share. It also means that we respect our co-workers and their views, and have respect for the task we have set ourselves.

Willpower

Willpower means first agreeing on mutual objectives and then not letting anything actually stand in the way of actually achieving them. In other words, it means we know exactly what we want, and our desire to get it should be irrepressible.

Simplicity

Behind this value are ideas like efficiency, common-sense and avoiding complicated solutions. Simple habits, simple actions and a healthy aversion to status symbols are part of IKEA.

Source: www.ikea.com. Used with the kind permission of IKEA.

Questions

1. In what ways could an employer seek to assess qualities of togetherness, humbleness, willpower and simplicity among candidates in the course of a recruitment and selection process? How accurate do you think judgements made along these lines are likely to be?

2. What selection methods could IKEA employ to assess whether potential workers can 'develop skills' and 'take on new directions and responsibilities'?

3. To what extent should an organisation like IKEA attempt to recruit and select workers who embody their organisational culture? Give reasons for your answer. Identify some possible negative outcomes of aligning selection with organisational culture.

EFFECTIVE RECRUITMENT AND SELECTION

We have already referred to the potential importance of recruitment and selection as an activity. Pilbeam and Corbridge (2006, p 142) provide a useful overview of potential positive and negative aspects noting that: 'The recruitment and selection of employees is fundamental to the functioning of an organisation, and there are compelling reasons for getting it right. Inappropriate selection decisions reduce organisational effectiveness, invalidate reward and development strategies, are frequently unfair on the individual recruit and can be distressing for managers who have to deal with unsuitable employees.'

REFLECTIVE ACTIVITY

Getting it wrong

In an attempt to check the robustness of security procedures at British airports, Anthony France, a reporter for *The Sun* newspaper, obtained a job as a baggage handler with a contractor subsequently named by the newspaper. In the course of his selection, France gave bogus references, and provided a fake home address and bank details. Throughout the selection process he lied about his past while details of his work as an undercover journalist were available on the Internet.

France then proceeded to take fake explosive material onto a holiday jet airliner at Birmingham International Airport.

This case provides a good, albeit extreme, example of the possible consequences of flawed selection procedures, or as happened here, when agreed practices, such as checking personal details, are not put into effect. Such consequences are potentially wide-ranging and veer from the trivial and comic to possibly tragic outcomes. One can certainly reasonably anticipate many of the negative outcomes listed below to follow when the predictions made about a candidate for employment fail to be borne out.

It is undoubtedly true that recruitment and selection strategies and practices have important consequences for all concerned, so what are the keys to maximising the chances of effective recruitment and selection? Some important factors are listed below.

RECOGNISING THE POWER OF PERCEPTION

Perception is defined as the process by which humans receive, organise and make sense of the information they receive from the outside world (Buchanan and Huczynski, 2007; French *et al,* 2008; and Rollinson, 2008). The quality or accuracy of our perceptions will have a major impact on our response to a situation. There is much data suggesting that when we perceive other people – particularly in an artificial and time-constrained situation like a job interview – we can make key mistakes, sometimes at a subliminal level. One key to enhancing effectiveness in recruitment and selection, therefore, lies in an appreciation of some core principles of interpersonal perception and, in particular, of some common potential mistakes in this regard.

- Selective perception. Our brains cannot process all of the information which our senses pick up so we instead select particular objects – or aspects of people – for attention. We furthermore attribute positive or negative characteristics to the stimuli: known as the 'halo' and 'horns' effect respectively. For example, an interviewee who has a large coffee stain on their clothing, but is otherwise well-presented, may have difficulty creating a positive overall impression despite the fact that it might be that their desire for the new job that resulted in nervousness and clumsiness.

- Self-centred bias. A recruiter should avoid evaluating a candidate by reference to himself or herself because this may be irrelevant to the post in question and run the risks of a 'clone effect' in a changing business environment. The sentence 'I was like you 15 years ago' may be damaging in a number of respects and should not be the basis for employment in most situations.

- Early information bias. We often hear apocryphal stories of interview panels making very early decisions on candidates' suitability and spending the remaining time confirming that decision. Mythical though some of these tales may be, there is a danger of over-prioritising early events – a candidate who trips over when entering an interview room may thus genuinely be putting themselves at a disadvantage.

- Stereotyping. This is a common short cut to understanding an individual's attributes, which is a difficult and time-consuming process, because we are all unique and complex beings. The logic of stereotyping attributes individuals' characteristics to those of a group they belong to – for example, the view that because Italians are considered to be emotional, an individual Italian citizen will be too. Stereotypes might contain elements of truth; on the other hand they may be entirely false since we are all unique. Everyone is different from everyone else. Stereotyping may well be irrelevant, therefore, and if acted on, also discriminatory.

It should be stressed that these, and other, perceptual errors are not inevitable and can be overcome. Many HR professionals study subjects like organisational behaviour as part of their career qualifications in which they are made aware of the dangers of inaccurate perception. Nonetheless, it remains the case that an understanding of this subject area is an important building block to effective recruitment and selection.

TAKING A STAGED APPROACH

Much prescriptive writing on recruitment and selection advocates viewing the process as sequential with distinct and inter-linked stages. This model is referred to as the *resourcing cycle*. The resourcing cycle begins with the identification of a vacancy and ends when the successful candidate is performing the job to an acceptable standard: ie post-selection. It is a two-way process. Organisations are evaluating candidates for a vacancy, but candidates also observe the organisation as a prospective employer. Conducting the process in a professional and timely manner is necessary for normal effectiveness in helping to ensure that not only is the 'best' candidate attracted to apply and subsequently accepts the post, but also that unsuccessful candidates can respect the decision made and possibly apply for future vacancies, along with other suitable candidates.

The first step in the recruitment process is to decide that there is a vacancy to be filled. Increasingly a more strategic and questioning approach may be taken. If, for example, the vacancy arises because an employee has left, managers may take the opportunity to review the work itself and consider whether it could be undertaken in an alternative way. For example, could the work be done on a part-time, job-share or flexi-time basis? Alternatively, could the job could be automated? The financial services sector in the UK provides one example of where technological developments have resulted in both significant job losses and changed patterns of work since 1990.

On the assumption that a post does need to be filled it will be necessary to devise specifications. Whether a competency-based approach (this concept will be defined later in the chapter) or the more traditional method of formal job descriptions and person specifications is chosen, a CIPD report (2007c) notes that specifications need to reflect the duties and requirements of the job along with the skills, aptitudes, knowledge, experience, qualifications and personal qualities that are necessary to perform the job effectively. Consideration should also be given to how the recruiter intends to measure and elicit information regarding those skills. Are they essential to job performance or merely desirable, and can they be objectively measured?

ATTRACTING CANDIDATES

The next stage in the recruitment cycle is the attraction of candidates, as one important objective of a recruitment method is to produce an appropriate number of suitable candidates within reasonable cost constraints. Pilbeam and Corbridge (2006, p 151) note that 'There is no ideal number of applications and no intrinsic value in attracting a high volume of candidates.' Neither is there a single best way to recruit applicants. Rather the chosen recruitment medium needs to ensure that there are a sufficient number of suitably qualified candidates from which to make a selection without being overwhelmed with large numbers of unsuitable applications. Using a recruitment agency to find a small number of suitable candidates, particularly for senior or specialised posts, may prove a significantly more cost-effective and efficient method than a major advertising campaign which generates a large response from unsuitable candidates. The choice of method will also be influenced by the availability of candidates – that is, is there likely to be a shortage or surplus of candidates? For example, in the period around 2005 there was a large pool of Polish migrant workers wanting to work in Britain, but within four or five years this had significantly diminished as employers found some applicants were being more selective, while other potential Polish workers had returned home after the financial and economic crisis took hold in the UK after 2008.

REFLECTIVE ACTIVITY

Look at the recruitment section of your local newspaper. What sort of vacancies are typically advertised here? Compare and contrast these with the types of vacancies advertised in broadsheet newspapers such as *The Times* or *Daily Telegraph*. What indicators are there in the wording of advertisements as to whether there is a surplus or shortage of candidates?

Which method of recruitment should be adopted? There is no single best way, and a contingency approach involving an analysis of what might be effective in particular circumstances is advocated: ie 'it all depends'.

Some organisations, for example in the local government sector, will always advertise all vacancies to ensure equality of opportunity whilst manufacturing organisations tend to rely on recruitment agencies (CIPD, 2007c). Human resources professionals should carefully consider and review which methods have been most effective in the past and which method or methods would be most appropriate for the current vacancy. They should also, critically, keep new methods under review, including, for example, the growing trend towards Internet-based recruitment.

SELECTION

One of the last stages in recruitment and selection is selection itself, which includes the choice of methods by which an employer reduces a short-listed group following the recruitment stage, leading to an employment decision. For most people, this is the only visible stage of the resourcing cycle because their experience of it is likely to be as a subject – or candidate – rather than involvement in planning the entire process. While recruitment can be perceived as a positive activity generating an optimum number of job-seekers, selection is inherently negative in that it will probably involve rejection of applicants.

It would be prudent to argue that selection decisions should be based on a range of selection tools as some have poor predictive job ability. While it is almost inconceivable that employment would be offered or accepted without a face-to-face encounter, many organisations still rely almost exclusively on the outcome of interviews to make selection decisions.

To have any value, interviews should be conducted or supervised by trained individuals, be structured to follow a previously agreed set of questions mirroring the person specification or job profile, and allow candidates the opportunity to ask questions. The interview is more than a selection device. It is a mechanism that is capable of communicating information about the job and the organisation to the candidate, with the aim of giving a realistic job preview, providing information about the process, and thus can minimise the risk of job offers being rejected. Organisations seeking high performance in their selection processes should therefore give considerable attention to maximising the uses of the interview and, ideally, combine this method with other psychometric measures where appropriate.

VALIDITY OF SELECTION METHODS

It may appear self-evident that organisational decision-makers will wish to ensure that their recruitment (and in this case) selection methods are effective. We have already suggested, however, that making judgements on an individual's personal characteristics and suitability for future employment is inherently problematic and that many 'normal' selection methods contain significant flaws. There is also the question of what is meant by the terms 'reliability' and 'validity' when applied to recruitment and selection.

Reliability in the context of workforce selection can refer to the following issues:

- Temporal or 're-test' stability where the effectiveness of a selection tool is assessed by consistency of results obtained over time. An individual could for example complete a personality inventory or intelligence test at different times over a period of several years, although in the latter case it would be important to isolate the impact of repeated practice on results.

- Consistency – that is, does the test measure what it sets out to? Some elements of IQ tests have for example been criticised for emphasising a person's vocabulary which might in turn be influenced by their education and general background rather than by their innate intelligence.

Validity in this area is typically subdivided into the following aspects:

- Face validity has an emphasis on the acceptability of the selection measure, including to the candidate himself or herself. For example, it is possible (although extremely unlikely) that there is a correlation between a person's hat size and his/her job competence. However, you would be reluctant to measure candidates' heads as part of their selection due to their probable scepticism at the use of this measure.

- Content validity refers to the nature of the measure and in particular its adequacy as a tool. For example, the UK driving test could be criticised for not assessing ability in either night driving or travelling on motorways.

- Predictive validity centres on linkages between results or scores on a selection measure and subsequent outcome – most commonly, job performance at a future point. Here it is important to identify when the comparison will be made – ie immediately in the case of a simple job requiring little training, or more commonly, at an intermediate point, possibly after a suitable probationary period.

We argue here that validity, along with fairness, should be the overriding indicator of a selection method for high performance organisations and that it is important to obtain sophisticated data on validity in all its forms. Pilbeam and Corbridge (2006, p 173) provide a summary of the predictive validity of selection methods based on the findings of various research studies.

1.0	Certain prediction
0.9	
0.8	
0.7	Assessment centres for development
0.6	Skilful and structured interviews
0.5	Work sampling
	Ability tests
0.4	Assessment centres for job performance
	Biodata
	Personality assessment
0.3	Unstructured interviews
0.2	
0.1	References
0.0	Graphology
	Astrology

However, they suggest that these validity measures should be treated with caution because they can be affected by the performance indicators used, and by the way the tools were applied. They indicate nonetheless both variability between measures and some overall degree of uncertainty when predicting future work performance during the selection process.

While it is recommended that validity should be the prime factor in choosing selection tools, it would be naïve not to recognise that other factors such as cost and applicability may be relevant. How practical, therefore, is it to conduct any particular measure? As indicated earlier, an organisation aiming for high performance is recommended to adopt valid measures as opposed to merely practical or less costly ones. Again, one should recognise that recruitment and selection is contingent upon other factors such as the work itself. A 'high performance' organisation in the fast-food industry may legitimately decide not to adopt some relatively valid but expensive methods when selecting fast-food operatives. It should be noted that the oft-derided method of interviewing can in reality be a relatively valid method if conducted skilfully and structured.

RECRUITMENT AND SELECTION: ART OR SCIENCE?

Systematic models of recruitment and selection based on a resourcing cycle should not necessarily imply that this process is underpinned by scientific reasoning and method. As we have seen, Pilbeam and Corbridge note that even the most valid methods fall some way short of complete predictive validity. Thompson and McHugh (2009) go further, taking a critical view on the general use and, in particular, the validity of employee selection methods. In commenting on the use of personality tests in selection, these authors state that in utilising such tests employers are essentially 'clutching at straws' and on this basis will probably use anything that will help them make some kind of systematic decision. These authors identify now discredited selection methods, such as the use of polygraphs to detect lying and other methods such as astrology, which are deemed more appropriate in some cultures than in others. It is indeed important to keep in mind that today's received wisdom in the area of recruitment and selection, just as in the management canon more generally, may be criticised and even widely rejected in the future.

The process of recruitment and selection continues nonetheless to be viewed as best carried out via sequential but linked stages of first gathering a pool of applicants, a screening-out process, followed by the positive step of actual selection. This apparently logical ordering of the activities is largely viewed as essential to achieve minimum thresholds of effectiveness.

INDUCTION AND TRANSITION

It is not always the case that selected employees are immediately capable of performing to the maximum level on their allotted job(s): important stages in the resourcing cycle occur post-selection. Many organisations when selecting are making a longer-term prediction of a new employee's capability. This accounts for many organisations' imposing a probationary period in which employees' performance and future potential can be assessed in the work setting. The resourcing cycle extends into this post-selection phase and the induction period and early phases of employment constitute a critically important part of both successful integration into the workplace culture and development as a fully functioning worker. The final stage of the resourcing cycle involves evaluation of the process and reflection on lessons learned from the process and their implications for the future.

RECRUITMENT COSTS

A concern with effectiveness in recruitment and selection becomes all the more important when one considers the costs of getting things wrong. We begin with apparent costs, which centre on the direct costs of recruitment procedures, but one might also consider the so-called opportunity costs of engaging in repeated recruitment and selection when workers leave an organisation. An excessive preoccupation with recruitment and selection will divert a manager from other activites he or she could usefully be engaged in. It is also useful to consider the 'investment', including training resources, lost to the employer when a worker leaves prematurely. The CIPD survey report *Recruitment, Retention and Turnover* (2009d) estimates the average direct cost of recruitment per individual in the UK in 2009 as £4,000 – increasing to £6,125 when organisations are also calculating the associated labour turnover costs. For workers in the managerial and professional category, these costs were considerably higher: £7,750, rising to £11,000.

Implicit costs are less quantifiable and include the following categories:

- poor performance
- reduced productivity
- low-quality products or services
- dissatisfied customers or other stakeholders
- low employee morale.

The implicit costs mentioned here are, in themselves, clearly undesirable outcomes in all organisations. In high-performing organisations 'average' or 'adequate' performance may also be insufficient and recruitment and selection may be deemed to have failed unless workers have become 'thinking performers'.

CONTEMPORARY THEMES IN RECRUITMENT AND SELECTION

THE COMPETENCY APPROACH

Typically, decisions on selecting a potential worker are made primarily with a view to taking on the most appropriate person to do a particular job in terms of their current or, more commonly, potential competencies. In recent years this concept has been extended to search for workers who are 'flexible' and able to contribute to additional and/or changing job roles. This approach contrasts with a more traditional model which involves first compiling a wide-ranging job description for the post in question, followed by the use of a person specification, which in effect forms a checklist along which candidates can be evaluated on criteria such as knowledge, skills and personal qualities. This traditional approach, in essence, involves matching characteristics of an 'ideal' person to fill a defined job. There is a seductive logic in this apparently rational approach. However, there are in-built problems in its application if judgements of an individual's personality are inherently subjective and open to error and, furthermore, if these personal characteristics are suited to present rather than changing circumstances.

The competencies model in contrast, seeks to identify abilities needed to perform a job well rather than focusing on personal characteristics such as politeness or assertiveness. Torrington *et al* (2008, p 170) identify some potentially important advantages of referring to competencies in this area noting that:

> 'they can be used in an integrated way for selection, development, appraisal and reward activities; and also that from them behavioural indicators can be derived against which assessment can take place.'

Competency-based models are becoming increasingly popular in graduate recruitment where organisations are making decisions on future potential. Farnham and Stevens (2000) found that managers in the public sector increasingly viewed traditional job descriptions and person specifications as archaic, rigid and rarely an accurate reflection of the requirements of the job. There is increasing evidence that this popularity is more widespread. A CIPD report (2007c) found that 86 per cent of organisations surveyed were now using competency-based interviews in some way; and in another survey, over half of employers polled had started using them in the past year (William, 2008). It is suggested that the competency-based model may be a more meaningful way of underpinning recruitment and selection in the current fast-moving world of work and can accordingly contribute more effectively to securing high performance.

FLEXIBILITY AND TEAMWORK

Many commentators refer to significant changes in the world of work and the implications these have for the recruitment and selection of a workforce. Searle (2003, p 276) notes that:

> 'Increasingly employees are working in self-organised teams in which it is difficult to determine the boundaries between different jobholders' responsibilities. The team undertakes the task and members co-operate and work together to achieve it. Recruitment and selection practices focus on identifying a suitable person for the job, but . . . isolating a job's roles and responsibilities may be difficult to do in fast-changing and team-based situations.'

There is here an implication both that teamworking skills could usefully be made part of employee selection and also that an individual's job specification should increasingly be designed and interpreted flexibly. It can plausibly be posited that we now inhabit a world of work in which unforeseen problems are thrown up routinely and on an ongoing basis and where there is seldom time to respond to them in a measured fashion (Linstead *et al*, 2009). In this type of business environment, decisions made can be 'rational' in terms of past practice and events but may in fact be revealed to be flawed or even obsolete when they are made in the new context.

If we accept this analysis of work in the 21st century, there is therefore an implication that organisations aiming for high performance may need to use selection methods which assess qualities of flexibility and creative thinking (irrespective of whether they are using a traditional or competency recruitment and selection model). Of course, many jobs may still require task-holders to work in a predictable and standardised way, so one should exercise caution when examining this rhetoric. Interestingly, however, recruitment and selection practices should themselves be kept under constant review if we accept the reality of a business world characterised by discontinuous, rather than incremental, change.

CASE STUDY

AN ALTERNATIVE APPROACH: 'TALENT PUDDLES' AT NESTLÉ

Many organisations are faced with the problem of how to create a pool of talent from which to select candidates. Jobs requiring specialist skills and knowledge can often take several months and considerable costs to fill, yet often suitable candidates have slipped through the organisations net because there wasn't a vacancy at that particular time. Creating 'talent pools' or databases of good applicants is one way organisations have tried to keep potential candidates interested but in many cases this has been no more than keeping CVs on file which are never referred to or seen again. Nestlé, the large global food and beverage manufacturer, has taken a more radical approach to managing talent by creating 'talent puddles'. Whilst these are similar to talent pools, Nestlé's approach has focused on creating a talent bank in specific areas of the business where there is a shortage of skilled applicants. Talent puddles focus on 'talent gaps' – specific jobs and difficult-to-fill roles – by creating a small puddle of talent that can be readily brought into the business, thus reducing the costs and speeding up the recruitment process.

The initiative began with the supply chain function which now contains 120 shortlisted candidates and has placed eight people but has since been extended to other areas of the business. This approach to resourcing has also changed the recruiters' role. A significant portion of their time is now spent calling people and sifting through CVs from the talent puddle. When people apply, recruiters look at the quality of the applications and assess what level/grade they are operating at, ranking and recording them accordingly. Candidates are met and interviewed by the recruitment team and line managers before being placed in the talent puddle. One could argue that in effect the organisation has created its own internal recruitment agency and there is no doubt that this approach has significantly reduced the company's reliance on recruitment agencies over the past five years. However, just like recruitment agencies, one could also question how you keep 120 highly skilled potential candidates interested if you don't have an actual vacancy.

Adapted from CIPD Annual Survey Report 2007(c) *Recruitment, Retention and Turnover*, p 10. London: CIPD.

RECRUITING IN THE VIRTUAL WORLD

The rise in the use of the Internet is probably the most significant development in the recruitment field in the early 21st century. Various surveys (CIPD, 2007c; IRS, 2008) now suggest that this is fast becoming employers' preferred way of attracting applicants. For example, 75 per cent of companies are now using their corporate website as their most common method (along with local newspaper advertising) of attracting candidates (CIPD, 2007). There is, however, little evidence that the Internet produces better-quality candidates, but it does deliver more of them and more employers report that online recruitment made it easier to find the right candidate (Crail, 2007). Candidates themselves are increasingly choosing this medium to search for jobs, with 89 per cent of graduates only searching online for jobs (Reed Employment, reported in *People Management*, 20 March 2008).

The benefits of online recruitment to employers include the speed, reduced administrative burden and costs, and no geographical limits. The benefits to applicants are that it is easier, faster and more convenient to post a CV or search a job site online than to read a selection of printed media (Whitford, 2003). This is all very well if you have skills that are highly in demand, but if employers are tending to post vacancies on their own websites, candidates still have to trawl the web in order to find vacancies and even 'web savvy' applicants may be deterred by the perceived impersonal nature of online recruitment. Also there are still some people who are either not comfortable using the Internet or do not have ready access to a computer. Thus there is still a role then for conventional advertising (IDS, 2006).

Whatever the pros and cons, online recruitment continues to expand and employers are now combining more traditional methods with online recruitment by using printed adverts to refer jobseekers to an Internet vacancy (Murphy, 2008). Other employers such as Microsoft are enhancing its brand visibility and credibility by having a wider Internet recruitment presence. Microsoft uses its online tools to impact and influence its public image and reach a broader audience and thus create a diverse workplace with varied skills and talents. One initiative is the introduction of 'corporate recruitment blogs'. The idea is that potential job candidates may be attracted to the company through what they see on the blog and make contact through the specific blogger who will initiate the recruitment process on behalf of the company (Hasson, 2007). See also the Cadbury Schweppes example below.

REFLECTIVE ACTIVITY

Is online chat the way forward with recruitment?

Graduates today have a higher expectation of being able to use social networking as a primary source of information and communication. In response to this Cadbury Schweppes launched its 2008 UK graduate recruitment campaign with a new online chatroom to give potential applicants the chance to interact with the company's current graduates. The confectionary giant has created an easy-to-use site that allows potential graduates the opportunity to chat online and put questions to its graduate recruitment team. The site builds on the success the company had with its graduate blogs in 2005 and MP3 downloads in 2006. Chatroom sessions are advertised on the firm's graduate recruitment calendar and the team have about eight hours of online dedicated chat to interested graduates (Berry, 2007). Would you use an employer's chatroom?

FAIRNESS IN RECRUITMENT AND SELECTION

One factor shared by both traditional and competence models of recruitment and selection is that both are framed by an imperative to take on the most appropriate person in terms of their contribution to organisational performance. This is, of course, unsurprising given the preoccupation of organisations in all sectors with meeting objectives and targets. However, when we consider what is meant by making appropriate selection decisions, other factors, including fairness, can also be seen to be important.

Decisions made in the course of a recruitment and selection process should be perceived as essentially fair and admissible to all parties, including people who have been rejected. There is evidence to support the view that applicants are concerned with both procedural justice – that is, how far they felt that selection methods were related to a job and the extent to which procedures were explained to them – and distributive justice, where their concern shifts to how equitably they felt they were treated and whether the outcome of selection was perceived to be fair (see Gilliland, 1993).

Fairness in this regard can be linked to the actual selection methods used. Anderson *et al* (2001) found that interviews, résumés, and work samples were well-regarded methods, while handwriting tests (graphology) were held in low regard. Personality and ability tests received an 'intermediate' evaluation. This is linked to the concept of face validity: how plausible and valid does the method used appear to the candidate under scrutiny? It is reasonable to suggest that employers should take care in choosing selection methods in order to maintain credibility among applicants as well, of course, as assessing the predictive value of the methods.

Fairness in selection also extends to the area of discrimination and equal opportunities, as we saw in Chapter 4. In the UK, for example, current legislation is intended to make unlawful discrimination on the grounds of age, race, nationality or ethnic origin, disability, sex, marital status and sexual orientation. The law identifies both direct discrimination, where an individual is treated less favourably on the sole grounds of their membership of a group covered in the relevant legislation, and indirect discrimination which occurs when a provision applied to both groups disproportionately affects one in reality. The Equality and Human Rights Commission highlights headhunting as one area in which indirect discrimination may occur. Headhunters may, in approaching individuals already in jobs, contravene this aspect of the law if existing jobs are dominated by one sex or ethnic group, for example. Compliance with equal opportunities legislation provides one example of performance infrastructure and would, it is surmised, reap business benefits – ie recruiting from the truly qualified labour pool and avoiding negative outcomes such as costly and reputation-damaging legal processes.

High-performance organisations may seek to go beyond the compliance approach and work towards a policy or even strategy of managing diversity (see also Chapter 11). As defined by the CIPD (2006) a managing diversity approach:

> 'is about ensuring that all employees have an opportunity to maximise their potential and enhance their self-development and their contribution to the organisation. It recognises that people from different backgrounds can bring fresh ideas and perceptions, which can make the way work is done more efficient and make products and services better. Managing diversity successfully will help organisations to nurture creativity and innovation and thereby to tap hidden capacity for growth and improved competiveness.'

It is thus important to ensure such a policy is operationalised in the field of recruitment and selection because staff involved in this activity can be said to act as 'gatekeepers' of an organisation.

OPPORTUNITIES FOR ALL AT ASDA

CASE STUDY

The following statement is an extract from the 'Opportunities for All' section of Asda's corporate website, accessed September 2004.

At Asda we endeavour to discriminate only on ability and we recognise that our organisation can be effective if we have a diverse colleague base, representing every section of society.

We want to recruit colleagues and managers who represent the communities in which we operate and the customers we serve.

Ethnic minorities

We have been working at all levels to make sure that ethnic minorities are represented across all levels of our business and we operate a policy of Religious Festival Leave so that any colleague can apply to take up to two days unpaid leave to attend their Religious Festival.

Women

We recognise that there are mutual benefits in making sure we employ women in our workplace. Besides our equal opportunities recruitment policy we have a number of other initiatives which support our commitment, particularly our flexible working practices which include job shares and part time working at all levels, parental leave, shift swaps and career breaks.

Disability

It is our aim to make sure that our stores are accessible for disabled people to both work and shop in. As a company we have been awarded the Two Tick symbol and we have a good working partnership with Remploy and we work together to help disabled people get back into the work place. We offer people with disabilities a working environment which is supportive and we operate an equal opportunities policy on promotion.

If, due to your disability, you need some help whether completing your application form or during the interview process, please contact the people manager in your local store or depot who will be pleased to help.

Age

The proportion of older people in the population is steadily increasing and we're seeing this reflected in the age profile of our workforce. We want to encourage the recruitment and retention of older, experienced colleagues, many of whom welcome the opportunity to work beyond the traditional retirement age, to work flexibly and enjoy a phased retirement.

We've been encouraging stores and depots to recruit more mature colleagues or 'Goldies' and in one new store in Broadstairs we opened with over 40 per cent of our colleagues aged 50 or over. And we have seen a reduction in both labour turnover and absence well below average in the store.

To further reinforce our commitment we also offer a number of flexible working schemes such as Benidorm Leave where older colleagues can take three months unpaid leave between January and March, or grandparents leave where colleagues who are grandparents take up to a week off unpaid to look after a new arrival.

Used with the kind permission of ASDA Ltd.

Questions

1. To what extent does this statement from Asda's website indicate that this organisation has a strategy for diversity management? What has led you to your conclusion?

2. How do Asda seek to safeguard their 'Opportunities for All' policy in the area of recruitment and selection? ·

3. Produce a statement for use by companies setting out employment policy in the area of age discrimination and indicate how this could take effect in the recruitment and selection of workers.

THE EXTENT OF PROFESSIONAL PRACTICE

SMALL AND MEDIUM-SIZED ENTERPRISES

There is evidence to suggest that many human resources management (HRM) practices often prescribed in the academic literature are more common in some sectors of business than others, and that the small and medium-sized enterprises (SME) group, in particular, are less likely to have in-house HR expertise and sophisticated systems in place (Cully *et al*, 1999). A study carried out by Cassell *et al* (2002) in SMEs in the north of England focused on both the use and perceived value (by employers) of a range of HRM procedures. In the area of recruitment and selection, only 31 per cent of firms in the sample used wide-ranging employee development and recruitment and selection procedures. Interestingly, 38 per cent of the sample questioned said that they did not use recruitment and selection procedures at all. In the companies that did make use of them, 50 per cent found that the procedures helped 'entirely' or 'a lot' in over half of the instances in which they are used. This is some way from the picture of widespread use and the assumed universal benefits conveyed in some sources.

The reality of the context faced by managers of SMEs will cause them to frame their responses in an entirely understandable way, and prescriptive 'textbook style' approaches may be viewed as inappropriate. It would, of course, be as damaging for SMEs as for any other organisation if a lack of 'high-quality' practices in recruitment and selection were seen to inhibit performance and, indeed, SMEs have often been criticised for the lack of a proactive and integrated approach to managing people. However, any assumption that universally applicable approaches to recruitment and selection are needed may ignore the distinctive processes and practices faced by particular organisations.

REFLECTIVE ACTIVITY

Lack of skills a major factor in UK recruitment and selection difficulties

A CIPD survey (2008c) reported that 86 per cent of British organisations were having difficulty filling vacancies in spite of the financial and economic crisis which hit in that year. In part, this was the result of a 'skills crunch' with 70 per cent of the research sample citing a lack of necessary candidate skills as the main reason for recruitment difficulties. However, only half of the surveyed companies had a formal resourcing strategy to counter the skills-gap problem and struggled to recruit top talent.

Deborah Fernon of the CIPD also pointed to the importance of the retention of talented workers, noting that 'Organisations should have a look at their learning and development strategies which can help met business demands in two ways. Firstly, those employers who have development opportunities are more likely to stay, which reduces turnover. Secondly, a good learning and development culture will foster a strong employer brand, helping to attract key talent.'

This research highlights the importance of referring to contemporary evidence when analysing recruitment and selection in general terms, and also points to the importance of the post-selection phase in retaining staff.

RECRUITMENT AND SELECTION: A CONTINGENCY APPROACH

The underlying principle that organisational policies and practices need to be shaped within a particular context is often referred to as the contingency approach. The argument put forward within this viewpoint is that successful policies and strategies are those which apply principles within the particular context faced by the unique organisation.

One example of a 'contingent factor' which can impact upon recruitment and selection is national culture. French (2010) draws attention to important cross-cultural differences in the area. For example, different cultures emphasise different attributes when approaching the recruitment and selection of employees. It is also the case that particular selection methods are used more or less frequently in different societies – see also Perkins and Shortland (2006). So in individualistic cultures such as the USA's and UK's, there is a preoccupation with selection methods which emphasise individual differences. Many psychometric tests can indeed be seen to originate from the USA. Furthermore, in a society which emphasises individual achievement as opposed to ascribed status (eg through age or gender), one might expect a raft of legislation prohibiting discrimination against particular groups. Here the expectation is that selection should be on the basis of individual personal characteristics or qualifications. This may contrast with more collectivist societies, for example China, where personal connections may assume a more prominent role. Bjorkman and Yuan (1999) conducted one of several studies which reached this overall conclusion. It may also be true that selection methods are given varying degrees of face validity in different societies. A CIPD survey (2004c) on graphology discovered that while relatively few companies in the UK used graphology as a trusted method of selecting employees, its adoption was far more widespread, common and therefore accepted in other countries, including France.

In summary, the contingency approach with the underlying message that managing people successfully depends on contextual factors – 'it all depends' – can readily be applied to the area of recruitment and selection. The increasingly large number of organisations operating across national boundaries, or who employ workers from different cultural backgrounds, can benefit from formulating policies within an awareness of cultural difference.

RECRUITMENT AND SELECTION AND ORGANISATIONAL CULTURE

It is unsurprising that the culture of a particular work organisation will influence selection decisions, with recruiters both consciously and unconsciously selecting those individuals who will 'best fit' that culture. In some organisations recruitment policy and practice is derived from their overall strategy which disseminates values into the recruitment and selection process. Mullins (2007, p 727) provides the example of Garden Festival Wales, an organisation created to run for a designated and short time-period. This organisation's managers were particularly concerned to create a culture via recruitment of suitable employees. This is an interesting example because this organisation had no prior history and it indicates the power of recruitment and selection in inculcating particular cultural norms.

Other research has demonstrated that individuals as well as organisations seek this 'best fit', providing evidence that many individuals prefer to work in organisations that reflect their personal values. Judge and Cable (1997) and Backhaus (2003) found that job-seekers may actively seek a good 'person-organisation fit' when considering prospective employers. This, of course, provides further support for the processual two-way model of recruitment and selection. However, justifying selection decisions on the basis of 'cultural fit' means that there are ethical issues to consider in terms of reasons for rejection: are organisations justified in determining who does and does not 'fit'? It may be that practical concerns also emerge – for example, in the danger of maintaining organisations in the image of current role models – which may be inappropriate in the future. Psychologists have also long recognised the threat posed by 'groupthink' where innovation is suppressed by a dominant group and an 'emperor's new clothes' syndrome develops, with individuals reluctant to voice objections to bad group decisions.

 REFLECTIVE ACTIVITY

Return to the IKEA case study at the start of this chapter.

IKEA put great stress upon recruiting employees who will complement their organisational culture.

● What are the potential benefits of selecting a workforce in terms of an organisation's culture?

● What are the philosophical and practical arguments against selection based on values and work culture?

CONCLUSION

This chapter indicates the key importance of recruitment and selection in successful people management and leadership. An awareness of issues and concepts within this area is an important tool for all those involved with leading, managing and developing people – even if they are not human resource managers *per se*. A recognition of the importance of this aspect of people management is not new, and 'success' in this field has often been linked with the avoidance of critical failure factors including undesirable levels of staff turnover and claims of discrimination from unsuccessful job applicants.

It has been argued here that it is also possible to identify aspects of recruitment and selection which link with critical success factors in the 21st century context, differentiating organisational performance and going some way to delivering employees who can act as 'thinking performers'. It is proposed, for example, that a competencies approach focusing on abilities needed to perform a job well may be preferable to the use of a more traditional matching of job and person specifications. In addition, many organisations may increasingly wish to identify qualities of flexibility and creative thinking among potential employees, although this may not always be the case; many contemporary jobs do not require such competencies on the part of jobholders. It is also the case that organisations should be preoccupied with the question of validity of selection methods, ideally combining methods which are strong on practicality and cost, such as interviewing, with other measures which are more effective predictors of performance. It is maintained, finally, that a managing diversity approach, welcoming individual difference, may enhance organisational performance and create a climate in which thinking performers can emerge and flourish.

However, it is maintained that a contingency approach to recruitment and selection, recognising that organisational policies and practices are shaped by contextual factors, remains valid, and that 'effectiveness' in recruitment and selection may vary according to particular situational factors. In this regard it is noted that cultural differences could be an important factor in predicting the relative success of recruitment and selection measures.

KEY LEARNING POINTS

- Managers involved in the recruitment and selection of workers have a key 'gatekeeper' role in giving or denying access to work.
- Effective recruitment and selection is characterised by a knowledge of social science topics such as perception.
- A staged logical approach to recruitment and selection, seeing it as a process, is recommended.
- We should examine the validity of different selection methods.
- Fairness is a fundamentally important principle reflecting the ethically-loaded nature of the activity.

REVIEW QUESTIONS

1. Indicate with examples three ways in which recruitment and selection policies and practices can be used by an organisation aiming to develop staff as part of a talent management strategy.

2. Evaluate the evidence regarding the potential validity of biodata and personality assessment as tools for selecting employees.

3. What do you understand by the contingency approach to recruitment and selection? Provide two examples, from academic sources or your own experience, to illustrate this approach.

EXPLORE FURTHER

Gilmore, S. and Williams, S. (2009) *Human Resource Management*. Oxford: Oxford University Press. Chapter 5 takes a themed approach to the topic of employee selection.

Thompson, P. and McHugh, D. (2009) *Work Organisations: A critical approach*, 4th ed. Basingstoke: Palgrave Macmillan. In Chapter 19 entitled 'Masks for Tasks', the authors take a critical perspective on the topics of how we assess others' attributes and how such perceptions are used in employee selection.

Arnold, J. *et al* (2005) *Work Psychology: Understanding human behaviour in the workplace* 4th ed. Harlow: FT Prentice Hall. Chapter 5 provides a clear and interesting discussion of different selection techniques and their validity.

CHAPTER 10

Developing Employees

Alex Tymon *and* Margaret Mackay

LEARNING OUTCOMES

After reading this chapter, you should be able to:

- explain the terms:

  — human resources development

  — learning, training and development

  — career management and career development

  — continuing professional development

- understand the organisational and economic need for development activities referring to contemporary debates and research

- identify where responsibility for development lies and why this is contested

- critique some of the more frequently-used development techniques

- explain the difference between career management and career development using three models

- identify the rationale for career development from an organisational and individual view

- evaluate the practice of continuing professional development.

OVERVIEW

The business case for investment in employee development is built on the need to sustain organisational performance, and adapt to a dynamic environment. The impact of a knowledge economy and resultant demand for a skilled workforce underpins the workplace as a critical learning environment. Proactive support for employee development differentiates an organisation's knowledge and skill capability. This is an offensive strategy for organisational growth, industry leadership and engagement of superior employee performance.

This chapter focuses on how individuals can adapt through learning, and expand their skill capability to deliver innovative practices, products and customer commitment. We begin by defining key concepts, before going on to highlight the evolving emphasis on work-based and individual learning – in contrast to more formal traditional training approaches. In this chapter, we also review perceptions of learning responsibility and talent development. This is mirrored through a shift from corporate career management to individual career development. The chapter ends by considering the promotion of continuing professional development (CPD) as key to building flexibility and agility.

INTRODUCTION

CREATING THE FUTURE AND ADAPTING TO CHANGE

Despite the tough operating conditions in the recent recession, it is interesting to note that many successful and well-known organisations actually increased their spend on learning, training and development, including PricewaterhouseCoopers, KPMG and Wyeth, who all appeared in the top five of the 2009 Training Top 125 (Freifeld, 2009). This tells us that developing employees is regarded as an essential organisational activity for success. According to Cho *et al* (2009, p 263), 'The success of tomorrow's most effective organisations will lie in their capacity to learn.'

The ways in which organisations develop their employees evolve in response to changes in the world of work, and these changes are making the task of developing employees increasingly challenging. For example: the top ten jobs in demand in 2010 did not even exist in 2004. Over the last ten years there have been twelve jobs created in knowledge industries for every one job created elsewhere (DCSF, 2009). Thus, organisations and individuals today may need a completely different skill set from that required just ten years ago, and will almost certainly need different or additional skills in the future.

However, it is not just organisations which need to be flexible and adaptable in their approach to learning and development. The Leitch Report (2006) highlighted the issues with skills shortages in the UK and the potential impact it could have on the economy and therefore society as a whole, suggesting that skilled and knowledgeable individuals who are able and willing to contribute were essential.

Above all, it will be the individual person for whom development is most important in the future. It is estimated that a school leaver in 2010 will have between ten and fourteen jobs by the time they are 38 years old, and by 2020 there will be five million fewer lower-skilled jobs in the UK (DCSF, 2009). Thus it will be increasingly rare for individuals to remain in the same occupation for their whole working life and certainly not in the same organisation. The employment security and success of individuals will increasingly depend upon continuous lifelong learning and skills flexibility. Taking responsibility for one's own development will be a necessity, with career management and continuing professional development growing in importance. It is therefore this need to be adaptable and flexible in learning that we have chosen to focus upon in this chapter.

DEFINITIONS OF KEY TERMS

We begin this chapter by defining some of the key terms which underpin developments and debates in the area of employee development.

HUMAN RESOURCE DEVELOPMENT (HRD)

In simple terms HRD can be viewed as developing the capabilities of people within an organisation in order to improve current and future efficiency, effectiveness and output.

There are many development methods, but the intended outcome is always learning and the application of learning. It is therefore valuable to consider what is really meant by the term 'learning' and how it happens.

LEARNING

Definitions of learning suggest it results in a relatively permanent change in behaviour (French *et al*, 2008) and comes about through the acquisition of new knowledge, skills and attitudes (KSA). A useful description of these terms can be found in Gold *et al* (2010, pp 109–114).

However, with this definition of learning there are several caveats which should be considered because they make a difference for the HRD practitioner, three of which are:

Caveat 1: Behaviour change as a result of learning may not be visible or sustained.

Employees may, via the process of learning, have changed their capabilities and motivation, but what if the opportunity to use them is missing? Does a lack of visible behaviour change mean that learning has not occurred? For those involved in HRD, this issue of opportunity to use new learning or a transfer of learning is a vital part of the process and as such is discussed more fully later in this chapter.

Caveat 2: The change in behaviour as a result of learning may not always be positive or desired.

The concept that all learning is good is not necessarily the case with adult learners. Employees learn short cuts and poor behaviour when they join an organisation just as quickly as desired behaviours, via informal learning. Formal learning takes place in the context of organised training or learning activities and generates explicit knowledge and skills (overt knowledge and skills that are capable of being shared with a wider audience). Informal learning occurs through daily workplace activities, leading to 'implicit' or 'tacit' knowledge or skills (knowledge and skills taken for granted or unconsciously held in the minds of employees). Burns (2008) reviewed numerous studies and surmised that the majority of workplace learning is in fact informal. The power of informal learning is an important consideration for those involved in organisational HRD: from a positive perspective it presents opportunities to provide timely and cost-effective learning; from a negative perspective it has the power to undermine formal interventions.

Caveat 3: Not all adult learning requires the acquisition of new KSA.

In fact it could be argued that for the majority of adult learning there is only a requirement for a slight adaptation in existing KSA. For example, an update in technology will probably only require a small amount of new knowledge and it may actually require less skill than the old version, a classic example being the introduction of EPOS till systems in supermarkets, which it has been argued deskilled the jobs of cashiers, stock controllers and finance staff. The case study below provides an example of this.

Similarly, most poor conduct issues are driven by inappropriate attitudes, with the employees often being perfectly skilled, knowing and able to display the expected behaviour, but choosing not to. This is important for those who are involved in HRD as changing embedded skills and attitudes can be difficult and more time-consuming than providing new ones.

 TELEWEST COMMUNICATIONS

CASE STUDY

During the 1990s Telewest Communications was one of several companies growing a new cable TV and telephone network in the UK. At the same time as new geographical areas were being developed, the products, services and systems needed to support customers in existing areas were also being upgraded and improved. A 'mobile training team' was used to both train new staff in new areas and provide upgrade training for staff in existing areas. In all cases trainers reported how much more difficult and time-consuming it was for existing staff to learn new systems compared to new staff, due to embedded KSA.

Question

Provide three examples of things you have learnt in the last year. What opportunities have you had to use this new learning? How did this learning occur: was it formal or informal? To what extent did you need completely new knowledge, skills or attitudes as opposed to adaptation of existing ones?

TRAINING, EDUCATION AND DEVELOPMENT

Training, education and development are all methods to enable learning, and are techniques at the disposal of the HRD professional and individual. The definitions of these terms can best be explained using an analogy:

> Schools in the UK are required to provide sex and relationships education to children, and whether or not we approve, most of us have a view of what it involves – certainly the passing on of information, but in a very general way. Most definitions of occupational education concur that it is focused on inputs and therefore has non-specific outcomes. It involves a planned process of providing access to concepts, ideas and knowledge.

However, what if your child was to come home saying, 'We had sex training at school today'? What images could flash through your mind? Such images may be

disquieting, because training is very different from occupational education. It is still a formal process but it is focused on outputs not inputs, such as the output of skill development. To quote Holst (2009, p 332), 'training is the mastery of action (practice) . . . it is about building skills, understanding and confidence of people.'

Consider too your reaction if your child said 'We had sex development at school today'. What images might be created now? Again they could well be alarming ones. Development is also focused on outputs and implies getting better at something or becoming more advanced. It is the process of growing an individual and preparing them or equipping them for different, better or bigger things.

The inter-relationships between these terms are important. It could be argued that training has clear outcomes and adopts a shorter-term perspective compared to development, which will have desired outcomes, but these are likely to be less specific than those for training and could adopt a longer-term, nurturing perspective. But this argument could depend upon the organisational context. If a medical consultant takes 13 years to qualify, would this be considered to be 'training' or 'development', or possibly both? What is probably most important is that training, education and development are all considered tools to be used within HRD in order to facilitate learning.

It is also useful for the HRD practitioner to be familiar with models of how people learn, from the early behaviourist theories of the 1920s through to more recent theories of cognitive, social and experiential learning. Wilson (2006, pp 201–51) provides three useful chapters on these topics.

KEY PRINCIPLES OF HRD

Until very recently, it was assumed that employers were responsible for the skill development of employees, and indeed many organisations took this responsibility seriously and provided comprehensive training and development interventions. Training was something that was 'done to employees' because it was good for the organisation and the employees accepted this because it was part of the psychological contract (see Chapter 7). In some organisations this is still the case, with the employer taking the lead role. At least this may be the case for development of skills that the organisation needs, but perhaps not so for skills that are of greater benefit to the employee as organisations might possibly be wary of developing their staff to the extent they become highly attractive to other employers. But the lines are becoming blurred and it is increasingly difficult to be clear where responsibility for skills and career development sits. One way to clarify this might be to establish who benefits most from the skills development and then assign responsibility accordingly.

IDENTIFYING WHEN LEARNING MAY BE NEEDED

The Magic Model (Figure 10.2) is a tool which can be used to identify when it might be necessary for an employee to undergo a learning experience, and

therefore it might be prudent to consider carrying out a learning needs analysis. Learning needs analysis is a new angle on the traditional process of training needs analysis, which is extensively covered in most training and development textbooks. Learning needs analysis is the process of identifying a gap in KSA that can and should be filled by a training, education or development intervention.

WHO BENEFITS FROM THE LEARNING?

Knowing who benefits from the learning may help to identify who should be responsible for its provision and it may also dictate the methods of development chosen. Clearly, if the organisation is the main beneficiary, it will be responsible for the training or learning provision, and it is likely to be more formal and structured so that it can be guaranteed that those employees who need the learning get it. On the other hand, if the employee is the main beneficiary, themselves, they must take some responsibility for its provision themselves, and because the learning will be much more individual in nature, the development techniques may be less formal and structured.

Provision of mandatory KSA and corrective coaching is very clearly in the interests of the organisation if it wants optimal performance from its employees. Very few organisations would argue that basic job training for new employees and corrective coaching for employees who are underperforming are anything other than a business necessity.

Learning for growth, on the other hand, could be viewed as much more in the interests of the employee, because it will lead to enhanced employment prospects, which could be outside the organisation, even if the organisation will also benefit through more robust succession planning.

Figure 10.1 Times when consideration should be given to learning needs analysis

Mandatory skills and knowledge are those required by all *new* employees and include induction/orientation, basic job learning to reach competent employee status and legislation-driven learning such as in health and safety. So whenever a new employee comes on board, thought should be given to learning needs analysis.

Adapting to changes in processes, materials, equipment, demand levels etc could all lead to a need for new or amended KSA. So whenever any organisational changes are planned, learning needs analysis should be considered.

Growing into a new role or developing for future career moves will inevitably demand changes and development of KSA. So learning needs analysis should be part and parcel of any career planning activities, either company or individually driven.

Improvements to current work practices and activities may require new or amended KSA. So both day-to-day performance management and the formal review process should include learning needs analysis as standard.

Corrective coaching for shortfalls in performance may require an intervention to increase or refocus KSA. So any poor performance or conduct issues may flag up the need for learning needs analysis.

Learning in order to adapt to change or to improve performance is less clear in terms of beneficiaries. Adapting to change could be viewed as in the interests of both organisation and employee, dependent upon the specifics. For example, training or developing employees in an upgrade to a software package could be essential for some workers and nice to have for others, dependent on their job role. In the earlier case study example of Telewest, training call centre operatives in changes to the customer management system was essential because the system was an inherent part of the day-to-day job and thus important for the business. In this case a structured refresher training programme was supplied.

However, for other employees – installers or sales people, for instance – this was not essential and therefore no formal training was provided for these employees. Yet changes to the product offering were considered essential for all employees by the organisation, although this was not necessarily the view of all employees. The sales teams, whose income was dependent on this knowledge, were clearly beneficiaries, but many of the technicians were far less interested.

Similarly, streamlining or improving how employees do their jobs could benefit both employee and organisation. For example: enabling a call centre operative to be more confident when dealing with irate customers could improve customer satisfaction and company profitability whilst at the same time affording greater job satisfaction for the employee, hence a shared benefit. But getting the same operatives to shorten the call durations would be of benefit to the organisation because this would increase productivity by enabling the operatives to take more calls. Yet for the same reason it could be viewed as a negative for the operatives themselves, if the only reward for efficiency was more work.

These examples begin to demonstrate that deciding who benefits from learning is not as straightforward as at first it may seem, as demonstrated in Figure 10.2. Mandatory KSA and corrective coaching are overtly in the interests of the organisation, but they are covertly also in the interests of the employee, as without them the employee lacks the skills to be employable.

Development of skills for growth may overtly be in the interests of the employee, but covertly it also benefits the organisation by providing a better skilled and potentially more motivated employee.

What is becoming increasingly clear is that in the 21st century it is unrealistic to expect employers to be totally responsible for HRD activities. The Leitch Report (2006) recognised this and called for a tripartite approach involving employers, government and individuals. However, what is of interest is that skills development is much more effective and successful if it is viewed as a partnership approach between the organisation and the learner; this is highlighted by the literature on the move from training to learning. The following case study gives an example of this approach.

Figure 10.2 *MAGIC* Model overt benefit or covert benefit

CASE STUDY

FENMARC PRODUCE LTD

Fenmarc Produce Ltd (a major food supplier to ASDA) see investing and developing their people as a strategy enabler. They introduced a learning solution called 101 to improve their market position, embed a new company culture and support the change-readiness of the organisation. However, the programme was also the starting point for personal development which focused on the individual. The outcome has been success for the company with profit per employee growing fivefold,

but only because employees have also benefited by increasing their skills and confidence.

Source: Human Resource Management International Digest (2007)

Question

What training, education and development are provided by your organisation? How does this fit into the MAGIC Model? Who benefits from these opportunities or interventions?

FROM TRAINING TO LEARNING

The historical view of training as an activity that is 'done to' an employee is making way for more contemporary approaches contrastingly (Anderson, 2007) which emphasise learning as initiated and driven by the individual employee. To appreciate this change we need to identify some key phases and concepts which underpin macro-level policy in the UK.

THE SYSTEMATIC TRAINING CYCLE

The Industrial Training Boards, stimulated by the 1964 Industrial Training Act, pushed for an improvement in the quality and quantity of organisational skills training provisions. One of the tools heavily promoted was the four-stage Systematic Training Cycle (STC). The STC comprises: training needs analysis, design, delivery and evaluation carried out in a systematic way, the intention being to ensure that training provision is both effective and efficient – ie the right things are trained in the most appropriate way. Numerous authors provide detailed descriptions of the four stages (Buckley and Caple, 2007; Harrison, 2009; Reid, Barrington and Brown, 2007) and the STC is by no means the only systematic model in existence: Cowell *et al* (2006) provide an overview of seven alternative systematic training models.

Despite stringent criticism of the cycle including the fundamental charges that it is unresponsive to change, slow and costly in terms of resources, and more generally, cold and clinical with a basis in scientific management (Rayner and Adam-Smith, 2009) the STC is still very much in use in many organisations today. Allen and Swanson point out that although there are many alternatives, 'systematic training is at the core of HRD and is by far the largest HRD investment year after year' (2006, p 428). Indeed, there are many examples of organisations that continue to use the STC, achieving some excellent results. A visit to the website of UK Skills www.trainingdatabank.com will provide case studies of organisations who have won a National Training Award as recognition of 'exceptional training'. These awards use the STC as a foundation of their judging criteria, which can also be found on the web: www.nationaltrainingawards.com.

The positive examples could imply that it is not the STC model that is faulty but the way in which it is used, or rather, misused. There is a wealth of evidence to suggest that few organisations fully use all the stages, with the most poorly completed stages being training needs analysis and evaluation. Gold *et al* (2010) explore why training needs analysis is often not done or not done well, and most textbooks on this topic lament the lack of proper evaluation of training.

Experience of being a judge for the National Training Awards (2009) supports these findings, whereby most entrants were easily able to explain the design and delivery of their learning intervention. However, they were not so clear on the original need for it, and were generally weak on demonstrating value as a result. So it could be argued that the STC is still a valuable tool when used correctly, but there are of course alternatives.

ALTERNATIVES TO SYSTEMATIC TRAINING

It could be argued that most organisations would prefer not to have to provide training: it is not a core activity and requires investment of scarce resources, and there are alternatives. For example (McClernon, 2006):

- recruit people who already have the KSA needed

- align compensation and reward more closely with performance to improve motivation

- improve communications and performance management to ensure effort is appropriately focused

- redesign work methods, increase technology or outsource, to reduce or remove the internal need for KSA

- improve work climate to increase engagement and commitment.

Sutherland (2009) also suggests organisations should make better use of the skills that their employees already have. In his survey more than 50 per cent of employees said their skills were greater than those demanded by their current job.

Supporters of the STC might claim that these activities are not really alternatives but could in fact be outputs of a thorough training or learning needs analysis, yet again suggesting that it is the use or misuse of the STC that is at fault. However, even if an organisation were to make full use of the alternatives, it is still highly likely there would be a need for employee development and learning which the traditional systematic approach may not be suited to address.

 REFLECTIVE ACTIVITY

- How is learning or training needs analysis carried out in your organisation?

- To what extent does training needs analysis identify alternatives to learning or training interventions?

AWAY FROM SYSTEMATIC TRAINING

In recent years there has been increasing interest in the concept of moving away from systematic training towards a more learner-centred approach, not least because research appears to show that competitive advantage can be gained when individuals are proactive in the learning process (CIPD, 2005b; Drucker, 2005; Sloman, 2007). Beard and Wilson (2006, p 4) propose a model called the 'learning combination lock' which highlights the complexity of learning for an individual and the multitude of factors which can affect its success. This model demonstrates how the 'one size fits all' approach of traditional training cannot hope to meet the needs of individual learners. The suggestion is thus a move from an instructor-led content-based intervention to a self-directed work-based process (CIPD, 2005). This supports the idea of androgogy by Knowles (1990), who speculated that adult learners such as employees within organisations need much more involvement in the learning process for it to be effective.

TOWARDS SELF-DIRECTED LEARNING

Research into self-directed learning attempts to quantify what steps need to be taken to encourage this approach. Of interest to HRD professionals may be the paper by Ellinger (2004) which discusses the implications for integrating self-directed learning into HRD practices. Self-directed learning requires certain organisational features, which are likely to be embedded within the culture of the organisation, in order to make success more likely – including the following (Confessore and Kops, 1998; CIPD, 2005b; Harrison, 2009):

- tolerance for errors and experimentation
- a supportive environment
- using everyday work as an opportunity to learn
- participative leadership and delegation
- fit with business goals
- open communications
- systems that encourage teamworking
- individual motivation and commitment.

The CIPD has produced a diagnostic tool which could provide the basis for organisations to start the move from training to learning: www.cipd.co.uk.

 REFLECTIVE ACTIVITY

Consider your organisation. To what extent are the features listed by Confessore and Kops above embedded in its culture? How ready is it to adopt self-directed learning?

In addition, much of the literature stresses the idea of helping individuals 'learn how to learn' or the concept of ownership for personal development – a recurring theme of this chapter. An analogy for this type of sustainable development could be:

> 'Give a man a fish and you feed him for a day. Teach a man how to fish and you feed him for life' (*attributed to Lao Tzu the founder of Taoism*).

If learners can become more adept and better at learning, not only will organisations find it easier to train and develop them, but the individuals themselves will find it easier to embark on the journey of 'lifelong learning'. The twin themes of contribution to organisational effectiveness, and personal development, have made lifelong learning a topical concept and a theme which is continued later in this chapter. The focus on moving from training to learning leads one to consider the methods of development which might enable this to happen.

CHOICE OF LEARNING AND DEVELOPMENT TECHNIQUES

Choosing a development technique, and the choice is vast, will be strongly influenced by a number of factors such as organisational culture, resources available and learner-related factors including learning theories and models, which are well explained in many HRD texts.

Peter Honey (1998) describes over 100 different techniques in his *Manager's Guide to Workplace Learning* text. Cheetham and Chivers (2001) list almost as many in their paper 'How professionals learn'. Both are useful sources of ideas for those planning development activities. But there is also evidence to show that some techniques are much more widely used than others and some are regarded as being more effective than others.

Interestingly, despite the supposed shift from training to learning, traditional off-job training courses are still widely used, with the CIPD survey (2008d) showing 64 per cent of people had participated in an event of this type in the previous 12 months. However, the same survey showed these courses were not well liked by learners, with only 15 per cent of people ranking them as most appealing, and critically, only 20 per cent of respondents feeling it was the most effective method to use. These respondents are not alone (Freifield, 2009b:14):

> 'My attention span since college has shortened considerably and now hovers around that of a gnat, so classroom instruction often can be a cure for insomnia for me.'

Being trained on-job was the most appealing learning method for 46 per cent of recipients and, vitally, was regarded as being most effective by 43 per cent. The effectiveness of on-job learning is almost certainly due to the in-built ability to practise and gain feedback in real time. This links into the unconscious-incompetent-to-unconscious-competent theory of learning (Howell, 1982) which shows how essential practice and feedback are in order for new skills to become embedded. This supports the argument for less formal and more learner-centred activities.

But it is far more complex than this. E-learning has long been heralded as the ultimate individualised learner-centred technique. In 2008 it was used by 57 per cent of organisations, but popularity does not equal effectiveness. Only 7 per cent of respondents in the 2008 survey regarded it as the most effective method, adding that it was not a substitute for other forms of learning and was only effective when used in combination (CIPD, 2008).

 REFLECTIVE ACTIVITY

Consider your own decision to take an instructor-led learning event as opposed to an e-learning alternative – for example, a CIPD qualification. What influenced your decision? What are the issues with e-learning?

Now consider the positives. In what ways can e-learning be used to add value to organisational and individual development?

How can some of the negatives be overcome or managed so that e-learning can be used more effectively?

Whatever development technique is selected there is one factor that appears to be essential if it is to be effective and that is *transfer of learning*. Indeed, most of us could cite examples of where a training intervention in itself has been enjoyed and the participants may well have changed their KSA – but there has been no marked change in job performance. Consider the manager who returns from a two-day management skills workshop brimming with enthusiasm to use new 'project management techniques' or to start 'coaching and mentoring' their team, but within days the enthusiasm is gone and the new techniques put on the back burner. This could be due to lack of transfer, which Yorks, Lamm and O'Neil (1999, p 56) tell us 'has long been the Achilles' heel of HRD'. There are multiple reasons for this lack of transfer: time pressures, resource shortages and culture mismatch being just a few. However, probably the biggest issue is related to organisational support and how much the newly trained employee is encouraged to use his or her new knowledge or skill.

Transfer is far more difficult to achieve with traditional systematic training, where trainees undergo a 'one size fits all' intervention, often off-job and therefore not tailored to them and lacking the realism of their everyday work experience. This could be the key to why on-job learning and self-directed learning are regarded as more effective, because they address this issue: learning is completely tailored and is much more likely to take place on-job in real time with in-built practice and feedback. See the illustration below for an example.

ILLUSTRATION

Dene Magna School introduced a 'Reflective Practitioner Programme' in order to improve teaching standards. The purpose of the scheme was to empower teachers to become their own leaders. The techniques used included peer observation, coaching, toolbox meetings and toolbox resources, all providing very real and relevant opportunities to learn with high levels of transfer. The results exceeded expectations.

www.investorrsinpeople.co.uk

 REFLECTIVE ACTIVITY

Think about training programmes you have attended. How was learning transfer facilitated?

From your experience of work-based development and training, what methods are employed to assist in translating experiential and other learning into relevant workplace activity?

CAREER AND PROFESSIONAL DEVELOPMENT

The debate about responsibility for learning leads on to a discussion about investment in career and professional development. This is the focus of the rest of this chapter.

WHAT IS A CAREER?

The term 'career', in its most general sense, is interpreted as upward progression through a series of job roles with increasing levels of responsibility or managerial control. In essence, a career is a structured sequence of work experiences that promote employee development and advance organisational capability.

WHAT DOES A CAREER LOOK LIKE?

The concept of a career is useful in providing a focus for employment and a future goal that drives a sense of purpose. There is no doubt that a perspective on career significance is uniquely personal and for some people of resounding meaning: 'careers are what we judge our lives by' (Inkson and Arthur, 2001, p 48).

By contrast some individuals attest that they have never had a career – rather 'a series of bits and pieces', or 'a chapter of accidents'. How can these opposing views be reconciled?

REFLECTIVE ACTIVITY

1. How does a career differ from a job?
2. What are the distinctive features of a career?
3. What does a career mean to you?

Individuals often make sense of their employment history by a retrospective construction of career decisions. These career stories may grant a coherence to a serendipitous employment experience of different roles or sectors. Media coverage of overnight career success often belies the years toiling for recognition. Even Harrison Ford, known for his remarkable good fortune in transitioning from carpenter to leading actor after a chance encounter with the film producer George Lucas, had previously spent 15 years as a cabinet-maker trying to start an acting career.

The rise in different employment contractual relationships, as highlighted in the introduction, through increasing part-time working, outsourcing and the use of flexible working arrangements, has altered assumptions about careers (Greller, 2006; Harrison, 2009). Hall (1996) declared the career in terminal decline, yet there is limited evidence of the widespread abandonment of career structures in organisational practice (Baruch, 2004, 2006). The relevance of career models then needs to be questioned in a global economy where a variety of employment patterns emerge, in particular as contemporary career patterns often transcend occupational and national boundaries.

CONTEMPORARY CAREER MODELS

Three prominent career concepts follow: the traditional career, the boundaryless career and the self-managed career. These academic constructs provide a useful framework from which to explore the thinking around career development.

TRADITIONAL CAREER

The image of a traditional career is of a pattern of jobs within a single organisation that follow a linear and predetermined path. This is often depicted as a hierarchical ladder that an employee climbs acquiring greater levels of expertise and managerial accountability (see Figure 10.3). In this model the employer assumes a parental role and employees' self-worth is defined by the organisation (Kissler, 1994).

Key characteristics of a traditional career structure are specific entry criteria linked to education and qualification attainment, a planned and coordinated structure of job experience, and a coherent reward strategy. Reward is provided through the extrinsic acceleration of pay, increased benefits, and role seniority. Additionally, intrinsic rewards flow from public recognition of an individual's promotion and achievement.

Traditional career ladder

Employee success is measured in progressive movement up the career structure that mutually satisfies organisational objectives and individual career growth. Examples of careerists flourishing within a single organisation are firstly Lord Browne who began work with the oil giant BP as a graduate trainee and rose to become Chief Executive, and secondly Sir Terry Leahy, CEO at Tesco. Leahy joined Tesco in 1979 as a management trainee and has never worked anywhere but in the supermarket chain. Such examples evidence the value of company-specific knowledge to career progression, and are a potent indicator of these particular individuals' worth to the business.

Figure 10.3 Traditional career ladder

This traditional model is equally valid within the public sector (Baruch, 2004a). The employer provides relative security of employment and career advancement in exchange for superior performance and firm allegiance to the organisation. However, the removal of many mid-level positions has affected the available rungs in the career ladder.

BOUNDARYLESS CAREER

The unpredictability of lifetime employment has affected expectations of a stable career pattern. DeFillippi and Arthur (1994) introduced the concept of career growth free of organisational restrictions. The boundaryless career crosses multiple companies and contexts unlike the traditional career path within a single company. An individual creates a career in various organisations through a process of development along a path of experience (Baruch and Rosenstein, 1992). The boundaryless career is multidirectional shaped by opportunity. An individual example is Adam Crozier who in public interviews has joked that his career path might suggest someone who doesn't quite know what he wants to do. Crozier began employment as a graduate trainee at Mars Pedigree Petfood, and has moved across diverse organisations from the *Daily Telegraph* to Saatchi & Saatchi, to the Football Association, to Royal Mail and to Chief Executive at ITV. Crozier's industry switching is connected by the transfer of integrated business and change management skills.

SELF-MANAGED CAREER

The self-managed career emphasises the individual as master of his or her own destiny rather than the organisation. A Protean career was a concept Hall developed (1996), named after Proteus, the early Greek god of the sea, who changed form to match the environment. As the business environment evolves and requirements change, individuals, following the analogy, must similarly adapt by renewing their skills and updating their knowledge. A Protean career is inevitably characterised by continuous learning. Success is gauged by the individual's vision and values as the career contract is an agreement with oneself and one's work (Hall, 1996). Sir Richard Branson, founder of the Virgin Group, is arguably Britain's best-known example of such adaptation. Branson has directed Virgin's evolution from music to airlines, shops, telecoms, drinks and even bridalwear.

Similarly, a 'portfolio career' is where an individual makes a deliberate choice of personal independence, working on a variety of contracts with clients and organisations (Handy, 1994). The freelancer identifies with clients, groups or collaborators, and this working identity forms a career (Ibarra, 2004). The professional with expertise for hire is a free agent, at liberty to showcase skills and competence as saleable commodities (Bridges, 1995).

> 'More than a quarter of all American workers now classify themselves as "free agents", and half of America's temps are professionals of one kind or another' (Talent on tap: the fashion for hiring temps has reached the executive suite', 10 December 2009, *The Economist*).

In this fluid environment an individual needs criteria for effective career management to shape an 'intelligent career' (Arthur, cited by Baruch, 2006, p 128). These are framed as open career questions.

- Know why – values, attitudes, internal needs, identity and lifestyle
- Know how – career competencies: skills, expertise, capabilities; tacit and explicit knowledge
- Know whom- networking, relationships, how to find the right people
- Know what – opportunities, threats and requirements
- Know where – entering, training and advancing
- Know when – timing of choices and activities.

Another perspective on career is one that embodies learning as a 'repository of knowledge' (Bird, cited in Arthur and Rousseau, 1996). This collected learning constitutes a career rather than the biographical succession of work experiences. Sir Alan Sugar, as a government appointed enterprise tsar, dispensed his own career advice as being that the most important thing is the experience you have amassed (BBC News, interview, 19 November 2008). From this perspective every worker has a career built through successive jobs of his or her working life. Yet there is tension in such a view, because it implies that all individuals are equally capable of deriving skill enrichment from accumulated experience. Individual entrepreneurs such as Stelios Haji-Ioannou, easyJet founder, demonstrate that some are more skilled than others in making use of their experience.

WHAT IS THE BUSINESS RATIONALE FOR CAREER MANAGEMENT?

The rationale for career management is the effective nurturing of talent, specific company knowledge and the successive deployment of workforce capabilities to best serve the business. Companies such as McDonalds, Walt Disney and the Hilton Group spend considerable time, money and effort turning fresh recruits into loyal company men and women who will internalise and promote organisational values. Although 'career management' and 'development' are often used interchangeably, they are differentiated by career ownership and direction.

Career management is the formal systematic process through which the organisation nurtures the human capital that can provide competitive advantage (Porter, 1998). It is marked by managerial interventions such as succession planning, formal mentoring and secondments. Effective career coaching embedded in the performance review process links an individual's development planning to the organisational charting of future resource allocation. Review the CIPD 'Guide to Career Management' (King, 2004) for further examples of career management.

Organisations invest in employees' education providing work experiences that expand competences and target development through in-house training and corporate universities. Return on this career investment is assessed against expected career trajectories. For example, in a global bank executive officers' career progress was measured against a predicted speed of reaching branch manager position within a number of years. If this position had not been reached, early severance was encouraged. This demonstrates the organisation's risk management of a career to assess whether an individual remains an increasing asset.

Many organisations need to build expertise through successive job experience and exposure to distinct environments. For example, the medical and legal profession demand intensive training and applied practice to achieve operational competence. Organisational investment in developing pilot skills may be questioned, as technological advances and auto-piloting have decreased individual skill reliance. However, the emergency US Airways jet landing on the New York Hudson River in 2009 dramatically demonstrates the value of an individual pilot's seasoned expertise. The pilot Sullenberger, a captain of 29 years' airline experience, saved the lives of all 150 passengers and crew members.

Although the concept of career management is straightforward, the execution may be more complex. Career oversight is often shared by different business units, managers and mentors and the locus of control for career management may vary in practice. Consider this view of a career structure: 'The career management is really about who knows who at the moment. There's no real formal structure to the career management' (CIPD, 2010c).

- What are the career interventions in your organisation?
- Who develops the career path?
- What navigates you through the maze?
- What are the challenges of career paths developed in distinct operating areas?

There is an apparent tension between organisations' promoting career opportunities to attract new recruits and the reality of what a promised career delivers. An employment climate affected by recession has further obscured career structures through recruitment and promotion freezes. Read the following example (CIPD, 2010c), and consider the implications for an individual employee:

'The career path that we are describing for the future is more come to us, learn some things, gain some skills, go somewhere else, move on and maybe rejoin us later in your career as a senior leading scientist.'

This is an opaque route and places the map firmly in the hands of the individual protagonist to chart his or her course. In addition, mergers and acquisitions can affect a maturing career plan that runs counter to the changed requirements of the business. Pressing business demands may include sourcing external expertise to find the right skill-sets. Accordingly, commitment may shift from the organisation to the team leader, to the project or to the profession (Baruch, 2006). If employers are ceding control of career management, then increasingly individuals are encouraged to be proactive in their own career development. This echoes the theme of self-directed learning.

Career development marks a shift from directing to enabling development that increases or sustains employees' current productivity (Robbins, 1993). Career development is a critical lever in attracting, engaging and retaining talent. As noted earlier, economic fluctuations demand career resilience as defined by Waterman *et al* (1994). Resilience is acquired by a constant updating of skills that enables employees to anticipate change and remain competitive. This assures an individual's employability within the company and outside (Ghoshal, Bartlett and Moran, 1999). Positive career development resonates with the need for continual learning, as highlighted in Protean and self-managed careers, and summarised in the CIPD model shown as Figure 10.4.

Career development is portrayed as symbiotic, offering the potential for both individual career advancement and the enhancement of organisational capability. The CIPD depicts this as positive career development.

Figure 10.4 Rationale for career development

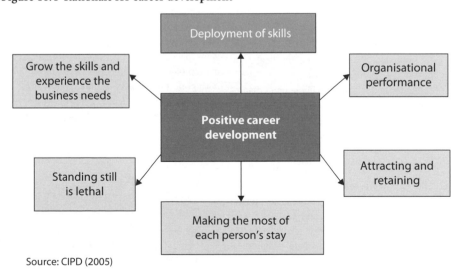

Source: CIPD (2005)

Read the case study below and answer the questions beneath.

CAREER DEVELOPMENT IN PRACTICE: A ROADMAP FROM WASHINGTON DC

The US government agency, Enduring Defense, based in Washington, DC, recognised employee retention was an issue. The agency employed over 3,000 staff combining government civilians, military personnel, and contractor employees. Attracting talented scientists and bright engineers was not a problem, but holding on to them was challenging. Many specialised staff were frustrated by a slow climb up the agency career pyramid. Some felt that if they couldn't move up, they would move out. As a result they took their cutting-edge technical knowledge and unique skills out of the door.

In the past the agency had always funded staff requests for training and development. Some conferences in Hawaii or Australia appeared to be remote from their departmental job focus. Staff looked at this funding as a networking opportunity for future external consultancy work. Expenditure control and development consistently anchored to mission objectives was a problem.

To address these issues, the agency set up a new corporate university as an umbrella for professional development specifically linked to mission goals. External consultants designed and implemented an organisation-wide competency framework. A set of Career Guides was rolled out for each function defining job broadbands and relevant resources for individual development.

Stan Allport worked in the facilities function in charge of logistics. He had attended the Career Guides roadshow, and was optimistic about his career track. Stan had worked for the US Air Force before joining the agency, and after two tours in Afghanistan felt entitled to protected employment in a steady job. After all, it was his due after such active stints.

But when Stan looked through his Career Guide he didn't find what he wanted. The Guide featured employees' self-improvement through mentoring and on-the-job projects. There were suggestions for skill updating, continuous learning and knowledge acquisition. Skill proficiency assessments were designed for the line manager and employee to agree on a Personal Development Plan. Stan was disappointed by a lack of specific job vacancies. The Guide emphasised employees' development aligned to the mission, not the plan for his career. Rumour was spreading that the severe restrictions on defence spending meant relocation of the agency to Huntsville, Alabama. This was not in Stan's vision of the future. He knew that his wife Kelly, a doctor at the children's hospital, and twin daughters would never leave the vibrant capital city for a sleepy southern state.

Stan emailed his line manager for an urgent meeting. He wanted to underline to her that the agency had promised him a career when he signed up. This self-improvement was a fuzzy concept; it was too uncertain. Where was the career map? He didn't really want to work on special assignments or extra projects. Stan had done his years of hard graft. It was payback time. Stan really wanted to know when he'd get his next promotion, and how his career mapped out until retirement.

Questions

1. What are the benefits of this development approach from an agency perspective?

2. What are some of the tensions for individual career development in practice?

3. If you were Stan's line manager, how would you explain the career guidance?

As can be seen from the above case study, the extent of the employer's responsibility in providing career development tools, opportunities and funding is debatable. Although it is assumed that HR practitioners will provide career support, this may vary in practice. 'HR departments are, of course, heavily involved in giving career advice and information to individuals, and assessing and advising on their development needs' (CIPD 2009e). Moreover, financial results or conflicting business priorities may overtake development needs. Similarly, line managers differ widely in their competence level as career coaches, and in their enthusiasm for acting as organisational guide. Factors critical for employee career development support and success are summarised below:

- managerial support
- mentoring guidance
- peer and organisational network support
- organisational investment
- opportunity for extending skills
- inclusive access to development experience
- diversity of staff profile in expected career progress
- harmony of business needs and individual aspirations.

Alternatively, an individual not finding opportunities or support may encounter barriers that limit career growth. Line managers may inhibit career movement, as the employee seeking guidance may become a rival for promotion. Research by the Work Foundation indicates that access to development and training opportunities is skewed, with managers and professionals five times more likely to receive work-based training than people with no qualification or in an unskilled job.

CAREER DEVELOPMENT STRUCTURES

Career success is in the eye of the beholder with progression implicit in the psychological contract. Boxall and Purcell (2008) argue that the construct of a deal is in the mind of individual employees and therefore cannot be viewed as contractual. Career success is complex because career aims change over time. Success may be measured in progress consistent with personal aspirations, the achievement of professional excellence or preference for meaningful work (Sullivan, 1999).

For some it is the extrinsic reward of power and remuneration, for others reward through internal feelings of worthiness and achievement (Baruch, 2006). Line managers and HR practitioners need to provide clear plans for career progression so that employees are aware of what is required to gain career advancement.

Employee expectations may be satisfied through the trade-off of long journeying hours for the future assurance of career uplift – for example, to achieve partnership status in accountancy firms. Yet the 'big four' accounting firms Deloitte Touche Tohmatsu, Ernst & Young, KPMG and PricewaterhouseCoopers all have predominantly male senior partner staffs. Professional women spend more time working flexibly, and have more non-linear career paths. Moreover, although the organisation wants to nurture talent and fast-track potential leaders, it may also need to balance this growth with the intake of fresh blood. For example, the fashion house Givenchy broke from reliance on in-house expertise by hiring the young designer Alexander McQueen to reinvigorate the company's style.

A trust in career fulfilment may be undermined by business survival as organisations are increasingly unable or unwilling to promise career opportunities (Dries and Pepermans, 2008, p 87).

Career promotion may be a simple case of managerial expediency in response to operational requirements rather than reward for effective performance.

Thus three pertinent questions emerge about career development structures:

- Is there a match between the organisation's needs and the individual's aspirations?
- Is the career framework transparent to all?
- Can the career offer remain valid and affordable for the business?

THE OWNERSHIP OF CAREER DEVELOPMENT

Career ownership revolves around control and direction. The orientation towards career perceptions of control may be more a result of mindset than external environment (Briscoe and Hall, 2006). Yet there is ambiguity in the commonality of purpose of career development for the organisation and for the individual. It is doubtful whether 'me-learning' can always transfer to 'us-expansion'.

International career development may call for distinct approaches in managing across borders. Expatriation is managed according to the organisational strategy for particular expertise – for example, international career structures at the oil company Shell, the Foreign and Commonwealth Office, and Nestlé. Research in international careers has found that the primary motives for going abroad are personal interest, a search for new experiences and an interest in the external environment (Suutari and Brewster, 2000). Consequently, there may be a mismatch between individual values and organisational pressure that provoke a career crisis. For example, a BBC journalist may refuse a political assignment in Israel when the individual's interests are focused on social development in Brazil. These individual career aspirations can change with family circumstances, educational requirements, health, financial commitments and personal interests.

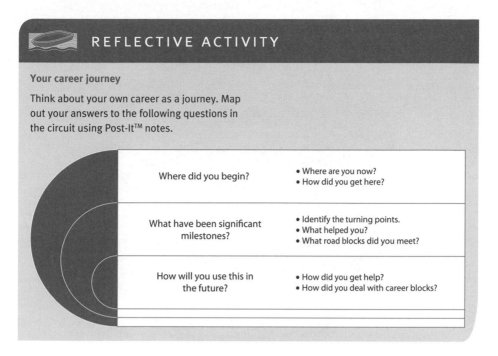

REFLECTIVE ACTIVITY

Your career journey

Think about your own career as a journey. Map out your answers to the following questions in the circuit using Post-It™ notes.

Where did you begin?	• Where are you now? • How did you get here?
What have been significant milestones?	• Identify the turning points. • What helped you? • What road blocks did you meet?
How will you use this in the future?	• How did you get help? • How did you deal with career blocks?

A self-managed career demands high levels of self-awareness and personal responsibility (Hall, 1996). It also makes significant demands on an individual's ability to adapt in terms of performance and learning, as evidenced in this statement: 'It is up to you how much you make of the fantastic training and development opportunities that are available to you here at IBM. It will only be limited by your imagination' (Source: IBM University Recruitment 2009/10). Certain individuals have a greater tolerance for ambiguity that suits an entrepreneurial approach to career invention. For others, self-directed career management is a burden resulting in mounting stress levels (Cooper, 2005). This reveals why many employees wish to keep the traditional psychological contract for the job security that it offers (McDonald *et al*, 2006). Workers at Cadbury's chocolate factory in Bourneville may have believed their specific company knowledge and experience would secure future employment until Kraft's takeover undermined such prospects.

Notwithstanding, there is debate as to how much individual development and learning can be effectively harnessed by the organisation, and managed as an organisational resource (Senge, 1993). The unpredictability of organisational career paths shifts the emphasis to individuals' personal investment through continuing professional development.

THE CONCEPT OF CONTINUING PROFESSIONAL DEVELOPMENT (CPD)

Continuing professional development has been defined as 'a constant updating of professional knowledge throughout one's working life by means of systematic,

Figure 10.5 Professional expansion

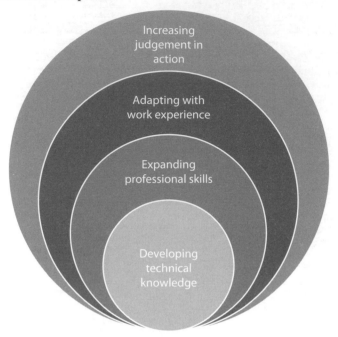

on-going, self-directed learning' (CIPD, Sept 2009). This professional enrichment is depicted in Figure 10.5.

UNDERSTANDING CPD

CPD promotes the ongoing attainment of effective job performance through targeting current and emerging development needs. The 'P' in CPD is used for 'professional' and 'personal' development as the two are often conflated. It can be argued that the product of CPD is essentially 'personal property'. Inkson and Arthur (2001) support the validity of self-interested professional development in what they termed career capitalism ie – the return on investment in a career. The understanding is that by recognising and taking advantage of development opportunities this will lead to career success (Arthur, Inkson and Pringle, 1999; DeFillippi and Arthur, 1996, cited in Briscoe and Hall, 2006, p 5). As a result an individual who understands the marketplace, and can adapt to what is in demand, can increase the yield on personal capital.

Continuing professional development can therefore be seen as a virtuous circle of improvement (see Figure 10.6). We can assume that development momentum is generated by individual and economic self-interest to improve professional capability and performance (Megginson and Whitaker, 2007).

However, the tangible evidence of such improvement can be questioned, as many performance reviews witness the annual listing of the same developmental needs. When does the circle devolve into a recurring nightmarish task? Could this be a Sisyphean prospect of refining competencies for skills that may not have a future

Figure 10.6 Virtuous circle of improvement

```
                    ┌─────────────┐
                    │  Applying   │
                    │ competence  │
                    └─────────────┘
      ┌─────────────┐           ┌─────────────┐
      │  Refining   │           │Assessing self│
      │   skills    │           │             │
      └─────────────┘           └─────────────┘

  ┌─────────────┐                    ┌─────────────┐
  │   Making    │                    │   Seeking   │
  │ connections │                    │  feedback   │
  │  updating   │                    │from peer/   │
  │  knowledge  │                    │  manager    │
  └─────────────┘                    └─────────────┘

      ┌─────────────┐           ┌─────────────┐
      │   Gaining   │           │  Reviewing  │
      │   support   │           │   choices   │
      │   funding   │           │  planning   │
      └─────────────┘           └─────────────┘
```

demand? British steel workers formerly employed by the Anglo-Dutch Corus plant may wonder if their company skills will in future only be in demand in the Far East.

As noted earlier, the Leitch Report (2006) recognised the importance of skills for productivity, and noted that gaps in learning and skills were a collective reason for organisations' failure to compete in global markets. Furthermore, the Department of Innovation, Universities and Skills in 2007 identified skills and learning gaps as the primary cause for individual lack of participation in economic activity (Gold *et al*, 2010, p 381). This corroborates continuing professional development as an organisational defensive strategy against the prospect of sector decline or industry changes. In addition CPD offers the protection of employability for the individual.

 REFLECTIVE ACTIVITY

1. Provide examples of CPD from your own experience.

2. What has this learning enabled you to do differently?

3. Who, in your opinion, is the prime beneficiary of this development?

EVALUATING CPD

Given organisational investment in training and education, the business wants to harness professional learning to affect improved performance. The Confederation of British Industry's Education and Skills Survey (2009) reported that 43 per cent of employers believed that investing in skills has improved their profitability and productivity. This suggests that CPD practice can serve as a tool in achieving this objective of increasing skill level, and continual learning is often embedded as a performance requirement and reinforced as a core competence.

CPD AND PROFESSIONAL BODIES

Many professional bodies enforce the practice of CPD as a condition of active membership, and to ensure consumer protection. Professional status is accredited, and assures the public of their role as a legitimised expert. In certain cases CPD is a legal requirement and represents individual professional liability: for example, the Association of Chartered Certified Accountants (ACCA).

Review the following example of CPD from the Royal College of Veterinary Surgeons (Source: www.rcvs.org.uk):

> 'The RCVS Guide to Professional Conduct makes it very clear that veterinary surgeons have a responsibility to ensure that they maintain and continue to develop their professional knowledge and skills. CPD is therefore the personal obligation of all responsible veterinary surgeons and should be seen as the continuous progression of capability and competence.
>
> The recommended *minimum* CPD is 105 hours over three years with an average of 35 hours per year. It is appreciated that most veterinary surgeons will do considerably more than this.'

By contrast the Chartered Management Institute declares a broad approach to CPD (http://www.managers.org.uk/): 'The Institute is not prescriptive as to the content, approach or effort an individual member puts into their development but offers advice and practical support.'

 REFLECTIVE ACTIVITY

Review a range of professional bodies for examples of CPD practice. You might want to look at the Royal Institute of British Architects (RIBA), the Institute of Fisheries Management (IFM) or the Chartered Institute of Environmental Health (CIEH).

Then in a study group answer the questions below by comparing your findings of CPD requirements and methods of recording evidence.

Questions

1. What are the advantages of identifying specific CPD categories?

2. Discuss the possible limitations of such an approach.

Here is an example from the Chartered Institute of Plumbing and Heating Engineering (CIPHE), in the table below, which requires a plumbing engineer to participate in and log 30 hours of CPD annually (http://www.ciphe.org.uk).

CPD category	Maximum hours for CPD claim
Training courses and workshops	30 hours
Conferences and seminars/lectures	14 hours
Attending exhibitions	8 hours
Technical writing	15 hours or 30 for books
Mentoring	20 hours
Private study	8 hours
Qualification studies	30 hours

CPD PRACTICE: STICK OR CARROT?

Two models of continuing professional development are evident in professional bodies: the compulsory or the voluntary approach. Whereas voluntary practice appeals to members' enlightened self-interest, obligatory practice allows for CPD record auditing. A recent survey found that 50 per cent of professional bodies made CPD mandatory (*Personnel Today*, 2008). CPD was measured by task hours or study units completed, and sanctions included suspension. Of those surveyed 25 per cent did not measure CPD in any respect. The resistance to compulsory CPD can denote the balance of professional power – for example, in the medical field (Sanker, 2003, cited in Megginson and Whitaker, 2007, p 5).

CONSTRAINTS OF CPD

Even if CPD practice and recording is systematic, the outcome and application of such development remains subjective. An inspection framework attempts to judge professional development through quantitative measures. Clocking learning hours and course attendance is easy to verify. Yet exposure to specialist knowledge through conferences may be insufficient for professional advancement in context. Improvement through CPD participation is difficult to evaluate without an assessment of learning.

This highlights an inherent conflict between the demonstration of competence levels and the ongoing need for further development. It is in the interest of the professional body to promote its members' competence, and generate demand for management learning in its role as a provider of professional courses or a learning academy. There may be little inclination to publicise members' skill gaps or atrophying knowledge. The risk is of CPD deteriorating into a form-filling exercise dominated by process. CPD must be a meaningful account of learning development and skill acquisition beyond a record of attendance at training events. Transforming CPD into a conversation rather than a monologue remains a challenge.

Figure 10.7 Subjective reward of CPD

BENEFITS OF CPD

The main benefits of CPD for the individual are updating, increasing competence and enhancing mobility (Sadler-Smith *et al*, 2000). Within organisations CPD serves as an auditable record of development activities and agreed development planning. The potential rewards of CPD must be apparent to both the individual and the organisation. For an individual it can expand their options and develop transferable skills (Bradshaw, 1985). The individual incentives for CPD are shown in the thought bubbles of Figure 10.7.

From an organisation's perspective of manageable resource CPD can cultivate talent and capitalise on exponential learning. Is there then evidence of a convergence of interest for employers and employees in the widespread adoption of CPD?

An expansive concept of CPD is as an alternative to a linear career path. Organisations offer structured opportunities for employees to break from the daily routine and follow altruistic desires to serve the community. Thus sabbatical leave building classrooms in Cambodia may coincide with the organisational fulfilment of corporate social responsibility (CSR). Such volunteer work can satisfy personal brand values.

Skill currency and knowledge offer possibilities for a self-managed career. However, the individual imperative to update skills and acquire qualifications is often a response to job demands that will ensure contract renewal. Despite the heralded benefits of professional development as self-empowering, individuals may be entirely instrumental in learning as they seek to demonstrate career relevance. CPD is therefore increasingly an investment for employment continuity. An individual between jobs needs to acquire marketable experience that will differentiate them from other job candidates, such as herding elephants in Kenya. The individual works on CPD as a personal venture for investment (Peters, 1999) illustrating agility and self-reliance through a colourful CPD portfolio.

The CIPD points to continuing professional development as 'an essential part of professional life, not as an optional extra' (CIPD Professional standards, 2009). Because CPD represents such an integral feature of contemporary working life, it can be illustrated (Figure 10.8) as interconnecting gears within the organisation.

Figure 10.8 The dynamics of learning and development

 REFLECTIVE ACTIVITY

How can an organisation maintain the smooth interplay of the three cogs (LEG) in this model?

As evident from this reflective activity, mutual commitment is required to meet the demands of a dynamic economic environment and adapt to constant movement. Learning can increase capability for potential earning. Earning sustains business competitiveness and continuous growing. Growing can expand learning and be life-enhancing.

CONCLUSION

Learning and effective employee development can maximise opportunities for business survival and success. Managing talent and harvesting dedicated organisational knowledge can be vital. Yet such development activities are often challenged by a dynamic environment.

A one-size-fits all approach is unlikely to succeed. If HR is to be effective, it has to be broad, potentially ranging from traditional training provision to harnessing informal learning for both employee career development and organisational advantage. HR has a role to play in raising awareness of the value of learning and enhancing workforce skills. It must also focus on tacit knowledge management and the capture and transfer of unique company specific skills.

A renewed interest in career management and innovative support for professional development can retain talent and foster engagement. Workplace learning offers mutual benefits for both the organisation and the individual; it increases organisational capability whilst enhancing individual employability. A starting point for HR practitioners is to embrace the concept of lifelong learning, to ensure their own skill-sets are current and relevant, thus providing a role model for their organisations.

KEY LEARNING POINTS

In the light of the main theories and implications, key learning points that emerge are that:

- There is a robust business case for investment in employee development to increase competence and ensure organisational competitiveness.
- The impact of the knowledge economy demands continuous learning and skill currency.
- Successful employee and talent development demands a tripartite approach.
- The emphasis for employee development has shifted from formal training to broader concepts of learning, and values the impact of informal learning.
- Organisations need to proactively support career development to increase motivation and retain talent.
- The individual is increasingly responsible for learning and career initiatives.
- Continuing professional development is integral to expanding individual learning.

REVIEW QUESTIONS

1. How can informal learning be managed in order to capitalise on talent development?

2. How can the HR function address the demands of business leaders who only value formal training?

3. How can HR promote sustained professional development?

4. What is the business rationale for investment in career management and development?

5. How can line managers address the tensions of organisational needs and self-directed development?

6. How can HR practitioners encourage talent development that embraces a diversity of education and experience?

EXPLORE FURTHER

Gold, J. *et al* (2010) *Human Resource Development: Theory and Practice*. Palgrave Macmillan. Take a look at definitions of knowledge, skills and attitude and evidence for and against the systematic training cycle

Wilson, F. L. (2006) *Organisational Behaviour and Work*. Oxford University Press. View the different theories and models of how people learn.

Megginson, D. and Whitaker, V. (2007) *Continuing Professional Development*, 2nd ed. London: CIPD. Extend strategies for continuous professional development.

Pedler, M., Burgoyne, J. and Boydell, T. (2007) *A Manager's Guide to Self Development*, 5th ed. Maidenhead: McGraw-Hill. Explore self-development activities to support individual career planning and development.

CHAPTER 11

Managing the Employment Relationship

Derek Adam-Smith *and* Sally Rumbles

LEARNING OUTCOMES

After reading this chapter, you should be able to:

- specify the importance of the contract of employment and its limitations for the management of employees

- explain differences in how conflict at work is viewed and some of the implications for managerial action

- assess the key implications for managers of recognising trade unions as representatives of employees

- understand the importance of management style and management practice to the effective management of employees

- understand the difference between equal opportunities and diversity

- appreciate the complexity of managing a diverse workforce.

OVERVIEW

The objectives of organisations may be expressed in different ways. In the private sector these typically relate to profitability or market share, while in the public sector account must be taken of budgetary constraints imposed by politicians. Voluntary bodies may express their objectives in terms of service delivery to vulnerable groups in society. All organisations, however, employ people to achieve their objectives irrespective of how they are expressed. Employees, also, have needs that they want to meet from their work, and expectations about how they will be treated. In this chapter we explore some key features that shape the employment relationship between employers and employees. Some of these elements are determined by employment law which places constraints on management action. However, there still remains considerable choice in the way that employees may be managed, and this choice is influenced by managers' beliefs and their attitudes towards their staff. One key decision that must be made is whether employees are to be treated in the same way as other organisational resources, or are viewed as a special kind of resource that can provide a competitive advantage. Much contemporary human resource management literature is based upon the latter view, and we identify three current themes that are consistent with this perspective: partnership, employee engagement and diversity management.

INTRODUCTION

THE NATURE OF THE EMPLOYMENT RELATIONSHIP

The employment relationship is concerned with relations between an employer and an employee: its features and the ways in which it can be managed. Thus an understanding of employment relations is important for those who are responsible for the effective management of people at work.

In essence, employment relations is concerned with the 'wage-work bargain' – that is, what work an employee will do in return for the wages paid by the employer. The term 'wages' refers not just to the pay received, but also to other terms of employment such as holiday entitlement and sick pay. It may also refer to other rewards that the employer may provide, such as subsidised private health insurance and free childcare places. Similarly, 'work' has a wider meaning than the employee's job. Employers have expectations about both the quantity and quality of the work. Some explicitly define specific behavioural characteristics of tasks, particularly in what are called 'customer-facing' jobs. One example can be found in the fast-food outlet McDonald's, where employees are expected to acknowledge customers, create a friendly atmosphere, be courteous and have high standards of personal appearance (HRMID, 2007). An expectation for the exercise of this type of labour has been referred to as 'emotional labour' (Gilmore, in Gilmore and Williams, 2009).

THE CONTRACT OF EMPLOYMENT

A useful starting point for our understanding of the terms of the wage-work bargain is through the concept, or idea, of the contract of employment. Each individual has a contract of employment with his or her employer, and the contract specifies the terms and conditions under which the employee works. However, the nature of the contract of employment is often misunderstood. Very few employees in the UK have a written contract which contains all their terms and conditions of employment in one document: most of us have a contract whose terms can be found in a number of sources. Figure 11.1 depicts some of the main sources of the contract of employment.

When employees refer to their 'written contract of employment', what they often mean is a formal written statement of the main terms of employment. This document is not the contract, as shown in a judgement by the Employment Appeal Tribunal (EAT). In their judgement on a case, the EAT concluded that

Figure 11.1 Some possible sources of the contract of employment

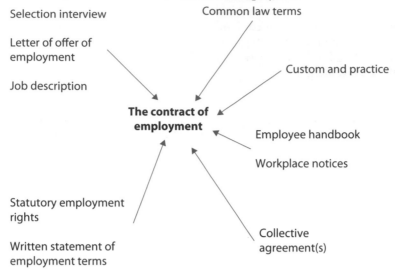

'this statement did not constitute a written contract between the parties. It was merely a document that stated the employer's views of the terms' (Sargeant and Lewis, 2008, p 75).

The written statement is important, nonetheless, since the Employment Relations Act 1996 requires it to specify the most important terms of employment, including pay, hours of work, holidays and sick pay.

The Act also allows employers to refer employees to other documents that contain these terms, or which provide more details. Thus, the other possible sources shown in Figure 11.1 may need to be examined if we are to have a clearer picture of the terms of the contract.

 REFLECTIVE ACTIVITY

Sources of the contract of employment

Obtain copies of as many of the documents shown in Figure 11.1 as you can, but especially offer letters, written statements and employee handbooks.

Read through these, and try to identify examples of statements that refer to employees' duties or responsibilities – ie what is expected of the employee. Also, identify examples of the pay and other benefits that an employee will be entitled to under the contract of employment.

It is common, especially in larger organisations, for the Human Resource (HR) department to produce an employee or staff handbook. This often contains details of employees' rights and duties. For example, it might explain what an employee is to do if they are unable to work through illness and what pay they will receive while sick. Similarly, employees who have a work roster may find that their actual times of work are provided by a notice.

Where an organisation uses job descriptions, these include the main duties and responsibilities of an employee: thus they seek to clarify the 'work' element of the wage-work bargain. At the selection interview, there may be discussion about the terms of employment. These may cover both the work expected of an employee and the pay they will receive. For example, a candidate might ask about opportunities for overtime work and be told by the line manager how that is arranged. Although such 'spoken promises' can become terms of the contract, the problem is that it may not be easy to be sure what was said. The avoidance of such problems was one of the reasons why legislation requires employers to provide the written statement so that there is less doubt over the terms of the contract. Similarly, the need to formalise what is agreed with an employee accounts for HR departments providing letters of employment offers and specifying details in employee handbooks.

However, some terms may still not be written down. Custom and practice refers to possible employment terms that arise because they have operated for some while. For example, an office may have a custom that all workers finish at lunchtime on Christmas Eve, but this has never been written down in any formal documentation. Suppose, then, a manager tells her staff that they will need to work till 17.30, their normal finishing time. Is this lawful? If an employee challenges this decision in a court, it may be decided that the custom is part of the terms of employment.

 REFLECTIVE ACTIVITY

Custom and practice

In the example of custom and practice given in the text about finishing work early on Christmas Eve, what factors do you think the courts might take into account to decide if it was reasonable for the employees to finish at lunchtime?

Other terms may be implied by judges to exist in a contract of employment. These are sometimes referred to as the 'common law terms'. For example, all employees have a duty to use reasonable skill and care in their work. It will be for the courts to decide what is reasonable, but, as we have seen above, job descriptions might be used to specify the standard of work expected of an employee. Another duty of employees is to give faithful and honest service and not commit misconduct. Many organisations will produce a list of disciplinary rules which seek to clarify what this common law term means for employees in reality, and these are often included in the employee handbook. The important point to note, however, is that even if these are not specified in any document, the duties still exist as part of the employee's contract of employment.

Statutory employment rights refer to those that are provided through legislation, emanating from both national and supra-national – eg European Union (EU) – levels. Their purpose is to provide a minimum 'floor of rights' for all employees, and employers cannot offer terms that are worse than those provided by legislation. Some of these relate to specific parts of the wage-work bargain – for example, the UK National Minimum Wage and the EU Working Time Directive, which was implemented in the UK through the Working Time Regulations. The latter specifies maximum hours of work. Other statutory employment rights are concerned with the way in which employees are managed. These include the right not to be unfairly dismissed, and thus how disciplinary action should implemented by a manager, and legislation that seeks to prohibit unlawful discrimination on certain grounds – for example, race, sex, religion and belief. We explore discrimination in more detail later in the chapter, and also deal with the issue in Chapters 4 and 9.

The final source of employment terms shown in Figure 11.2 below is collective agreements. These can be found in organisations that recognise a trade union or unions, and where terms of employment such as pay and holidays are negotiated between the union and the employer. The outcomes of the negotiations are called collective agreements since they cover the collective group of workers represented by the trade union. A collective agreement normally covers all the employees in a particular occupation or grade, whether or not they are union members. Where unions are recognised, the employer has a relationship with both individual employees and the trade union.

Collective agreements are not normally legally enforceable between the employer and trade union. However, the substantive terms of these agreements – for example, pay and hours – are incorporated into individual contracts of employment. Where an employer has collective agreements with a trade union these agreements can be an important source of an employee's contractual terms.

THE WAGE-WORK BARGAIN REVISITED

The effective management of the employment relationship requires managers to understand the nature of the contract of employment. In particular, it is important to recognise that the terms of the contract may be found in a number of different sources. However, Williams and Adam-Smith (2010) point out that there are two major problems with viewing the employment relationship simply

Figure 11.2 The relationship between the contract of employment and collective agreements

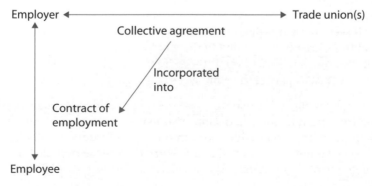

as a contractual one. First, a contract implies that the two parties come together in a free and equal way. However, those seeking work are clearly in a weaker position than the employer who has the freedom to offer the job to a number of applicants – see also Chapter 9. Furthermore, once an employee has taken a job, she or he is then required to obey the employer's commands or orders. The second problem with a simple contractual view of the relationship is that it is not possible to specify, at the outset of the relationship, all the obligations of the parties. The contract is thus open-ended, and the relative power of the parties will be important in deciding how the relationship is shaped. Thus, it is also important to recognise that the employment relationship has a power dimension, and that there is potential for differences, or conflict, to emerge in the relationship. Of course, the relationship is also characterised by co-operation between the employer and employees. The latter have an interest in the success of their employer which will help secure their jobs.

TRADE UNIONS AND COLLECTIVE BARGAINING

Union membership has declined significantly in the UK since its peak of some 13 million in 1980 when over half of all employees were members of a trade union, and collective agreements set the terms and conditions of about three-quarters of the UK workforce. Overall, some seven million workers are now union members which accounts for around 27 per cent of the workforce (Barratt, 2009). Union membership remains particularly strong in the public sector, though, where about two-thirds of employees are members. In the private sector membership is under 20 per cent and mainly confined to larger employers.

As we saw above, collective agreements arrived at through negotiation between trade unions and employers can be a major source of an employee's contractual terms. Collective bargaining refers to the process where employers and unions jointly agree the terms and conditions of employees. For the employer, collective bargaining can be an efficient means of determining contractual terms since it does not require negotiation with each individual employee, and can assist in containing the conflict that may arise over employment terms. In addition, since the union has made the agreement, it has an interest in ensuring its members (the employees of the organisation) accept the terms that are agreed. Collective bargaining, then, is a key function of trade unions, and is a process that can provide greater equality of power in the employment relationship.

Collective bargaining is concerned with both parts of the wage-work bargain. It determines important parts of the wage the employee receives. As well as pay, hours and holidays it may cover matters such as overtime and shift premiums, sick pay, redundancy payments, pensions and health insurance (Kersley *et al*, 2006). These terms are the 'economic' aspects of the contract, or 'wages'. However, collective bargaining can also determine 'work' issues. For example, as well as redundancy pay, a collective agreement may specify how staff would be selected for redundancy, should that situation arise. In addition, it is not uncommon for there to be collective agreements covering staffing plans, equal opportunities and performance appraisal schemes. Thus, collective bargaining has a 'managerial' aspect which means that these matters are determined by joint agreement, not by managers alone. This provides an example of how gaps in the open-ended contract may be filled.

As well as collectively bargaining with employers on behalf of employees, trade unions have other functions. First, they may provide specific services to their members as individuals. These may include legal and financial advice for both work and personal matters. Trade unions in the UK also seek to represent their members outside the workplace in wider social matters. This might include lobbying for improved employment legislation such as the introduction of the National Minimum Wage, and campaigning to improve the employment conditions of migrant workers.

One further role of trade unions, important to those managing employment relations, is the involvement of unions in formal grievance, disciplinary and similar matters where union officials typically represent their members at interviews.

 REFLECTIVE ACTIVITY

Find out more details of the role of trade unions. The easiest way to do this is to go to the unions' websites. If your employer recognises a union or unions, this would be a good starting point. If not, perhaps visit the web pages of a union you have recently heard about in the news. Most can be found simply by typing their name into a search engine or visiting the Trades Union Congress website, www.tuc.org.uk, which lists many unions. For each union, identify how it describes its role and seeks to achieve its objectives, the types of workers it recruits and how many members it has.

THE ROLE OF PROCEDURES

Grievance and disciplinary procedures are two of the most common ones found in organisations. However, there may be separate procedures covering specific employment matters: harassment and bullying; equal opportunities; pay grading if a job evaluation scheme is used; and appeals against performance appraisal ratings, especially if this is linked to pay. The purpose of a procedure is to create a 'problem-solving pathway'. In many cases this means allowing managers to consider an employee complaint, or, in the case of disciplinary action, providing managers with the opportunity to change or correct an employee's behaviour. The main reason for having employment relations procedures is so that appropriate action can be taken to solve a problem, rather than leave employees feeling they must express their disagreement with management through other means – for example, by being absent from work or performing below their capability. Procedures seek to ensure that managers deal with employment issues in a fair and consistent way, and are one of the ways in which managers seek to control or contain conflict in the employment relationship.

CONFLICT AND THE EMPLOYMENT RELATIONSHIP

We have noted the potential for conflict to arise in the employment relationship, so how do managers view the reasons for its existence? Before exploring the answer to this question, undertake the following Reflective Activity.

REFLECTIVE ACTIVITY

Conflict at work

For this activity, you are asked to reflect on each of the four following statements on conflict between employers and employees. For each, identify the values or beliefs of those people who hold this view. Which of these views most closely reflects your own view? Why?

Conflict between an employer and employee is:

1. a dysfunctional factor in an otherwise healthy organisation

2. largely preventable, provided organisations take a proactive approach to developing policies and practices which take account of employees' needs and expectations from work

3. an inherent feature of organisational life, but one that can be largely institutionalised and managed through recognising that differences of interests exist between the two parties

4. a reflection of the fundamental divisions and inequalities in the wider society.

Each of the four views reflects different explanations of the causes of conflict between employers and employees and how they are to be managed. These views are based on 'frames of reference': a term first attributed to Fox (1966, 1974) to distinguish between the beliefs held by managers that influence their approach to the management of employees.

Those that believe that conflict is dysfunctional are characterised as holding a 'unitary' view. Often using the team or family analogy, those with unitary perspective expect cooperation from their staff since the goals of the organisation and employees are the same: employees must understand and accept their role, and also accept that the leaders of the organisation are best-placed to make the important decisions. With its emphasis on cooperation, the unitary view would see conflict as a result of poor communications, or, significantly, as the result of trouble-makers, like trade union activists, who generate conflict in an otherwise harmonious organisation.

As human resource management theory and practice has developed, some authors have coined the term 'neo-unitary' to capture the beliefs that underpin this approach to managing the employment relationship (Farnham and Pimlott, 1995). This perspective has much in common with the traditional unitary view in that cooperation and harmony between employers and employees is believed to be the normal state of affairs. However, as the statement in the activity suggests, conflict can be prevented, but only if managers are proactive in developing policies and practices that take account of the needs and expectations of employees. Managers will thus need to utilise the knowledge provided by the

Human Relations school of thinking to engender employees' commitment to their work and the organisation's objectives (Edwards, 2003).

Those who believe that conflict in the employment relationship is inevitable are said to hold a 'pluralist' perspective. While not disputing that there is scope for cooperation between managers and employees, pluralists point to the differences in interests between employers and employees. For example, employers will naturally wish to minimise wages while employees will, equally naturally, wish to maximise their pay. The key concern of pluralists in the employment relationship is to find ways to manage the conflict so that disruption – for example, in the form of strikes – is limited. For those with a pluralist perspective, trade unions are not the cause of conflict. Rather they have a legitimate role in representing one interest group, employees, in the relationship. The task for managers is to build a relationship with trade unions, and develop procedures so that disputes and differences can be resolved through the process of negotiation.

Those holding a Marxist view of conflict see this as the result of workers being exploited in the employment relationship. The development of procedures with trade unions to prevent and resolve expressions of conflict is, at best, only a temporary solution. Conflict, it is argued, will be eliminated only when the distinction between the owners of capital and workers is removed.

MANAGEMENT STYLE AND EMPLOYMENT RELATIONS

The distinction between unitary and pluralist perspectives provides a basis for understanding different management styles. According to Purcell and Ahlstrand (1994, p 177) '[management] style implies the existence of a distinctive set of guiding principles, written or otherwise, which set parameters to and signposts for management action regarding the way employees are to be treated. . . .' 'Style', then, describes the choice that is made as to how the employment relationship is to be managed. These authors identify two dimensions of management style: individualism and collectivism.

INDIVIDUALISM

Two broad extremes of individualism can be identified, based on the extent to which managers view employees as individuals with needs and aspirations. Those that are described as having 'high individualism' or an 'investment orientation' towards staff would typically emphasise the following policies and practices:

- employees seen as an important resource
- a focus on internal labour markets
- employee development, appraisal and individual systems of reward
- empowerment.

This management style is based on a neo-unitary view where conflict and differences can be prevented, and, as we will see later, is aimed at generating employee engagement.

In contrast, managers who have a low concern with individual employees, a traditional unitary view, would adopt a 'cost minimisation' approach with the following characteristics:

- labour as a commodity to be bought from, and returned to, the external labour market as economic activity dictates
- an emphasis on numerical flexibility
- limited, if any, training
- tight control over pay.

COLLECTIVISM

Purcell and Ahlstrand (1994) also draw a similar distinction on the collective dimension of management style which seeks to capture the extent to which managers accept that employees have a right to act collectively – for example, by joining a trade union – and are willing to negotiate and consult with employee representatives. At one extreme, typical of the traditional unitary approach, there would be resistance and hostility towards trade unions. At the other end of the spectrum the relationship sought by management is highly cooperative with the union, and would include: regular consultation with union representatives on strategic plans; extensive information exchange; and the use of joint working parties to manage employment matters. The contemporary term for this approach is 'partnership', and we examine this later in the chapter. Between these extremes lies what Purcell and Ahlstrand (1994) refer to as 'adversarial relations'.

Such relationships may exist in organisations where unions have been recognised by the employer for many years, but where managers would prefer not to have to negotiate with them. The primary concern of managers in these firms will be to protect their right to make decisions without the involvement of unions, sometimes called the 'managerial prerogative' (Storey, 1983). Control and stability of the employment relationship, through formally agreed procedures, are important characteristics in such businesses, and the issues on which unions can negotiate are usually carefully and tightly drawn.

ADVERSARIAL EMPLOYMENT RELATIONS AT BRITISH AIRWAYS?

Employment relations in British Airways (BA) are conducted through collective bargaining with a number of trade unions representing the different groups of workers it employs. Cabin crew staff, those providing in-flight services to passengers, are mainly organised by the British Airlines Stewards and Stewardesses Association (BASSA) which is part of the Unite trade union.

During the 1990s, in response to increased competition both from airlines like Virgin Atlantic on its long-haul routes, and low-cost operators such as Easyjet and Ryanair, BA sought to reduce its operating costs. With employment accounting for 30 per cent of total costs, changes to employment terms offered a potential solution for the company. The proposals made by BA led to a number of disputes with the trade unions, including strike action by BASSA members, amongst others.

Faced with substantial losses during 2009 the company proposed reducing the number of cabin crew on long-haul lights from 15 to 14 and the introduction of a two-year pay freeze. The airline also proposed changed contracts of employment for newly-recruited and promoted cabin crew that included setting pay at market rate plus 10 per cent: the latter meaning that new staff will be paid significantly less than current workers. These proposals were rejected by cabin crew members in the summer.

In November 2009 BA introduced a pay freeze and new staffing levels. BASSA claimed that BA could not unilaterally make these changes, and balloted its members on strike action. Although an overwhelming majority voted in favour of going on strike, which was planned around the Christmas period, the High Court declared the ballot unlawful. A second ballot in early 2010 produced another majority in favour of a strike. Two four-day strikes took place in March. As the dispute became more acrimonious there were allegations that BA saw the dispute as a way of weakening BASSA and that the Unite leadership were unhappy with the way BASSA were conducting the dispute. BA had also informed its staff that those who took strike action would lose their travel concessions which allow them and their family to travel standby for 10 per cent of the normal airfare.

Questions

1. What does this dispute tell you about employment relations between BA and its cabin crew?

2. Do you think BA was right to insist on making changes to employment terms given its financial position? Why do you think employees did not accept these changes?

3. Would you have advised BA managers to do anything differently?

PARTNERSHIP AGREEMENTS

We have already noted the importance of collective agreements as a source of employment terms, and that these can be arrived at through either adversarial or cooperative relationships between the employer and trade unions. In recent years there has been increased attention given to 'partnership agreements' between employers and unions which appear to be the result of a more cooperative approach between the two parties. As Williams and Adam-Smith (2010, p 236) note: 'at the heart of partnership working is the notion that it benefits the employer, the recognized union, and the workforce at large too.' However, while pointing out that the concept is 'rather ambiguous', they suggest that studies of such agreements identify some common elements:

- a shared commitment between the employer and trade union to the success of the organisation
- the development of new forms of communication and consultation arrangements
- some form of employer guarantee on job or employment security
- union acceptance of the need for its members to work flexibly.

 REFLECTIVE ACTIVITY

Partnership agreements

List what you believe to be the benefits of partnership agreements to: the employer, the trade union, and the employees of the organisation.

Each of the elements of partnership agreements justifies a little more explanation. The first can be little more than empty rhetoric. However, if it genuinely reflects a greater level of trust between the parties, it may lead to improved employment relations. The development of communication and consultation processes can take different forms. Such processes may, for example, provide for trade unions to be more closely involved in the decision-making processes of the organisations, at least to the extent that union representatives are consulted on those matters that may have an impact on employees. Also, they may provide for representatives of all employees, not just those that are union members, to be informed and involved in business decisions.

The final two elements seek to meet the key needs of the employer and employees. Employees may be reluctant to be more flexible in their working arrangements if they believe that this could put jobs at risk. Thus flexibility comes if the employer is willing to agree to some level of employment security. Not, perhaps, a commitment that employees will keep those specific jobs as a result of organisational change, but that alternative jobs will be available – hence 'employment security'. These two components, then, combine to establish a degree of mutuality in the partnership agreement since each meets the respective key need of the employer and the employee.

As businesses struggle in the difficult economic climate, we have a good opportunity to see how well partnership agreements work in practice. Do they allow the business to survive when faced with poor trading conditions, and provide employees with higher levels of job security than would have been the case without it? Alternatively, are the espoused benefits of partnership working only enjoyed when economic conditions are favourable for organisations? This suggests that the central plank of partnership is the trust needed between the parties in the employment relationship. Without this, partnership is unlikely to succeed.

EMPLOYEE ENGAGEMENT

As we pointed out at the start of this chapter, the management of employment relations implicitly includes three current themes. We have referred to the first of these, namely partnership, in the preceding sections. We go on to look at the third of these – diversity management – in greater detail later in this chapter. We now turn to our second theme of employee engagement.

The management of the employment relationship characterised by an 'investment orientation' towards employees is designed to elicit their commitment to the organisation. Where managers are able to achieve an engaged workforce it is claimed that this can lead to both organisational success and employee well-being (MacLeod and Clark, 2009). A recent CIPD-commissioned research report (Alfes *et al*, 2010, p 5) identified engagement as having three dimensions:

- intellectual engagement – thinking about the job and how it might be done better

- affective engagement – positive feelings about doing a job well

- social engagement – actively seeking opportunities to discuss work-related issues.

Where organisations are able to effectively engage their employees on these dimensions, the authors claim that three important outcomes can be identified which can assist organisations in the achievement of their objectives. First, engaged employees are likely to perform better than those who are not. Respondents in the survey claimed to have good levels of job and social skills, were willing to take on extra work and tended to have high ratings in their performance appraisal. Secondly, engaged employees are more likely to be innovative at work. This might include searching out new methods of working, generate enthusiasm for innovative ideas and transform such ideas into meaningful applications. Thirdly, engaged employees are more likely to want to stay with their employer.

How then can organisations generate employee engagement? Alfes *et al* (2010, p 55) propose six drivers of engagement:

1. meaningfulness of work

2. employee voice

3. senior management communication and vision

4. line management

5. person-job fit

6. supportive work environment.

'Meaningfulness' refers to being able to relate one's own tasks to a broader context and to feeling able to make a difference (see also Chapters 8 and 12), and is identified as the most important driver of engagement.

Employee involvement mechanisms were found to be the second most important factor affecting engagement. Engagement levels increased when employees felt that they had a voice in decisions that were being made about their work. The importance of management style on employee engagement, and, thus, performance is underlined by the significance of these two factors. Through communication, managers can help employees place their own work in the context of the 'bigger picture' of the organisation's objectives. Similarly, establishing and maintaining effective communication and consultation channels can both reinforce employees' view of the value of their work and enhance social engagement.

It is perhaps no surprise then that the Alfes report (2010) emphasises the importance of the style of both line and senior managers in employee engagement. While the relevance of the latter has been outlined above, line managers, it is suggested, are the crucial link between the employer and employees, and their behaviour is central to levels of engagement. Their key tasks in this respect are selecting the correct people for the job (the person-job fit), regular communication with their staff, relevant training and development, and ensuring reciprocity of effort and reward.

DIVERSITY AT WORK

INDIVIDUAL DIFFERENCES AND MANAGEMENT STYLES

Management style also affects the way in which managers handle the individual characteristics of employees. We would expect those who have an 'investment orientation' towards employees to take account of individual differences to the benefit of the organisation. Such an approach is analogous with the management of diversity. Before examining the meaning of diversity we briefly consider the legal provisions on discrimination.

We noted earlier that statutory employment rights are an important source of an employee's terms, and that specific legislation makes for unfair discrimination if it is based on the grounds of sex, race, age, religion, belief, sexual orientation or disability. As we have seen in Chapters 4 and 7, managers regularly discriminate between employees, for example in choosing between job applicants. The legislation prohibits discrimination which has no connection with the work to be done, and distinguishes between direct and indirect discrimination. An example of direct discrimination would be a job advertisement that states that only women can apply for the post. Indirect discrimination arises when a requirement or condition that cannot be justified is applied to a situation where members of one or more of the protected groups cannot comply. An example from the authors' own experience involved a hospitality company that required bar staff to have GCSEs in English language and mathematics. Many of its existing staff, performing the job competently, did not have this qualification, so it was not a necessary requirement. It was judged unlawful since anyone educated outside England or Wales would not have taken these examinations.

EQUAL OPPORTUNITIES

The concept of equal opportunities underpins many organisational approaches to equality in the UK which have been developed in response to the legislation introduced by successive UK governments since the mid-1970s to address unfair discrimination in the pursuit, obtaining and retaining of employment, as well as other workplace practices. The result is a legal framework developed around a definition of inequality that draws heavily on the idea of indirect discrimination: 'discriminating against people on grounds that are irrelevant to the jobs they doing or for which they are applying' (Chryssides and Kaler, 1996, p 89). To reduce the disparate treatment by managers, the HR profession has focused on establishing specific procedures to ensure legal compliance and demonstrate equal treatment (Harris, 2005). Thus the 'neutral treatment' principle of much anti-discrimination legislation has become the cornerstone of organisational policies and procedures which are designed to achieve sameness of treatment in resourcing decisions (Foster and Harris, 2005, p 6).

An equal opportunities approach is seen as one of 'compliance' with the law. It typically focuses attention on groups that may be unlawfully discriminated against, and features such initiatives as target-setting, positive action and redressing past discrimination. Its attraction for line managers is that it offers a certain simplicity and ease of application by reducing the scope for exercising discretion and providing the essential means of defending their decisions against claims of less favourable treatment (Wilson and Iles, 1999). Its limitation is that it has led HR specialists and operational managers alike to focus on consistency of process or procedural justice, even though consistency is a relative principle, whose pursuit alone will not act as a catalyst for progressive employment practice (Foster and Harris, 2005). Relying on a principle of consistency is problematic as it does not require individuals to be treated well, only alike, and allows for situations where all employees are treated equally, but equally badly (Fredman, 2001).

In order to meet its EU membership requirements, equality legislation in the UK has expanded to take account of a growing number of specific groups in the workforce. The EU continues to be highly influential in this respect since managing diversity is a key component of the 2009 Lisbon Treaty. In the UK there will be a single Equality Bill, due to become law in October 2010. This is expected to introduce rights that relate to personal circumstances rather than to personal characteristics: for example, parental leave rights. The resultant increased legal complexity has meant that managers need to be aware not only of individual rights, but, as we saw with an 'investment orientation' to employees, a concern with individual needs at work. In other words, a managing diversity approach. Managing diversity in this context is framed as a strategic response arising from demographic change, and is differentiated from equal opportunities on the basis that organisations should focus on the individual rather than the potentially disadvantaged group to which the employee belongs. Thus diversity encompasses a whole range of differences beyond those associated with disadvantage or covered by anti-discrimination legislation (Tomlinson and Schwabenland, 2010).

REFLECTIVE ACTIVITY

Equality and diversity in practice 1

Go online and research the equality and diversity statements on the websites of the TUC, www.tuc.org.uk, and one or two of the largest trade unions such as Unite, www.unitetheunion.com or Unison, www.unison.org.uk. What evidence can you find about their view on equal opportunities? Read the next section on 'the nature of diversity' and research the websites to see if there is any indication of a diversity focus.

THE NATURE OF DIVERSITY

Equal opportunities (EO) initiatives in the UK are aimed at developing a level playing field for disadvantaged groups, but it is claimed that they have failed to achieve the goal of greater organisational inclusion of minorities for two reasons. First, they do not cover adequately all disadvantaged groups, and those that they do (such as women and non-white employees) are treated as homogeneous, often stereotyped, groups. Second, EO fails to generate the involvement and commitment of managers who perceive it simply as a compliance issue (Ahmed, 2007). Managing diversity is claimed to overcome these limitations, and to provide a powerful set of arguments with which to mobilise management interest in the needs of members of minority groups (Kandola and Fullerton, 1994). At the same time writers such as Belbin (1991) found that culturally diverse teams were more effective than homogeneous ones, thus providing the basis of a business case for diversity. French (2010) summarises research showing that the performance of multicultural groups at work was typically either much better than that of mono-cultural groups, or significantly worse, highlighting the importance of careful management of such groups, if they are to be effective.

Unlike EO initiatives, a diversity approach recognises that everyone is different even though some may share certain characteristics such as ethnic origin, gender, etc. Diversity therefore consists of visible factors – eg race, age – but also non-visible personal characteristics including background, culture, personality and preferred work-style. The diversity argument is founded on the premise that 'harnessing these differences will create a productive environment in which everybody feels valued, where their talents are being fully utilised and in which organisational goals are met' (Kandola and Fullerton, 1994, p 40). The CIPD defines diversity as 'valuing everyone as an individual – valuing people as employees, customers and clients' (CIPD, 2010d, p 2). In principle, diversity management encourages the development of more innovative HR policies and practices which offer greater reciprocity in the employment relationship by addressing individual needs. This HR approach appears more relevant to the flexible behaviour required of employees in the less predictable work roles that are a feature of contemporary working life (Foster and Harris, 2005). The problem for today's managers then is that there is no single best way of treating employees, because each one will have their own personal needs, values and beliefs.

ORGANISATIONAL BENEFITS OF DIVERSITY

Three main reasons are typically used to justify an organisational approach for making equality and diversity an important management issue:

- the business case
- the impact of the demographic time-bomb
- the social justice argument.

The business case for diversity

According to the CIPD (2010d), there are three business reasons for organisations exceeding legal requirements on discrimination: people issues, market competitiveness and corporate reputation.

1. People issues – creating an open and inclusive workplace culture in which everyone feels valued helps to recruit and retain good people. People aspire to work for employers with good employment practices and to feel valued at work. To be competitive, organisations need to derive the best contributions from everyone. Skills shortages and difficulties in filling vacancies are forcing organisations to recruit from more diverse pools and to offer different working arrangements in the 'war for talent'. Managing diversity creates a recruitment pool that improves the chances of getting the right person for the right job. Diversity also creates engaged employees working in a climate of productivity and commitment, with low turnover and sickness absence rates. In turn, creativity and innovation are increased.

2. Product market competitiveness – a diverse workforce can help to inform the development of new or enhanced products or services, open up new market opportunities, improve market share and broaden an organisation's customer base.

3. Corporate reputation – healthy businesses flourish in healthy societies and the needs of people, communities and businesses are interrelated. Social exclusion and low economic activity rates limit business markets and their growth. Thus businesses need to consider corporate social responsibility (CSR) in the context of diversity. The overall image of an organisation can be important in attracting and retaining both customers and employees.

Arguably, the business and social justice cases for diversity are complementary, because unless people are treated fairly at work they will feel less committed and may under-perform. Despite many criticisms of the business case, researchers claim that it and social justice arguments can coexist to produce a case for diversity that is capable of achieving greater social equality. In some organisations – for example, in the voluntary sector – the business case and social justice is largely the same thing (Tomlinson and Schwabenland, 2010).

Studies have found that not all HR diversity practices are associated with increased workforce diversity and that attitudes to diversity in large corporations have been, at best, mixed. For example, managers in some organisations have tended to see its value in recruitment and selection, but have not applied it to other working practices. There is also a wide recognition of the supposed value of workforce diversity, but mixed evidence on its impact on business performance. The CIPD (2005c) claims that there is evidence that indicates improved financial performance in organisations which take diversity seriously. However, others argue that there is limited empirical data to prove an association between the outcome of HR diversity practices and improved organisational performance (Shen *et al*, 2009). Despite the apparent attractiveness of the business case it appears that organisations still see legislation as the main driver for making changes in practice, and view diversity management as a cost rather than a driver of organisational success. If that is the case, it suggests that arguments for the business case need to be communicated more effectively and its profile raised as a strategic business lever (CIPD, 2007d).

 REFLECTIVE ACTIVITY

Equality and diversity in practice 2

Go online and research the equality and diversity statements of your employer and one or two other employers. What indication do they give as to whether their approach is more equal opportunities or diversity focused? Identify some examples of the business case for diversity for your chosen organisations.

Demographic changes

The UK workforce is ageing; the proportion of the working population aged between 50 and 64 is at its highest level since the 1970s. This trend is continuing, with predictions that by 2033, 23 per cent of the population will be aged 65 and over with only 16 per cent aged 16 or younger. In addition, there is a sharp tapering of people in the workforce between 30 and 40 years old due to low birth rates in the 1970s, and there are fewer white able-bodied men under 45 years of age (ONS, 2010). Put simply, changing demographics mean that if there are fewer white males available for employment, employers need to consider broadening their search for employees. In the view of the then Department of Trade and Industry: '21st century organisations require a flexible, highly skilled workforce, adaptable to change and able to compete in the global marketplace. Employers need to be fishing in the widest possible talent pool to ensure they have access to the breadth and depth of skills available, which meet their business needs' (DTI, 2001, p 3). The demographic time-bomb created by falling birth rates and longer life-spans means that fewer younger people will be employed to provide the taxes to support an ageing population. Even though changes in retirement ages may enable people to have the right to work longer, the statistics predict that proportionately fewer people will be in paid employment.

MANAGING DIVERSITY — HOW TO MOVE EQUALITY FORWARD

One of the main criticisms of managing diversity is that it requires significant resources with no guarantee of success. There is no instant formula for its achievement because it is a complex task and every organisation will approach it differently. The CIPD (2005c, 2007d and 2010d) suggests that, in common with other strategies for employee engagement, it needs to be led from the top of the organisation. Further, it requires systematic management action that moves from minimal legal compliance to a focus on the development of an open workplace culture in which everyone feels valued and can add value. The key is to make managing diversity a mainstream issue, owned by everyone so that it influences all employment policies, practices and drivers.

The CIPD suggests the following tips for implementing a successful managing diversity strategy:

- ensure that initiatives and policies have the support of senior management
- remember managing diversity is a continuous process, not a one-off initiative
- develop a diversity strategy to support the achievement of business goals which addresses the diverse needs of customers
- focus on fairness and inclusion, ensuring that merit, competence and potential are the basis for people decisions
- review policies and update with changes in law

 REFLECTIVE ACTIVITY

How diverse is the workforce?

Diversity: the state of play.

- Unemployment is twice as high among people from ethnic minorities, and there are proportionately more unemployed Chinese, Indian and Black African graduates than white graduates. Interestingly, however, only 12 per cent of white men are in professional occupations, as opposed to 21 per cent of Chinese and Indian men.

- White men have the lowest rate of participation in full-time education between the ages of 16 and 24 (37 per cent) followed by white women (40 per cent).

- 41 per cent of white women in employment work part-time, but only 7 per cent of white men do so, as opposed to 38 per cent of Bangladeshi men.

- Black and Asian people are 2.5 times less likely to have jobs than whites.

- Ethnic minorities account for 8 per cent of the overall population. Because they are relatively younger, it was projected that ethnic minorities would account for half the growth in working population to 2009.

- In the past ten years, the employment rate of the over-50s has risen by almost 25 per cent. The number of people aged over 60 is forecast to rise by 40 per cent in the next 30 years (CIPD, 2010d).

Consider the above statistics about diversity and compare them with those in the organisation for which you work. How diverse is your organisation in comparison to these statistics? What initiatives are taken by your employer to encourage diversity – for example, part-time working, flexible hours, etc? What initiatives could your employer consider in future to encourage a more diverse workforce?

- address work-life balance needs to the benefit of the organisation and the employee by offering suitable choices and options
- encourage ownership, creating a culture of empowerment so that decisions are not passed up without good reason
- develop guidelines for managers to help them respond flexibly and appropriately to diversity needs
- link diversity management to other initiatives such as Investors in People and quality management
- be aware of the international context and the influence of national cultures on work.

The social justice argument has been examined in more detail in Chapter 4. It is essentially an ethically-driven approach incorporating corporate social responsibility. It is often associated with compliance measures directed at disadvantaged groups, target-setting and positive action (Rayner and Rumbles, in Gilmore and Williams, 2009). As such, the social justice argument has frequently been linked with equal opportunities measures targeting groups rather than the individually-focused orientation of diversity management.

FORD: DRIVING DIVERSITY AND INCLUSION

CASE STUDY

'You are unique. That is important to us, and we value the abilities and perspectives all of our employees bring to their work. From the boardroom to the design studio, from the plant floors to the engineering centres, each employee is part of Ford's collective strength as a company. Ford has always taken steps to develop a workforce which reflects the communities in which we do business.

Today we continue to attract a highly skilled and committed workforce that reflects the diversity within our society. Such variety only helps us better reflect and cater to the needs and requirements of our diverse customer base. Diversity is not only a reality of our workforce, it is a distinct advantage. Ford's comprehensive diversity strategy has helped to create an inclusive environment, which meets the diverse needs of its people and adds value to the business. Our inclusion policies are supported by strong management commitment, robust procedures and effective measurement tools.

Ford believes in corporate social responsibility and is committed to diversity and inclusion in all aspects of our business, including suppliers, contractors, and dealerships. All business partners are required to meet the standards outlined in our diversity and dignity at work policies.

Throughout our history, inclusion has been as much a part of our success as our great products. By choice, Ford is committed to a diverse workplace not simply because it's good for business, but because it is the right thing to do.'

Source: Ford website www.ford.co.uk/About Ford/ Ford Careers/WhyJoinFord/Diversity&inclusion

Questions

1. Examine the practicalities of managing a diverse workforce in a traditional production environment like Ford.

2. How might you reconcile the needs of individuals such as workers with caring responsibilities (children or elderly parents) with the needs of a production-line environment?

3. How far should employers adapt workplace practices to accommodate individual needs?

CONCLUSION

The management of the employment relationship is a complex task. Managers have considerable choice in the way in which they structure the relationship, including the extent to which they view employees as a resource, and whether to deal with trade unions as representatives of employees. One key factor that may influence that choice is the market within which the business operates. Employers with tight product or service margins may decide that the costs of investing in employees cannot be afforded. Similarly, they may decide that trade unions will limit flexibility and add to labour costs. It is also important to note that although an investment orientation that includes recognition of individual differences is claimed to improve business performance, there is mixed evidence about the extent of this success.

KEY LEARNING POINTS

This chapter has examined a number of issues important to the management of the employment relationship, and has made the following key points:

- Employment law places some constraints on how managers can treat their employees.

- Beliefs shape management style and influence whether employees are seen as a resource or a factor of production, and whether trade unions are perceived to be legitimate representatives or a source of conflict.

- To achieve a workforce that is trusting of management and committed to the success of the organisation requires managerial initiatives to develop an appropriate culture supported by relevant policies and practices.

- Three contemporary developments which reflect strategies to achieve the commitment of employees are partnership agreements with trade unions, employee engagement and diversity management.

- Discriminatory decisions taken at work need to be made on factors relevant to the work itself and not on personal characteristics such as age, sex, race, etc.

- An equal opportunities approach can be portrayed as one that seeks compliance with legislation, and typically focuses on identifiying the groups who are more susceptible to unfair discrimination. It utilises procedures that are designed to meet legal requirements on equal treatment.

- The managing diversity approach focuses on the individual with the aim of creating a work environment where everyone feels valued, where their talents are fully utilised and where organisational goals are met.

REVIEW QUESTIONS

1. With regard to the following scenarios, identify what you consider to be typical features present in respect of the management of the employment relationship:

   — where employees are seen as a resource that can provide competitive advantage

   — where trade unions are recognised for collective bargaining

   — where employees are viewed as a 'factor of production'

   If possible, you should draw on your own work experience.

2. What action can an HR manager take to prevent conflict arising within an organisation? If it does arise, what options exist for its resolution?

3. A line manager has asked you to help her understand the importance of the contract of employment, and how far she can rely upon it to ensure she gets 'the best out of her staff'. How would you reply?

4. Evaluate the evidence that managing diversity is good for business using examples from academic sources or from your experience. If you were an HR professional, what arguments could you make to your employer in support of the business case?

5. How might trade unions and other employee representative groups reconcile the needs of their collective body (equal treatment for all) with the needs of individuals (valuing individual needs)?

EXPLORE FURTHER

Gennard, J. and Judge, G. (2010) *Employment Relations*, 5th ed. London: CIPD is the CIPD text on the subject.

Gilmore, S. and Williams, S. (eds). (2009) *Human Resource Management*. Oxford: Oxford University Press, Chapters 10 and 11.

Kirton, G. and Greene, A. (2006) *The Dynamics of Managing Diversity: A critical approach*, 2nd ed. Elsevier.

Konrad, A., Prasad, P. and Pringle, J. (eds). (2006) *A Handbook of Workplace Diversity*. London: Sage.

Williams, S. and Adam-Smith, D. (2010) *Employment Relations: A critical introduction*. Oxford: Oxford University Press, 2nd ed. Takes a thematic approach to the subject area.

Websites

The Department for Business, Innovation and Skills (BIS) www.bis.gov.uk/what we do/employment matters. This is the Government Department responsible for employment policy.

Trades Union Congress www.tuc.org.uk. The TUC is the umbrella organisation for most of the trade unions in the UK.

Confederation of British Industries www.cbi.org.uk. The CBI is the national representative body for UK employers.

Advisory, Conciliation and Arbitration Service, www.acas.org.uk. ACAS provides a range of impartial advice and publications on employment relations.

CIPD website www.cipd.co.uk contains research and other documents on employment relations and managing diversity.

Commission for Equality and Human Rights website www.equalityhumanrights.com. The Commission has responsibility for monitoring the effect of equality legislation.

CHAPTER 12

Performance Management, Motivation and Reward

Alex Tymon *and* Gary Rees

LEARNING OUTCOMES

After reading this chapter, you should be able to:

- understand the assumptions which underpin the application of performance management (PM)
- identify the different ways that PM can be defined and interpreted by organisations
- recognise the contribution of organisational theory, industrial engineering and behavioural science systems to the development of PM
- understand the relationship between performance, motivation and reward
- evaluate the extent to which PM can assist in improving organisational effectiveness and efficiency
- consider the contribution that HR can make to performance management.

OVERVIEW

Organisational effectiveness and efficiency has rarely been off the management agenda of all organisations, and becomes a higher priority during times of economic austerity. Performance management (PM) is one process that enables organisations to produce greater quality of product or service.

However, PM must not be considered to be the universal panacea to improving organisations. This chapter places PM in context, and weighs up the pros and cons of adopting PM as a means to improve productivity or service by motivating employees to perform better, and at the same time considers the arguments for the use of reward.

Contemporary issues such as employee engagement and commitment are discussed by focusing on motivation theories and approaches, with a view to how HR can make a difference in adding value through PM.

INTRODUCTION

There is little doubt that most organisations in the 21st century share some common objectives in order to ensure their survival, so that by producing a consistent product and/or service, which raises more in revenue than it costs to provide, they will attract customers, retain customers and encourage customers to keeping spending.

Not-for-profit organisations share some of these aims, such as the need for consistency and the requirement to minimise costs for the provision of their product or service. What is also beyond doubt is the role of people in helping to meet these objectives. There is a wealth of research (Huselid, 1995; Patterson, 1997; Guest, 1998; Holbeche, 2005) which demonstrates that well managed employees increase revenues and decrease costs and that performance management (PM) is all about managing employees well.

The economic turmoil of 2007 to 2010 has further increased the spotlight on PM, with questions posed as to the robustness of PM in the light of the 'reward for failure' practices that accompanied the collapse of the banking industry.

Wain (2009, p 17) cites the CIPD's research, which demonstrated that 92 per cent of its survey thought that closer scrutiny of poor performance accounted for the rising interest in PM.

In this chapter we consider the concept of PM and the theories of motivation that underpin it, along with its implications for managing and leading employees.

WHAT IS PERFORMANCE MANAGEMENT?

There are a myriad definitions of performance management, but one of the best known is that of Armstrong and Baron (2004) and adopted by the CIPD (2009):

> 'A process which contributes to the effective management of individuals and teams in order to achieve high levels of organisational performance. As such, it establishes shared understanding about what is to be achieved and an approach to leading and developing people which will ensure that it is achieved.'

This definition informs us of two important factors. Firstly, the all-encompassing nature of performance management, where it has been suggested that all activities within a business should be contributing towards better performance and that managing the performance of employees is 'running the business' (Mohrman and Mohrman, 1995). Secondly, this definition implies that performance management can be viewed as a 'process'.

The extent to which performance management impacts upon performance is contingent upon the context and the interconnectedness and interlocking of various supporting mechanisms. The ultimate aim is to maximise organisational effectiveness within the current and changing context (Jones, 1995).

The all-encompassing nature of performance management can be seen by examining the people-performance link. A classic approach adopted may take the form of the Boxall and Purcell AMO model (2008) – see Figure 7.3. If we consider that performance is a function of ability, motivation and opportunity, then the role of the employer or their agent, or the manager, has to be to maximise these three elements, in order to maximise performance. However, it could be argued that the terminologies adopted by Boxall and Purcell (2008) need to be brought into line with current HR thinking and practice. Concepts such as able, committed and engaged allow us to explore the AMO model in a different light.

In the context of high-performing organisations (HPWO), research indicates that the activities presented in Figure 12.1 are representative of activities demonstrated in HPWOs. For example, Jamrog *et al* (2008) found that in a survey of 1,369 organisations, HPWOs are clear about what behaviours employees need to exhibit to execute organisational and departmental strategies. In addition to managers setting clear goals, they need to understand employees' abilities and guide their performance. HPWOs have well established values that are the key drivers of employee behaviour, and are typically well understood by most employees.

THE STRATEGIC NATURE OF PERFORMANCE MANAGEMENT

The PM process includes the alignment of objectives and performance through measurement, assessment and monitoring. Where there is a gap between objectives and performance, appropriate HR supporting mechanisms are required (Figure 12.2).

Figure 12.1 Attempts to identify some of the activities which could maximise the three elements

ACE employees: Able, committed and engaged + opportunity, resources and support = High performance

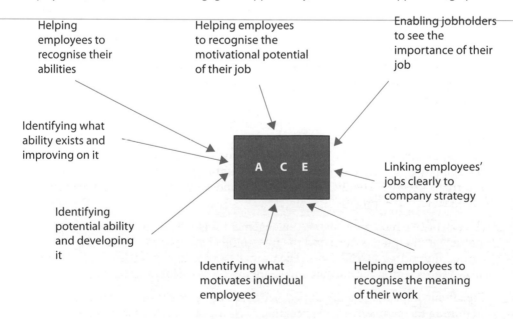

Figure 12.2 Human Resource supporting mechanisms

It could therefore be argued that HR as a function can add value through the range of supporting mechanisms that it can provide.

Another method of considering the strategic nature of performance management is through the 'balanced scorecard', which attempts to link employee rewards to performance in the areas of finance, customers, internal business processes and innovation, learning and growth. According to Chavan (2009, p 396), 'In some instances, companies see the non-financial measures as of such importance that a threshold level of performance is set for each of the non-financials. Only if an individual exceeds these threshold levels can they qualify for performance-related rewards linked to financial performance results.' The importance of organisational culture and vision also has a part to play in how the organisation considers and addresses performance.

PERSPECTIVES ON PERFORMANCE MANAGEMENT

From a managerialist perspective, where the manager has to ensure the most effective and efficient use of resources (including people) in achieving business objectives, PM can be seen as an issue of control and manipulation, and very much a top-down process.

The assumption underlying this perspective of PM is that the organisation, in the form of a controlling manager, can make a positive impact upon an individual's work performance. Within this assumption, managers are expected to demonstrate both general management skills as well as skills directly related to the PM process. The latter could include task skills such as objective-setting, understanding technical aspects of the job, monitoring progress and measuring results.

General management skills, in contrast, could include leadership, mentoring, coaching, and interpersonal relationships. Managers may demonstrate strong task skills but are often lacking confidence in the softer interpersonal and social skills (Bowles and Coates, 1993).

The managerialist perspective also assumes a hierarchy of control, with a direct relationship between manager and subordinate. This is more difficult to achieve in complex organisational structures, such as multi-dimensional matrix structures. For example, a subordinate may report to several different line managers, who are all based in different locations. The control aspect of PM is legitimised through the perceived objectivity of the process. This objectivity then becomes the driving force for achieving performance outputs (Levinson, 1970; 1976).

THE ETERNAL TRIANGLE

Herzberg (1968) presents the eternal triangle perspective, whereby there are three general philosophies of personnel (or HR) management: namely, organisational theory, industrial engineering and behavioural science.

The organisational theorist Weber (1947) believed that human needs are either so irrational or so varied and adjustable that personnel management has to be as pragmatic as the occasion demands. Herzberg cites the example of job design, where, if jobs are organised in a proper manner, the result will be the most efficient job structure, and the most favourable attitudes will follow. Alternatively, within the eternal triangle theory, the industrial engineers (Taylor, 1911) believe that humankind is mechanistically orientated and economically motivated, and therefore we need to attune the individual to the most efficient working process. Here we need to design the most appropriate incentive system and design the most appropriate working system for the human machine. Behavioural scientists (Schein, 1984) focus on group sentiments, attitudes of individual employees and the organisation's social and psychological climate, with the emphasis on instilling healthy employee attitudes and an appropriate organisational climate. This model illustrates a useful analogy for the use and possible misuse of PM as means to improve performance in organisations.

PERFORMANCE MANAGEMENT AS A PROCESS

Performance management can also be viewed as a process by looking at the employee lifecycle and the performance management activities which could contribute to improved performance at each stage. The advantage of this approach is that it can provide guidance to organisations on which activities to introduce and when.

With regard to Table 12.1, when considering the time-line and action:

Before the recruitment and during the selection process, some of these activities are understood and are embedded in many organisations, others less so. For example, how many organisations provide sufficient information to enable prospective employees to 'self-select' themselves out of the recruitment process and potentially save the costs and effort of managing employees who cannot or will not be successful? How many organisations are explicit in looking for employees whose values are aligned to that of the business and are therefore more likely to be committed? How many organisations make the conscious effort to test for potential at the recruitment stage?

Research around the 'induction crisis' identifies problems which may manifest themselves in both the short term and long term. For example, the Reed Consulting Survey (2004) demonstrated that 4 per cent of new starters walk out of the job because of poor or non-existent induction programmes, and 93 per cent of the 5,700 respondents in their survey believed that a poor induction has a continual adverse effect on their productivity at work.

During formal induction, when organisations run induction or orientation schemes, to what extent is the robustness of these schemes measured, and potential subsequent action taken? Is there recognition that this is the stage at which employees learn the rules of behaviour and the difference between the overt or stated set expectations of the organisation, and the reality of what will be tolerated in practice? A robust induction process can be invaluable in making performance standards and expectations explicit.

During the probation period, to what extent do line managers appreciate the true value of the probationary period? All too often, it consists of a form-filling exercise initiated by the HR department, where the manager signs to say that the new employee should have their position confirmed, without having any idea of how they are actually performing. Then a few months later they are complaining that the employee is underperforming, or worse still, are asking HR how they can remove them.

During the formal reviews and appraisals, how many managers recognise the value of feedback, constant feedback both positive and developmental? Behaviourist learning theory (Skinner 1953, cited in French *et al*, 2008, pp 123–4) demonstrates the power of positively reinforcing desired behaviours: employees are much more likely to repeat actions which gain them positive recognition. Positive reinforcement has been shown to increase employees' 'self-efficacy beliefs', which in turn, has been shown to increase performance (Bandura, 1993).

The power of positive feedback is the theory supporting 'appreciative inquiry' (see below). How many managers appear to spend their time and effort looking for and acting on the 5 per cent of jobs that people do badly, whilst ignoring the 95 per cent that they do effectively? There appears to be a blockage against

Table 12.1 Performance management as a process

Employee activity	Time-line and action	Manager/employer activity
Gains knowledge of expectations and culture Self-selects in or out	Before recruitment: Job descriptions, person specifications, adverts, company information	Gives signals of expectations on jobs performance standards, conduct standards and culture
Demonstrates ability and motivation Conscious or subconscious alignment with values Self-selects in or out	During selection process: Interviews/assessment etc	Tests ability and motivation Checks values alignment Seeks potential
Learns conduct expectations Adapts to the culture	During formal induction/orientation	Formalises conduct expectations, terms and conditions/handbook etc
Learns performance standards Develops knowledge and skills	During mandatory training	Provides standards of job performance Provides knowledge and skills Provides feedback
Becomes a productive employee Adapts to the culture	During probation period	Team briefing and communications Reinforces performance and conduct standards Provides feedback One-to-one reviews Provides on-going training and coaching
Reviews performance Agrees objectives Identifies learning needs Considers aspirations Possibly gains reward	During formal reviews and/or appraisals: Annual or more regularly	Reviews performance Sets objectives Agrees learning needs Identifies potential and aspirations Possible links to reward
Continuous improvement Develops self-feedback mechanisms Achieves potential	Ongoing: Business as usual	Team briefing and communications Reinforces performance and conduct standards Provides feedback One-to-one reviews On-going training and coaching

At any time:
Possible poor performance or poor conduct intervention

recognising when an employee has performed to standard, a belief that employees should exceed before they receive recognition. A typical comment on supervisor training courses is: 'Why should I recognise an employee who has just reached the standard? That is their job.' But if we employ someone and ask them to reach a certain standard and they do, then this should be recognised and the danger of not doing so is that performance and standards will slide. The balance between allowing experimentation and providing appropriate feedback needs constant review. An excuse sometimes cited for lack of feedback is the idea that people learn from mistakes, and it is certainly true that allowing people to fail can be useful in some circumstances. Control theory (Carver, Sutton and Scheier, 2000) had indicated that failure can even motivate more than success.

Learning Organisation theory (Ellinger, 2004) suggests that freedom to fail is an important factor to enable an organisation to grow, but there is a lot of difference between giving employees space to experiment accompanied by constructive feedback and abdication management. According to Geal and Johnson (2002, p 26):

> 'What do people learn from mistakes? What not to do, so they need to try something else. But, what else? A manager able and willing to give developmental feedback so they can improve is both necessary and motivating when handled well.'

So using the excuse of allowing people to learn from mistakes could be viewed as lazy at best, and at its worst could be incredibly costly for the organisation.

 REFLECTIVE ACTIVITY

Drawn from research into positive psychology (Seligman, 1998), Appreciative Inquiry suggests that when employees are encouraged to focus on their strengths, then they are more likely to succeed and enjoy greater job satisfaction (Bryce, 2007). For a practical example, see Arkin's article 'Mr Bright Side' in *People Management*, May 2005, p 28.

At any time there may be the need to manage poor performance or conduct, and this raises the question of how many managers are able and willing to manage poor performance or conduct in a positive way before it becomes a major issue. An organisation may well have a 'capability and conduct' procedure, which will undoubtedly espouse the wisdom of dealing with performance and conduct issues in an informal way as being the most effective route. But how many organisations train and support their managers to run 'improving poor performance/poor conduct' discussions?

 REFLECTIVE ACTIVITY

Think about an organisation with which you are familiar. Using Table 12.1 as a guide, consider what evidence there is that it has a clear performance management process in place. What evidence is there that it has been implemented in an effective manner?

However, there is more to PM than just the actions involved. Effective PM is not only dependent upon what is done but also upon how it is done. Purcell *et al* (2003) provide research evidence to support the proposition that no one particular HR practice is critical to organisational success, but good management by line managers, applying various approaches effectively and appropriately according to the context, is the key factor. Committed and capable line managers are, therefore, essential to successful PM (Hutchinson and Purcell, 2003). These managers need to know the 'how' of PM as much as the 'what' – the answers to questions such as:

1. How can we define performance?

2. Who should define performance?

3. How can we measure performance?

4. What is the link between motivation and performance?

DEFINING PERFORMANCE

For performance to be managed it has to be defined and measured. This demonstrates the organisation's values (Johnson and Scholes, 2002), as measuring is a mechanism of communicating that a particular activity is valued.

There is no single, universal definition of performance. The definition of performance depends very much on the particular perspective adopted. For example, some definitions of performance relate to the organisation and various expectations in terms of outputs:

> 'Performance should be defined as the outcomes of work because they provide the strongest linkage to the strategic goals of the organisation, customer satisfaction, and economic contributions.' (Bernadin *et al*, 1995)

Other definitions emphasise behavioural aspects, in addition to outputs or results:

> 'Performance means both behaviours and results. Behaviours emanate from the performer and transform performance from abstraction to action. Not just the instruments for results, behaviours are also outcomes in their own right – the product of mental and physical effort applied to tasks – and can be judged apart from results.' (Brumbach, 1988, p 389)

WHO DEFINES PERFORMANCE?

It is not only a question of how performance is defined, but also who within the organisation is, or are, responsible for defining performance standards. Often, it is the organisation itself that determines performance and how it will be measured. Performance requirements are often part of a strategic planning process, cascading top-down through the organisation from senior management (Humble, 1972). However, this does not have to be the case. Semler (1993) describes a bottom-up approach, where employees at Semco were allowed to set their own performance targets and define appropriate rewards. There is also the possibility of a combined top-down and bottom-up approach, with mutual adjustment of goals and objectives (Nonaka and Takeuchi, 1995).

Other stakeholders, such as shareholders, and customers, will have their own views on performance standards or achievements and these different views may be contradictory. The different parties involved have different perspectives, expectations and experience of performance. For example, shareholders are interested in long-term value of stocks and assets. Middle management may have an interest in protecting and advancing their own position, power and rewards. Customers are increasingly demanding high quality, customised products and services. In addition, all of these stakeholders may adopt different roles at different times or have multiple, simultaneous roles. Therefore, the agreement of what constitutes effective performance may be difficult to reach.

A more integrated approach may help to overcome some of the problems inherent in defining performance and performance standards. It is generally accepted that involving employees in the setting of objectives and targets is more likely to gain commitment to their achievement. Fundamentally, though, for the organisation to succeed, someone, somewhere needs to combine the targets to ensure that the organisational objectives are indeed being met. This is a line management responsibility, but HR might need to ensure and empower that process's taking place. If it is not achieved the organisation's future may be at risk.

WHAT ASPECTS OF PERFORMANCE CAN BE MEASURED?

It is impossible to measure all aspects of an employee's performance. Similarly, there are areas that will prove difficult to measure in themselves. For example, how does an organisation measure knowledge-creation and use creativity and innovation?

Similarly, PM assumes explicit performance measures and cannot always incorporate tacit inputs, throughputs and outputs at individual, group and organisational levels. The temporal argument relating to PM needs to be considered in order to make an accurate assessment of performance. Performance targets are typically set in time and the time-scale might in itself affect accurate measurement. How does one allow for long-term performance improvements and outcomes within an annual appraisal cycle, for example? The critical issue then becomes when we measure and record performance.

What an organisation chooses to measure depends on the PM framework adopted within the organisational context. This depends on what the organisation values in its employees. To what extent is learning valued as part of the PM process, for example? However, a robust PM process typically relies on the setting of goals and targets, which are themselves definable, and measurable.

PITFALLS OF DEFINING PERFORMANCE TARGETS

There are many pitfalls with objectives and targets. Reeves (2008) uses the term 'targetology' to describe the fixation of the British Government and many organisations with targets. He agrees that targets can be helpful, citing the reduction in hospital waiting times as an example. But he questions the number of targets which are used:

> 'Targets are not intrinsically bad: clear objectives for any organisation, expressed as specific goals should improve performance. . . . One or two clear targets can be powerful. A hundred targets is a recipe for confusion, stress and disaster. . . Just because targets are good, it does not mean that more targets are better.'

The number of targets used is not the only pitfall. Research by Professor Yves Emery (2008) identifies some common issues with both defining targets and attaining them: policy deployment, quality versus quantity targets, goal displacement, individualisation effect, goal override and limited influence. An example of each is provided in Table 12.2.

Hall (2009, p 10) argues that 'Focusing organisation and individual activity on what really matters, through the use of targets linked to strategic aims, can be a powerful management "tool" but careful consideration needs to be given to what is targeted, how targets are applied and who targets are applied to.'

In addition there is the challenge of the traditional PM emphasis on the individual, whereas the increasingly interdependent nature of work, and the consequent emphasis on team and groups, makes measurement more challenging. It is not just individual performance that is important, but also the contribution that the individual makes towards group effort, and the combined output of the group as a whole. So team targets are an area that needs to be explored.

 REFLECTIVE ACTIVITY

Analyse the targets or objectives that you have been set during a performance management process. To what extent do the pitfalls listed in Table 12.2 apply to these? How could your targets be improved upon?

www.XpertHR.co.uk

MEASURING PERFORMANCE

The performance management process (Table 12.1) shows that measurement or performance review and feedback should be an on-going activity, so that positive reinforcement or corrective action can be supplied as soon as it is justified. Normal management activities such as walking the floor and one-to-one reviews can enable this measurement to happen and ensure that one of the 'golden rules' of appraisals is followed: 'No surprises' – ie anything discussed in a period review or appraisal concerning performance should be expected by both parties.

Another measurement technique, which is often overlooked, is that of 'self-measurement'. The research that supports the idea of autonomy and participation

Table 12.2 Pitfalls of target definition

Issue	Example
Policy deployment The difficulties of translating strategic goals into meaningful bottom line targets. Not all objectives are easily split and can become meaningless if broken down too much	A common strategic goal, such as 'increase market share', which may well translate into specific objectives for senior managers, but is almost impossible to be a meaningful objective for a back office employee such as a payroll data entry clerk
Quality versus quantity targets With quantity targets being easier to set and therefore being used in place of quality targets which may be more beneficial	An HR officer may be set a target to ensure 95 per cent of employees who leave the organisation complete an exit interview, a very SMART target. But actually what is really wanted is quality of data from exiting employees about why they are leaving, so that meaningful decisions can be made
Goal displacement Where the measures become seen as the goal	In a call centre the goal may be to improve customer service and one measure of this is to answer calls more quickly. It is easy for employees to 'lose calls' – ie drop them as soon as they are answered – in order to improve the call answering statistics, which actually results in even worse customer service
Individualisation effect Where competing goals set up unintended competition between staff, especially competition for scarce resources	A cable TV sales team may be measured on the number of customers they sign up, and to ensure quality of sales the customers have to stay for a minimum time period of six months. However, the technicians who install the product in the customer's home are measured on speed of install and the quicker the install, the more likely there will be a problem, which in turn leads to customers disconnecting
Goal override Where employees only focus on goal achievement and neglect other important responsibilities. It may become necessary to have a relatively complex measurement system in order to ensure that the 'day job' carries equal weight	A hotel maintenance team may be targeted on the completion of reported repairs and may go flat out to achieve these targets. As a result they may neglect the preventative maintenance jobs, which are a part of their job description, because they are not overtly measured
Limited influence Where employees have very little control over the targets set, or at least perceive this to be the case	In a retail environment where product range, price and advertising are all centrally controlled a shop assistant may easily perceive that they really have very little control over the actual sales that they make and this perception may actually be real. It has also been argued that employees are just the delivery system and that 90 per cent of the impact of their endeavours comes from the system!

in goal-setting is well known and includes the work of Herzberg (1968), Hackman and Oldham (1980), Locke and Latham (1990), to name but a few. Although the different theorists may argue why, they do mostly conclude that participation in goal-setting can lead to improved performance. But the effects of 'self-regulation' or self-measurement and management are perhaps less well known.

Motivation theories

Content theories focus on what motivates people, whereas process theories concentrate on how people are motivated. Content theories assume links between job satisfaction, motivation and performance, whereas process theories don't automatically assume a link between job satisfaction and performance, but do assume links between motivation and job satisfaction and motivation and performance.

Herzberg (1967) distinguishes between motivation and movement. Offering an inducement may simply be movement, whereby the employee 'moves' or acts in order to achieve an outcome (eg a reward), but may not be motivated (internally driven to want to do it, other than to achieve a reward).

Locke (1968) in Hollyforde and Whiddett (2002) identified the value of goals as a motivator and performance enhancer. Specific rather than general goals and participation in goal-setting, together with knowledge of achievement, are important in improving performance.

Hackman and Oldham's (1975) Job Characteristics model in French *et al*, 2008, links five job characteristics, namely: skill variety, task identity, task significance, autonomy and feedback, to three critical psychological states – meaningfulness, responsibility and knowledge of outcomes, which lead to higher levels of motivation and performance.

Bandura (1993, p 128) states that:

> 'Most human motivation is cognitively generated. People motivate themselves and guide their actions anticipatorily by the exercise of forethought. . . . Forethought is translated into incentives and appropriate action through self-regulatory mechanisms.'

Latham (2007) provides a useful summary of some of the research around this area but the message appears to be that although the effects are mediated and moderated by other factors such as personality, involving employees in goal-setting and facilitating self-feedback can and does result in higher performance. This perhaps provides an argument for the use of more self-appraisal. It presents an argument for developing ways employees can access their own feedback on performance.

MEASUREMENT AT WHAT COST?

Performance measurement is not without potentially significant costs in terms of staff time and administration. Not only are implementation costs to be considered but also the long-term maintenance costs of any PM system once established. To what extent do organisations consider the total costs of the PM system versus the impacts, both positive and negative, on performance outcomes? An example would be the internal focus of systems within the automotive manufacturing industry, where the needs of customers were ignored to the long-term harm of the organisation. Organisations may assume that a PM system will have a positive impact but any improvement needs to be offset against the often substantial costs of running the system itself.

APPRAISAL AS A PERFORMANCE MANAGEMENT TOOL

Although PM is more than simply appraisal, some form of performance appraisal is central to PM (Fletcher, 2004) and is most often undertaken with the aim of improving performance, motivating employees and/or allocating rewards. An honest and accurate assessment of current performance can be a strong driver for further learning, development and performance improvement. The process of performance feedback and the setting of improvement targets can itself be a strong motivator (Locke and Latham, 1990), and for there to be equitable distribution of rewards some fair method of comparing contributions between individuals is required. Otherwise, unfair systems will fall into what Herzberg termed 'hygiene factors' and be demotivators (Mullins, 2005). The impact of fairness is also highlighted by Adams' equity theory:

> Equity theory contends that employees compare the inputs, abilities and effort they bring to work, and the outputs and rewards they gain as result of their ability and effort, with others in a similar situation, using the concept of distributed justice. A perceived injustice motivates the individual to take action. They can increase or decrease their inputs, or seek to increase or decrease the inputs of others. Alternatively, they can seek to change the outputs for either themselves or others. It is important to note the part that perception plays in equity theory, so the injustice may not be actual.
> (Hollyforde and Whiddett, 2002)

The whole performance management system, therefore, should ensure that employees perceive equity of treatment and fairness, none more so than in the appraisal process. This supports the argument that PM and reward policies need to be transparent and understandable. The part that perception plays in this means extra attention may have to be paid to communication about the process to ensure the message is clear.

Different types of appraisal include: top-down, self-appraisal, peer appraisal, bottom-up and multi-rater, such as 360-degree and 720-degree feedback. The most common is a top-down approach with the inclusion of self-appraisal, usually as a preparatory activity for the employee. There are many benefits of a multi-rater approach which in theory will produce a more rounded outcome, but the time and expense involved often rules this out as an option.

Appraisal methods can be divided into two main approaches: those oriented towards results (outputs); and those oriented towards competencies (inputs). Results-oriented appraisal is based on the setting of quantifiable, achievable and time-bounded objectives, most often in a participative process between manager and subordinate, and geared to achieving organisational objectives. Competency-oriented appraisal takes a different approach, with assessment based on the demonstration of certain key skills and behaviours thought to be associated with high performance, this may also involve just manager and employee, but often this is where multi-rater instruments are most likely to be used. The trend is towards combining both results- and competency-based approaches in an attempt to deliver the dual benefits of achieving immediate performance targets and supporting longer-term development of key skills and capabilities.

In addition, PM systems differ in the emphasis they give to rewards or development. The trend is for increasing emphasis on development rather than reward, and de-emphasising the link between PM and pay in particular (Armstrong and Baron, 2005). There is also a move away from purely performance-related or competence-related pay and towards 'contribution-related' pay, which takes into account all aspects of an individual's contribution, including both performance (results) and competence (Brown and Armstrong, 1999). This mirrors the similar trend seen in appraisal methods, as described above.

Performance management and development are overlapping and inter-dependent processes. Performance reviews, whether they are periodic appraisals or continuous, day-to-day, interactions between managers and employees, provide encouragement and substance for learning and development. This might be as informal training, self-managed learning by the individual employee, coaching by the manager, or more structured training and development interventions. Whatever the form, development is intended to have a direct impact on performance capabilities and can also have a powerful motivational effect (Tamkin *et al*, 1995).

However, these multiple perspectives on appraisals lead to some difficult conflicts. Reconciling PM as a developmental process and as a pay decision-making process is not straightforward. That closely linking performance appraisal to pay reduces the focus on development and performance improvement is well understood (Kessler and Purcell, 1992). An employee is less likely to describe a development need if it might be seen as a weakness and detrimentally affect their pay award.

POTENTIAL PITFALLS WHEN EVALUATING EMPLOYEES

Appraisals ask for evaluations to be made, and accordingly there are potential pitfalls, some of which are highlighted below.

Rating scale issues

In appraisal systems where a rating scale is used, there are constant issues with people being unhappy with the 'average' rating. Standard distribution dictates that not everyone will be at the top, some people will be at the bottom and most people will be in the middle. But being rated as 'competent', 'satisfactory', 'C' or '3/5' is unsatisfactory for people who can see 'exceptional', 'A' or '5/5' on the scale.

The Swiss Federal Administration trialled a new system with the following grades:

A++   Far beyond expectations

A+   Beyond expectations

A   Objectives fully reached

B   Objectives partially reached

C   Objectives missed

Although people psychologically still want to be A++, most employees will be rated as an A, which is psychologically better than a C (Yves Emery, 2008).

Appraiser bias

Appraisers all have their own biases. Some have tendencies to rate everyone kindly or everyone harshly, which can raise issues, especially when rewards are linked and comparisons are made with other teams, whose managers have rated differently. In addition there are those who struggle to differentiate between any employees, wanting something for everyone, known as the 'watering can effect'. Furnham (1997) identified 13 different 'perception errors', which he said could negatively influence an appraisal system. These pitfalls can severely affect an employee's sense of equity and cause dissatisfaction with the system, which in turn is likely to diminish performance.

Furnham's 13 systematic perception errors are:

1. First impressions – rather than how the appraisee performs.
2. Halo effect – favourable comparison to one quality.
3. Horns effect – contrary to halo effect, a negative rating.
4. Contrast error – comparison with selected employees.
5. Differing from appraiser.
6. Same as me – sharing common attributes with appraiser.
7. Recency effect – judging recent behaviour, then generalising.
8. Central tendency – everyone in the middle of the scale.
9. Leniency in rating – generous to avoid conflict.
10. Strict rating – consistently strict in appraising performance.
11. Performance dimension error – where two aspects of the appraisal follow, score two distinct qualities the same.
12. Spillover effect – based on previous appraisal.
13. Status effect – based upon higher-level positions, and giving better appraisals.

Reward pitfalls

Whilst not all formal appraisal systems are overtly linked to rewards, there are many potential issues with appraisal systems being linked to rewards. Fixed quota systems, where evaluation is based on the amount of reward available and not on actual levels of performance, can lead to meaningless appraisals for employees.

The total amount of money available may not be sufficient. Research evidence suggests that less than 10 per cent of the annual salary has a very limited effect on motivating people to higher performance (Emery, 2007). In the current economic climate, the question has to be asked as to how many organisations can make budgetary arrangements for this amount of money. Similarly, are managers willing or able to differentiate enough between their employees to enable a smaller 'pot' to be distributed in such a way as to offer more than 10 per cent to some employees? Do employees who are less confident and think they cannot achieve the standards to attain a bonus actually work less hard, so in effect the reward becomes a de-motivator? Reward brings with it a range of pitfalls in differing contexts.

Dependent upon organisational structure and context, the practice of team reward may inhibit or adversely affect individual motivation (for further reading, see the CIPD website).

A more fundamental issue may centre around whether rewards such as pay and other recognition schemes actually motivate employees at all.

According to Kuvaas (2006) performance appraisal satisfaction is directly related to effective commitment and turnover intention and the relationship between performance appraisal and work performance is mediated and moderated by employees' intrinsic motivation.

PAY: THE MOTIVATOR TO PERFORM?

Latham (2007) argues that all through the 20th century, theorists argued about the capacity of money to motivate employees towards greater performance. Money or what it can supply (money can be a status symbol or a sign of recognition) appears in all of the 'content' theories of motivation and therefore it is implied that money is a motivator (see Reflection theory).

Lawler (2009, p 29) argues that 'In rewards, most organisations still have job descriptions and merit pay systems, and fail to use knowledge-based pay, profit sharing and stock ownership plans that create high levels of involvement in the success of the organisation.'

 REFLECTIVE ACTIVITY

Reflection theory – why is pay important to an individual member? Does pay provide the mirror by which an employee reflects images of power, status, value and succession? The meaning that pay holds is largely deduced from employees' personal characteristics (values), pay level (relative to others) and the level of familiarity the person experiences with the pay system (pay system knowledge). These meanings are expected to influence employee outcomes such as satisfaction, motivation and performance (Thiery, 2001, in Salimäki et al, 2009).

Research by Barber and Bretz (2000) suggests that money is among the most important factors for people when deciding on a job. Some practitioners will point to exit interview data and proclaim that lack of money is the reason for people leaving an organisation and moving to pastures new. However, more detailed analysis may produce a different picture. People who have decided to leave an organisation may well quote the 'bigger and better' pay packet as the reason for them moving, but if a different exit interview question is asked, 'What made you start looking for another job to start with?', then other factors begin to emerge. People become dissatisfied with a job due to poor management, lack of opportunities, boredom and in fact, most of the 'satisfiers' in the Herzberg list, or if money is a factor it is linked to equity theory – ie they decide that others with whom they compare themselves are paid more.

REFLECTIVE ACTIVITY

Think about yourself and talk to others you know. What was it that made you and them think about looking for a new job?

There is also an argument that money, an extrinsic motivator, may actually decrease long-term intrinsic motivation and so have a detrimental effect on performance. There is some evidence for the potential negative performance impacts of contingent pay schemes in practice (Marsden and French, 1998).

Deci *et al* (2001) and Cameron *et al* (2001) both carried out meta-analyses to try to establish the link between extrinsic rewards and intrinsic motivation, and the results are mixed. Frey and Jegen (2001) question the degree to which extrinsic incentives such as performance-related pay crowd out the intrinsic motivation to do a good job. According to Deci, Ryan and Koestner (2001), the use of rewards as a motivational strategy is a risky proposition, as this disengages interest and self-regulation. Cameron, Banko and Pierce (2001) counteracted this by stating that rewards are not harmful to motivation to perform a task.

Thomas (2009, p 196), in Chalofsky, and Krishna, argues that the four most critical intrinsic rewards are: a sense of meaning and purpose, a sense of choice, a sense of competence and a sense of progress – ie the work itself. Intrinsic rewards can lead to more engaged and committed employees.

In terms of meaningfulness, people with the highest levels of productivity and fulfilment view themselves as inseparable from their work, intrinsically motivated by the work itself and professionally committed to and engaged with the organisation.

There is evidence to suggest money can reduce the effectiveness of intrinsic motivation and there are circumstances when it appears not to. The deciding factor as is so often the case is not what is done, but how it is done. This is a reason to consider another of the process theories of motivation: Expectancy theory.

EXPECTANCY THEORY

A process theory of motivation which seeks to explain how an individual is motivated to increase performance. Vroom's Expectancy theory is explained through the formula:

$F = E \times I \times V$,

where F is the force of motivation, E is expectancy – the belief that extra effort will result in better performance (if I work harder, my output will increase);

I is instrumentality – the belief that better performance will lead to a reward (if my output increases, I will get a reward);

V is valence, the perceived value of the reward (how much I want the reward).

The valence links back to content theories of motivation, as these tell us that individuals are motivated by a multitude of things (needs and wants).

Source: Buchanan and Huczynski (2007)

EXPECTANCY THEORY IN ACTION – PERFORMANCE-RELATED REWARD

A classic use of Expectancy theory is in defining and executing a performance-related reward scheme, in order to improve short term performance. An example could be an attempt to increase sales of sports shoes in a sports shop on the lead up to Christmas. For this to work employees have to:

- believe that putting in extra effort, talking to customers etc will result in making extra sales **(Expectancy),** so they need training, goal-setting and feedback to this effect.

- believe that the extra sales they make will be recognised and will result in a reward. This could be extra pay, prizes, recognition, promotion etc **(Instrumentality)**, so there needs to be systems for individuals to record their sales that actually result in the promised reward being given.

- believe the reward is worth having **(Valence)**. They need to want the reward on offer, a good reason to offer a choice of rewards if possible.

All of this needs to be fairly and clearly communicated.

So the question of whether money is a motivator which can lead to improved performance is a very complex one and the answer is by no means clear (Latham, 2007). At best, it can be said that there is a connection between money and satisfaction which may under certain circumstances increase commitment and perhaps performance.

More important is the fact that all employees will be motivated by different things, as highlighted by the 'content theories'. The effective manager will recognise this and work towards helping employees gain maximum motivation at work, using the principles of expectancy theories and equity theory to make this happen.

The resurgence of interest of intrinsic factors such as meaning, purpose, spirituality and commitment, and more recently engagement, has emphasised the importance of work as a motivator in the organisation (Csikszentmihalyi, 1990; Fox, 1994; Lockwood, 2007; Meyer and Herscovitch, 2001).

As indicated earlier, perhaps one of the more contentious areas for debate lies within the issue of whether to link pay and performance. Heneman (1992, p 258) argues that 'the results to date on the relationship between merit pay and subsequent motivation and performance are not encouraging,' and this view is supported by Williams (1998, p 172), who reports that 'there is negligible evidence of a rigorous kind which supports the positive benefits commonly claimed for merit pay.'

As both performance and motivation are affected by many factors, performance-related pay (PRP) (or any other intervention) cannot be linked in a causal manner. Williams (1998, p 173) argues that managers' and employees' views need to be considered in order to analyse the effect of PRP on motivation and performance. Whilst the debate of PRP or not PRP goes on, it is worth considering some of the operational difficulties that have been associated with reward practice.

The following set of questions has been raised by Williams (1998, p 176) and adapted to fit the categories provided:

With regard to organisational culture, teams and individual attitudes to PRP:

- Is PRP appropriate to all organisations?
- Is there a climate of trust (particularly in line managers – subordinate relations)?
- What effect does PRP have on team and cooperative building?
- Does a focus on individual performance lead employees to place self-interest ahead of those of the organisation generally?
- Does PRP create divisiveness?
- Does PRP encourage short-termism?

He similarly raises questions about the PM process itself:

- What criteria should be used for measuring performance? Outputs? Inputs? Both?
- Can individual performance be measured objectively and fairly?
- Can performance be defined comprehensively?
- Do line managers have the willingness and ability required to operate PRP?
- How much of performance is within the individual's control?
- How should average performers be treated?

Questions related to the value of rewards also need to be addressed:

- What amount of pay constitutes a significant increase in the eyes of employees?
- Will PRP diminish the value of intrinsic rewards?

It may be relatively simple to provide an answer to each of these individual questions. However, when considered together, the complexity of linking PRP to performance becomes much more evident. Thus simple, prescriptive solutions cannot be found.

TOTAL REWARD AT ARUP

CASE STUDY

Arup is a global design and engineering consultancy. The company employs around 10,500 people in 37 countries, around half of whom are based in the UK. At Arup, which is employee-owned, the reward package includes a global profit-sharing scheme as well as a range of other benefits.

Although the organisation did not formally publish a total reward policy until 2007, Arup has been practising a total reward strategy for much longer, and offers online total reward statements to its employees around the world. Tony Hatton-Gore, Director, Group Remuneration and Benefits joined Arup in 2001. At that time, there was an awareness of total reward within the organisation and, soon afterwards, Arup decided to adopt this approach.

There were three key reasons behind the decision to introduce total reward statements:

- total reward statements were seen as an effective way to ensure staff understood the make-up and the value of their employment package

- in line with its values of honest and fair dealings with staff and in the interests of transparency, Arup wanted people to understand what was available within the organisation as an employee-owned firm

- as an engineering and design consultancy, the organisation wanted to take a holistic 'total design' approach to reward.

Total reward statements

Hatton-Gore explains that although there are some elements of the benefits package – such as the global profit-share scheme and global retirement policy – that are determined centrally, the benefits vary by country, and are based on the company values in combination with what Arup needs to compete in the local labour markets.

The total reward statements are tailored for each individual employee. They include details of salary, profit-share payments and in some cases more than 20 items to which the employee is entitled. The items included are mainly those on which a value can be placed, and these are totalled to give a monetary value for the overall employment package.

Other benefits, such as holiday allowance or the availability of flu vaccinations, are included on the statement but not given a cash value. Hatton-Gore notes that some of the benefits listed on the statement are included because the organisation wants to make sure that employees are aware of what is available: for example, the employee assistance programme. He says: 'We have not attempted to put a monetary value on these things.'

However, while training and development opportunities are viewed as part of the employment package, these are not included on the total reward statement. Hatton-Gore explains that reward in a monetary sense is just one part of what working for the organisation is about; the career and personal development opportunities, and the chance to work on interesting projects, are part of the overall experience rather than another element in the reward list.

Arup's formal total reward policy combines both the monetary and the non-monetary benefits of working for the organisation.

The policy was published in a company magazine when it was formally launched in 2007, and is also available to employees via the intranet.

Hatton-Gore says if somebody finds a way to put a value on some of the other, less tangible, elements of the employment package – such as career opportunities – this would be a 'very interesting idea', but says it is a challenge that has not yet been cracked.

Questions

1. To what extent can Arup's total reward strategy be truly transparent?

2. How will this reward approach be received across all 37 countries?

Source: Sharp, R. (2009)
www.XpertHR.co.uk

ARGUMENTS AGAINST THE USE OF PM

There is increasing evidence that PM can have a positive impact on employee commitment and organisational performance (Fletcher and Williams 1996; Guest 1997). However, evidence is not universally positive, and some studies suggest performance appraisal and pay to be the least effective HR policies, as perceived by the employees (Hutchinson and Purcell, 2003). This mixed picture probably reflects the spectrum of different PM approaches adopted across organisations. Rather than adopting mechanistic, off-the-shelf approaches, organisations need to fit whatever they do to their current and future context. For example, organisations need to consider how appropriate reward strategies fit within their context. The CIPD reward management survey (2003) showed that organisations seem to be moving more towards flexible benefit packages, thereby allowing staff to make some choices that suit their personal circumstances and preferences. The same argument applies to appraisal, with organisations moving away from top-down, descriptive systems to more participative, self-evaluative and developmental approaches.

WHAT HAPPENS AFTER PM?

If a standard formal appraisal interview occurs with the appraisee, a range of actions or options is available to superiors and subordinates alike. As we have suggested already, there may be a portfolio of approaches that interact within the PM process, such as 360-degree feedback, self-appraisal, upward appraisal, coaching and mentoring interventions, etc.

Companies may operate a system of forced ranking, or forced distribution, whereby groups of employees are compared against each other and ranked from best to worst, instead of being judged against independent performance standards. Although this approach is more common with appraising managers, it can be applied to any area of work. Employees who are placed in the lowest category (for example, the lowest 5 per cent) may be dismissed from the organisation or given a fixed time to improve their current performance to the expected organisational standards. Conversely, the top-performing employees may be provided with significant learning opportunities, career growth and perhaps significant financial and personal rewards (Boyle, 2001).

HOW CAN PERFORMANCE BE IMPROVED?

Dependent upon the source(s) of the performance problem, the organisation needs to decide on the type and scope of problem intervention. There may need to be consideration of the macro level issues affecting the broader organisational context, or attention given to micro level, individual issues.

Some of the techniques available include:

- learning
- development
- training
- coaching, mentoring
- team-building
- culture change programmes
- reward schemes
- structure, process, systems, job redesign, etc
- management approach.

CONCLUSION

Perhaps the 'expiry date' of the philosophy of fitting people to jobs, expecting them to do their jobs and be compliant to organisation needs, is close. If organisations expect employees to act as business partners and business performers, then perhaps they need to have more involvement in the running of the business. If employers expect employees to think for themselves, then by definition, they have to delegate, trust, nurture and develop (all) employees.

The question of equal treatment for all employees also has to be taken into account. Harrison and Kessels (2004) discuss the notion of the 'knowledge worker' and the 'non-knowledge worker', a point further emphasised by Drucker (1993), who differentiates between knowledge workers who contribute to the core of the economic activity in a knowledge-intensive organisation, and service workers who facilitate that contribution. Implicit in these descriptions is the understanding that some employees contribute more than others to the success of the organisation, and they should be managed and rewarded accordingly, receiving a proportionately higher amount of management time, resources, recognition and reward.

Apart from the employer perspective, employee expectations continue to change. Arnold (1996) argues that the traditional working relationship has changed, with a movement away from the old to new deals.

Under the new deal, what are the implications for PM, and does the archetypal individual match the 'knowledge worker' analogy described above? Whilst there may not be a universally accepted definition of a knowledge worker, they need to generate knowledge that adds value to the organisation. Harrison and Kessels (2004) further argue that 'knowledge workers form a vital part of the knowledge economy, and it is logical to predict that they will pay increasing attention to their own employability and economic attractiveness as they become more aware of their market value.'

From a human resource development perspective, the emphasis should be on developing people rather than on the job itself. However, the challenge for employers may be in retaining employees for the duration of their most productive work (while they add value) and no longer.

The HR strategy has to encompass all aspects affecting performance, at contextual, organisational, team and individual level. To do this, it has to be part of the main business strategy, closely aligned to organisational culture and supported by appropriate mechanisms such as organisational structure, HR policies and procedures, and be strongly aligned to the HRD strategy.

More flexible and fluid arrangements will be necessary, within which there is a greater appreciation of the subjective, tacit, multi-stakeholder aspects of performance. From a more strategic perspective, the resource-based view of HR (Boxall, 1996; Boxall and Purcell, 2003) suggests ways in which organisations can build upon unique clusters or 'bundles' of human and technical resources in order to improve levels of performance and thereby achieve competitive advantage in the marketplace. The agility highlighted by Dyer and Shafer (1999) and adapted by Boxall and Purcell (2003, p 202) may provide an insight as to how organisations can use PM within a bundle of HR activities.

The significance of maintaining competitive advantage is further highlighted in a CIPD report (CIPD, 2003e), where it is argued that organisations need to strive to be knowledge-intensive firms. The report's findings stated that among other factors, PM is central to the success of knowledge-intensive firms.

The HRD strategy could also be enhanced, to incorporate ways in which HRD and HRD professionals can assist in motivating employees (Buchner, 2007), and move away from what is 'being done' to employees and move towards how the employees can grow in their capabilities, skills and competences.

Performance management may contribute to the success of the firm, but the vital issue is how the talents of employees can be retained, developed and utilised so as to add value to the organisation. Whilst we may concentrate on the output measurement from PM and deal with its consequences, the question to be answered is 'How do we increase performance?' The answer may take us back to developing and nurturing the organisation's greatest asset – employees: a theme developed in Chapter 10.

- Performance management is only a process. The perspective that senior management adopts will impact significantly on how the process is implemented and the consequences of the process followed through.

- Emphasis needs to be placed upon the employees' expectations throughout the whole performance management and appraisal process. These expectations may link to the psychological contract and organisational culture influences.

- When it comes to setting performance targets, there is a strong requirement to readjust to contextual changes and maintain a realistic perspective, or the targets themselves may negatively impact upon performance.

- The question of who defines performance is a critical part of the performance management process. The relationship between the appraiser and appraisee needs to be clearly defined and professionally maintained.

- There needs to be a sensitive and pragmatic balance of performance management, motivation and reward systems to effect appropriate performance outcomes.

- Managers (including HR professionals) need to understand not just what motivates employees, but why they are motivated.

REVIEW QUESTIONS

1. Critically assess the role and contribution that HR makes to the PM process.

2. What motivates you at work, and how would you classify these motivators in terms of content and process theories?

3. To what extent is 360-degree feedback a fad that is unsustainable as a true and workable practice (when it comes to manager/employee interactions)?

4. Do you believe that everthing surrounding and including performance management places too much emphasis upon the individual, at the expense of teams, divisions, organisational cultures etc?

EXPLORE FURTHER

Armstrong, M. and Baron, A. (2004) *Managing Performance: Performance management in action*. CIPD. Remains the front runner of performance management texts. Particularly useful on the 'how to' approaches.

Buytendijk, F. (2008) *Performance Leadership: The next practices to motivate your people, align stakeholders, and lead your industry*. McGraw-Hill Professional. This text provides a broader perspective on performance management and is strong on highlighting its pitfalls.

Cokins, G. (2004) *Performance Management: Finding the missing pieces (to close the intelligence gap)*. Wiley and SAS Business Series. This text provides a pragmatic approach to performance management and introduces a range of techniques and approaches that HR professionals should find both interesting and useful.

Read the latest edition of the CIPD Annual Reward Survey for insights as to what is changing and what is remaining the same in relation to benefits and rewards available and adopted.

Part 5: Conclusion

CHAPTER 13

Summary Themes and Future Trends

Ray French *and* Gary Rees

LEARNING OUTCOMES

After reading this chapter, you should be able to:

- identify some of the key challenges and themes impacting on HR
- indicate some possible future HR developments
- highlight key research findings that impact upon HR (this learning outcome is embedded throughout the chapter).

OVERVIEW

The purpose of this final chapter is to highlight recurrent themes in our book in order to identify the key challenges facing those who lead, manage and develop people in the contemporary workplace. As we have seen, responsibility in this area may fall to a designated Human Resource (HR) function. In some cases, though – for example, in many smaller organisations – line managers take the leading role in managing workers. An alternative model is to outsource this activity to specialist providers. We have argued that in reality, a combination of line and HR expertise is required in many situations in order to effectively manage people at work. In Chapter 2 we examined the possible shape of HR activity – that is to say, *who* carries out the work – in greater detail.

In conclusion, though, *whoever* undertakes the people management role will be required to operate in a pressured situation in the early 21st century. Based on consistent trends over the past 20 years, they will almost certainly be faced with competing demands to secure high worker performance leading to perceived added value, while at the same time securing employee engagement. As we noted at the very start of this book, managing people within such a demanding context is no easy task. We look again at key external developments facing HR in this final chapter, together with suggestions for effective people management in a challenging era.

How can we most effectively lead, manage and develop people? While we counsel against regarding the latest fad (whatever that may be) as a panacea, there is a need to evaluate major contemporary research in HRM and HRD as well as valid theories and models in areas such as motivation and how people learn. Sometimes these models highlight central findings which have remained valid over many decades, while in other cases recent research points to new and developing insights. The challenge for students, and of course managers, is to appreciate what is changing and what is enduring in this subject area. In this chapter we highlight findings and theories which can help aspiring and existing managers.

The chapter concludes with a look at the possible future of HR with reference to recent research such as the CIPD 2010 'next generation' report.

As the core book for CIPD's Leading, Managing and Developing People module, we trust that this chapter will serve as a useful revision tool for both students and tutors. Please also refer to our website www.cipd.co.uk for additional resources.

INTRODUCTION

In this book we have examined a very wide range of topics. The breadth of coverage reflects the all-encompassing nature of leading, managing and developing people. When examining the management of employees we have considered the nature of the employment relationship (Chapter 11), recruitment and selection (Chapter 9), training and development (Chapter 10) and performance management and reward (Chapter 12). There are, in short, many different and varied aspects to employing workers – although in Chapters 2 and 3 we saw how such disparate threads might be subsumed within a strategic focus or 'bundles' of connected policies.

Beyond the specific subdivisions of HR work listed above, we have also stressed the broader importance and role of leadership as an activity (Chapter 5). Linked with leadership are the ethical and professional aspects of leading and managing people (Chapter 4).

We have also argued that the ways in which people are managed is influenced in a most profound way by wider economic, political and social developments. The drive for flexibility (Chapters 7 and 8), emanating from work organisations – and externally from national governments and supra-national bodies – has been particularly influential in this regard. Increasingly, flexibility becomes part of the mindset of employees too and we have shown how the desire, or even expectation, for flexible working can impact on workers' psychological contracts. Managing flexible work arrangements sensitively and efficiently brings a new focus to HR.

It is also necessary to consider the role and place of HR within organisations as all the topical knowledge and cutting-edge skills possessed by managers would be ineffective if HR does not have a defined role and status within a workplace. Only if this role and status exists can those who manage people have a positive influence on organisations' people management strategies, policies and practices.

We have seen how HR can be both a specialist and 'line' role and how it has developed from a support administrative function focused on compliance to, in many cases, a fully-integrated business partner role.

In view of the broad topic coverage of this book, implicit in the subject area, we will select particular areas for further scrutiny in this final chapter.

Although key external factors facing HR are numerous and ever-changing we have highlighted the concept of globalisation and its potentially wide impact on employment, both in terms of creating clusters of key knowledge workers but also the continued presence of more routine work and standardised workers. We also focus on the role of macroeconomic factors, specifically the economic downturn which began in 2008, on managing people in different contexts such as the private and public sectors, drawing on material presented in Chapter 3.

We also return to look at particular themes which are threaded through the book. It is increasingly a routine part of HR managers' life to work with a diverse workforce and we summarise issues surrounding diversity raised in previous sections, particularly Chapters 4 and 11. The theme of conflict is also revisited, because although types of conflict may ebb and flow with time, some degree of conflict is inevitable within workplaces. Conflict is by no means a negative phenomenon and can be managed to drive up organisational performance. We deal also with the phenomenon of outsourcing and the sensitive areas this flags up for HR.

One overriding important theme is change. In Chapter 6 we concluded that it is vital to plan, communicate and execute change successfully if a business was to survive. Organisations may wish to change or, alternatively, are compelled to, due to altered legal obligations or some other changing external driver. As change is ultimately about people, HR in partnership with line managers has a key role in change management. In this chapter we identify some important changing trends as they affect people management. However, what is more important than identifying specific examples of change is the recognition that HR managers need to have a positive attitude or mindset towards change *per se,* given the inherently changing nature of leading, managing and developing people.

HR CONTEMPORARY CHALLENGES

GLOBALISATION AND TALENT CLUSTERS

All organisations need to confront the key issues emanating from the external environment. In the early 21st century one key environmental factor is globalisation, powered by the strategic aim of companies to seek out new market opportunities, while attempting to use changes in the environment to their advantage. Such an evolutionary trend reflects better communication and accessibility provided by the Internet, development of sophisticated and standardised software (so-called microsoftisation), improvements in infrastructure, and decades of tough competition necessitating cost-cutting in all sectors. As these trends evolve, all organisations become challenged to achieve sustainability in their marketplaces.

In essence, globalisation is underpinned by profoundly important economic, socio-cultural, technological and political factors. It is a deep-rooted phenomenon which has impacted on business in different but always important ways and is predicted to evolve – paradoxically in unpredictable ways – in future.

Linstead, Fulop and Lilley (2009) characterise globalisation as an increased blurring of boundaries of all sorts including those between nation states, economies, industries and work organisations. A sense of greater interconnectedness between different parts of the world has implications for all aspects of business. For our purposes, though, we can identify two: first the pressure to drive down employment costs in the face of significant overseas competition, and second, freer movement of workers across the globe resulting in a more diverse workforce.

Profound consequences for HR can follow. For example, some private sector organisations in Western economies have recognised the lower cost-base of other economies such as India and responded by relocating particular business operations there. This is by no means an inevitable process. Bawden (2009) notes how companies including BT, Powergen, Abbey and Orange have repatriated call centre jobs back to the UK from India in recent years.

However, there has been a clear trend since the mid-1990s to relocate white-collar jobs from the UK to emerging and developing economies.

At the same time, much routine manufacturing work has similarly been outsourced or otherwise moved to developing countries like China. One can predict that these emerging economies, built on relatively low-cost provision, will themselves develop as the cycles of wealth creation and increased opportunity begin to take their course.

KNOWLEDGE WORKERS

What are the implications of a trend like this for the HR manager? Clegg *et al* (2008) note that one consequence of globalisation has been the concentration of clusters of world-class expertise in particular sectors by location. These authors cite high-technology clusters in Silicon Valley in northern California, parts of Japan and Cambridge in the UK. Much of the net inflow of workers to London (170,000 in 2006), prior to the 'credit crunch' of 2008, can be attributed to the status of London as a 'magnet for talent'.

In Chapter 8 we recorded the view that an up-skilling of the UK's workforce could be accompanied by a workforce desiring greater autonomy and control in their jobs – see Hutton (2004).

The term 'knowledge workers' has come to denote people engaged in non-repetitive results-oriented work, who require continuous learning and the exercise of creativity (see Bratton and Gold, 2007). It is argued that the demands of such high-level employees can be dealt with more effectively by those organisations which lead and manage workers in imaginative ways and develop them to a very high level of competence.

REFLECTIVE ACTIVITY

A Greater London Authority press release on 13 May 2009 gave a clear indication of how Mayor Boris Johnson envisaged the future development of the London workforce. He set out a vision of London as a global centre of excellence in a range of sectors including high technology industries, medical services and the creative industries. The Mayor went on to note that a highly-skilled pool of talent was critical to London's competitiveness. If this strategy was successful he claimed that the city would enter a virtuous circle, acting as a magnet for talent which would in turn drive further innovation.

Questions

1. What principles of organisational and job design would be appropriate when managing talented knowledge workers? Give reasons for your answers.

2. To what extent might it be more useful to refer to the terms 'meaningfulness', 'engagement' and 'commitment' – as opposed to the traditional term 'motivation' – when considering high-performing talented workers?

3. Identify two leadership styles which could be used to ensure high performance by this type of worker.

When answering these questions, refer to relevant chapters within this book.

As we saw in Chapter 9, the concepts involved in recruiting, retaining and retraining knowledge workers have changed considerably in recent years. Less emphasis is placed on recruiting and training knowledge workers for specific jobs because jobs are changing so quickly. Instead, employees are recruited and developed who can contribute in a flexible way to an organisation's future. If HR adopts more of a fit-the-job-to-the-person (FJP) approach, as opposed taking an FPJ (fit-the-person-to-the-job) stance, there may be additional benefits in terms of performance and future performance.

Perhaps HR needs to be more innovative in terms of capturing talent, and then nurturing it. The extent to which HR adopts a risk-averse approach by following standardised processes and not 'thinking beyond the box' could result in the loss of talent. Emphasis needs to be placed upon seeking talent, with contribution to performance – a key criteria for recruitment and selection, not just in the job/role being filled following a prescriptive process, including possible avoidance of legislative malpractice and concerns over potential discriminatory practice.

Getting the best from knowledge workers is dependent on their having the autonomy and discretion to contribute to their maximum ability. Clearly, this can be risky for the organisation and requires a certain level of trust and more subtle (and probably informal) forms of performance management. A full system thus comprises hired, empowered and bright, well-managed knowledge workers with managers who have commensurate skills and abilities. If the whole 'system' does not work from a process point of view, however, sustainability and the high-performance working ideal is lost.

Whilst there are many challenges facing HR, as we have seen throughout the book, there has been a recent preoccupation with managing 'high-end', multi-skilled, highly qualified, high-contributing talent. However, not all jobs are prescribed as high end, and inevitably, many workers and managers will occupy 'standard' jobs, and in some cases, what could be deemed 'dirty' jobs.

Concepts such as 'knowledge management', 'knowledge workers', 'talent', 'talent pipeline' and 'talent management' may be commonplace in many organisations. To what extent these terminologies are rhetoric rather than reality may come down to definition.

MANAGING ROUTINE WORK AND THE 'STANDARDISED' WORKER

Much HR literature – for example, Harrison and Kessels (2003) and Holbeche (2008) – focuses on achieving the best from knowledge workers. As the authors of several chapters have pointed out, in so doing we can be in danger of ignoring the less glamorous, often worse-paid staff who occupy more routine functions. Some would argue, especially from a total quality view, that all jobs can be treated as holding knowledge and all staff should be seen as knowledge workers, and this is probably true. For the most part, however, our rhetoric fails to meet that reality, and in many instances standardised jobs are, potentially, just that.

Beardwell (2010) indicates that the term 'talent' has typically been used to identify individuals who make a difference to organisational performance. As such this could, and arguably should, refer to *all* employees, in addition to the more specific connotation of key positions that are important to fill for an organisation. In summary, talent management is a broad term referring to all important workers and roles which are pivotally important to organisational success.

Certain tasks (such as serving at a food counter) have been through the mill of cost-cutting. Sections of employment have very often been de-skilled, to the point where workers feel alienated from their tasks (see Chapter 8). These workers experience pressures different from those of the uncertainties connected to knowledge workers, which include the pressure from high-volume repetitive work with little control and the associated dangers of work intensification.

Managing standardised workers is usually more straightforward because the tangible outputs are measurable (Chapter 12). In reality one is often looking to neutralise or minimise the damage that can be caused by staff not bothering (consciously or unconsciously) to undertake routine tasks effectively. In such instances a person-job fit approach (Chapter 8) is appropriate in order to align expectations on both sides of the employment relationship. Clearly, this strategy has consequences for the psychological contract, which was discussed in Chapter 7.

While performance management of standardised workers might be straightforward (because their tasks are straightforward), reward is not. In Chapter 12 Tymon and Rees described wages as an important aspect of reward, up to a point. For many standardised workers, wages are of high importance. However, an organisation must ensure that it does not create an escalating cost-drain from year-on-year wage increases at high levels because these are difficult to correct at a later stage.

Traditionally, HR is mainly associated with fitting the person to the job (FPJ), where a standardised procedure includes a job description, person specification and a set of guiding rules and principles around matching the 'best' candidate to a job. To recruit and retain standardised staff, the 'cocktail' of benefits has to be thought through carefully to match the needs of a targeted set of available staff. Simple financial rewards can be used in an uncomplicated contract that has supervisors who are strong in 'management' using conventional performance management processes.

Alternatively, one might try to cut the wage bill and offer other types of inducements, such as prospects of internal development and promotion (used commonly by media companies), a strong sense of positive-value culture (illustrated by the supermarket Asda in Chapter 9), or promote positive aspects of the work – as commonly seen in parts of the voluntary sector, where the nature of a jobholder's contribution makes a difference to vulnerable people. The 'leadership' aspect of our text would be more important if such non-wage angles were adopted in order to provide proximal reinforcement of the offer.

Regarding leadership in such contexts (Chapter 5), it is likely that selection of managers who deal mainly with standardised workers will depend on strength in 'management' with 'leadership' (at a high level) being less crucial. However, managers who are in this situation really do need to have skills in leading, managing and developing people. The importance of focusing effort on business objectives and the need for a clear direction and purpose is crucial in order to ensure that the managing and leading of staff has a clear aim, and thus provides the basis for performance management. Staff will detect any absence of a clear direction, and its lack will undermine efforts of leading (nowhere?) and managing (for what purpose?). This presents a fundamentally important but difficult task.

 REFLECTIVE ACTIVITY

'Exploited' work experience students forced to make tea

Paton (2010) in an article in the *Daily Telegraph* newspaper reported a study conducted by academics from the University of Westminster on the experiences of work placement students on undergraduate degrees during the recession. The survey sample was of around 100 students from the London area. Over 70 per cent reported that they felt unfulfilled by their working experiences and also saw themselves as 'exploited'. A majority claimed that they spent most of their time filing, scanning and photocopying with one quoted as saying that the only thing they learned was how many sugars their colleagues took.

The Director of the National Council for Work Experience, Heather Collier, noted that 'These

are difficult times for everyone but it's not a green light for employers to act unethically.'

Questions

1. With reference to Chapter 4 of our book, indicate whether or not you agree that the students were subject to unethical treatment. Do you feel that their managers were acting professionally and were they in any meaningful sense 'exploited'? Give reasons for your conclusions.

2. If you had responsibility for organising students' work placement experience, would you approach this by regarding them as standard or knowledge workers – or a mix of the two? How would your perspective impact on their planned work experience?

MANAGING DURING ECONOMIC HARDSHIP

It could be argued that HR faces heightened challenges during an economic recession (see the McDonald's case study in Chapter 1). In 2007 much of the world began to experience the onset of an economic downturn, fuelled by a crisis in sub-prime mortgage lending in the USA. In itself the ensuing crisis demonstrated the interconnectedness of national economies as the crisis rapidly took hold in diverse parts of the planet. There were documented job cuts in many sectors. Indeed, many businesses failed in the course of the recession, leading to job losses in companies with progressive HR policies and practices swept away in the economic and financial maelstrom. However there is evidence that many organisations have re-considered their HR policies during the downturn while attempting to maintain their overall strategic focus. The CIPD (2009c) thus quoted a corporate HR leader from a financial services group:

> 'Our talent management initiatives are robust and believed to add value to the organisation. We therefore believe that the attraction and retention of talent is even more important in the current economic environment than it has been at any time in the past.'

The CIPD (2009c) presented findings from a research study carried out among a sample of 705 members who held senior roles across the private, public and third (or not-for-profit) sectors. Some findings resulting from reduced budgets were perhaps predictable with concerns regarding employee development initiatives, coupled with the macro-level economic situation impacting on pay and, recruitment and selection – with many respondents reporting a shift of focus from recruitment to employee retention.

The impact of economic recession has also resulted in some more innovative strategic re focusing according to this report. Findings include:

- Organisations focusing more of their time on engaging, motivating, retaining and fully using the skills of existing employees.

- Recognition of increasing opportunities to recruit talent discarded by competitors.

- As noted earlier, renewed scrutiny on talent management systems and processes.

- More honest and frequent communications between managers and other employees with greater individual understanding of the situation faced by the business.

- Reconsideration of pay and reward with more creative thinking about non-financial rewards.

- Greater emphasis on ethical leaders who are able to lead and motivate in both bad and good times.

REFLECTIVE ACTIVITY

Ulrich – see Brockett (2010) – has highlighted the central role that HR can play in making businesses more sustainable in the wake of the economic crisis which began in 2008. Ulrich proposes that HR leaders can equip organisations for the longer term by investing in skills of people and exercising quality leadership. However, Ulrich suggests that while the top 20 per cent of HR departments were 'already there' in terms of building sustainability and another 60 per cent were moving in the right direction, the bottom 20 per cent would 'never get it'.

Question

Choose an organisation that you are familiar with – ideally your current employer. Which bracket do you think HR falls into: *already there, in the right direction* or *will never get it?* Give reasons for your conclusion.

TURBULENCE AND HARDSHIP IN THE PUBLIC SECTOR

We saw in Chapter 3 that while differences in HR between the private and public sectors may not be great in many instances, the high proportion of staff costs in many public sector institutions meant that HR had a fundamental role in determining expenditure levels. At the time of writing, in the run-up to a UK general election, the main political parties were setting out policies intended to reduce costs, at the very least by asking the same staff to do more. Few expected the years following 2010 to be anything other than tough for public sector employees, whichever political party – or combination of parties – took power.

In 1992 a leading HR academic, John Storey, published a scheme which differentiated between traditional personnel management/industrial relations and the emerging term of human resource management (HRM). Storey provided 27 points of difference which would locate the characteristics of personnel/IR and HRM in relation to each other. Such differences included beliefs and assumptions, strategic aspects and key levers exhibited by both traditions.

Storey's scheme identified the following points. While in the personnel/IR model the manager would be preoccupied with developing and enforcing contractual obligations, in HR there was a move to get employees to go beyond contract. The HR role was seen as transformational as opposed to transactional (see Chapter 5 for a summary of these terms). There was also a difference in that HRM was concerned to foster a greater link between performance and reward in contrast to highly regulated pay. It can be argued that the personnel/IR tradition as outlined here is strongly reminiscent of the way in which people were managed in the public sector. The flagging up of the HRM alternative opened the way to a reconsideration of how people were to be led, managed and developed in the sector.

In the same period from roughly 1990, a revolution occurred within UK local government and public service providers. Political agendas comprising reduction in taxes (local and national) together with advances in transparency and public audit resulted in generational change in the sector. UK governments of all political persuasions have consistently rewarded those organisations which do well and public service providers are now used to a variety of 'league tables'. Such processes increase expectation to perform in ever-spiralling demands. The more recent downturns in global and local economies have, as indicated earlier, squeezed the public sector still further as governments seek to balance expenditure.

Such pressures have changed the nature of leadership and management in the sector. Hospitals and universities now attract a different type of chief executive from what was expected 20 years ago. The same is true of most of the public sector and the expanding voluntary sector. Top leaders now need to 'drive' the organisation in more senses than one: steering has always been a function, but chief executives are pressing the accelerator for change and achievement as never before.

One can conclude that linked developments in the academic and political spheres led to a situation whereby the nature of people management in the UK public sector was reviewed and in many cases took on a new direction emphasising a performance focus combined with an attempt to engage workers and to derive added value from employees. The HR function itself came under pressure with new roles evolving and a need to demonstrate relevance in terms of performance, together with cost savings and efficiencies.

 REFLECTIVE ACTIVITY

In Chapter 1 we referred to the attempts by Wychavon District Council to put overall management principles into effect through policies and styles designed to engender employee engagement. Among the Council's stated strategic management principles were:

- adopt an entrepreneurial not municipal culture

- apply good performance management as a cornerstone of the Council's management

- invest to save where there are robust cases to do so

- focus on resident and customer satisfaction as a principal objective

- continually develop and challenge to remain excellent.

Wychavon Council's objectives could only be achieved by a change in organisational culture. Refer back to Chapter 1 and summarise the ways in which they sought to engage their employees in this change programme.

Question

What type of leadership would be most appropriate in such a situation? Give reasons for your conclusion, with reference to material set out in Chapter 5 of our book.

KEY THEMES

Having outlined some of the key external factors confronting those who manage people in organisations, we now turn to identify some of the important *themes* contained within this book which, we have argued, underpin people management in contemporary workplaces.

MANAGING DIVERSITY

How organisations approach and manage diversity – introduced in Chapter 4, and explored in greater depth in Chapter 11 – will be a 'differentiator' for the future. It is much easier, and tempting, to hire similar people who get on easily. A homogeneous workforce might be thought to be an easy option thus avoiding the 'diversity issue'. However there is much evidence suggesting that enhancing diversity within groups and teams has a potential pay-off in terms of performance – see Belbin (1993).

Notwithstanding this classic finding from the field of social psychology, it is also true that a diverse workforce needs *careful managing* if the benefits of diversity are to be secured. In examining the specific case of cultural diversity, French (2010) recorded the consensus view of research in this area – namely, that multicultural work teams will either perform much better than mono-cultural groups or much worse. So the key to securing performance is good management. Surowiecki (2004) made a similar point in highlighting the potential *wisdom of crowds*. He noted for example that if one wanted to guess the weight of an ox, the average of a crowd's guesses would always give the best estimate. The more diverse the crowd the more accurate they would be.

Surowiecki also recognised, however, that if a high-performing team were left to their own devices, they may come to feel invincible and hence vulnerable to making blatant mistakes. This is an important finding reminiscent of the notion of 'groupthink' (Janis, 1982). A seemingly excellent work team, or trouble-free work environment more generally, should never be taken for granted, therefore, and both their outcomes and processes should be monitored with a view to swift intervention if problems are signalled.

So we see that managing diversity is a challenging activity offering both the promise of enhanced worker performance while at the same time containing in-built dangers. More generally, the recent findings outlined above point to another key theme within this book: namely, the need to review evidence and to be open to new research insights.

In view of persistent global economic and social trends, it remains unlikely though that any sector can survive without embracing diversity, depending on the level of supply of specific workers. Where there are staff shortages, finding homogeneous workers will require either specialised recruitment and selection (Chapter 9), selective internal promotion through learning, training and development (Chapter 10), or increasing rewards (Chapter 12).

We have also suggested that diversity can be a source of competitive advantage (see the Tesco case study in chapter 4 and the Ford case study in chapter 11), despite the caveats in the last but one paragraph. It is hard to see how an organisation can only partially adopt the changes needed to cope with a diverse organisation and still remain effective. For example, if current trends continue, the UK and other markets with high employment levels will continue to be net importers of skilled workers, with most entrants having a diverse range of backgrounds. The 2005 UK Labour Government's adoption of a 'points system' for immigration enabled focused replenishment of the overall workforce, but remains to be tested. A changed political climate after 2010 may alter the situation. Notwithstanding this, those organisations which learn how to take advantage of new pools of talent – wherever they come from – have potential for differentiation.

MANAGING DIFFICULTY

We conclude this section of the chapter by highlighting several further areas which can prove problematic for those engaged in HR, together with some suggestions for overcoming problems.

Hand-in-hand with diversity come the effort and challenge involved in managing the inevitable conflicting interests that difference produces – which can lead to actual conflict. The effective manager will ensure that any ensuing problems are limited to constructive and task-related conflicts – see Chapter 11 – and do not degenerate into damaging interpersonal disputes. As we have suggested, diverse groups can produce innovative and smart solutions that provide (differentiated) competitive advantage. To be successful such staff will need context- or contingency-based leadership styles (Chapter 5) rather than one-best-way. Managers who can cope with such demands will have to be recruited or developed.

BULLYING IN THE WORKPLACE

CASE STUDY

Hobson (2009) cites a survey conducted by the trade union Unison, which stated that bullying at work had doubled in the past ten years with one in three staff surveyed claiming to have been bullied in the previous six months. The most common forms of bullying included excessive monitoring and criticism, exclusion/isolation, intimidation, public humiliation and being treated in a rude or disrespectful manner.

Bullying assumed a bigger media profile in 2010 due to allegations of bullying in senior UK politicians' offices and the controversy surrounding the Head of the Bullying Helpline's alleged role in publicising these claims.

Hobson concludes that 'anyone who manages people should remember that there is a very fine line between being demanding and being a bully.'

Question

Find three definitions of the term 'bullying'. How easy is it to differentiate between demanding and bullying behaviour? Locate any one organisation's policy on bullying and summarise its main features.

There is evidence that an increasing number of organisations have outsourced activities, for example to subcontractors in order to concentrate on their own core capabilities (Child, 2005). In an important sense outsourcing has become normal and accepted practice within the notion of flexibility and its associated benefits – see Chapter 7. Subcontractors, offering a better price than can be generated internally, might be using legitimate means (such as economies of scale) in their cost-cutting, but they might not. How far the contracting organisation should (and does) investigate the terms and conditions of subcontracted workers is an area ripe for investigation as the structure of our economy changes. HR is likely to be at the forefront when such investigations do become routine. They will have to be well placed in terms of their investigating skills and extend their understanding of all aspects of managing and leading people beyond the legal issues into the ethical dimensions of employment – see Chapter 4.

ENDURING THEORIES AND MODELS FOR LEADING, MANAGING AND DEVELOPING PEOPLE

CONTINGENCY APPROACHES

Which concepts and models are especially relevant when leading, managing and developing people? One important insight is that there are few universally applicable principles and prescriptions. Throughout this book we find numerous examples of policy measures which can work very well – but only in particular situations. A contingency perspective provides the guiding philosophy that the best way to organise and manage – in this case lead, manage and develop people – will all depend on the particular circumstances which obtain. This insight is itself not new as several British and American studies which concluded that organisations should be designed and structured according to their size or technology employed or the turbulence they encountered in their market are now five decades old – see Burns and Stalker (1961) and Lawrence and Lorsch (1967). So a contingency approach to business and management is part of mainstream thought. Returning to the area of leading, managing and developing people in the early 21st century, we find examples of the continuing value of the essential contingency insight in this book.

In Chapter 3 we saw how HR practices and their delivery could themselves vary according to the organisational context. Charlotte Rayner and Liza Howe-Walsh note, for example, that the recruitment and retention of volunteer workers in the third sector (charitable and voluntary organisations) was especially tough, together with funding and reward of employees. Meanwhile the particular circumstances surrounding small and medium-sized enterprises (SMEs) led to much HR work being outsourced. Growing organisations also faced specific issues with Greiner's (1972) model of crises in such organisations pointing to possible variances in how people were managed. We saw, finally, how the field of international HRM was associated with specific strategic decisions – eg whether to adopt an ethnocentric or global approach to managing people and the use of particular methods, such as mentoring for expatriate managers.

In Chapter 5 on leadership, we again saw how some academics – see Hersey and Blanchard (2001) and Kreitner (2001) – found that particular leadership styles would be more appropriate in some situations than others. Gill Christy suggests in her chapter that contingency perspectives remain highly relevant for the exercise of leadership in modern organisations. She concludes that the contingency perspective should inform training of leadership and management skills and that leadership might change hands in response to changed circumstances.

Contingency perspectives form the main thrust of the conclusions to Chapters 8 and 9, with the implication that principles of, and actual practices in, job design and recruitment and selection respectively could and should alter according to the situation. In Chapter 10, Alex Tymon and Margaret Mackay find value in applying the contingency principle to the area of developing employees. They indicate that the choice of learning and development techniques is strongly influenced by contingent factors such as prevailing organisational culture, resources available and learner-related factors. In Chapter 12 Alex Tymon and Gary Rees conclude that what an organisation chooses to measure within its performance management policies (an important underpinning factor) will depend on the organisational context – for example, what it really deep down values in its employees. In this chapter we also encounter expectancy theories of motivation which show how individual workers evaluate the link between effort, performance and reward, thereby suggesting that workers might vary considerably in terms of what motivates them and how.

ENDURING PRINCIPLES

While contingency theory is undoubtedly alive and kicking in the field of people management, we do not wish to suggest that effective leadership, management and development of people can be attained by adopting a pure 'pick and mix' of those strategies and practices which we diagnose as fitting a situation at any one time. To do so would be both simplistic and misleading, since there are undoubtedly core principles and insights which should inform managers no matter what situation they find themselves in. We set out below some of these enduring principles which have been associated with successful management over a long period.

There is a need first to ensure that all people management initiatives are seen to add value to an organisation. In Chapter 3 we presented findings of research by Truss and Gill (2009) who noted that HR was perceived as adding value if it delivered services reliably and on time. Stronger performance was correlated with a strong sense of identity and purpose amongst HR practitioners. A CIPD report (2010c) found that high-achieving HR departments were embedded in the core business of their organisations. So, in summary, the success of *any* policy initiative, as applied to leading, managing and developing people, will be dependent on other key managers' perceptions of how it adds value and also their pre-formed views on the credibility of the people who put forward that initiative. It is also important to employ measures and techniques which are *valid* – see our discussion of recruitment and selection techniques in Chapter 9 – and also *relevant*, as shown by the necessity of transferring learning to the workplace in Chapter 10.

In Chapters 4 and 11 we saw how the management of people was influenced by employment law, so there is a need always to ensure that existing and new measures are compliant with both national and supra-national (eg European Union) legal frameworks. The effective management of the employment relationship, as set out in the first part of Chapter 11, underpins the work of all those involved in managing people. Managers' perception of this relationship should ideally go beyond ensuring minimum legal compliance. If the relationship is characterised by a proactive investment orientation towards employees, we saw that it is more likely to result in employee engagement and organisational success. This long-standing conclusion has been reinforced more recently by MacLeod and Clark (2009) and Alfes *et al* (2010).

Workers' perceptions of how they are treated continue to influence their sense of identity with the employing organisation and motivation to their work. In Chapter 12 we saw how performance management must be carried out in a fair and equitable way – for example, in an appraisal process. Performance management and reward policies should be transparent and understandable. Equity theory dates from the work of Adams (1965) and continues to receive support – see Hollyforde and Whiddett (2002). If workers perceive an injustice when they compare their own inputs and outputs – eg effort and reward – with those of others, the resultant unpleasant feeling will motivate them to take action. In Chapter 7 Simon Turner reviewed the concept of the psychological contract, which again indicates that we all make a mental comparison between inputs and outcomes at work and that a balanced state is desirable in this regard. In Chapter 4, Charlotte Rayner and Richard Christy began their discussion of ethics and professionalism by emphasising that human beings are special and can reasonably demand to be treated in certain ways by employers. They go on to conclude that managers have an important role to play in terms of acting with integrity, going beyond that which is required by the law. There is no more enduringly important and relevant principle in leading, managing and developing people than that of fair treatment.

THE FUTURE OF HR?

Management fads emerge and re-emerge continually. Perhaps there may come a time when HR turns full circle, or perhaps rebrands itself. Whilst HR should not be considered a fad, like Madonna it needs to re-present itself in a credible light continuously. Sarah Bridge reported in the *Times* (2007) that the future of HR lies in its ability to add value and avoid being outsourced.

The CIPD *Next Generation* HR Report (2010f) argues that HR needs to embrace the role of agent provocateur in order to add value to organisations. The authors of this report suggest that HR needs to be insightful in order to add value, so that HR can 'find new ways of meeting current and future challenges' (p 4). This approach assumes close contact with senior management, and in essence, 'helping to educate a class of business leaders who are also able to see business as an applied HR discipline'. The level of insight can range from strategic to tactical to operational, and may vary from company to company and be context-specific.

The argument surrounding the extent to which organisations are strategy-driven then emerges. One approach to strategy formulation may consider the development of a corporate strategy, followed by the development of an HR strategy (and marketing strategy, financial strategy etc). HR's representation at board level and strategic decision-making level is critical here, but it could be argued that a more 'bottom up' approach to strategy formulation could be taken. Assessment of internal competence and capability may prove to be a stronger starting point when considering strategy, than the traditional environmental scanning, accompanied by external threats, etc. The extent to which the internal assets, namely employees, are valued and considered to be the bedrock of strategic decision-making may determine the success or not of the organisation. Concepts such as employee engagement and the strength of the employment relationship, coupled with the development of employees, may prove to be stronger determinants of strategic decision-making.

Sullivan *et al* (2009) from the Work Foundation argue that the employment relationship, together with the employer-employee relationship, trust and employer branding and segmentation are critical areas for the future of HR.

Over the last decade the CIPD has developed its thinking from HR professionals demonstrating the necessary knowledge and operational indicators adding value to business, to business partners, to business leadership. HR needs to focus on three key factors. First, the core value drivers (what makes a business successful or not), described in the *Next Generation* Report (2009, p 15) as 'business savvy'. Second, HR needs to show understanding of the market trends and forces that affect the business now and in the future, together with a broad understanding of the macroeconomic and societal factors influencing the organisation now and in the future (referred to as 'contextual savvy'). Third, understanding the impact of people, culture and leadership within a change context is vital, combining the 'hard' and 'soft' factors that 'enable or derail business' (p 15). This is referred to as 'organisation savvy'.

If HR contributes business, contextual and organisation savvy, then it could be asked if the marketing, finance and other functions do so too. Similarly, these set of expectations could equally be applied to directorate roles (including non-executive directorate roles).

The degree to which HR adopts a managerialist approach also comes into question when issues of morality and ethicality of practice are called into question. The moral compass may become less effective if the overriding objective is a commercial one. The agent provocateur role may not sit comfortably with the upholder of corporate social responsibility role, as do poacher and gamekeeper. HR may therefore have to commit itself to one of these roles or perhaps a different role altogether!

To paraphrase wording from a report by Deloitte (2009, p 5), 'People working in HR have to believe that they are not only partnering with the business, but that they *are* the business.' By definition, HR is an integral part of the company brand.

CONCLUSION

We began this book by stating that leading, managing and developing people is a tough topic. It is not possible to manage people effectively by adhering to a checklist. One size does definitely not fit all. Managing people is hard work which requires thought, care and considerable attention to detail in every interaction and decision made. The sheer breadth of sub-topics covered by the chapters in this book is impressive, and expertise is developing in all areas. The ideas presented in this book provide the reader with a wide set of options to take into their own work environment. 'The basics' are needed to survive, but with changes to people's psychological contracts and changes in employee expectations, 'the basics' are likely to become more complex and demanding.

This text is being written at a time when it is widely acknowledged that change is a constant feature of our work context and all sectors are under pressure to produce results within a negative economic environment. The resource-based view of organisations, summarised by Pilbeam and Corbridge (2010), has helped in placing 'people' at centre-stage in the achievement of competitive advantage. Mobilising this potential should be a fundamental task in leading, managing and developing people.

Solutions are increasingly geared to process (how we do things) rather than content (what we do). This trend is reflected in all chapters, and provides a considerably more sophisticated challenge than previously.

Leading, managing and developing people is demanding due to the inherently problematic nature of people as 'resources', taken together with a challenging external context. The other side of the coin is that it is also rewarding on a whole range of levels for yourselves as practising or aspiring HR managers. Leading, managing and developing people can be a source of fulfilment even when it involves taking tough decisions. Helping employees to fulfil their potential can be the most rewarding task within any workplace.

EXPLORE FURTHER

Throughout this book we have stressed the importance of keeping abreast of current research. Indeed this is one important theme within the CIPD Leading, Managing and Developing People unit. You are recommended to search appropriate websites in order to be aware of emerging reports and data surveys. Suitable websites include those listed below:

- www.cipd.co.uk Chartered Institute of Personnel and Development.
- www.peoplemanagement.co.uk CIPD magazine
- www.employment-studies.co.uk Institute for Employment Studies
- www.ilo.org International Labour Organisation

- www.bis.gov.uk Department of Business, Innovation and Skills
- www.ons.gov.uk Office of National Statistics
- www.europa.eu/employment European Union Employment and Social affairs
- www.managers.org.uk Chartered Institute of Management
- www.tuc.org.uk Trades Union Congress
- www.independent.co.uk *Independent* Newspaper
- www.telegraph.co.uk *Daily Telegraph* Newspaper
- www.bbc.co.uk/news/
- www.cnn.com/BUSINESS CNN Business News

References

Adair, J. (1983) *Effective Leadership*. London: Pan Books.

Adair, J. (2003) *The Inspirational Leader: How to motivate, encourage and achieve success*. London: Kogan Page.

Adler, P. S. (1999) 'The emancipatory significance of Taylorism', in Cunha, M. P. F. and Marques, C. A. (eds) *Readings in Organization Science – Organisational Change in a Changing Context*. Lisbon: Instituto Superior de Psicologia Aplicada.

Aguilar, F. J. (1967) *Scanning the business environment*. New York: Macmillan.

Ahmed, S. (2007) The language of diversity. *Ethnic and Racial Studies*, Vol. 30, No. 2: 235–56.

Alfes, K., Truss, C., Soane, E. C., Rees, C. and Gatenby, M. (2010*) Creating an Engaged Workforce: Findings from the Kingston Employee Engagement Consortium Project*. London: CIPD.

Alimo-Metcalfe, B. (1995) An investigation of female and male constructs of leadership and empowerment. *Women in Management Review*, Vol. 10, No. 2: 3–8.

Allio, R. J. (2008) C. K. Prahalad heralds a new era of innovation. *Strategy and Leadership*, Vol. 36, No. 6: 11–14.

Alvesson, M. and Willmott, H. (2000) Identity regulation as organizational control: producing the appropriate individual. [Electronic version.] *Journal of Management Studies*, Vol. 39, No. 5: 619–44.

Anderson, N., Born, M. and Cunningham-Snell, D. (2001) 'Recruitment and selection: applicant perspectives and outcomes', in Anderson, N., Ones, D. and Sinangil, H. K. (eds) *Handbook of Industrial Work and Organizational Psychology*, Vol. 1. London/New York: Sage.

Anderson, V. (2007) *The Value of Learning: From return on investment to return on expectation*. London: CIPD.

Anderson, V. and Boocock, G. (2002) Small firms and internationalisation: learning to manage and managing to learn. *Human Resource Management Journal*. Vol. 12, No. 3. 5-24.

Anderson, V. and Skinner, D. (1999) Organisational learning in practice: how do SMEs learn to operate internationally? *Human Resource Development International*, Vol. 2, No. 3: 235–58.

Anell, B. and Wilson, T. (2000) The flexible firm and the flexible co-worker. *Journal of Workplace Learning: Employee Counselling Today*, Vol. 12, No. 4: 165–70.

Argyris, C. (1960) *Understanding Organizational Behaviour*. London: Tavistock.

Arkin, A. (2005) Power play. *People Management*, Vol. 11, No. 5: 40–2.

Armstrong, M. and Baron, A. (2005) *Managing Performance: Performance management in action*. London: CIPD.

Arnold, J. (1996) The psychological contract: a concept in need of close scrutiny? *European Journal of Work and Organisational Psychology*, Vol. 5, No. 4: 511–20.

Arnold, J., Cooper, C. L. and Robertson, I. T. (2005) *Work Psychology: Understanding human behaviour in the workplace*, 4th ed. Harlow: FT/Prentice Hall.

Arrata, P., Despierre, A. and Kumra, G. (2007) Building an effective change team. *McKinsey Quarterly*, November.

Arthur, M. and Rousseau, D. (1996) *The Boundaryless Career: A new employment principle for a new organisational era*. Oxford: Oxford University Press.

Atkinson, J. (1984) Manpower strategies for flexible organisations. *Personnel Management*, August: 28–31.

Avolio, B. J., Kahai, S. and Dodge, G. E. (2000) E-leadership implications for theory, research and practice. *The Leadership Quarterly*, Vol. 11, Issue 4: 615–68.

Avolio, B., Walumbwa, F. and Weber, T. (2009) Leadership: current theories, research and future directions. *Annual Review of Psychology*, Vol. 60: 421–49.

Backhaus, K. (2003) Importance of person–organisation fit to job-seekers. *Career Development International*, Vol. 8, No. 1: 221–6.

Baker, K. (2009) Whitehall HR business partners get skills refresher to deal with cuts. *Personnel Today*, 17 November. Accessed through XpertHR, 27 April 2010.

Ballantyne, I. (2009) 'Recruiting and selecting staff in organizations', in Gilmore, S. and Williams, S. (eds) *Human Resource Management*. Oxford: Oxford University Press.

Balogun, J., Gleadle, P., Hope Hailey, V. and Willmott, H. (2005) Managing change across boundaries: boundary-shaking practices. *British Journal of Management*, Vol. 16: 261–78.

Bandura, A. (1993) Perceived self-efficacy in cognitive development and functioning. *Educational Psychologist*, Vol. 28, No. 2: 117–48.

Barber, A. and Bretz, R. (2000) 'Compensation, attraction and retention', in Rynes, S. L. and Gerhart, B. *Compensation in Organisations*. San Francisco, CA: Jossey-Bass.

Barney, J. B. and Hesterly, W. S. (2008) *Strategic Management and Competitive Advantage*, 2nd ed. Harlow: Pearson/Prentice Hall.

Barratt, C. (2009) *Trade Union Membership 2008*. London: Department for Business Enterprise and Regulatory Reform.

Baruch, Y. (2004) 'The desert generation', *Personnel Review*, Vol. 33, No. 2. 241-256.

Baruch, Y. (2006) Career development in organisations and beyond: balancing traditional and contemporary viewpoints. *Human Resource Management Review*, Vol. 16, No. 2: 125–28.

Baruch, Y. and Rosenstein, E. (1992) Career planning and managing in high tech organisations. *International Journal of Human Resource Management*, Vol. 3, No. 3: 477–96.

Bass, B. M. (1985) *Leadership and Performance Beyond Expectations*. New York: Free Press.

Bawden, T. (2009) BT returns call-centre jobs to Britain from India, *The Times*, 16 July.

BBC Radio 4 (2008) Interview with Prof. Joseph Nye, *The Today Programme*, broadcast on 23 April.

Beardwell, J. and Claydon, T. (2010) *Human Resource Management: A contemporary approach*, 6th ed. Harlow: FT/Prentice Hall.

Beaumont, P. and Harris, R. (2002) Examining white-collar downsizing as a cause of change in the psychological contract: some UK evidence. *Employee Relations*, Vol. 24, No. 4: 378–88.

Becker, B. and Huselid, M. A. (2006) Strategic human resource management: where do we go from here? *Journal of Management*, Vol. 32, No. 6: 898–925.

Beer, M. and Spector, B. (1989) 'Corporate-wide transformations in human resource management', in Walton, R. E. and Lawrence, P. R. (eds) *Human Resource Management, Trends and Challenges*. Boston, MA: Harvard University School Press.

Beer, M., Spector, B., Lawrence, P. R., Mills, D. Q. and Walton, R. R. (1984) *Managing Human Assets*. New York: Simon & Schuster, Free Press.

Belbin, M. R. (1990) *Team Roles at Work*. Oxford: Butterworth-Heinemann.

Belbin, M. R. (1991) *Management Teams – Why They Succeed or Fail*. Oxford: Butterworth.

Belbin, M. R. (1993) *Team Roles at Work*. Oxford: Butterworth-Heinemann.

Bentley, R. (2008) Where did the business partner model go wrong? *Personnel Today*, 31 March. Accessed through XPertHR, 27 April 2010.

Bernadin, H. K., Kane, J. S. and Ross, S. (1995) 'Performance appraisal design, development and implementation', in Ferris, G. R., Rosen, S. D. and Barnum, D. J. (eds) *Handbook of Human Resource Management*. Cambridge, MA: Blackwell.

Berry, M. (2007) Cadbury-Schweppes launches UK graduate recruitment campaign with a new online chatroom. *Personnel Today*, 7 November. Available online at: www.personneltoday.com [accessed 16 May 2008].

Biggs, D. and Swailes, S. (2006) Relations, commitment and satisfaction in agency workers and permanent workers. *Employee Relations*, Vol. 28, No. 2: 130–43.

Bjorkman, I. and Yuan, L. (1999) The management of human resources in Chinese–Western joint ventures. *Journal of World Business*, Vol. 34, No. 2: 1–19.

Blake, R. R. and McCanse, A. A. (1991) *Leadership Dilemmas – Grid Solutions*. Houston: Gulf Publishing.

Blake, R. R. and Mouton J. S. (1964) *The Managerial Grid*. London: Gulf Publications.

Blanchard, P. N. and Thacker, J. W. (2004) *Effective Training: Systems, strategies and practices*. New Jersey: Pearson/Prentice Hall.

Bloisi, W., Cook, C. and Hunsaker, P. (2003) *Management and Organisational Behaviour*. London: McGraw-Hill.

Blyton, P. and Morris, J. (1992) 'HRM and the limits of flexibility', in Blyton, P. and Morris, J. (eds) *Reassessing Human Resource Management*. London: Sage.

Boatright, J. R. (2000) *Ethics and the Conduct of Business*, 3rd ed. London: Prentice Hall.

Bollaert, H. and Petit, V. (2010) Beyond the dark side of executive psychology: current research and new directions. *European Management Journal* (in press): doi:10.1016/j.emj.2010.01.001.

Bond, R. (2004) Call centre is 'my dream job'. BBC News on Line website, 14 April.

Boselie, P., Brewster, C. and Paauwe, J. (2009) In search of balance – managing the dualities of HRM. *Personnel Review*, Vol. 38, No. 5: 461–71.

Bowen, D. E. and Ostroff, C. (2004) Understanding HRM–firm performance linkages: the role of 'strength' of the HRM system. *Academy of Management Review*, Vol. 29: 203–21.

Bowles, M. L. and Coates, G. (1993) Image and substance: the management of performance as rhetoric or reality? *Personnel Review*, Vol. 22, No. 2: 3–21.

Boxall, P. (1996) The strategic HRM debate and the resource-based view of the firm. *Human Resource Management Journal*, Vol. 6, No. 3: 59–75.

Boxall, P. and Purcell, J. (2000) Strategic human resource management: where have we come from and where should we be going? *International Journal of Management Review*, Vol. 2, No. 2.

Boxall, P. and Purcell, J. (2003) *Strategy and Human Resource Management*. Basingstoke: Palgrave Macmillan.

Boxall, P. and Purcell, J. (2008) *Strategy and Human Resource Management*, 2nd ed. Basingstoke: Palgrave Macmillan.

Boyle, M. (2001) Performance reviews: perilous curves ahead. *Fortune Europe*, Vol. 143, Issue 11.

Bradshaw, D. (1985) Transferable intellectual and personal skills. *Oxford Review of Education*, Vol. 11, No. 2: 201–16.

Bramley, P. (1996) *Evaluating Training Effectiveness*. Maidenhead: McGraw-Hill.

Bratton, J. and Gold, J. (2007) *Human Resource Management Theory and Practice*, 4th ed. Basingstoke: Palgrave Macmillan.

Braverman, H. (1974) *Labour and Monopoly Capital: The degradation of work in the twentieth century*. New York: Monthly Review Press.

Brech, E. F. L. (1975) *Principles and Practice of Management*, 3rd ed. Harlow: Longman.

Bridge, S. (2007) What's the future of HR? *Times* Online, 7 February.

Bridges, W. (1995) *JobShift: How to prosper in a workplace without jobs*. London: Nicholas Brealey.

Briscoe, J. and Hall, D. (2006) The interplay of boundaryless and Protean careers: combinations and implications. *Journal of Vocational Behaviour*, Vol. 69: 4–18.

Brockett, J. (2010) See HR as a professional services firm, says Ulrich. *People Management*, 25 March: 11.

Brown, D. and Armstrong, M. (1999) *Paying for Contribution*. London: Kogan Page.

Brumbach, G. B. (1988) Some ideas, issues and predictions about performance management. *Public Personnel Management*, Winter: 387–402.

Bryce, V. (2007) Give me strength. *People Management*, 8 February: 7.

Buchanan, D. and Badham, R. (1999) *Power, Politics and Organizational Change: Winning the turf war game*. London: Sage.

Buchanan, D. and Boddy, D. (1992) *The Expertise of the Change Agent*. London: Prentice Hall.

Buchanan, D. and Huczynski, A. (2007) *Organizational Behaviour*, 6th ed. London: FT/Prentice Hall.

Buchanan, D. A. and Wilson, B. (1996) 'Next patient please: the operating theatres problem at Leicester General Hospital NHS Trust', in J. Storey (ed.) *Cases in Human Resource and Change Management*. Oxford: Blackwell Business.

Buchner, T. W. (2007) Performance management theory: a look from the performer's perspective with implications for HRD. *Human Resource Development International*, Vol. 10, No. 1, March: 59–73.

Buckley, R. and Caple, J. (2007) *The Theory and Practice of Training*. London: Kogan Page.

Burnes, B. (2004) *Managing Change*, 4th ed. Harlow: FT/Prentice Hall.

Burns, J. (2008) Informal learning and transfer of learning: how new trade and industrial teachers perceive their professional growth and development. *Career and Technical Education Research*, Vol. 33: 3–24.

Burns, T. and Stalker, G. M. (1961) *The Management of Innovation*. London: Tavistock.

Burns, T. and Stalker, G. M. (1994) *The Management of Innovation*, new ed. Oxford: Oxford University Press.

Caldwell, R. (2008) HR business partner competency models: re-contextualising effectiveness. *Human Resource Management Journal*, Vol. 18, No. 3: 275–93.

Caligiuri, P., Lepak, D. and Bonache, J. (2010) *Managing the Global Workforce*. Chichester: Wiley.

Cameron, J., Banko, K. M. and Pierce, W. D. (2001) Pervasive negative effects of rewards in intrinsic motivation: the myth continues. *The Behaviour Analyst*, Vol. 24: 1–44.

Cantrell, S. and Benton, J. M. (2007) The five essential practices of a talent multiplier. *Business Strategy Series*. Vol. 8, No. 5: 358–64.

Carnall, C. (2003) *Managing Change in Organizations*, 4th ed. Harlow: FT/Prentice-Hall.

Carver, C., Sutton, S. and Scheier, F. (2000) Action, emotion and personality: emerging conceptual integration. *Personality and Social Psychology Bulletin*, Vol. 26: 741–51.

Cassell, C., Nadin, S. and Gray, M. (2002) Exploring human resource management practices in small and medium-sized enterprises. *Personnel Review*, Vol. 31, No. 6: 671–92.

Caulkin, S. (2003) How to catch a rising star. *The Observer* Business pages, 9 November 9: 15.

CBI (2009) Education and Skills Survey, accessed from: http://www.cbi.org.uk/ndbs/ content.nsf/b80e12d0cd1cd37c802567bb00491cbf/e83f616f81370ce880256dc60047ede9 on 29 April 2010.

Chalofsky, N. and Krishna, V. (2009) Meaningfulness, commitment and engagement: the intersection of a deeper level of intrinsic motivation. *Advances in Developing Human Resources*, Vol. 11: 189–203.

Chavan, M. (2009) The balanced scorecard: a new challenge. *Journal of Management Development*, Vol. 28, No. 5: 393–406.

Cheetham, G. and Chivers, G. (2001) How professionals learn in practice: an investigation of informal learning amongst people working in professions. *Journal of European Industrial Training*, Vol. 25: 250–88.

Chhokar, J. S., Brodbeck, F. C. and House, R. J. (eds) (2007) *Culture and Leadership Across the World*. New Jersey: Lawrence Erlbaum Associates.

Child, J. (2005) *Organisation*. Oxford: Blackwell.

Cho, Y., Cho, E. and McLean, G. N. (2009) HRD's role in knowledge management, advances in developing human resources. OnlineFirst, published 14 July 2009 as doi:10.1177/1523422309337719.

Chryssides, G. and Kayle, J. (1996) *Essentials of Business Ethics*. Maidenhead: McGraw-Hill.

CIPD (2003a) *Maximising Employee Potential and Business Performance: The role of high-performance working*. Report. London: CIPD.

CIPD (2003b) *Reward Management 2003: A survey of policy and practice*. London: CIPD.

CIPD (2003c) *People and Performance in Knowledge-Intensive Firms*. London: CIPD.

CIPD (2004a) *Human Capital Reporting: An internal perspective*. London: CIPD.

CIPD (2004b) *High-Performance Working*. Fact sheet. Available online at: www.cipd.co.uk/ subjects/corp/strategy/general/highperfwk.htm [accessed 10 January 2005].

CIPD (2004c) *Graphology*. Fact sheet. London: CIPD.

CIPD (2005a) *Managing the Psychological Contract*. Fact sheet. London: CIPD.

CIPD (2005b) *Training to Learning*. Change agenda. London: CIPD.

CIPD (2005c) *Managing Diversity: People make the difference at work – but everyone is different*. London: CIPD.

CIPD (2006) *Diversity: An overview*. Fact sheet. Available online at: www.cipd.co.uk/subjects/ dvsequl/general/divover.htm?Issrchres=1 [accessed 8 May 2008].

CIPD (2007a) *The Changing HR Function*. Survey report. London: CIPD.

CIPD (2007b) *Leadership and Management Standards*. Available for download from CIPD website at http://www.cipd.co.uk [accessed 21 April 2008].

CIPD (2007c) *Recruitment, Retention and Turnover*. Annual survey report. London: CIPD.

CIPD (2007d) *Diversity in Business a Focus for Progress*. Survey report. London: CIPD

CIPD (2008) *Who Learns at Work?* Annual survey report. London: CIPD.

CIPD (2008a) *Code of Professional Conduct and Disciplinary Procedures*. London: CIPD.

CIPD (2008b) *Work–Life Balance*. Fact sheet. London: CIPD.

CIPD (2008c) Flexible working 'boosts staff performance. *People Management*, 6 May.

CIPD (2008d) *Recruitment, Retention and Turnover*. Annual survey report. London: CIPD.

CIPD (2008/9) *Employment and Economic Trends*. Survey report, Deloitte/CIPD Ireland. London: CIPD.

CIPD (2009a) *Employee Outlook* (online). Quarterly survey report. London: CIPD. Available online at: http://www.cipd.co.uk/surveys [accessed 20 March 2010].

CIPD (2009b) *Organisation Development*. Fact sheet. London: CIPD.

CIPD (2009c) *The War on Talent: Talent management under threat in uncertain times*. London: CIPD.

CIPD (2009d) *Recruitment, Retention and Turnover*. Annual survey report. London: CIPD.

CIPD (2009e) *Succession Planning*. Fact sheet. Available online at: http://www.cipd.co.uk/subjects/hrpract/general/successplan.htm [accessed 30 April 2010].

CIPD (2010a) *HR Business Partnering*. Fact sheet. London: CIPD.

CIPD (2010b) *Learning and Talent Development*. Report. London: CIPD.

CIPD (2010c) *Creating an Engaged Workforce*. London: CIPD.

CIPD (2010d) *Diversity: An overview*. Fact sheet. London: CIPD.

CIPD (2010e) *Next Generation HR: Time for change – towards a next generation of HR*. London: CIPD.

CIPD (2010f) *Sustainable Organisation Performance: What really makes the difference*. Shaping the Future Interim Report. London: CIPD.

Clark, J. (1993) 'Full flexibility and self-supervision in an automated factory', in Clark, J. (ed.) *Human Resource Management and Technical Change*. London: Sage.

Clarke, C. and Pratt, S. (1985) Leadership's four-part progress. *Management Today*, March: 84–6.

Clegg, S., Kornberger, M. and Pitsis, T. (2008) *Managing and Organisations*. London: Sage.

Collings, D. G., Scullion, H. and Dowling, P. J. (2006) Global staffing: a review and thematic research agenda. *International Journal of Human Resource Management*, Vol. 20, No. 6: 1253–72.

Confessore, S. J. and Kops, W. J. (1998) Self-directed learning and the learning organisation: examining the connection between the individual and the learning environment. *Human Resource Development Quarterly*, Vol. 9: 365–75.

Conger, J. (1999) Charisma and how to grow it. *Management Today*, December: 78–81.

Conger, J. (2002) Danger of delusion. *Financial Times*, 29 November.

Cooper, C. (2005) The future of work: careers, stress and wellbeing. *Career Development International*, Vol. 10: 396–99.

Cowell, C., Hopkins, P. C., McWhorter, R. and Jorden, D. L. (2006) *Advances in Developing Human Resources*, Vol. 8, No. 4: 460–75.

Coyle-Shapiro, J. and Kessler, I. (2000) Consequences of the psychological contract for the employment relationship: a large-scale survey. *Journal of Management Studies*, Vol. 37, Issue 7: 903.

Crail, M. (2007) Online recruitment delivers more applicants and wins vote of most employers. *Personnel Today*, 20 November. Available online at: www.personneltoday.com [accessed 16 May 2008].

Crane, A. and Matten, D. (2010) *Business Ethics*, 3rd ed. Oxford: Oxford University Press.

Crook, C. (2005) The good company. *The Economist*, 22 January: 3–4.

Csikszentmihalyi, M. (1990) *Flow: The psychology of optimal experience*. New York: Harper Perennial.

Cully, M., Woodland, S. and O'Reilly, A. (1999) *Britain at Work, as depicted by the 1998 Workplace Employee Relations Survey*. London: Routledge.

Cunningham, I. (2008) A race to the bottom? Exploring variations in employment conditions in the voluntary sector. *Public Administration*, Vol. 86, No. 4: 1033–53.

Dany, F., Guedri, Z. and Hatt, F. (2008) New insights into the link between HRM intergration and organizational performance: the moderating role of influence distribution between HRM specialists and line managers. *International Journal of Human Resource Management*, Vol. 19, No. 11: 2095–2112.

Davenport, T. H. (1993) *Process Innovation: Re-engineering work through information technology*. Boston, MA: Harvard Business School Press.

DCSF [Department for Children, Schools and Families] (2009) *14-19 Briefing: Making change happen*. www.dcsf.gov.uk/14-19.

Deci, E. L., Ryan, M. and Koestner, R. (2001) The pervasive negative effects of rewards on intrinsic motivation: response to Cameron. *Review of Educational Research*, Vol. 71: 43–51.

DeFillippi, R. and Arthur, M. (1994) The boundaryless career: a competency-based prospective. *Journal of Organisational Behaviour*, Vol. 15, No. 4: 307–24.

Deloitte (2009) *Shaping Up: Evolving the HR function for the 21st century*. New York/London: Deloitte MCS Limited.

Devanna , M. A., Fombrun, C. J. and Tichy, N. M. (1984) 'A framework for strategic human resource management', in Fombrun, C. J., Tichy, M. M. and Devanna, M. A. (eds) *Strategic Human Resource Management*. New York: John Wiley.

De Vos, A. and Meganck, A. (2009) What HR managers do versus what employees value. *Personnel Review*, Vol. 38, No. 1: 45–60.

De Wit, B. and Meyer, R. (2004) *Strategy: Process, content and theory*, 3rd ed. London: Thomson Publishing.

Donaldson, T. and Preston, L. (1995) The stakeholder theory of the corporation: concepts, evidence and implications. *Academy of Management Review*, Vol. 5: 265–9.

Dowling P. J., Festing, M. and Engle A. D. (2008) *International Human Resource Management*, 5th ed. London: Thomson.

Doz, Y. L. and Prahalad, C. K. (1988) 'A process model of strategic redirection in large complex firms: the case of multinational corporations', in A. M. Pettigrew (ed.) *The Management of Strategic Change*. Oxford: Blackwell.

Dries, N. and Pepermans, R. (2008). Real high-potential careers. *Personnel Review*, Vol. 37, No. 1: 85–108.

Drucker, P. F. (1993) *Post-Capitalist Society*. Oxford: Butterworth-Heinemann.

DTI (2001) *Diversity Best Practice in the Corporate World: A guide for business*. London: Department of Trade and Industry, Women and Equality Unit.

DTI (2005) *High Performance Work Practices: Linking strategy and skills to performance outcomes*. London: DTI in association with the CIPD.

Dyer, L. and Shafer, R. (1999) 'Creating organizational agility: implications for strategic human resource management', in Wright, P., Dyer, L. and Boudreau, J. (eds) *Research in Personnel and Human Resource Management* (Supplement 4: Strategic human resources management in the twenty-first century). Stamford, CT: JAI Press.

The Economist (2009) Talent on tap: the fashion for hiring temps has reached the executive suite. 10 December.

Edwards, P. (2003) 'The employment relationship and the field of industrial relations', in Edwards, P. (ed.) *Industrial Relations*, 4th ed. Oxford: Blackwell.

Egan, J. (2009) *HR Roles and Responsibilities*. IRS Employment Review survey (2nd ed., January). Accessed through XPertHR: http://www.xperthr.co.uk/searchresults.aspx?s=egan on 8 June 2010.

Eglin, R. (2004) Cash is not king in holding on to staff. *Sunday Times* (London) Appointments, 15 February: 7.

Eikhof, D. R., Warhurst, C. and Haunschild, A. (2007) Introduction: What work? What life? What balance? Critical reflections on the work–life balance debate. *Employee Relations*, Vol. 29, No. 4: 325–33.

Ellesworth, R. E. (2002) *Leading with Purpose: The new corporate realities*. Palo Alto, CA: Stanford University Press.

Ellinger, A. (2004) The concept of self-directed learning and its implications for human resource. *Advances in Developing Human Resources*, Vol. 6: 158.

Elliott, L. (2004) Job flexibility can tie you up in knots. *Guardian Weekly*, 25–31 March: 16.

Emery, Y. (2004) Rewarding civil service performance through team bonuses: findings, analysis and recommendations. *International Review of Administrative Sciences*, Vol. 70, No. 1: 157–68.

Emery, Y. (2008) Lecture presentation at Portsmouth University, based upon three research articles by Emery, Y. and Glauque, D. (2005), *Paradoxes de la gestion publique*. Paris: L'Harmattan.

Emery, Y. and Gonin, F. (2007) *Dynamiser la gestion des ressources humaines.* Lausanne: Presses polytechniques et universitaires romandes.

Engle, A. D., Dowling, P. J. and Festing, M. (2008) Globalisation of SMEs and implications for international human resource management research and practice. *European Journal of International Management*, Vol. 2, No. 2: 153–69.

Evans, J. (2008) Leaders need to be humble, not heroes. *People Management Online*, 17 April. Available online at: http://www.peoplemanagement.co.uk [accessed 20 March 2010].

Farndale, E. and Brewster, C. (2005) In search of legitimacy: personnel, management associations worldwide. *Human Resource Management Journal*, Vol. 15, No. 3: 33–48.

Farnham, D. and Pimlott, J. (1995) *Understanding Industrial Relations*, 4th ed. London: Cassell.

Farnham, D. and Stevens, A. (2000) Developing and implementing competence-based recruitment and selection in a social services department. *International Journal of Public Sector Management*, Vol. 13, No. 4: 369–82.

Fayol, H. (1949) *General and Industrial Management*. London: Pitman.

Festing, M. (2007) Globalisation of SMEs and implications for international human resource management research and practice. *International Journal of Globalisation and Small Business*, Vol. 2, No. 1: 5–18.

Fincham, R. and Rhodes, P. (2005) *Principles of Organizational Behaviour*. Oxford: Oxford University Press.

Fitzgerald, C. and Howe-Walsh, L. (2008) Self-initiated expatriates: an interpretative phenomenological analysis of professional female expatriates. *International Journal of Business and Management*, Vol. 21, No. 3: 156–75.

Fletcher, C. (2007) *Appraisal, Feedback and Development: Making performance review work*, 4th ed. London: Taylor & Francis.

Fletcher, C. and Williams, R. (1996) Performance management, job satisfaction and organisational commitment. *British Journal of Management*, Vol. 7: 169–79.

Fombrun, C. J., Tichy, M. M. and Devanna, M. A. (eds) (1984) *Strategic Human Resource Management*. New York: John Wiley.

Foot, M, and Hook, C. (2005) *Introducing Human Resource Management*, 4th ed. Harlow: FT/Prentice Hall.

Foote, D. (2001) The question of ethical hypocrisy in human resource management in the UK and Irish charity sectors. *Journal of Business Ethics*, Vol. 34: 25–38.

Foster, C. and Harris, L. (2005) Easy to say, difficult to do: diversity management in rctail. *Human Resource Management Journal*, Vol. 15, No. 3: 4 17.

Fournier, V. (1999) The appeal to 'professionalism' as a disciplinary mechanism. *The Sociological Review*, Vol. 47, No. 2: 280–307.

Fox, A. (1966) *Industrial Sociology and Industrial Relations*. Research Paper No. 3. Royal Commission on Trade Unions and Employers' Associations. London: HMSO.

Fox, A. (1974) *Beyond Contract: Work, power and trust relations*. London: Faber & Faber.

Fox, M. (1994) *The Reinvention of Work: A new vision of livelihood for our time*. New York: HarperCollins.

Francis, H. and Keegan, A. (2006) The changing face of HRM: in search of balance. *Human Resource Management Journal*, Vol. 16, No. 3: 231–49.

Fredman, S. (2001) Equality: a new generation? *Industrial Law Journal*, Vol. 30, No. 2: 145–68.

Freifeld, L. (2009) Brain sells. *Training*, Vol. 46, No. 6: 9.

French, J. and Raven, B. (1968) 'The bases of social power', in Cartwright, D. and Zander, A. (eds) *Group Dynamics: Research and theory*. London: Harper & Row.

French, R. (2010) *Cross-Cultural Management in Work Organisations*, 2nd ed. London: CIPD.

French, R., Rayner, C., Rees, G. and Rumbles, S. (2008) *Organisational Behaviour*. Chichester: Wiley.

French, W. L. and Bell, C. H. (1999) *Organizational Development: Behavioural science interventions for organizational improvement*, 6th ed. Upper Saddle River, NJ: Prentice Hall.

French, W. L., Kast, F. E. and Rosenzweig, J. E. (1985) *Understanding Human Behaviour in Organizations*. London: Harper & Row.

Friedman, M. (1970) The social responsibility of business is to increase its profits. *New York Times* Magazine, 13 September: 32ff.

Furnham, A. (1997) *The Psychology of Behaviour at Work*. Hove: Psychology Press, Taylor & Francis.

Furnham, A. (2005) Where egos dare. *People Management*, Vol. 11, No. 3: 40–2.

Garcia, M. F., Posthuma, R. A. and Colella, A. (2008) Fit perceptions and the employment interview: the role of similarity, liking and expectations. *Journal of Occupational and Organizational Psychology*, Vol. 81, No. 2: 173–89.

Geal, M. and Johnson, B. (2002) Management performance: a glimpse of the blindingly obvious. *Training Journal*, October: 24–7.

Gershon Efficiency Review (2004) accessed from http://www.hm-treasury.gov.uk/spend_sr04_index.htm on 29 April 2010.

Ghoshal, S., Bartlett, C. and Moran, P. (1999) A new manifesto for management. *Sloan Management Review*, Vol. 40, No. 3: 9–22.

Giles, C., Guha, K. and Atkins, R. (2010) At the sharp end – the failings of flexibility. *Financial Times*, 22 January. Available online at: www.ft.com. [accessed 1 February 2010].

Gilliland, S. W. (1993) The perceived fairness of selection systems: an organizational justice perspective. *Academy of Management Review*, Vol. 18: 694–734.

Gilmore, S. (2009) 'Conclusions', in Gilmore, S. and Williams, S. (eds) *Human Resource Management*. Oxford: Oxford University Press.

Gilmore, S. E. and Williams, S. (2003) Constructing the HR professional: a critical analysis of the Chartered Institute of Personnel and Development's professional project. Third International Critical Management Studies Conference. Lancaster University Management School.

Gilmore, S. and Williams, S. (2007) Conceptualising the 'personnel professional': a critical analysis of the Chartered Institute of Personnel and Development's professional qualification scheme. *Personnel Review*, Vol. 36, No. 3: 398–414.

Gilmore, S. and Williams, S. (eds) (2009) *Human Resource Management*. Oxford: Oxford University Press.

Gioia, D. A. and Thomas, J. B. (1996) Identity, image and issue interpretation: sensemaking during strategic change in academia. *Administrative Science Quarterly*, Vol. 41: 370–403.

Glen, C. (2006) Key skills retention and motivation: the war for talent still rages and retention is the high ground. *Industrial and Commercial Training*, Vol. 38, No. 1: 37–45.

GMAC (2008) www.expatica.com/nl/.../Global-relocation-trends-2008-.htm

Gold, J., Holden, R., Iles, P., Stewart, J. and Beardwell, J. (2010) *Human Resource Development: Theory and practice*. Basingstoke: Palgrave Macmillan.

Goldthorpe, J. H., Lockwood, D., Bechhofer, F. and Platt, J. (1968) *The Affluent Worker: Attitudes and behaviour*. Cambridge: Cambridge University Press.

Gould-Williams, J. (2003) The importance of HR practices and workplace trust in achieving superior performance: a study of public sector organizations. *International Journal of Human Resource Management*, Vol. 14, No. 1: 28–54.

Gratton, L. (2000) *Living Strategy: Putting people at the heart of corporate purpose*. Harlow: FT/Prentice Hall.

Greiner, L. (1972) 'Evolution and revolution as organizations grow'. *Harvard Business Review*, July-August.

Greller, M. (2006) Hours invested in professional development during late career as a function of career motivation and satisfaction. *Career Development International*, Vol. 11, No. 6: 544–59.

Grey, C. (2009) *A Very Short, Fairly Interesting and Reasonably Cheap Book About Studying Organizations*, 2nd ed. London: Sage.

Grint, K. (1997) *Fuzzy Management*. Oxford University Press.

Grundy, T. (1993) *Managing Strategic Change*. London: Kogan Page.

Gubbins, C. and Garavan, T. N. (2009) Understanding the HRD role in MNCs: the imperatives of social capital and networking. *Human Resource Development Review*, Vol. 8: 245–75.

Guest, D. (1997) Human resource management and performance: a review of the research agenda. *International Journal of Human Resource Management*, Vol. 8, No. 3: 263–76.

Guest, D. (1998) Is the psychological contract worth taking seriously? *Journal of Organizational Behaviour*, Vol. 19: 649–64.

Guest, D. (2004) Flexible employment contracts, the psychological contract and employee outcomes: an analysis and review of the evidence. *International Journal of Management Reviews*, Vol. 5/6, No. 1: 1–19.

Guest, D. E. and Conway, N. (2002) *Pressure at Work and the Psychological Contract*. London: CIPD.

Hackman, J. R. and Oldham, G. R. (1980) *Work Redesign*. New York: Addison-Wesley.

Hall, D. (1996) *The Career Is Dead, Long Live the Career*. San Francisco, CA : Jossey-Bass.

Hammer, M. and Champy, J. (1993) *Re-engineering the Corporation: A manifesto for business revolution*. London: Nicholas Brealey.

Handy, C. (1976) *Understanding Organisations*. London: Penguin Books.

Handy, C. (1989) *The Age of Unreason*. London: Business Books.

Handy, C. (1994) *The Empty Raincoat: Making sense of the future*. London: Hutchinson.

Hanlon, G. (1998) Professionalism as enterprise: service class politics and the redefinition of professionalism. [Electronic version.] *Sociology*, Vol. 32, No. 43.

Hardy, C. (1994) *Managing Strategic Action: Mobilizing change – concepts, readings and cases*. London: Sage.

Hardy, C. 1996. Understanding power: bringing about strategic change. *British Journal of Management*, Vol. 7, Special issue: S3–S16.

Harris, L. (2005) 'Employment law and human resourcing strategies', in Leopald, J., Harris, L. and T. J. Watson (eds) *The Strategic Managing of Human Resources*. Harlow: Pearson Education.

Harrison, R. and Kessels, J. (2004) *Human Resource Development in a Knowledge Economy*. Basingstoke: Palgrave Macmillan.

Harrison, R. (2005) *Learning and Development*, 3rd ed. London: CIPD.

Harrison, R. (2009) *Learning and Development*, 5th ed. London: CIPD.

Hasson, J. (2007) Blogging for talent. *HR Magazine*, Vol. 52, No. 10: 65–8.

Hays-Thomas, R. (2004) 'Why now? The contemporary focus on managing diversity', in Stockdale, M. S. and Crosby, F. J. (eds) (2004) *The Psychology and Management of Workplace Diversity*. Oxford: Blackwell.

Heenan, D. and Perlmutter, H. (1979) *Multinational Organizational Development: A social architecture perspective*. Reading, MA: Addison-Wesley.

Henderson, S. (1997) Black swans don't fly double loops: the limits of the learning organisation. *The Learning Organisation*, Vol. 4, No. 3: 99–105.

Heneman, R. L. (1992) *Merit Pay: Linking pay increases to performance ratings*. Reading, MA: Addison-Wesley.

Hendry, C. (1995) *Human Resource Management*. Oxford: Butterworth-Heinemann.

Hersey, P., Blanchard, K. and Johnson, D. (2001) *Management of Organisational Behaviour: Leading human resources*, 8th ed. London: Prentice Hall.

Herzberg, F. (1968) One more time: how do you motivate your employees? *Harvard Business Review*, January–February: 109–20.

Hiltrop, J.-M. (1996) Managing the changing psychological contract. *Employee Relations*, Vol. 18, No. 1: 36–49.

Hobson, J. (2009) Bullying in the workplace. *Personnel Today*, 5 March.

Hofstede, G. (1991) *Cultures and Organizations*. Maidenhead: McGraw-Hill.

Hofstede, G. (2001) *Culture's Consequences: Comparing values, behaviours, institutions and organizations across nations*. London: Sage.

Holbeche L. (2008) *Aligning Human Resources and Business Strategy*. Oxford: Butterworth-Heinemann.

Holden, N. (2002) *Cross-Cultural Management: A knowledge management perspective*. Harlow: Pearson.

Hollyforde, S. and Whiddett, S. (2002) *The Motivation Handbook*. London: CIPD.

Holst, J. D. (2009) Conceptualizing training in the radical adult education tradition. *Adult Education Quarterly*, Vol. 59, No. 4: 318–34.

Honey, P. (1998) *101 Ways to Develop Your People Without Really Trying: A manager's guide to work-based learning*. Maidenhead: Peter Honey Publications.

Howe-Walsh, L. J. and Schyns, B. (2010) Self-initiated expatriates: implications for HRM. *International Journal of Human Resource Management*, Vol. 21, Issue 2: 260–73.

HRMID (2007) McDonald's serves up better customer care and lower employee turnover: Two-stage training for more than 4,000 staff. *Human Resource Management International Digest*, Vol. 15, No. 1: 23–6.

Huczynski, A. and Buchanan, D. (2007) *Organisational Behaviour: An introductory text*, 6th ed. Harlow: Pearson Education.

Hughes, M. (2006) *Change Management: A critical perspective*. London: CIPD.

Humble, J. (1972) *Management by Objectives*. London: Management Publications.

Hunt, B. (2007) Managing equality and cultural diversity in the health workforce. *Journal of Clinical Nursing*, Vol. 16: 2252–9.

Huselid, M. A. (1995) The impact of human resource management practices on turnover, productivity and corporate financial performance. *Academy of Management Journal*, Vol. 38: 635–72.

Hutchinson, S. and Purcell, J. (2003) *Bringing Policies to Life: The vital role of front-line managers in people management*. London: CIPD.

Hutton, W. (2004) Got those old blue-collar blues. *The Observer*, 22 August.

Ibarra, H. (2004) *Working Identity: Unconventional strategies for reinventing your career*. Boston, MA: Harvard Business School Press.

IDS (2006) *Online Recruitment*. IDS study 819, April. London: Incomes Data Services.

Iles, P., Forster, A. and Tinline, G. (1996) The changing relationships between work commitment, personal flexibility and employability: an evaluation of a field experiment in executive development. *Journal of Managerial Psychology*, Vol. 11, No. 8: 18–34.

Inkson, K. and Arthur, M. (2001) How to be a successful career capitalist. *Organisational Dynamics*, Vol. 30, No. 1: 48–61.

Jamrog, J. J., Vickers, M., Overholt, M. H. and Morrison, C. L. (2008) High-performance organizations: finding the elements of excellence. *People and Strategy, The Human Resource Planning Society Journal*, Vol. 31, No. 1: 29–38.

Janis, I. L. (1972) *Victims of Groupthink*. Boston, MA: Houghton Mifflin.

Janis, I. L. (1982) *Groupthink: Psychological studies on policy decisions and fiascos*. New York: Free Press.

Jehn, K. (1994) Enhancing effectiveness: an investigation of advantages and disadvantages of value-based intragroup conflict optimising performance by conflict stimulation. *International Journal of Conflict Management*, Vol. 5, No. 3: 223–38.

Jenner, S. and Taylor, S. (2007) Employer branding – fad or the future for HR? Research Insight Paper. London: CIPD.

Johnson, G. and Scholes, K. (2002) *Exploring Corporate Strategy*, 6th ed. London: FT/Pitman.

Johnson, G., Scholes, K. and Whittington, R. (2007) *Exploring Corporate Strategy; Texts and cases*, 7th ed. London: FT/Pitman.

Jones, T. W. (1995) Performance management in a changing context. *Human Resource Management*, Fall: 425–42.

Judge, T. A. and Cable, D. M. (1997) Applicant personality, organisational culture and organisation attraction. *Personnel Psychology*, Vol. 50, No. 2: 359–94.

Judge, W. Q., Naoumova, I. and Douglas, T. (2009) Organizational capacity for change and firm performance in a transitional economy. *International Journal of Human Resource Management*, Vol. 20, No. 8: 1737–52.

Kandola, R. and Fullerton, J. (1998) *Diversity in Action: Managing the mosaic*. London: CIPD.

Kang, D., and Stewart, J. (2007) Leader-member exchange (LMX) theory of leadership and HRD. *Leadership and Organization Development Journal*, Vol. 28, No. 6: 531–51.

Katou, A. A. and Budhwar, P. S. (2009) Causal relationship between HRM policies and performance: evidence from the Greek manufacturing sector. *European Management Journal*, Vol. 28: 25–39.

Kelliher, C. and Anderson, D. (2010) Doing more with less? Flexible working practices and the intensification of work. *Human Relations*, Vol. 63, No. 1: 92–4.

Kersley, B., Alpin, C., Forth, J., Bryson, A., Bewley, H., Dix, G. and Oxenbridge, S. (2006) *Inside the Workplace: Findings from the 2004 Workplace Employment Relations Survey*. London: Routledge.

Kessler, I. and Purcell, J. (1992) Performance-related pay: objectives and application. *Human Resource Management Journal*, Vol. 2, No. 3, Spring: 6–33.

Kiessling, T. and Harvey, M. (2005) Strategic global human resource management research in the twenty-first century; an endorsement of the mixed-method research methodology. *International Journal of Human Resource Management*, Vol. 16, No. 1: 22–45.

King, Z. (2004) *Guide to Career Management*. London: CIPD.

Kissler, G. (1994) The new employment contract. *Human Resource Management*, Vol. 33, No. 3: 335–52.

Knowles, M. (1990) *The Adult Learner: A neglected species*. London: Gulf Publications.

Kotter, J. P. (1996) *Leading Change*. Boston, MA: Harvard Business School Press.

Kotter, J. P. (1999) *What Leaders Really Do*. Boston, MA: Harvard Business School Press.

Kreitner, R. (2001) *Management*, 6th ed. Boston, MA: Houghton Mifflin.

Kreitner, R. and Kinicki, A. (2001) *Organisational Behaviour*, 5th ed. New York: McGraw-Hill.

Kuvaas, B. (2006) Performance appraisal satisfaction and employee outcomes: mediating and moderating roles of work motivation. *International Journal of Human Resource Management*, Vol. 17, No. 3, March: 504–22.

Ladkin, D. (2008) Leading beautifully: how mastery, congruence and purpose create the aesthetic of embodied leadership practice. *The Leadership Quarterly*, Vol. 19: 31–41.

Ladkin, D. and Taylor, S. (2009) Enacting the 'true self': towards a theory of embodied authentic leadership. *The Leadership Quarterly*, Vol. 21: 64–74.

Lashley, C. (1995) Towards an understanding of employee empowerment in hospitality services. *International Journal of Contemporary Hospitality Management*, Vol. 7, No.1: 27–32.

Latham, G. (2007) *Work Motivation: History, theory, research and practice.* London: Sage.

Lawrence, P. and Lorsch, J. (1967) *Organisation and Environment.* Boston, MA: Harvard Business School Press.

Lawler, E. (2009) The knowing-doing gap. *Conference Board Review*, Vol. 46, Issue 3, May/June: 29.

Leanna, C. and Barry, B. (2000) Stability and change as simultaneous experiences in organizational life. *Academy of Management Review*, Vol. 25, No. 4: 753–9.

Leach, D. and Wall, T (1994) *What Is – Job Design?* Sheffield: Institute of Work Psychology.

Legge, K. (2005) *Human Resource Management: Rhetorics and realities*, 2nd ed. Basingstoke: Palgrave Macmillan.

Leitch, S. (2006) *Review of Skills: Prosperity for all in the global economy – world-class skills.* Final Report. Norwich: HMSO. Available online at: www.hm-treasury.gov.uk/leitch [accessed November 2009].

Lessem, R. (1989) *Global Management Principles.* Harlow: Prentice Hall.

Levinson, H. (1970) Management by whose objectives? *Harvard Business Review*, July-August: 125–34.

Levinson, H. (1976) Appraisal of what performance? *Harvard Business Review*, July--August: 30–46.

Lewin, D. (2001) IR and HR perspectives on workplace conflict: what can each learn from the other? *Human Resource Management Review*, Vol. 11, No. 4, Winter: 453–85.

Lewin, K. (1947) Frontiers in group dynamics. *Human Relations*, Vol. 1: 5–42.

Lewin, K. (1951) *Field Theory in Social Science.* New York/London: Harper & Row.

Linstead, S., Fullop, L. and Lilley, S. (2009) *Management and Organisation: A critical text*, 2nd ed. Basingstoke: Palgrave Macmillan.

Lloyd, M. and Maguire, S. (2002) The possibility horizon. *Journal of Change Management*, Vol. 3, No. 2: 149–57.

Locke, E. A. and Latham, G. P. (1990) *A Theory of Goal-Setting and Task Performance*. Englewood Cliffs, NJ: Prentice Hall.

Lockwood, N. R. (2007) *Leveraging employee engagement for competitive advantage: HR's strategic role*. Alexandria, VA: Society for Human Resource Management.

Lupton, T. (1991) Organisational change: top-down or bottom-up management? *Personnel Review*, Vol. 20, Issue 3: 4–10.

MacDonald, D. J. and Makin, P. J. (2000) The psychological contract, organisational commitment and job satisfaction of temporary staff. *Leadership and Organization Development Journal*, Vol. 21, No. 2: 84–91.

Mackie, J. L. (1977) *Ethics – Inventing Right and Wrong*. Harmondsworth: Penguin.

Macleod, D. and Clark, N. (2009) *Engaging for Success: Enhancing performance through employee engagement*. London: Office of Public Sector Management.

Maguire, H. (2002) Psychological contracts: are they still relevant? *Career Development International*, Vol. 7, No. 3: 167–80.

Mahoney, J. (1994) 'How to be ethical: ethics resource management', in Harvey, B. (ed.) *Business Ethics – A European Approach*. Hemel Hempstead: Prentice Hall.

Mammam, A., Akuratiyagamage, V. W. and Rees, C. J. (2006) Managerial perceptions of the role of the human resource function in Sri Lanka: a comparative study of local, foreign-owned and joint venture companies. *International Journal of Human Resource Management*, Vol. 17, 12 December: 2009–20.

Marchington, M., Grimshaw, D., Rubery, J. and Willmott, H. (2005) *Fragmenting Work: Blurring organizational boundaries and disordering hierarchies*. Oxford: Oxford University Press.

Marchington, M., Vincent, S., and Cooke, F. L. (2005) 'The role of boundary-spanning agents in inter-organizational contracting', in M. Marchington, D. Grimshaw, J. Rubery and H. Willmott (eds) *Fragmenting Work: Blurring organizational boundaries and disordering hierarchies*. Oxford: Oxford University Press.

Marks, A. (2001) Developing a multiple foci conceptualization of the psychological contract. *Employee Relations*, Vol. 23, No. 5: 454–69.

Marks & Spencer (2008) *About Plan A*. Company website: http://plana.marksandspencer.com [accessed 18 April 2008].

Marris, P. (1986) *Loss and Change*. London: Routledge & Kegan Paul.

Marsden, D. and French, S. (1998) *What a Performance: Performance-related pay in the public services*. London: Centre for Economic Performance.

Mayon-White, B. (1993) 'Problem-solving in small groups: team members as agents of change', in Mabey, C. and Mayon-White, B. (eds) *Managing Change*, 2nd ed. Buckingham: Open University/Paul Chapman Publishing.

McCalman, J. and Paton, R. A. (1992) *Change Management*. London: Paul Chapman Publishing.

McClernon, T. (2006) Rivals to systematic training. *Advances in Developing Human Resources*, Vol. 8, No. 4, November: 442–59.

McCracken, M. and Wallace, M. (2000) Towards a redefinition of strategic HRD. *Journal of European Industrial Training*, Vol. 24, No. 5: 281–90.

McDonald, P., Brown, K. and Bradley, L. (2005) Have traditional career paths given way to Protean ones? Evidence from senior managers in the Australian public sector. *Career Development International*, Vol. 10, No. 2: 109–29.

Megginson, D. and Whitaker, V. (2007) *Continuing Professional Development*, 2nd ed. London: CIPD.

Mercer Survey 2008/9. http://www.employeebenefits.co.uk/item/7971/23/319/3).

Meyer, J. P. and Herscovitch, L. (2001) Commitment in the workplace: towards a general model. *Human Resources Management Review*, Vol. 11: 299–326.

Miller, D. (2004) Building sustainable change capability. *Industrial and Commercial Training*, Vol. 36, No. 1: 9-12.

Millward, N., Bryson, A. and Forth, J. (2000) 'All change at work: British employment relations 1980–1998 as portrayed by the Workplace Industrial Relations Series', in Blyton, P. and Turnbull, P. (2004) *The Dynamics of Employee Relations*, 3rd ed. Basingstoke: Palgrave Macmillan.

Mitchell, L. (2009) David Fairhurst interview in *Managing People*, 30 July. Available online at: http://www.hrzone.co.uk.

Mohrman, A. M. and Mohrman, S. A. (1995) Performance management is 'running the business'. *Compensation and Benefits Review*, July-August: 69–75.

Mumford, E. (1995) Contracts, complexity and contradictions: the changing employment relationship. *Personnel Review*, Vol. 24, No. 8: 54-70.

Mullins, L. (2010) *Management and Organisational Behaviour*, 9th ed. Harlow: FT/Prentice Hall.

Murphy, N. (2008) Line manager's role in people management. *IRS Employment Review* survey, Issue 894, 3 April. Accessed through XPertHR, http://www.xperthr.co.uk/ article/ 84008/survey--line-span-span-classhighlightmanagers-span-span-classhighlightrole-span-in-people-span-classhighlightmanagement.aspx?searchwords=murphy_2008_line_managers_role, on 8 June 2010.

Murphy, N. (2008) HR roles and responsibilities. *IRS Employment Review* survey. Accessed through XPertHR, http://www.xperthr.co.uk/searchresults.aspx?s=murphy_2010, on 8 June 2010.

Murphy, N. (2008) Trends in recruitment methods in 2006 and 2007. *IRS Employment Review*, Issue 893. Available online at: www.xperthr.co.uk [accessed 16 May 2008].

Murray-West, R. (2002) Sunderland car workers are Europe's most productive. *Daily Telegraph*, 9 July.

Needle, D. (2004) *Business in Context*, 4th ed. London: Thomson Learning.

Nelson, L. (2003) A case study in organisational change: implications for theory. *The Learning Organization*, Vol. 10, No. 1: 18–30.

Nonaka, I. and Takeuchi, H. (1995) *The Knowledge-Creating Company*, Oxford: Oxford University Press.

Noon, M. and Blyton, P. (2002) *The Realities of Work*, 2nd ed. Basingstoke: Palgrave Macmillan.

ONS (2010) Office for National Statistics, www.statistics.gov.uk [accessed 24 March 2010].

Open University (1985) Block 1. *Managing and Messy Problems*. Course T244. *Managing in Organizations*. Milton Keynes: Open University.

Paauwe, J. (2009) HRM and performance: achievements, methodological issues and prospects. *Journal of Management Studies*, Vol. 46, No. 1: 129–42.

Paauwe, J. and Boselie, P. (2005) HRM and performance: what next? *Human Resource Management Journal*, Vol. 15: 68–83.

Paton, G. (2010) Exploited work experience students forced to make tea. *Daily Telegraph*, 11 January.

Paton, R. A. and McCalman, J. (2000) *Change Management: Guide to effective implementation*, 2nd ed. London: Sage.

Patterson, M., West, M., Lawthorn, R. and Nickell, S. (1997) *Impact of People Management Practices on Business Performance*. Issues in People Management, No. 22. London: Institute for Personnel and Development.

Perkin, H. (1989) *The Rise of Professional Society – England since 1880*. London: Routledge.

Perkins, S. J. and Shortland, S. M. (2006) *Strategic International Human Resource Management*. 2nd ed. London: Kogan Page.

Perlmutter, H. V. (1969) The tortuous evolutions of the multinational corporation. *Columbia Journal of World Business*, January-February: 9–18.

Perry, M. (2001) Flexibility pays. *Accountancy Age*, 6 December: 15–18; reprinted (2002) in *Human Resource Management International Digest*, Vol. 10, No. 4: 13–15.

Perry, E. and Kulik, C. T. (2008) The devolution of HR to the line: implications for perceptions of people management effectiveness. *International Journal of Human Resource Management*, Vol. 19, No. 2: 262 73.

Peston, R. (2007) *Rose Goes Green in Pursuit of Profit*. BBC News website, 15 January, at http:// news.bbc.co.uk [accessed 18 April 2008].

Peters T. J. (1999) *The Brand You 50; Or: Fifty ways to transform yourself from an 'employee' into a brand that shouts distinction, commitment, and passion!* New York: Knopf Publishing.

Pettigrew, A. (1985) *The Awakening Giant: Continuity and change at ICI*. Oxford: Blackwell.

Pettigrew, A. and Whipp, R. (1993) 'Understanding the environment', in Mabey, C. and Mayon-White, B. (eds) *Managing Change*, 2nd ed. London: Paul Chapman Publishing.

Pilbeam, S. and Corbridge, M. (2006) *People Resourcing Contemporary HRM in Practice*, 3rd ed. Harlow: FT/Prentice Hall.

Pilbeam, S. and Corbridge, M. (2010) *People Resourcing and Talent Management*, 4th ed. Harlow: FT/Prentice Hall.

Pitcher, G. (2008) Backlash against HR business partner model. *Personnel Today*, 29 January.

Pollert, A. (1991) 'The orthodoxy of flexibility', in Pollert, A. *Farewell to Flexibility?* Oxford: Blackwell.

Pollitt, D (2003) Shift-pattern switch improves staff turnover and recruitment at Seeboard. *Human Resource Management International Digest*, Vol. 11, No. 1: 12–14.

Porter, M. (1985) *Competitive Advantage: Creating and sustaining superior performance*. New York: Free Press.

Porter, M. (1998) *Competitive Strategy: Techniques for analyzing industries and competitors*. New York: Free Press.

Porter, M. E. and Kramer, M. R. (2006) Strategy and society: the link between competitive advantage and corporate social responsibility. *Harvard Business Review*, Vol. 84, No. 12: 78–92.

Price, A. (2004) *Human Resource Management in a Business Context*, 2nd ed. London: Thomson.

Price, D. (ed.) (2009) *Principles and Practice of Change*. Basingstoke: Palgrave Macmillan.

Priem, R. L., Butler, J. E. (2001) Is the resource-based theory a useful perspective for strategic management research? *Academy of Management Review*, Vol. 26, No. 1: 22–40.

Pugh, D. S. and Hickson, D. J. (1976) *Organizational Structure in Its Context*. Farnborough: Saxon House.

Purcell, J. and Ahlstrand, B. (1994) *Human Resource Management in the Multi-Divisional Company*. Oxford: Oxford University Press.

Rajan, A. (2002) Meaning of Leadership in 2002. *Professional Manager*, March: 33.

Rao, T. V. and Varghese, S. (2008) Trends and challenges of developing human capital in India. *Human Resource Development International*, Vol. 12, No. 1, February: 15–34.

Rayner, C. and Adam-Smith, D. (eds) (2009) *Managing and Leading People.* London: CIPD.

Reed Consulting survey 2004, accessed through http://www.shef.ac.uk/content/1/c6/ 05/87/73/Handout%20-%20Induction.doc on 28 January 2010.

Rees, D. and McBain, R. (2004) *People Management.* Basingstoke: Palgrave Macmillan.

Reeves, R. (2008) The trouble with targets. *Management Today*, 8 January.

Reid, M., Barrington, H. and Brown, M. (2007) *Human Resource Development*, 7th ed. London: CIPD.

Robbins, S. (1993) *Organisational Behaviour: Concepts, controversies and applications*, 6th ed. Englewood Cliffs, NJ: Prentice Hall.

Rodrigues, C. A. (1988) 'Identifying the right leader for the right situation'. *Personnel Today*, September: 43–6.

Rodwell, J. J., Noblet, A. J., Stean, P., Osborne, S. and Allisey, A. F. (2008) Investigating people management issues in a third sector health care organisation – an inductive approach. *Australian Journal of Advanced Nursing*, Vol. 27, No. 2: 55–62.

Rollinson, D. (2008) *Organisational Behaviour and Analysis: An integrated approach*, 4th ed. Harlow: FT/Prentice Hall.

Rose, S. (2007) Back in fashion: how we're reviving a British icon. *Harvard Business Review*, May: 51–8.

Rosener, J. (1990) Ways women lead. *Harvard Business Review*, November–December: 119–25.

Rosenfeld, R. and Wilson, D. (1999) *Managing Organisations: Texts, readings and cases*, 2nd ed. London: McGraw-Hill.

Rousseau, D. (1995) *Psychological Contracts in Organizations: Understanding written and unwritten agreements.* London: Sage.

Sadler-Smith, E., Allinson, C. and Hayes, J. (2000) Learning preferences and cognitive style: some implications for continuing professional development. *Management Learning*, Vol. 31, No. 2: 239–56.

Salimäki, A., Hakonen, A. and Heneman, R. (2009) Managers generate meaning for pay. *Journal of Managerial Psychology*, Vol. 24, No. 2: 161–77.

Sargeant, M. and Lewis, D. (2008) *Employment Law*, 4th ed. Harlow: Pearson.

Saunders, M. N. K. and Thornhill, A. (2006) Forced employment contract change and the psychological contract. *Employee Relations*, Vol. 28, No. 5: 449–67.

Schein, E. (1978) *Career Dynamics: Matching the individual and organisational needs*. Addison-Wesley. Reading, MA.

Schein, E. (1984) Coming to a new awareness of organizational culture. *Sloan Management Review*, Vol. 25, No. 2: 3–16.

Schuler, R. S., Dowling, P. E. and De Cieri, H. (1993) An integrative framework of strategic international human resource management. *Journal of Management*, Vol. 19, No. 2: 419–59.

Searle, R. (2003) *Selection and Recruitment: A critical text*. Milton Keynes: Palgrave Macmillan in association with the Open University.

Semler, R. (1993) *Maverick: The success story behind the world's most unusual workplace*. London: Arrow Books.

Sears, L. (2010) *Next Generation HR: Time for change – towards a next generation HR*. London: CIPD.

Seligman, M. (1998) *Learned Optimism*. New York, NY: Simon & Schuster.

Senge, P. (1993) *The Fifth Discipline: The art and practice of the learning organisation*. New York: Random House.

Sennett, R. (1998) *The Corrosion of Character: The personal consequences of work in the new capitalism*. London: Norton.

Senior, B. and Swailes.S. (2010) *Organisational Change*, 4th ed. Harlow: FT/Prentice Hall.

Sharp, R. (2009) Total reward at Arup. *IRS Employment Review*, Issue 916, 19 February.

Shen, J., Chandra, A., D'Netto, B. and Monga, M. (2009) Managing diversity through human resource management: an international perspective and conceptual framework. *International Journal of Human Resource Management*, Vol. 20, No. 2, February: 235–51.

Simpson, S. (2010) *Volcano Update: Seven things employers should be doing*. www.PersonnelToday.com. 22 April [accessed 23 April 2010].

Sparrow, P. R. (2005) 'Global human resource management', in Shams, M. and Jackson, P. (eds) *Developments in Work and Organizational Psychology: Implications for international business*. London, New York and Amsterdam: Elsevier.

Springett, N. (2002) The impact of corporate purpose on strategy, organisations and financial performance. *Human Resources and Employment Review*, Vol. 2, No. 2: 117–24.

Sternberg, E. (2000) *Just Business*, 2nd ed. Oxford: Oxford University Press.

Stewart, J. and McGoldrick, J. (eds) (1996) *Human Resource Development: Perspectives, strategies and practice*. London: Pitman.

Storey, J. (1983) *Managerial Prerogatives and the Question of Control*. London: Routledge.

Storey, J. (1989) 'From personnel management to human resource management', in Storey, J. (ed.) *New Perspectives on Human Resource Management*. London: Routledge.

Storey, J. (1992) *Developments in the Management of Human Resources*. Oxford: Blackwell.

Storey, J. (1995) *Human Resource Management: A critical text*. London: Routledge.

Strack, R., Caye, J., Leicht, M., Villis, U., Böhm, H. and McDonnell, M. (2007) *The Future of HR in Europe: Key challenges through 2015*. London: Boston Consulting Group.

Suff, R. (2008) Business partnering at the AA. *IRS Employment Review*, Issue 908.

Sullivan, S. (1999) The changing nature of careers: a review and research agenda. *Journal of Management*, Vol. 25, No. 3: 457–84.

Sullivan, J., Wong, W, Adusumilli, D., Alder, A., Blazey, L., Huggett, M. and Parkin, J. (2009) Deal or no deal? An exploration of the modern employment relationship. The future of HR Working Paper. London: The Work Foundation.

Surowiecki, J. (2004) *The Wisdom of Crowds*. New York: Doubleday.

Sutherland, J. (2009) WERS Report. Training and employee use of skills in Scotland: some evidence. *Fraser Economic Commentary*, Vol. 33, No. 1: 60–4

Suutari, V. and Brewster, C. (2000) Making their own way: international experience through self-initiated foreign assignments. *Journal of World Business*, Vol. 35, No. 4: 417–36.

Tamkin, P., Barber, L. and Hirsh, W. (1995) *Personal Development Plans: Case studies of practice*. Brighton: Institute for Employment Studies.

Tan, V. and Tiong, T. N. (2005) Change management in times of economic uncertainty. *Singapore Management Review*, Vol. 27, No. 1: 49–68.

Tannenbaum, R. and Schmidt, W. H. (1973) How to choose a leadership pattern. *Harvard Business Review*, May-June: 162–80.

Taylor, F. W. (1911) *Principles of Scientific Management*. New York: Harper.

Taylor, R. (2002) The future of work–life balance. *Human Resource Management International Digest*, Vol. 10, No. 4.

Tesco (2008) Tesco.com website [accessed 13 September 2004; 16 February 2005; 4 May 2008].

Tharenou, P. (2008) 'Self-initiated careers', in Baugh, S. G. and Sullivan, S. E. (eds) *Maintaining Focus Energy and Options Over the Career*. Charlotte, NC: Information Age Publishing

Thomas, R. M. (2001) *Recent Theories of Human Development*. Thousand Oaks, CA: Sage.

Thomas, R. (2009) 'The business environment of human resource management', in Gilmore, S. and Williams, S. (eds) *Human Resource Management*. Oxford: Oxford University Press.

Thomson, P. (2008) The business benefits of flexible working. *Strategic HR Review*, Vol. 7, No. 2: 17–22.

Thompson, P. and McHugh, D. (2009) *Work Organisations: A critical approach*, 4th ed. Basingstoke: Palgrave Macmillan.

Tomlinson, F. and Schwabenland, C. (2010) Reconciling competing discourses of diversity? The UK non-profit sector between social justice and the business case. *Organisation*, Vol. 17: 101–21.

Torrington, D., Hall, L. and Taylor, S. (2002) *Human Resource Management*, 5th ed. Harlow: FT/Prentice Hall.

Torrington, D., Hall, L. and Taylor, D. (2008) *Human Resource Management*, 7th ed. Harlow: FT/Prentice Hall.

Townsend, R. (1981) *Up the Organisation*. Greenwich, CT: Fawcett.

Toynbee, P. (2008) MPs must fulfil Labour's pledge to low paid and temporary workers. *The Guardian*, 23 February: 33.

Truss, C. and Gill, J. (2009) Managing the HR function: the role of social capital. *Personnel Review*, Vol. 38, No. 6: 674–95.

UKCES (2009) *National Employer Skills Survey 2009*. Key Findings Report. March. London: UK Commission for Employment and Skills.

Ulrich, D. (1997) *Human Resource Champions: The next agenda for adding value and delivering results*. Boston, MA: Harvard Business School Press.

Ulrich, D. and Brockbank, W. (2005) *The HR Value Proposition*. Boston, MA: Harvard Business School Press.

Ulrich, D. and Smallwood, N. (2004) Capitalizing on Capabilities. *Harvard Business Review*, Vol. 82, No. 6: 119–27.

Ulrich, D., Younger, J. and Brockbank, W. (2008) The twenty-first century HR organization. *Human Resource Management*, Vol. 47, No. 4: 829–50.

Vilanova, M., Lozano, M. and Arenas, D. (2009) Exploring the nature of the relationship between CSR and competitiveness. *Journal of Business Ethics*, Vol. 87: 57–69.

Von Bergen, C. W., Soper, B. and Parnell, J. A. (2005) Workplace diversity and organisational performance. *Equal Opportunties International*, Vol. 24, No. 3/4.

Wahrenburg, M., Hackethal, A., Friedrich, L. and Gellrich, T. (2006) Strategic decisions regarding the vertical integration of human resource organizations: evidence for an integrated HR model for the financial services and non-financial services industry in Germany, Austria and Switzerland. *International Journal of Human Resource Management*, Vol. 17, No. 10: 1726–71.

Wain, D. (2009) Command performance. *People Management*, 5 November.

Wainwright, S., Clark, J. and Griffith, M. (2006) *The UK voluntary sector almanac*. London: NVCVO Publications.

Walumbwa, F., Avolio, B. J., Gardner, W. L, Wernsing, T. and Peterson, S. (2008) Authentic leadership: development and validation of a theory-based measure. *Journal of Management*, Vol. 34, No. 1: 89–126.

Wang, G. G. and Sun, J. Y. (2009) Clarifying the boundaries of human resource development. *Human Resource Development International*, Vol. 12, No. 1: 93–103.

Wang, D. and Shyu, C. (2008) Will the strategic fit between business and HRM strategy influence HRM effectiveness and organizational performance? *International Journal of Manpower*, Vol. 29, No. 2: 92–110.

Warech, M. and Tracey, J. B. (2004) Evaluating the impact of human resources: identifying what matters. *Cornell Hotel and Restaurant Administration Quarterly*, Vol. 45: 376–87.

Warren, C. (2009) HR and OD 'should be one and the same'. *People Management*, 20 November.

Waterman, R., Waterman, J. and Collard, B. (1994) Toward a career resilient workforce. *Harvard Business Review*, July-August: 87–95.

Watson, T. J. (2006) *Organising and Managing Work*, 2nd ed. Harlow: FT/Prentice Hall.

Weber, M. (1947) *The Theory of Social and Economic Organization* (translated by Henderson, A. M. and Parsons, T.). Oxford: Oxford University Press.

White Paper (1999) http://archive.cabinetoffice.gov.uk/moderngov/download/modgov.pdf [accessed 27 January 2010].

Whitford, A. (2003) *Why You Can't Ignore Internet Recruitment: One-stop guide.* Reed Business Information. Available online at: www.xperthr.co.uk [accessed 16 May 2008].

Wight, G. (2007) Bending the rules: Surrey County Council embraces flexible working. *Development and Learning in Organizations*, Vol. 21, No. 4: 20–1.

Wignall, A. (2004) Work in progresss [Professor P. Nolan quoted]. *The Guardian*, 21 September.

Wiley, C. (2000) Ethical standards for human resource management professionals: a comparative analysis of five major codes. *Journal of Business Ethics*, Vol. 25: 93–114.

William, N. (2008) Competency-based interviews and online psychometric tests are best for choosing candidates. *Personnel Today*, 10 March [Accessed online 7 May 08].

Williams, R. S. (1998) *Performance Management: Perspectives on employee performance*. London: International Thomson Business Press.

Williams, S. and Adam-Smith, D. (2010) *Contemporary Employment Relations: A critical introduction*, 2nd ed. Oxford: Oxford University Press.

Wilson, E. and Iles, P. (1999) Managing diversity – an employment and service delivery challenge. *International Journal of Public Sector Management*, Vol. 12, No. 1: 27–48.

Wilson, F. L. (2006) *Organizational Behaviour and Work: A critical introduction*, 2nd ed. Oxford: Oxford University Press.

Wolff, C. (2008) Wychavon District Council: staff engagement proved vital to success. *IRS Employment Review*, Issue 909, 17 November.

Wood, J., Zeffane, R., Fromholtz, M., Wiesner, R. and Creed, A. (2010) *Organisational Behaviour*, 2nd Australasian ed. Milton, Queensland: John Wiley & Sons.

Woodall, J., Scott-Jackson, W., Newham, T. and Gurney, M. (2009) Managing the decision to outsource human resources. *Personnel Review*, Vol. 38, No. 3: 236–52.

Woodward, J. (1965) *Organisation and Technology*. Oxford: Oxford University Press.

Workforce Management (2004) http://www.workforce.com/section/09/feature/23/85/39/index.html [accessed 30 April 2010].

Work Foundation (2003) *The Missing Link: From productivity to performance*. Work and enterprise panel of inquiry. London: The Work Foundation.

Work Foundation (2009) *Quality People Management for Quality Outcomes: The future of HR review on evidence on people management*. Report. July.

Wright, C. (2008) Reinventing human resource management: business partners, internal consultants and the limits of professionalization. *Human Relations*, Vol. 61, No. 8: 1063–86.

Wright, P. M. and Haggerty, J. J. (2005) Missing variables in theories of strategic human resource management: time, cause and individuals. *Management Review*, Vol. 16: 164–73.

Wright, P. M. and McMahan, G. (1992) Theoretical perspectives for strategic human resources management. *Journal of Management*, Vol. 18, No. 2: 295–320.

Yorks, L., Lamm, S. and O'Neil, J. (1999) Transfer of learning from Action Learning programs to the organizational setting. *Advances in Developing Human Resources*, Vol. 1: 56.

Yukl, G. (2006) *Leadership in Organisations*, 6th ed. London: Prentice Hall.

Yukl, G. (2009) *Leadership in Organizations*, 7th ed. Harlow: Pearson International.

Zigurs, I. (2003) Leadership in virtual teams: oxymoron or opportunity? *Organizational Dynamics*, Vol. 31, Issue 4: 339–51.

Index